THE THREE LIVES
OF
CHARLES DE GAULLE

David Schoenbrun

THE THREE LIVES
OF
CHARLES DE GAULLE

Atheneum   New York

1968

For Lucy

*whose generation will find new reasons
to preserve and strengthen
old friendships*

Published by Atheneum
Reprinted by arrangement with David Schoenbrun
Copyright © 1965, 1966 by David Schoenbrun
All rights reserved
Library of Congress catalog card number 65-15921
Manufactured in the United States of America by
The Murray Printing Company,
Forge Village, Massachusetts
Published in Canada by McClelland & Stewart Ltd.
First Atheneum Paperback Edition

Contents

THE THREE LIVES
OF
CHARLES DE GAULLE

INCARNATION AND REINCARNATION

> *When leaders fail, new leaders are projected upward out of the spirit of eternal France: from Charlemagne to Joan of Arc to Napoleon, Poincaré and Clemenceau. Perhaps this time I am one of those thrust into leadership by the failure of others.*
>
> CHARLES DE GAULLE *to U.S. Admiral Stark, December 16, 1942, in London*

A SOLITARY FIGURE stood at attention facing the flag-draped catafalque, his body rigid, his head held high, his eyes closed in prayerful silent salute. He was a giant of a man, towering six and a half feet from his huge feet, broad as the base of a pedestal, up the full length of the greatcoat that enveloped him from ankle to chin to the hard crown of his kepi high above the ground. Two small stars on the kepi twinkled in the candlelight, but his own face looked waxen in the pale yellow glow.

The chill and silence of death filled the great hall. Its ancient, thick, stone walls muffled the howling gale outside, where the winds whipped rain cold as liquid ice on the bent backs of the Londoners huddled in long lines that serpentined through two miles of streets, from the steps of Westminster Hall to Lambeth Bridge and the Left Embankment beyond. London's weather was at its majestic worst, but Londoners were at their adverse best as they waited patiently for General de Gaulle to pay his last respects to Winston Churchill, so that they could follow him into the hall to bid farewell in their turn to the man who incarnated England in its darkest and finest hours.

The funereal scene on that stormy day of January 1965 was the

closing scene of a drama that began twenty-five years earlier, in
June 1940, with the same leading men—Winston Churchill and
General de Gaulle—and the same supporting cast—the patient,
unheroically heroic people of London. It was an epic that is not
likely to be performed again, the last of the passion plays of the
neo-Dark Ages of pre-thermonuclear man.

Back in those dark days men's weapons were crude casings,
containing low-yield dynamite, mounted on ponderous flying
machines. Such puny weapons could not determine by themselves
the outcome of a war. Wars had still to be fought and won by
hand-to-hand combat, and only extraordinary leadership could
rally men to so fearsome a battle. Winston Churchill and Charles
de Gaulle were such leaders, brave men themselves, able to inspire
fellow men to heroism. This was their role in the twin scene they
played in London on June 18, 1940.

Winston Churchill faced Commons on that day of disaster, his
feet braced apart, his body hunched forward, like a captain on the
bridge of a storm-tossed ship. The situation was desperate, and he
wasted no time in saying so: "What General Weygand called the
Battle of France is over. I expect that the Battle of Britain is about
to begin. Upon this depends the survival of Christian civilisation."
Winston Churchill then called upon his countrymen to prepare
for the ultimate test: "Let us therefore brace ourselves to our
duties, and so bear ourselves that, if the British Empire and its
Commonwealth last for a thousand years, men will say: 'This was
their finest hour.' "

Later that day, in a small studio of the BBC, General de Gaulle
sat before a microphone, his deep powerful voice raised in full
force as though all of France were there before him. Like a high
priest chanting a litany, he intoned these words, with a measured
beat: "For France is not alone. She is not alone. She is not alone.
She can form a solid bloc with the British Empire which commands the seas and continues the fight." Like Churchill, who
exhorted Britons to fight on despite the fall of France, de Gaulle,
in the same spirit, told Frenchmen, "This war has not ended with
the Battle of France. This war is a world war."

These twin appeals of June 18, 1940, launched a great adventure
that carried these men, their fellow countrymen and the entire
world from the darkness of the Nazi night to bright victory in the
greatest, most terrible and, most likely, last world war of human

history. If ever the world explodes in the nuclear age, it will be the end of the planet; if there is survival, the fused world will be unrecognizable to survivors and their progeny, who themselves will not bear much resemblance to human beings.

Those who argue that there have always been wars and always will be may be right, but if they are, they will not get the chance to say I told you so. If, however, they are wrong, and there are no new world wars, then our descendants will never know men like Churchill and de Gaulle. It is not because they were in themselves unique and inimitable—on the contrary, they incarnated their nations and reincarnated the classic hero types of their peoples—but rather because they achieved their greatness in unique, inimitable circumstances. They were warrior heroes, a genus of man that is now dead, the first class victim of the nuclear age.

General de Gaulle, Liberator of France, will thus go down in history as the last Frenchman ever to free his country, just as General Eisenhower is now the last of the line of Supreme Commanders to lead a mighty armada to the rescue of enslaved peoples. A nuclear war would not be fought by an armada, and any beach would be too hot to land upon in the aftermath of an atomic barrage whose deadly radiation would have a destructive duration of half a century and more. The last statues of the last of the liberators have surely been cast. What survivors of an atomic holocaust would want to cast a statue? And to whom? It is inconceivable that anyone would erect a heroic monument to The Finger That Pressed The Button.

* * *

Of the wartime giants, Roosevelt was the first to go, dying a few weeks before the victory he so longed to see. Stalin was the second to go, living just long enough to see his country enter the atomic age that made his kind of human giant an anachronism. Churchill lived long enough to witness the disintegration of the empire which he had fought so valiantly and futilely to build. Chiang Kai-shek was defeated and forced to flee into exile. Dwight D. Eisenhower retired to end his days as elder statesman and gentleman farmer. By 1960 only one of the giants of the past was still in power: Charles de Gaulle, lone ranger of the Western plains, sole survivor of the heroes of the last world war in the last war world of history.

De Gaulle encouraged mixed emotions about himself. He never sought to be merely "popular." He wanted to be respected and obeyed, and for this he had to exercise authority, a necessarily abrasive act. He rarely missed an opportunity to make the worst of a bad thing, and he was not averse to adding insult to injury in the conduct of world affairs. Not content with countering the policies of the great powers, he would jeer at Russian and American leaders. At one press conference, announcing that he had invited Khrushchev to visit France, he then ridiculed him by referring to him as a little man in the back row when he, de Gaulle, had visited Stalin in Moscow. He often referred to America in a condescending manner as "our daughter, America," an image meant to convey the impression that America was a young upstart compared with great old France. He has called China that "yellow dust of vast multitudes." It could be said, therefore, that if de Gaulle is undoubtedly a heroic figure, he knew how to play the role of a villain as well. For those who believe in the creation of an integrated United States of Europe, as for those devoted to the integration of the Atlantic Alliance, or those striving for a ban on atomic proliferation, or his fellow Frenchmen who chafe under his autocratic rule, Charles de Gaulle is the villain of their drama. In this sense he is a kind of evolutionary link between the hero and the antihero type that has more recently emerged in world affairs.

The antihero, a kind of heroic villain, first appeared in literature and then became prominent in the movies, with the Humphrey Bogart style of leading man—the snarling, tough, beautifully ugly hard guy with a soft heart. Many variations of this type have since evolved, from the amoral adventurer James Bond, a rebel hired for a cause, to the ultimate antihero Leamas, the middle-aged, mediocre, shabby spy who came in from the cold.

In the first nuclear decade the antihero emerged from fiction and entered into public life. He was in a way a product of the balance of terror, which paralyzed the giants and permitted little Napoleons to dress up and parade around as mock heroes. Nasser is that kind of antihero of Arabia. The great powers, Russia and America, aborted the Anglo-French invasion of Suez, permitting Nasser to strut about thereafter boasting of his "victory" over the aggressors. Nasser is a tall, athletic, dark and handsome man who overthrew a corrupt regime and fought for independence for his people. In this sense he is an Egyptian hero. But his vain posturings, his absurd schemes of pan-Arabism in Africa, his failure to make peace and his inability to make war with Israel, all these are the marks of a villain. He is, therefore, the prototype of the unheroic hero—that is, the antihero.

Antiheroes, like cactus, grow best in the desert or other underdeveloped soil: Nkrumah in Ghana, Sekou Touré in Guinea, Tshombé in the Congo, Makarios in Cyprus, Sukarno in Indonesia. The antiheroes of the Americas range from Juan Perón to Fidel Castro, all of whom have recognizable heroic qualities that somehow are distorted, deformed, degenerated or otherwise twisted into an antiheroic mold. Yet they have their cultists, not only among their own peoples, but throughout a continent, such as Nasser in Africa and Castro in America. The human hunger for a hero to worship is apparently so fundamental that when no genuine hero is available, an antihero, genuine or not, is created by mass self-delusion.

Great powers, like little countries, have their antiheroes as well. Khrushchev was an impressive example. No national leader elevated to hero status ever looked and acted less like a hero than the funny little fat man with the incongruously childish pet name of Nikita. Even when he banged on the world's desk with his shoe, he seemed more like a circus clown than a monster. It was hard to believe that he was a power-mad bully. Even after the Cuban missile crisis, when it could no longer be doubted that his act was the real thing, there were millions, including many of his chosen targets in America, who found it hard, and still find it hard, to see the villain in the antihero of the Soviet Union. Perhaps it is because, with all his faults, he was human, or at least inhuman, but not nonhuman like his successors, the faceless robots, the non-men of the collegial councils. Even the most terrible tyrants are humanly comprehensible and thereby less frightening than the mysterious midgets of committeeism.

Whatever else his faults, Charles de Gaulle is the antithesis of midgetism. He is a giant in every sense of the word: in his huge, ungainly body and in his great spirit; in his historic achievements and in his dismal failures; in his services to his country and in his disservices to his countrymen. Charles de Gaulle loves only France and cares little about Frenchmen. In fact, he cared little about any men, regardless of race, color or creed. With a kind of inverse tolerance, Charles de Gaulle never discriminated against anyone; he simply opposed everyone. He is not particularly anti-American or anti-British; he is just pro-French. He is a kind of heroic antihero, a blend of the first and last specimen of each type, an example of self-sublimation unique in the literature of leadership in our times. None of his contemporaries, remarkable men all, had quite his special blend of good and evil or, if those words are too strong, of positive and negative elements of heroism.

His career was as filled with paradox as his personality was overlayed with contradictions. He came to power when his country was no longer a great power. Born in the nineteenth century, raised and educated by nineteenth-century men, steeped in the Victorian romanticism of those times, he found himself alone when the reign of nineteenth-century men came to an end in the year 1960. In that year all of the candidates for the office of president and vice-president of the United States were men born and bred in the twentieth century: John F. Kennedy, Lyndon Johnson, Richard Nixon and Henry Cabot Lodge. In November 1960 John F. Kennedy became America's youngest president-elect, succeeding to the person and the generation of Dwight D. Eisenhower, who had been the oldest president in American history. The succession of Eisenhower by Kennedy signaled the advent of a centurial changing of the guard.

From that moment on, the old guard gave way to the new throughout the world: in England the changes went from right to left as well as from nineteenth- to twentieth-century men: Macmillan to Home to Wilson. In Germany, Adenauer, a contemporary of the Iron Chancellor Bismarck, gave way to Ludwig Erhard, some forty years his junior. In Russia, Khrushchev, one of the original bolsheviks, was deposed by Brezhnev and Kosygin, the first Soviet leaders who had not been old enough to fight against the cossacks of the Czar. As the old guard faded away, Charles de Gaulle became the oldest leader of a major power, the Senex Primus of the world. The title of first elder is only a fictional honor, yet is is not without real effect on world politics. It conferred a special dignity and authority that President de Gaulle skillfully exploited in his exercise of leadership.

Even the new, young leaders, psychologically inclined to dismiss anachronistic old men, could not help but be impressed by de Gaulle's awesome ancientness. President Kennedy deferred to him most respectfully in their meeting in Paris and even asked him to draw upon the wisdom of his long experience to advise the young President on the basic principles of statesmanship. The younger man was not merely flattering his difficult elder, although a Kennedy was quite capable of trying his Gaelic charm on an old Gaul.

The author of *Profiles in Courage* was sincerely interested in Charles de Gaulle as a case history of power politics and the human potential for leadership. He told this writer a few days before his death that he had been deeply disappointed at de Gaulle's failure to send him, as de Gaulle had promised, his mature reflections on leadership and statesmanship. When General de Gaulle heard of Kennedy's disappointment, he expressed his own regrets with the comment, "I meant to write to him. I thought I had time."

There was much about Kennedy that de Gaulle admired and even envied, and much that he could understand in the catholicity and idealism of the man, but there could be no very close human contact between the eldest and the youngest statesmen of the world. Lyndon Johnson, a parliamentarian, a prairie politician, a pragmatist and a Protestant, was a total mystery to an autocratic, urban, Catholic mystic like de Gaulle. An intellectual, a socialist and a technocrat like Britain's Harold Wilson and a stolid German burgher like Ludwig Erhard were merely bureaucrats, not chiefs, in the eyes of a de Gaulle. All his life he had chosen to remain aloof, in a solitude he deemed necessary for a chief, but in his twilight years Charles de Gaulle had no choice but to be lonely. All his peers had disappeared.

The disappearance of the class of 1890 coincided with the disappearance of the world of 1890, in one of those rare periods of history in which there is not a normal continuation of culture from one generation to the next, but rather an ending of one culture and a beginning of a new one. In this break in history Charles de Gaulle was not just an older man watching younger men come to power in an evolutionary cycle of succession; he was a man of an old world watching a revolutionary new world come into being.

The world of 1890 into which Charles de Gaulle was born was fundamentally the same in its philosophy and its sciences as the world of his father and his father's father. There had certainly been progress, even great advances, from Lavoisier to Becquerel, from Pascal to Bergson. But these were advances along the same line of history, progress from the same original point of departure rather than fundamental change.

The fundamental change, from one world to a different world, a change not only of degree but of nature, came when Captain de Gaulle was a man of thirty, his personality and character already formed by the world of his youth. When the change came, he was not immediately aware of it, nor were most men of his age. He would only discover much later in life that a mathematician and physicist named Albert Einstein had opened the way to a new world. Einstein's theories were not just advances on Newton's world, they were a break with Newton's world that presaged the end of de Gaulle's world.

In Newton's world what went up had to come down; that was the law of gravity. In Einstein's world what went up high enough stayed up and orbited around the planet or went shooting off into limitless space; that was a law that imposed an entirely new gravity on the old rules of power politics of de Gaulle's world. The time-space factor has changed all the classic concepts of war, including the very idea of war as a means of furthering the interests of nations.

There was a time in history when wars could resolve disputes and profit the victor at least temporarily. Charles de Gaulle was born only twenty years after such a war—the Franco-Prussian War. Twenty years after his birth he was commissioned a lieutenant and prepared with joy for another war which he knew to be coming and which he welcomed as a great opportunity.

Noting in his memoirs that war clouds were forming again over Europe at the turn of the century, Charles de Gaulle confessed, "I must say that in the prime of my youth I imagined without horror, and magnified by anticipation, that unknown adventure. . . . When I entered the army it was one of the greatest things in the world." That was young Charles de Gaulle and his world at the turn of the twentieth century. And that is a world now dead.

Young men of today may enter an army, which is still an essential element in national life, for if world war on the grand scale is impossible, limited forms of warfare have not yet disappeared from history. But few young men of today would consider the army to be "one of the greatest things in the world," and no one but a maniac could imagine the advent of war "without horror" in the thermonuclear age of man.

There are young men of today who also love their country and are prepared to dedicate their lives to serving it; but there are surely few who reincarnate the exalted nationalism and romantic heroism of a Charles de Gaulle and the men of 1890. The notion of the nation-state as the highest, immutable form of human society, exercising full, unrestricted sovereignty over its own affairs, is now as anachronistic a concept as the concept of war as a means of serving the national interest. As for the romance of war, that is a delusion of the past. The most patriotic of young Americans fighting in Vietnam for a cause in which they believe nonetheless call it "the dirty war." They do not parade with pennants flying; they sing no songs to war. Many are heroic; none strike the pose of a hero. They laugh at the posturing of a de Gaulle, last of the heroes of antiquity.

It could be said that Mao Tse-tung was equally a surviving giant of the past. But Mao was not quite comparable to the other giants who dominated the world of the mid-twentieth century. He was not one of the heroes of the victorious wartime coalition. If he had any classic role, it was the role of the villain. Anthropolitically, Mao was an unclassifiable mutant, something between the ancient warlords and the modern commissars of China. Quarantined and self-isolated, he lacked the one characteristic common to the classic giant heroes and giant villains alike: the charismatic projections of their images and personalities that made them universally and intimately known in the roles they played on the world stage. Throughout his career Mao was enigmatic, not charismatic; he was an off-stage character whose voice was heard and whose presence was felt, but who was rarely seen in the spotlight of history.

Charles de Gaulle possessed some of the qualities of each of the other leaders of his times. De Gaulle was as charismatic a personality as Roosevelt and Churchill, yet, in his own way, he was as self-isolated and unclassifiable as Mao. He bridged the worlds of the distant past and the far future, keeping alive the mythology of ancient Gaul, prophesying the advent of a new Europe, decrying only the mediocre present of an enfeebled France, which is no longer Gaul but not yet Europa. He was a tower of babelizing contradictions, both an anachronism and a visionary, exciting the world to alternate bursts of adulation and anathema. As one by one his allies and his adversaries expired or retired, he alone continued to stride across the world stage, declaiming with undiminished passion the grandeur of his nation, and claiming for it an equal place among the leading powers of the world. It was almost as though Charles de Gaulle knew that he was the very last of his kind and was inspired to a final heroic performance.

France has a highly varied collection of hero types. In the Pantheon, the official state mausoleum, there are no less than fifty-six more or less complete skeletons and six disembodied hearts of official heroes of France, ranging from the Revolutionary philosophers Voltaire and Rousseau, the oldest of the relics, to the newest official hero, entombed there in 1965, the martyr of the wartime underground, Jean Moulin, de Gaulle's personal delegate, who became chief of the resistance movement in occupied France. It is significant that Jean Moulin, the only man to be interred in the Pantheon during the presidency of Charles de Gaulle, was a resistant. The resistant is a hero type peculiarly French, and Charles de Gaulle, last of the giants of the pre-atomic world, was also the last in a long line of this supreme hero type of French legend.

The history of France from Gaul to de Gaulle has been a history of recurrent waves of invasion and countercurrents of resistance to the invaders. There were, of course, periods of French invasion of other countries, and a number of conquering hero types of the genus Napoleon, but the hero type dearest to the French heart and closest to the French temperament is not the emperor, it is the resistant, not the conqueror but the liberator. This is the hero typified by Charles de Gaulle. He is the last resistant-reincarnate of a two-thousand-year-old line that goes from Vercingetorix, the first resistant, who rallied the tribes of Gaul to rise up against General Caesar, through Charles Martel, who saved Europe from the Saracens; Genevieve, patron saint of Paris, who stopped the Huns of Attila at the city's gates; Joan of Orleans, who rallied the people against the English; Georges Clemenceau, who avenged the defeat by the Prussians and rescued the lost provinces of Alsace and Lorraine—to Charles de Gaulle, leader of Free France, liberator and guardian of the French nation, last of the great Gauls.

It is appropriate to call Charles de Gaulle a Gaul, for he himself constantly referred to the French people as "les Gaulois," just as he used such archaic terms as "les Germains" and "les Slavs" to designate the people of modern Germany, Eastern Europe and Russia, who are no more Germans and Slavs, as those people were constituted in the time of Caesar, than the British and Americans of today are anything like the ancient Anglo-Saxons, which was the only name by which Charles of Gaul referred to them.

To an American mind this kind of historical self-sublimation does not seem genuine. At best it sounds like deliberate political hokum, designed as historical justification for contemporary nationalistic policies; at worst it feeds the suspicion that the practitioner is a megalomanic Machiavel. Yet to a Gallic mind and, above all, to the very special Gaullist mind, this is the most familiar kind of history—the history of a family group, not merely learned from school books but kept ever fresh in daily life. The French live with history. All history is current in a city like Paris, where even a subway station is named Alesia in honor of the climactic battle of Vercingetorix against Caesar.

Ancient legend lived on as modern reality when the hero who arose to revive the nation was a man named "Gaulle." In old French the name of the land was often written with a double "l," so that Charles de Gaulle could present himself philologically as well as psychologically as the incarnation of eternal France and reincarnation of the heroic resistant.

* * *

Charles de Gaulle was born to the role of the resistant. His father, Henri de Gaulle, had been a soldier in the war against the Prussians, whose armies had defeated Napoleon III and annexed the provinces of Alsace and Lorraine. From his earliest childhood Charles de Gaulle was raised to avenge that defeat and drive the Germans out of France. His generation accomplished its historic mission, but its triumph was transient. Twenty years after victory in World War I, France was hit by World War II, and once again the Germans occupied the motherland.

In the course of his life Charles de Gaulle saw three republics rise and fall in France. He served all three, with the single, overriding mission of resisting the enemy and preserving the independence of France. But within that unifying mission Charles de Gaulle lived through three different lives, playing a different role in three different republics, in a constantly changing France.

In the first of his three lives Charles de Gaulle served as a soldier of the Third Republic. That life in that Republic came to an end on June 17, 1940, when a senile marshal took over a defeatist government and prepared to seek an armistice that would deliver France into the arms of the Nazis and replace the republic with a totalitarian state. On that day of disaster Charles de Gaulle faced a terrible choice between obedience to his chiefs and to the state or to his conscience and to the nation, a choice between surrender or exile. He chose his conscience, his nation and exile as the only honorable means of serving France and restoring a republic. He fled to London.

The French say that "to depart is to die a little." For Charles de Gaulle this flight to London on June 17, 1940, was a death-departure from a France that would never be the same again and from a life that he would never live again as a simple soldier. De Gaulle consciously experienced this sense of death. He noted in his diary that day, "I felt within myself a life coming to an end—the life I had lived within the framework of a solid France and an indivisible Army. At age forty-nine, I was embarking on a new adventure, a man whom destiny had propelled far from the beaten paths." That was the self-composed epitaph of Charles de Gaulle, soldier of the Third Republic.

On the very next day, June 18, General de Gaulle rose like a phoenix out of the ashes of the old life of Charles de Gaulle. No longer a subordinate soldier, he became the leader of Fighting France, the heroic resistant of historic legend and finally the liberator of France. General de Gaulle, like Charles de Gaulle, was, however, fated to an untimely demise. In July 1955, only ten years after his victorious liberation of France, he retired from politics, defeated in his attempt to rally a majority to his personal standards. He entered the shadows of the library to write the memoirs which were in effect his own obituary for history. At a news conference he took his leave of reporters with these parting words: "I say farewell to you. We shall not meet again until the tempest once again looses itself upon France." Those were the last words of General de Gaulle, savior of the Fourth Republic, who interred himself in the mausoleum of his memories.

Three years later, in May 1958, the tempest he foresaw blew up in Algiers and loosed itself upon France. Once again the people turned to Charles de Gaulle, resurrecting him from his library tomb. At the age of sixty-seven he was again reborn, in his third incarnation, as President of France. Like Charles de Gaulle, the President was a soldier; but this time he fought mainly against the French Army. Like General de Gaulle, he was a resistant; but President de Gaulle spent more of his time resisting his allies than his enemies. He was also a liberator; but it was not France he liberated, it was France's former colonies. Unlike either of the former de Gaulles, President de Gaulle was a master politician and statesman, the absolute sovereign of the Fifth Republic, holding the scroll of a constitution as a scepter but with as much power as any absolute monarch of modern history.

Each of these three de Gaulles incarnated France and each was the reincarnation of the other, but each played a different role as soldier, savior and statesman of France. France herself changed from a great world power to a European power. A biography of Charles de Gaulle is, thus, necessarily, also a biography of France. Since France, although no longer preeminent, is still an essential element in the world, the story is therefore also a universal story; it is the story of our own lives and of our own times. It is a true story, although there is no single, simple truth about this complex man. It is also a fable because he is a fabulous man, in whose lives mythology has played as great a role as reality.

This, then, is the true-to-life fable of the last of the giants in a world that has grown both too small and too big for his kind.

PART ONE
THE SOLDIER

French officers will always lead, if the soldiers will follow; and English soldiers will always follow, if their officers will lead.

> SAMUEL JOHNSON,
> *On the Bravery of the English Common Soldiers, c. 1760*

If my soldiers were to begin to think, not one would remain in the ranks.

> *Ascribed to* FREDERICK THE GREAT

Had not innumerable soldiers shed their blood, there would have been no Hellenism, no Roman civilization, no Christianity, no Rights of Man, and no modern developments.

> CHARLES DE GAULLE,
> *The Edge of the Sword*

CHAPTER ONE

THE IMMACULATE CONCEPT

*Peering down into the gulf into which the mother-
land has fallen, I am her son, calling her, holding
the light for her, showing her the way to salvation
... Ah! Mother, such as we are, we are here to
serve you.*

CHARLES DE GAULLE, *The Call to Honor*

WHAT A JOY it must be to celebrate the turn of a century! The
imagination soars at the expectation of the last New Year's Eve of
this century. A great cry will go up around the world as people
embrace one another, however fleetingly, to celebrate the advent of
January 1, 2000.

Charles de Gaulle was one of the fortunate ones who celebrated
the birth of a century—and what a century the twentieth promised
to be. It was the start of the age of man-made miracles. Young
inventors were tinkering with the first automobiles, the first flying
machines, the first cameras and telephones. Man was conquering
nature, discovering and, at the same time, seeking to disprove the
bestial origin of the species. It was an age of reason triumphant,
seeking new reasons for faith. This was the lesson taught to his
children by the Catholic intellectual Henri de Gaulle on the
night of November 22, 1900, as he gathered his family around the
table in his home on the Rue Princesse in Lille, to celebrate the
tenth birthday of his son Charles.

A professor of philosophy with a doctorate in science as well,
Henri de Gaulle was concerned with the need to reconcile reason
and religion. Family dinners were frequently turned into lecture
sessions. But on that night Henri de Gaulle kept his talk brief,

signaled to his wife to bring in the birthday cake and then nodded to his first-born son, Xavier, to make the toast to Charles. Xavier arose, smiled at his younger brother and said, "To Charles, on this first birthday of the twentieth century."

"Oh, no, that's wrong!" The protest was blurted out by their sister, Marie-Agnès, who blushed and then paled at her outburst.

Henri de Gaulle smiled at his children. He encouraged debate in his family, and none of his children was shy. He nodded at Marie-Agnès to continue.

"The twentieth century has not yet celebrated its own first birthday," she said. "It began on January 1, it is true, but it will not be a year old until December 31, next month. After all, our first birthdays came one year after we were born, so the twentieth century is now zero year old."

Charles sat silently, staring into the ten candles on his cake while Xavier and Agnès disputed the parallelism of the birth dates. Henri de Gaulle let his children debate a bit, as he would allow his students to conduct a discussion until the moment came for him to intervene and set it straight. When they began repeating their arguments, he tapped on a glass for attention and said, "Come now, let us examine this objectively. Xavier is right in saying that the year 1900 is the first year of the twentieth century, since the cycle of the last one hundred years was completed on December 31, 1899. From 1800 to 1899 is a hundred-year period just as there are ten numbers from zero to nine, including zero as the first number. Count from zero to nine on your fingers and you will use all ten fingers."

He paused and smiled as he watched the children counting and noted that Charles, still staring silently into the candlelight, kept his hands folded on his lap. He continued, "Let us not forget, children, that last December thirty-first the Pope celebrated a special mass to welcome the birth of the new century. However, Marie-Agnès is also right, in a sense. The twentieth century is not yet a year old, and so on this night it could be said that the tenth birthday of Charles has come before the first birthday of the twentieth century, as Marie-Agnès argues. And the Pope has decided to hold another special mass this December thirty-first to celebrate the first birthday of the new century. Surely it is better to welcome the new century twice than risk being impolite because, in any case, we are going to have to live with it."

The children silently reflected on the words of their father.

Suddenly young Charles came out of his reverie and said, "How strange! We know the names of all the stars in the heavens and how many days it would take to reach them by train, if a train could fly into the skies. And yet we do not know whether our century arrived yesterday or if it will only arrive tomorrow." As the others turned to stare at him in astonishment, he said, "It's absurd," biting off the words sharply, in a peremptory and professorial manner which so exactly, if unconsciously, mimicked his father's own classroom style that all the family roared with laughter while the ten-year-old Charles flushed with embarrassment, wondering what he had said that was so funny.

The family itself was not surprised at his outburst. They had become accustomed to the darkling moods and thunderclap personality of young Charles, about whom his father had said two years earlier, "From such a child as he we expect much." This is an expectation rarely voiced by sober-minded parents about a little boy of eight, and Henri de Gaulle, an autocrat and teacher, had less illusions about children than most parents. Yet he sensed very early that Charles was different from other children.

The de Gaulle family itself was anything but ordinary. One finds the name de Gaulle throughout French history, and often enough associated with heroic acts of patriotic resistance to an invader. Just how or when the ancient name "Gaule" became the family name "Gaulle" is a matter of conjecture. This type of family name is not a rare phenomenon. There are many families that have the name "France," just as there are Germans who bear the name "Deutsch." Some historians believe that the family may have originated in Brittany or Wales. The French word for Wales is "Pays de Galles," and an early ancestor may have been designated by the country of his origin, such as John from Wales, or Jean de Galles. One of the branches of the family of the ancient kings of Brittany was called Goëllo, a Breton name which would become Gaulle in translation into French.

In the fourteenth century a Chevalier de Gaulle, Lord and Governor of the city of Vire in Normandy, won special mention and immortality in the history books for his victorious defense of his city against an English invasion of the land. A Jean de Gaulle is cited in the chronicles of the historic battle of Agincourt. Legend has it that it was Sir Jean de Gaulle who warned his commanding officer, the Constable d'Albret, that the terrain favored the mobile British archers, who could outmaneuver the ponderously heavy, slow-moving French foot soldiers. The tradition-blinded high command of the day, refusing to heed the words of that prophetic de Gaulle and his wild talk of a war of movement, went down to disastrous defeat. Whether or not this legend bears any relationship to fact, or whether Jean de Gaulle is even remotely related to our Charles de Gaulle, whose own prophetic theories of blitzkrieg went similarly unheeded in France, matters less than the fact that the de Gaulle family believed the legend to be true and passed it on in all its romantic aura to the impressionable young Charles de Gaulle. What is important—indeed, of the greatest significance in understanding the man today—is that he not only believed the legends, adored the fairytales of family and school history books, but that he wrote them down in his copybooks and acted them out. His brothers recalled that he did not hesitate to rewrite history to suit his own concept of what should have taken place. In his version of Agincourt, the Constable d'Albret heeded the words of Jean de Gaulle, and redeployed his troops to outflank the English. In the fantasy world of young Charles de Gaulle it was the French who won the battle of Agincourt!

There was no lack of Gaullist heroes to emulate in play. One was a family hero, Jean-Baptiste de Gaulle, the great-great-grandfather of Charles de Gaulle; Jean-Baptiste was a legal counselor at the court of the King in 1750. And his cousin, also named Jean-Baptiste, but who spelled his family name in one word, "Degaulle," was a naval engineer who designed and constructed the jetties and the lighthouse of Le Havre and Honfleur. At the time of the French Revolution Jean-Baptiste de Gaulle, the petty nobleman of the robe, remained loyal to the King and was thrown in prison by the revolutionaries, there to remain until he was released by the new revolution of the IX Thermidor.

The name de Gaulle appears throughout French history, generally in minor roles, but, by an extraordinary coincidence, almost always connected with acts of resistance. In the year 1414, in the reign of Charles VI, one finds a Sire de Gaulle who was given the task of defending the Porte Saint-Denis gateway to Paris against the armies of the Duke of Burgundy. And, after the occupation of Normandy by the Plantagenets, history records the act of resistance of a Seigneur de Gaulle, who refused to take the oath of vassalage to the foreign lord. His goods and properties were confiscated, he was declared to be a traitor and a felon and he was sent into exile. The King of France awarded him a fief in

Burgundy, at Cuisery. His coat of arms features three nuts, "les noix de galle," a kind of growth found on oak trees, similar to the sacred trees of the ancient Gauls, a symbol of soul and resistance.

Loyalty to the nation and resistance to the enemy were leitmotifs of the de Gaulle family and the families allied to it. Charles de Gaulle's maternal grandmother was Julia Delannoy, who descended from the MacCartans of Ireland and the Flemings of Scotland. Young Charles had been raised on stories of the loyalty of the Flemings to the Stuarts and knew all about their flight into exile in France as they followed James II. The motto of the Fleming family was "Always and Everywhere Faithful." The motto of the MacCartan clan was "Hit hard!" These two sentiments were drilled into the boy's head by his father from his earliest age, so that it became second nature for Charles de Gaulle to regard faith to an ideal and strength to strike the enemy as being the highest attributes of man.

The young boy was particularly impressed by his namesake, his uncle, the first Charles de Gaulle, a historian of the Bretons and the Celts, who wrote a book called *The Celts in the XIXth Century* in which he advocated the union of the Breton, Scots, Irish and Welsh peoples. The uncle was a passionate nationalist who believed also in the preservation of regional and racial languages, cultures and groupings within the nation. In one of his pamphlets, "The Awakening of the Race," his nephew Charles found and cherished these lines: "In a camp, surprised by an enemy attack under cover of night, where each man is fighting alone, in dark confusion, no one asks for the grade or rank of the man who lifts up the standard and makes the first call to rally for resistance."

Official biographers of the Gaullist cult have earnestly burrowed through the records to find these phenomena that would seem to point to a predestination of the career of Charles de Gaulle, the Liberator, the First Resistant of France. The biographers' efforts to embroider the mantle lead them to stretch the material very thin, as in the instance of one biographer who points out that Sire de Gaulle, guardian of the Gate of Saint-Denis, carried out his mission just "fifteen years before Joan of Arc," as though, somehow, this established a link between Charles de Gaulle and the Maid of Orleans.

This kind of history twisting, so prevalent among French popularizers of national legends and myths, is not to be taken seriously in itself and would not be worth noting if it were not for the fact that the legends and myths of history are often more important in their influence upon a nation's thinking than the truth itself. A writer like Jacques Bainville, one of France's most respected and widely read historians, convinced millions of his fellow citizens that Germany was the historic enemy of France although the French had fought the British more often in national conflicts of interest than they had ever fought Germany as a nation. Indeed, the first war between France and Germany as nation-states was the Franco-Prussian War of 1870, for there was no German nation-state worthy of the name before that. But one cannot convince most Frenchmen of such facts. They consider Germany and Germans to be ancient enemies as far back as pre-Roman times.

De Gaulle himself subscribed to this notion. In one of his early essays, *Vers l'Armée de métier,* he wrote a brilliantly poetic passage about the constant conflicts between the two peoples whom he called "Gaulois et Germains," using the ancient names to describe Frenchmen and Germans: "Wherever it passes, the French-German frontier is the lip of a wound. Whence ever it blows, the wind that sweeps over it is heavy with hidden thoughts."

Heavy with hidden thoughts are the minds of many otherwise rational Frenchmen when they regard the myths and mystifications of the Gaullist cult. Those who live among the French and have traveled through the land in the wake of the General as he swept across the roads of France in periodic morale-building missions never cease to be astonished at the fervor, sometimes the frenzy, of the mobs whose passions he arouses and plays upon with the virtuosity of a great conductor who has become an evangelist. One feels the presence of a man of destiny, the very incarnation of all the men of destiny of mythology. In this sense the Gaullist myth is of the greatest importance in understanding the relationship between de Gaulle and France.

None was more impressed with the Gaullist myth than young Charles de Gaulle himself in the most impressionable years of his childhood. His history-teaching, yarn-spinning father taught him to read the history of France before he was five years old. By the time he was celebrating his tenth birthday at the turn of the century, Charles de Gaulle was reading the Chronicles of Froissart, the medieval historian, and was already keenly aware of the significance of his name, so deeply rooted in the ancient soil of Gallic France.

An intensive religious education by his devout parents linked in his mind and soul France and the Church, so that for de Gaulle France was not just a nation, it was a Catholic nation, under the special protection of God. The "chosen people" myth, so often attributed to the Jewish people, is seen and felt perhaps more intensely than anywhere else among the French. Their love for their beautiful, nature-blessed land is so lyrical that one sometimes feels that for the French the biblical line would read: And in the beginning there was France. This was particularly true of Charles de Gaulle, who always acted as though the world revolved around France, axis of the earth.

This reporter experienced personally de Gaulle's mystical religious nationalism in a conversation with the General in the spring of 1959. At one point in our talk I asked President de Gaulle why he so often referred to 1500 years of French history, whereas most Frenchmen consider their history to be 2000 years old. General de Gaulle replied:

> For me the history of France begins with Clovis, who was chosen king by the tribe of the Franks, who gave their name to France. Before Clovis we have the Gallo-Roman and Gallic prehistory of France. The deciding factor for me is that Clovis was the first king to be baptized a Christian. Mine is a Christian country and count the history of France from the accession of a Chr. tian king, who bore the name of the Franks.

This revealing answer to my question was given without a second's hesitation, without any pause for reflection, just as naturally as though it were the simplest question of fact, such as "Where were you born?" I am convinced that if de Gaulle had ever been awakened out of a deep sleep one night and asked to say where he was born, he would not have replied "On the Rue Princesse, in Lille," but would have said, with a frown at the stupidity of the questioner, "Why, in Christian France, of course!"

* * *

The brightest jewel in the crown of Christian France is the Cathedral of Notre Dame de Paris, and Notre Dame was a favorite playground of young Charles de Gaulle when his family moved to Paris in 1901. He never tired of visiting the Cathedral and climbing to the tower to look out over the city. He would stare proudly at the thirteenth-century frescoes which, he had been told by his father, had been restored by an artisan who was a namesake of his mother.

After Notre Dame, his favorite church was Saint Sulpice, where his parents took the children to listen to the world-famous organ music. After services at Saint Sulpice, the family would go to the lovely Luxembourg gardens, where Charles liked to visit the palace and listen to his father talk about his great-great-grandfather, Jean-Baptiste de Gaulle, counselor of the King.

Two of his family favorites were Jean-Baptiste's grandson Julien-Philippe de Gaulle, and his wife, Josephine-Marie-Anne Maillot, both of whom were writers whose books inspired young Charles and lit the literary fires within him. He loved to read and reread grandfather Julien-Philippe's *Nouvelle Histoire de Paris* and, above all, his impassioned *Vie de Saint Louis*. Equally delightful to him were the works of his gifted grandmother Josephine-Marie, whose Christian names were given to him by his parents among his four baptismal names.

His grandmother gave him more than just her Christian names. Her poems, *Songs for Marie,* gave him the passion of her Christian faith. Her social essay, *Strength through Work and Perseverance,* reaffirmed his own almost fanatic devotion to duty. Her *Life of Chateaubriand* introduced him to the writer who was to be the strongest literary influence upon his own style and thinking. Finally, her greatest gift was her romantic history, *The Liberator of Ireland, or The Life of Daniel O'Connell*. It remained for him a lifelong example of man's resistance to persecution, religious and national, an inspiring example that Charles de Gaulle never forgot.

The writings and influences of his grandfather and grandmother, and his namesake, Uncle Charles de Gaulle, are verifiable factors which, when added to the fancies of imaginative history writers, reveal to us a young boy raised to believe in God and country and his own family's tradition of outstanding service to both. The tradition is as royalist as it is religious. The ideal of noble resistance to the foreign enemy is coupled with the concept of patriotic dissidence from any authority other than that to which the de Gaulles chose to be loyal.

Charles de Gaulle, prophet of mechanized warfare, whose theories went unhonored by an unheeding high command, yet who never for a moment doubted that he was right and all others were wrong, is the man whose moral courage and self-confidence grew within the boy who played the role of the Knight of Agincourt, similarly unhonored, unheeded and right. There was never much point in saying to Charles de Gaulle that he might conceivably be wrong just because he was out of step with every-one else; as he saw it, he and his ancestors were often out of step and just as often right. His self-righteousness and sense of history were so deeply rooted that at times he used a turn of phrase that shocked listeners who got the impression that he really believed himself to be a living reincarnation of past heroes of France, if not eternal France herself.

* * *

Dreamers are always considered a bit strange by those who are too dull to dream, and little boys who prefer to play "history" rather than football are bound to be considered odd by their ball-playing fellows. Charles de Gaulle was always an odd one as a boy, as a young collegian and as a soldier. Tall and awkward, taciturn and shy, an introvert who on occasion betrayed a confident aggressiveness that left extroverts gasping, he was always a lonely, strange figure, never of or with the crowd.

Before he even started his schooling he was deeply engrossed in military strategy. He was struck by his mother's story of how, as a young girl during the war of 1870, she had broken down and cried when she had learned that Marshal Bazaine had capitulated. He questioned his father intensely about the Marshal's inept handling of his army in the critical engagements at Vionville and Mars-la-Tour. Young Charles knew all the details of the capitulation at Sedan leading to the ultimate surrender of Paris, after the siege in which his father had been wounded. He begged his father to tell him every detail of the battle and kept shaking his head and pounding his fists in frustration, saying, "But we should have won, we could have won!"

His father was both astonished and pleased by the passion and the brilliance of his boy's soul and mind. They spent hours together reliving the history of their beloved country and talking about the glorious future ahead, dreaming of the day when France would rise again in all her grandeur and liberate the lost territories of Alsace and Lorraine. Henri de Gaulle was not surprised to see his son organize neighborhood boys and schoolmates into opposing armies in historic war games. He looked on approvingly as he saw Charles play the roles of Napoleon or Joan of Arc, Louis XIV or Clemenceau, not suspecting, perhaps, that the boy was becoming an incurable romantic, living in a very special dream world of his own.

Henri de Gaulle encouraged his favorite son to pursue his military studies and to broaden them by reading the great philosophers. Charles found in his father's library the works of Goethe and Nietzsche, which opened up new worlds for him. In his teens he read Nietzsche the way other boys were reading Jules Verne. Long before his teachers mentioned their names, de Gaulle had read Socrates, Plato and Kant. The classic Greeks and the modern German philosophers had the most profound influence upon his thinking. The literary style he enjoyed most was the lyrical prose of Chateaubriand, whose works remained his favorite reading.

Young Charles tried his own hand at writing in his teens. He composed a one-act playlet in verse, which he entitled "Une Mauvaise Rencontre"—"A Bad Encounter." His family liked it so much that they had it privately printed at some expense. It was the story of a traveler accosted by a tramp who stopped him and demanded his hat, shoes, cape and purse. The tramp was a bandit who liked to pretend that his victim was really a good Samaritan charitably handing over his possessions. The bandit, a clever rogue, said to the traveler, "Won't you save a soul before it is seized with the blind desire to kill a fellow man?" With a cynical gesture of courtesy, the rogue offered to "exchange" his torn and filthy jacket for the traveler's handsome cape and, when his victim hesitated, added this final reason to prove it was a good exchange: "Moreover, look here: I have two pistols cocked!"

Charles de Gaulle was sixteen when he authored this interesting little morality in verse. It suggests a somewhat precocious understanding of the rationale of power. The thought expressed in the line "save a soul before it is seized with the blind desire to kill a fellow man" is a prophetic preview of a technique that Charles de Gaulle would learn to perfect in a turbulent career. Throughout his several careers, Charles de Gaulle often won his way by saying, in effect, "Do as I ask in order to prevent me from doing something terrible that I do not want to do but will do unless you yield."

As a young boy and a young man de Gaulle learned how to impose his will on bigger, stronger boys by sheer force of character. On summer holidays he would round up young farm boys and organize them in his favorite war games. At home he would play with his brother, Xavier, and his friends, three and four years older than himself, and they would follow the orders of the strong-minded, cocksure youngster.

Everyone knows the nickname he had at the Military Academy of St. Cyr: the "Big Asparagus." Less well-known, but far more revealing of his personality and the impression he made on his schoolmates were two other nicknames that his classmates still recall. The first name he was given, as a plebe, was "Le Coq," the fighting cock that is one of the historic symbols of France itself. Another nickname, given him by his commanding officer in his first stage of army duty, was "Le Connétable," the Constable, an ancient rank of the highest officer in the army.

De Gaulle was accepted for the St. Cyr Military College in the summer of 1909, just after a new regulation had been passed requiring every cadet to spend one year of service as a common soldier in the ranks before training to be an officer. It was at that very outset of his career that he began to earn his nicknames and the reputation of a brilliant but difficult and insubordinate individualist.

He chose the Thirty-third Regiment of Infantry, stationed in Arras, for his basic training. The commanding officer of the company de Gaulle was assigned to was a Captain de Tugny, who probably never forgot the year when it was his duty to give orders to Private Charles de Gaulle. When asked later why he had kept de Gaulle in the lowest rank and had never promoted him beyond private, long-suffering Captain de Tugny replied: "What use to make that young man a sergeant when the only military title that would interest him would be Grand Constable!" Thereafter de Gaulle's classmates at St. Cyr—among them a future Marshal of France, Alphonse Juin—never tired of calling him Grand Constable, when they were not calling him "Le Coq" or a variety of other names, including "Deux-mètres," which might be freely translated as "Mr. Two-Yards," referring, of course, to his height, which was only one of the characteristics that marked him for special attention.

Charles de Gaulle, according to the records, made a very poor common soldier, as one might expect from so uncommon a young man. His sergeant, like Churchill many years later, considered him a heavy cross to bear. For one long year an almost daily battle was waged between Private Charles de Gaulle and the martinet inspecting sergeant of his company, who found de Gaulle to be one of the most awkward, undisciplined recruits he had ever had the misfortune to train.

The Charles de Gaulle who knew his military history of France by heart, who had fought hundreds of mock battles, enacting the roles of the greatest heroes of France, had no patience with the plodding dullards who reigned over the common soldier of the ranks. He hated barracks life and the stupid regulations which most men hate when they are first subjected to basic army drill. It was not that de Gaulle rejected the very necessary discipline and constant drill that make for perfect teamwork and almost automatic reactions in time of battle. What he objected to were the old-fashioned, long-out-of-date, time-wasting procedures that were not merely dull but, even worse, dulling the best young material of the army.

His barracks mates used to wait with delight for each inspection, knowing that the inevitable would happen and that de Gaulle would so draw upon himself the wrath of the sergeant that they would all get off with only the most cursory glance from the harassed top-kick.

"De Gaulle!" the sergeant would bellow.

"Present," the giant recruit would reply, trying to stand at attention smartly but getting himself off balance as he struggled to hold his ungainly body in regulation position.

The sergeant would groan in despair as he watched the performance; then, lifting his eyes from the far-off peak of de Gaulle's cap, he would see on the rack behind him the recruit's field pack, loosely folded and bulging in places in which a regulation field pack is not expected to bulge. The sergeant would take his stick, poke the pack, which would come tumbling down, bursting open en route, shedding a very unregimental bundle of parade red trousers wrapped around the works of the philosopher Henri Bergson. The fact that Bergson, a friend of Henri de Gaulle and a frequent visitor to the de Gaulle home, was fond of young Charles, who had spent many afternoons listening to him discuss philosophy with his father, was probably not known to the inspecting sergeant. Even if it had been, one may well doubt that he would have viewed it as a reasonable excuse for a slovenly field pack.

It was undoubtedly in the first experience of army life that de Gaulle began to form his own opinion about the way the army was run and the caliber of some of its officers—a low opinion which he was never to revise as time and circumstances brought him into frequent clashes with authority. De Gaulle's opinion of the army, expressed freely even after the army had helped bring him back to power in 1958, is typified in a remark that had a wide circulation in Paris at the time: "The French Army has always been wrong."

De Gaulle's first clash with the army authorities, which had begun in that first period in Arras, seems in retrospect to have been an act of predestination, as do so many events in the life of this man of destiny. Stubborn and proud, Charles de Gaulle decided that he would return to Arras and the Thirty-third Regiment after his graduation from St. Cyr. The privilege of choosing a regiment is given only to honor students, but Charles de Gaulle never doubted that this would be his rank on graduation, as indeed it was. He was graduated among the first ten of a class of more than two hundred.

De Gaulle's decision to return as a second lieutenant to the regiment where he had suffered so many humiliations as a cadet was responsible for an association which was to influence his entire career. The colonel commanding the Thirty-third when de Gaulle returned was Henri-Philippe Pétain. There are the elements of a Greek tragedy in this first encounter and early friendship of these two men who were to play their roles almost thirty years later, when Pétain capitulated to Hitler and de Gaulle fled to London to raise the standard of resistance, in a real-life fulfillment of his childhood fantasies.

All the elements of greatness began to mature in the young officer who had been born with a great name and encouraged to believe in a destiny of grandeur. The teachings of great writers had been more than learned, they had been so absorbed as to permeate his being. His courage, self-confidence, crusading spirit, consciousness of personal mission—all were full-formed in the young sublieutenant who was the biggest man in his regiment in every meaning of the word. All that remained to permit this potential for greatness to be achieved was a great challenge, the opportunity to render "the signal service" he did not doubt would come.

The great challenge was not far distant when Sublieutenant Charles de Gaulle arrived in Arras and reported for duty to Colonel Pétain in October 1912. Thunderheads were forming in the skies over Africa as the imperial powers competed for colonies. They heralded the approaching storm that was to break out in full fury over Europe two years later. De Gaulle's class at St. Cyr had been convinced that its postgraduate studies would be taken not in any war college, but in war itself. During basic cadet-training in Arras, one of de Gaulle's constant quarrels with his company commander and the inspecting sergeant was the lack of preparation of the army for the coming war with Germany. He had argued that its training and equipment were inadequate for a conflict with a numerically superior adversary. De Gaulle had lectured his barracks mates and classmates on the need for new strategy and new equipment to permit French quality to triumph over German quantity.

On his graduation and return to Arras, at last with his own command, albeit a tiny squad of men, Sublieutenant Charles de Gaulle threw himself into his mission with a drive and sense of responsibility as though he were the commanding general of a huge army. The soldiers were astonished by a squad leader who talked to them about the glory and grandeur of France and lectured them on great battles of history with almost no interest in their ability to do a smart right-about turn. He commanded like an officer who never expected his men to do anything but march straight ahead and capture the Kaiser single-handed.

Colonel Pétain watched his most junior officer with amusement at first, then with growing respect, particularly after he himself had a first-hand experience of Charles de Gaulle's personal style of military reasoning and comportment.

Pétain was lecturing his officers on the historic battle of Arras in 1654, in preparation for deploying his regiment over that ancient battlefield in one of their war-game exercises. He was going over the course of the battle blow by blow, discussing the relative merits and mistakes of the Prince de Condé and Turenne. Despite Vicomte de Turenne's eventual victory at the head of the royal forces, Pétain argued that Prince de Condé had outmaneuvered him through much of the battle, and particularly at Hocquincourt.

The respectful silence of the officers was suddenly broken by the booming interruption of a powerful voice from the back of the room: "But, Colonel, no!"

Everyone turned to stare at the foolhardy officer who had interrupted the regimental colonel. It was Sublieutenant Charles de Gaulle, red-faced and embarrassed at his own temerity, but now obliged to carry on and explain his outburst.

"Surely, Colonel, the proof of the tactical skill is in the eventual result. You argue that Condé was right not to try to outflank Hocquincourt, after capturing La Ferté. But, sir, the answer is that the firepower of Turenne was so great and so well-handled that Condé was persuaded not to persist in the engagement, and thus Arras was saved."

All eyes turned back to the front of the room and to the Colonel on the lecture stand, to see how he would meet the challenge of the brash junior officer.

"Stand up, Lieutenant de Gaulle!" Pétain ordered.

There was a tense moment of silence as Pétain stared across the classroom with conflicting emotions, torn between irritation at the breach of military etiquette and admiration for the depth of feeling and learning of his young officer. The tension broke when the Colonel said, "Lieutenant, you have obviously studied your Siege of Arras very thoroughly. I applaud your diligence. We must talk over the lessons of this battle again some time."

From that day the older man and the youngster were drawn close together. In the officers' quarters, off-duty as well as in formal regimental exercises, Colonel Pétain was frequently seen in excited conversation with Sublieutenant de Gaulle, discussing the great battles of history and the coming test of strength that both men believed to be inevitable, indeed desirable, to reverse the results of the Franco-Prussian War and to regain the lost provinces.

De Gaulle was convinced that the invention of the machine gun and the rapid-firing cannon dictated a drastic change in tactics and strategy. This corresponded exactly with Pétain's own view. Both men believed that this increased firepower virtually doomed the cavalry and required a shift to semistatic positions, with the infantry carrying the brunt of the attack by rapid sorties, from well-dug-in positions, under cover of heavy bombardment and machine-gun fire. Their theory, presaging the trench warfare which was to be featured in the bloody conflict so near in the future, was to get its ultimate test at Verdun, where Colonel Pétain won his reputation as France's greatest field commander and young Lieutenant de Gaulle was cited for outstanding action and bravery.

When war broke out, the Thirty-third Regiment, rated by the general staff as one of the most efficient fighting units in the army, was thrown immediately into action in the first few days of the fighting to hold the advancing Germans outside Dinant. Pétain still commanded the Regiment, and Charles de Gaulle, promoted to full lieutenant, was a platoon leader.

The Fifth Army commander, General Lanrezac, a tradition-bound staff-college pedant, threw his units into action with colors flying and bugles sounding the charge—all very romantic and dashing, but an act of suicide in the face of the Germans' intense artillery bombardment and murderous machine-gun fire. French bayonets in a fixed charge were of no use against the fountain of flames spurting through the ranks. The Thirty-third was badly seared, while Dinant was reduced to rubble by cannon bombardment.

Charles de Gaulle, at the head of his platoon in every charge, was one of the first officers to be hit, on August 15, 1914. He was evacuated to the hospital just the day before the British Expeditionary Force, which was to rush up and stem the German advance, landed at Boulogne.

De Gaulle, convalescing from his wound, had time to study the tactical errors that he had seen in his first action at Dinant. Following the course of the fighting from daily communiqués, he became more and more convinced that the general staff was using the tactics of 1870 to fight the war of 1914, with little understanding of how new weapons affected tactics. He was outspokenly bitter against Joffre as he lectured fellow officers at the hospital on the faults of the high command. His mistrust of hidebound martinets and "drill-book generals," which had been sown in his mind from the very first moment of basic training and which was to mark and shape his entire career, hardened in the first few weeks of World War I.

As de Gaulle lay in bed, frustrated and angry, his worst predictions came true. The Germans broke through the lines of the Fifth Army and sent it in full retreat, while Lanrezac clung hopelessly to his outmoded tactics. Only when Joffre appointed Gallieni to organize the Sixth Army did the tide of battle begin to turn, until the French and British together halted the Germans in the first battle of the Marne and began to push eastward.

De Gaulle, his wound healed but still convalescent, asked to return to his old unit immediately; the request, which normally would have been turned down, was in this instance gratefully approved because the Thirty-third had been decimated in the early action. He returned to find many of his comrades dead, many more wounded and hospitalized. Losses had been severe. Charles de Gaulle was welcomed back but, because he had still not completely recovered, was assigned as adjutant to the chief of staff pending complete recovery which would permit his going back into the line.

He fussed and fretted at the paper work of an adjutant, the more so because he thoroughly disapproved of the policies and directives that came down to his desk from the higher command. Although still marked unfit for combat, he begged his superiors to let him lead reconnaissance patrols on intelligence missions. Finally, relieved to get rid of so vexing a staff officer, they granted de Gaulle permission to go out on patrol.

His years of mock battles as a youngster, his long hours of reading the German philosophers, his intensive study of the language at school and his fearlessness made Charles de Gaulle an ideal intelligence officer. He crawled repeatedly out of the trenches, across no man's land, right up to the German barbed wire and, crouching there under cover of darkness, listened to the conversations of the enemy in the trenches. De Gaulle's patrol won immediate fame as the finest, most fearless reconnaissance patrol of the division. Time and again he brought back invaluable intelligence on German attack plans. On January 20, 1915, after months of valorous patrol duty, de Gaulle was cited in an order of the day of the Second Division:

> Lieutenant Charles de Gaulle has carried out a series of reconnaissance missions of the enemy positions, and has brought back with him information of the greatest value.

The Thirty-third Regiment was famed as one of the bravest of the Fifth Army, and Charles de Gaulle was known as one of the bravest of the brave men in Pétain's command. None of his comrades would bet that he would last out the war. He took far too many chances and volunteered for the most dangerous missions. He acted like a man possessed—and indeed he was and always would be.

De Gaulle was possessed by the spirits of the French heroes of history. He fought as though he were immortal, as though nothing could kill him. The young officer already felt the emotions that the old man he was to become expressed so many battles later in his memoirs: death was preferable to mediocrity. He was prepared to excel or expire. This was ever his sentiment and it became stronger as he assumed greater leadership responsibilities. It was a genuine imperative, never a bluff. De Gaulle walked hand in hand with death, a constant reassuring companion, his ultimate protection against decline and defeat.

Death almost claimed him a second time when he was wounded once again during a patrol at Mesnils-les-Hurlus. His wounds, more severe than those suffered at Dinant, kept him out of the lines for four months. Healed and clamoring for more action, he was promoted to captain on September 4, 1915, and took command of his first company at a post with the forbidding name "Cholera Farm," on route 108, near Berry-au-Bac.

Cholera did not get him, but the Germans did again, for the third time, only not with bullets. Captain de Gaulle was blown up by a mine and had the narrowest escape from instant death. Despite severe wounds, de Gaulle came back to action once more as commanding officer of the Tenth Company and in February 1916 marched his men off to take part in the defense of Verdun, one of the greatest battles of military history and one in which both de Gaulle and his mentor Pétain covered themselves with glory and blood.

Pétain no longer commanded the Thirty-third Regiment. He had been promoted to general and had responsibility for a vital sector of the front at Douaumont. De Gaulle's immediate commander was Lieutenant-Colonel Boudhors, who recorded this observation about his brave captain: "I was instructed to send an officer to General Levy, commanding the sector of Douaumont, to inform him of the precise position in the light of all the information at our disposal. In view of the gravity of the situation and of the importance attached to the mission, I thought that only Captain de Gaulle was capable of fulfilling it."

Captain de Gaulle carried out his mission exactly as his Lieutenant-Colonel expected him to. He carried out many more missions of intelligence and reconnaissance at Verdun and was one

of the most dedicated of the many indomitable men in that army
who marched into the enemy fire shouting Pétain's unforgettable
order: "They shall not pass."

Pass they did not, but the wall that stopped the assault of the
crown prince of Germany was made of the bodies of hundreds of
thousands of valiant Frenchmen. And one of those bodies fester-
ing on the fields of Douaumont was the body of Charles de Gaulle,
left for dead after a vicious hand-to-hand fight with units of the
Brandenburger Regiment.

The men of the French Thirty-third had fought like demons as
the tide of battle flowed across the Douaumont defenses. In close-
quarter combat Captain de Gaulle used a pistol at point-blank
range while Germans surged all around and through his company.
At the height of the fighting a German reared up at his side, thrust
forward with his bayonet and pierced de Gaulle's thigh, bringing
him crashing down into the mud like a towering tree cut down by
a tempest. And just after his wounded body hit the ground, a shell
exploded only yards away, spraying red-hot jagged chunks of
metal across the field, one of which tore through the skull of the
felled giant as he lay helpless in the muck and blood.

Charles de Gaulle lay half-buried in the battleground, uncon-
scious and almost dead, for hours. When he came back to life he
was being carried through the darkness, but he knew that he
would not be seeing his own men for a very long time because the
voices he heard through the throbbing pain in his head were
speaking German. De Gaulle had been picked up by a German
reconnaissance patrol combing the battlefields after the action.

Many years later, when writing his memoirs, he recalled that
moment and remembered how he had reflected on the irony of
battle. "I realized that these men who were now saving my life
were those who, only a little time before, in the hand-to-hand
struggle, were trying desperately to kill me." De Gaulle was
always a fighter who understood and appreciated other men who
fight for their ideals. The de Gaulle who, cut by a bayonet and
ripped by shrapnel, could rise above himself when reflecting on the
captors who had maimed him was the same de Gaulle who, trying
to end another terrible war, had the courage to call the Algerian
rebels brave men and to offer them "la paix des braves" when no
other French leader would have dared publicly to call them
anything but terrorists or assassins.

Verdun was a milestone on de Gaulle's march to greatness.

General Pétain, lamenting the loss of his friend and valued officer, cited him in an order of March 2, 1916, issued at Verdun:

> Captain de Gaulle, commanding a company, reputed for his high intellectual and moral qualities, at a moment when his battalion was decimated under fire of a ferocious bombardment, and when the enemy was investing his company on all sides, carried his men into a furious attack and fierce hand-to-hand assault, the only solution which he judged to be compatible with his sentiments of military honor. He is an officer without equal in every respect.

The citation carried with it the award of the Cross of the Legion of Honor, one of the few honors that superior officers were to grant to this admirable but troublesome soldier of France who, despite his heroic combat record against foreign enemies, was to win his greatest victories and fight his most courageous battles against the French Army itself and, at times, against the majority of his fellow Frenchmen. Never did this paradox strike him as a contradiction, for it was not the army that he served. The army was only a means—one of many—to serve France. Such was his immaculate concept.

CHAPTER TWO

ADVICE AND DISSENT

> *Faced by a challenge, the man of character has recourse only to himself. Not that he wishes to ignore orders or neglect counsel but that he has a passion to impose his will and the jealousy of all other decisions.*
>
> CHARLES DE GAULLE, *The Edge of the Sword*

FOR ORDINARY MEN capture simply meant the end of the war. The only problem was to stay fit and find some way to pass the long, boring hours of imprisonment. For extraordinary men whatever happens is not an end, it is only the beginning of a new challenge and a new opportunity. Roosevelt toughened his mind and soul in his fight against paralysis; Stalin used prison as a time for more study and planning for the eventual day of revolution. Charles de Gaulle fought his way back to health from his terrible wounds, like Roosevelt, and, like Stalin, used his thirty-two months in prison for study and planning for the future.

Always a solitary man, he kept to himself in his first prison camp at Friedenberg, concentrating on exercising his stiff leg while the bayonet wound healed. He would walk painfully around the yard and then sit against the wall and massage his thigh and knee in his big, strong hands. During rest periods and in his cell he would read German newspapers and war communiqués, following the course of battle and improving his knowledge of the German language. De Gaulle was convinced that Germany would long be either a dangerous enemy in war or an equally dangerous competitor in times of peace, challenging France for leadership in Europe. And since he never doubted that some day he would be called upon to play a leading role in French affairs, he felt it imperative to make himself expert in all things

German. Being a war prisoner could, therefore, be a misfortune that might be turned to good use.

De Gaulle, the scholar and statesman, had the same gift of foresight that he possessed in the field of military tactics and strategy. Although he regarded Germany as a traditional enemy, he sensed the need to end this enmity some day and had a vision of the great things that the remarkable French and German peoples might do together instead of to each other.

In his military treatise, *Vers l'Armée de métier,* there is an extraordinary essay on the French and the Germans which reveals not only deep insights into the character of the two peoples but insights into the mind of the writer himself, as well as an example of a literary style that makes de Gaulle one of France's great poet-soldiers. In his writings Charles de Gaulle achieved, in reverse, the wish of Victor Hugo: "If I had not been a poet, I would have been a soldier."

Charles de Gaulle, soldier-poet, revealed himself in his essay on the French and German peoples. He revealed both his admiration for their fine qualities and his contempt for their base characteristics. He showed a deep understanding of both peoples and wrote with an objectivity that placed him above both, as though he were not a Frenchman himself, but some Olympian observer watching a strange breed that interested him but was not his kin. "Between Gauls and Germans, alternate victories have solved and settled nothing. Sometimes, worn out by war, the two peoples seem to come close together, but they are like two panting wrestlers leaning on each other only to catch their breath.

"It is not," de Gaulle argued, "that each underestimates the value of the other; there are moments when each dreams of the great things they could do together. But the way they think is so different that this keeps both peoples in a constant state of mistrust."

De Gaulle then went on to describe the Frenchman and the German in two of the most sharply etched pen portraits of contemporary literature.

> This Frenchman, who takes so much pain to be orderly in his thinking and so little in his actions, this logician always torn by doubt, this careless hard worker, this imperial adventurer who loves nothing more than his hearth at home, this fervent admirer of alexandrine verse,

tailcoats and royal gardens, who nonetheless sings popular songs, dresses sloppily and litters his own lawns, this Colbert who collaborates with Louvois, this revolutionary Jacobin who shouts "Long Live the Emperor!," this man beaten at Charleroi who dares mount the attack on the Marne, in short, how can the German ever join, understand or repose his confidence in this unstable, uncertain, contradictory people?

Charles de Gaulle had little illusion or love for the German, but his portrait, although etched in acid, betrayed an admiration for some of the German qualities he wished the French would possess. De Gaulle saw Germany as an "elemental force of nature, a matrix of powerful but confused instincts." His sharp pen slashed out the German characteristics:

These born artists without taste, these highly skilled technicians of a feudal society, these bellicose but loving fathers of families, whose dining rooms are designed as temples, whose toilets are Gothic palaces, who build their factories in forests, these oppressors who want to be loved, these servile warriors, these chivalrous knights who swill their beer until they vomit.

At times Germany appeared to de Gaulle as a "sublime but glaucous sea from which the fisherman's net can pull, pell-mell, monsters and treasures." At other times it was a "multi-colored cathedral" which "organizes into a symphony for the senses, mind, soul and emotions, the light and the religion of the world, but whose murky transept, echoing with the roars of barbarians, blinds the eyes, the spirit and the soul."

When one reads these lines one understands some of the paradoxes of de Gaulle himself: this untypical but very French Frenchman, this nationalist with so little illusion about his nation, this ally who admired, while ridiculing, his friends and foes alike, this man who loved his country but not his countrymen, this passionate iceberg, this hermit happy only in cheering crowds, this soldier who despised militarists, this politician who refused to join a party or even let one join him, this statesman who served no state and respected no man, this dreamer who wished to be a man of action!

* * *

All through the long days of his imprisonment in German camps the man of action in de Gaulle dreamed of returning to action, his very soul itching for freedom under the chafe of the rough prison garb. He seized every attempt to break out and often succeeded in evading his guards. But he never got very far. His makeshift German uniforms might get him quickly past careless patrols. His fluent German enabled him to ask for directions and food without arousing suspicion. There was, however, no way for him to disguise the frame that had won him the nickname of "Mr. Two-Yards." All patrols had to do was to look for a giant with a huge nose jutting out from an undersized head, walking with the ungainly gait of a young giraffe, who, when questioned, would answer with the voice of a bull. He never had a chance to evade search patrols. Charles de Gaulle was one of those men who could not get lost in a crowd.

Recapture and punishment had no effect on him. Solitary confinement he regarded as a pleasant way of life. He passed the hours reciting the Greek poets or declaiming aloud in German to perfect his fluency for his next attempt. He tried to break out of every camp they sent him to, from Friedenberg to Szuczyn to Magdeburg. Each escape attempt saw him try a new technique, the last of which was a tunnel, although it seemed the most difficult means of escape for a man with his huge and partially crippled body. He worked patiently, tirelessly at his tunnel until he was caught digging shortly before reaching the outer wall.

As penalty for that attempted escapade he was sent to the camp for hardened offenders, the gloomy fortress of Ingolstadt, an escape-proof prison surrounded by a sixty-foot wall and a wide moat. The cells, inside yet another moat in the interior of the fortress, were large rooms deep inside and underneath the fort, where six prisoners were put together in each room for greater security.

With escape almost impossible, with his wounds hurting and his leg stiffening in the dank, tomblike cells, de Gaulle for the first time experienced something close to despair, his spirit finally shaken badly. He once told his aide-de-camp, Lieutenant Claude Bouchinet-Serreulles, in London decades later, that he thought the end had come. "If I had not remembered my Greek poetry, I think I should have died," he confessed. Serreulles, now a banker in Paris, recalls his astonishment on learning that Greek poetry was the medicine that saved de Gaulle's life in prison camp.

It was in Ingolstadt that de Gaulle met some fellow prisoners who were destined to achieve great fame and with whom he spent long hours discussing the war and the postwar world.

One who had also been at another camp with him was France's ace flyer Roland Garros. It was Garros who explained to de Gaulle the importance of the airplane in modern combat. Garros was enthusiastic about its future as a major offensive weapon and saw it as a new type of cavalry reconnaissance. De Gaulle listened carefully, took pages and pages of notes on all types of aircraft and their capabilities. In its rudimentary stage of development he did not yet see the plane as an offensive weapon. The Germans were to develop that later in their screaming dive bombers. But de Gaulle, already enthusiastic about the tank as mechanized cavalry, immediately saw the value of the plane as a reconnaissance scout for artillery and intelligence, and incorporated it into his first theory of mechanized warfare.

Among the other fellow prisoners there was the writer Rémy Roure, who was to become one of the major voices of Free France and a leading journalist of France in the mid-twentieth century. The publisher Berger-Levrault, who later printed one of de Gaulle's masterpieces, his essay on leadership, *Le Fil de l'épée,* was another cellmate. Berger-Levrault was so impressed by de Gaulle's discussions of tactics and strategy that he said of him, "He is a remarkably gifted officer who will be without doubt one day one of the greatest exponents of the military art"—an opinion of de Gaulle shared by all his prison companions, including one who was to become the youngest general and then marshal of the Red Army before being executed in a purge—young Lieutenant Tukhachevsky of the Imperial Russian Army.

De Gaulle and Tukhachevsky became good friends after their first encounter, when the stocky gay Russian officer came over to the tall brooding Frenchman and asked, "Are you sad because the war is lost?"

The Frenchman glowered and growled, "It isn't lost! Why, it's almost already won!"

The Russian laughed and said, "No, no . . . I meant are you sad because you are out of it . . . it is lost to you." When de Gaulle, unanswering, lowered his head and turned away, Tukhachevsky continued, "What good is it to be sad? The present may not be ours, but perhaps the future will be." De Gaulle lifted his head, smiled in return, for these were words that went to his heart.

Yes, the future would be theirs, he said to the Russian, not
realizing how fatefully accurate that prediction would prove to
be.

* * *

Within a very short time the fellow prisoners and friends, de
Gaulle and Tukhachevsky, were fighting on opposite sides of the
barricades. Only a year after the defeat of Germany had liberated
them both, both were back at war: Tukhachevsky in the revolutionary bolshevik ranks, the new Red Army, and de Gaulle in the
allied interventionist forces that went to the aid of the White
Russian loyalists.

In May 1919 Captain de Gaulle reported for duty to General
Joseph Haller, commanding the Fifth Division of Chasseurs being
readied for service in Poland and Russia. The commander-in-chief
of the French Expeditionary Force was General Weygand, who,
like Pétain, was destined to clash bitterly later with the brilliant
young officer whom he first commanded, admired and decorated
for valor. Forty-six years after their first service together President
de Gaulle refused to permit military honors to be rendered to
General Weygand in a funeral ceremony that the family and
friends of Weygand requested to be held in Les Invalides. De
Gaulle would not forgive Weygand, even in death, for having capitulated to and collaborated with the Nazis. French generals do
finally die, but their hatreds never fade away.

Under Weygand's command in the Russian campaign, Charles
de Gaulle served as a combat intelligence officer and won his third
citation in an order of the day at the army level. General Weygand
cited him for "the particularly brilliant manner in which he
accomplished, in the most painful conditions, several missions for
the armies in the offensives of August 1920. Demonstrating a sure
judgment, exposing himself to direct contact with the enemy in
order to get precise intelligence (in operations against the Army of
Budremy and in the capture of Humbrezon) he was, for his chief,
a most invaluable support and, for his Polish comrades, the very
example of an accomplished officer."

The intervention, ill-conceived and ill-fated, did not last long,
but long enough for intelligence officer de Gaulle, always observing, always preparing for his day of responsibility, to take good
note of the vast expanses of the Russian land and the spirit of the
poorly equipped but inspired fighting men who were defending

their land against the invader. He never doubted that those men resented the allied intervention, not as bolshevik revolutionaries, but—more importantly, in de Gaulle's view—as Russians fighting for their motherland.

De Gaulle had nothing but contempt for Communism as an ideology and a strong mistrust of it as a subversive political force. Yet there were many qualities that he admired in the Communist leaders—not only in Stalin, whom he could not but admire as a powerful leader of a great people, but even in a colorless functionary like Molotov, the dreary prototype of Communist man. De Gaulle's description of Molotov during his first negotiation with him in London in 1942 betrays an astonishing appreciation, almost an envy, of a Russian like Molotov whom de Gaulle would have liked to have had as his own trusted aide:

> I found in Mr. Molotov a man who seemed both physically and mentally—lock, stock and barrel—made to fill the office which had been delegated to him. His tone serious, his gestures rare, his politeness thoughtful but stiff, his gaze directed within himself, the Soviet Minister for Foreign Affairs said what he had to say evenly and listened with attention. But he let nothing escape him that appeared spontaneous. Nothing would move him, make him laugh or irritate him.

Subconsciously de Gaulle may have been describing himself, or perhaps that part of himself which he would have liked to have re-created in the image of a perfect Gaullist foreign minister; a man not too unlike the one he finally did find, Maurice Couve de Murville, his foreign minister through the first seven-year term of his presidency, from 1958 through 1965. Without reference to Monsieur de Murville, one might note the very interesting conclusion that de Gaulle draws in his description of the Soviet Foreign Minister: "In Molotov, who was and wanted to be merely a perfectly adjusted cog in an implacable machine, I thought I had identified a complete success of the totalitarian system. I paid tribute to its greatness." De Gaulle added, almost as an afterthought and with an evident regret, "I could feel the melancholy of it."

Charles de Gaulle's admiration for the Russians inclined him to think of the Soviet Union as simply a modern manifestation of Mother Russia and to discount Communism as a secondary rather than a primary motivating force of Soviet world policies. Many an allied diplomat and statesman felt uneasy as he listened to de Gaulle expound his theory of the primacy of Russianism over Communism. Some unsubtle minds even began to suspect that de Gaulle might be "soft on Communism" or even pro-Communist, as though Charles de Gaulle could ever be soft on anything or pro-anything other than France.

In meetings with Stalin and Khrushchev, de Gaulle always acted on the assumption that these men were seeking advantage for Russia first and for Communism second. It was not that de Gaulle doubted that the Soviet leaders kept in mind the aim of world revolution, but he regarded Soviet leaders as Russian nationalists rather than fanatic missionaries, and he was convinced by first-hand experience that they would always put Russian security ahead of Communist proselytizing. More than once he saw Soviet statesmen sacrifice European Communist parties and betray Communist doctrines and dogma as they maneuvered in the game of world power politics. These experiences confirmed a theory that had already begun to take form in his mind very early in his career, dating back to his first experience with Tukhachevsky, who wore alternately the uniforms of the Czar and the Soviets, but who never at any time ceased to be a Russian.

* * *

The Polish General Staff, deeply impressed by the extraordinary intellectual and moral qualities of the French officer, whose exploits were known throughout the country, asked de Gaulle to stay on as an instructor in tactics and intelligence operations at the War College. De Gaulle, intensely interested in Poland and Russia, mindful of French interests in Eastern Europe, eagerly accepted the offer. But he was not able to stay very long, for his fame had spread back home in France and, in October 1921, he was recalled to serve as teacher of military history at St. Cyr, pending further study at the Superior Staff College, where officers of promise were prepared for higher command assignments.

He returned to France wearing a new decoration given him by the admiring Polish government, and he proudly showed his Cross of St. Wenceslas to the young bride whom he hardly knew, for he had married in France after a rapid courtship, between service in the Ukraine and his return to Poland to take part in the defense of Warsaw.

Captain de Gaulle had come back to France in November 1919, after the Russian campaign, for a short rest. It was at the Salon d'Automne, in Paris, that he saw a tall handsome girl smile and wave to one of his friends in the buffet of the museum. He asked who she was and his friend said that she was his cousin, offering to introduce de Gaulle to her if he wanted. He wanted, he said.

The two young men marched promptly through the crowd toward the table of the Vendroux family. Mr. Vendroux was a prosperous businessman from Calais who had brought his daughter to Paris for the year-end holidays. She was not a pretty girl in the popular conception, but de Gaulle was struck by her dignity, her calm repose and an inner beauty which shone through her eyes, at least as seen by his eyes. As he stepped forward to be introduced, he could hear the orchestra playing the latest hit song of the day, "The Destiny Waltz."

De Gaulle folded his long body into the small space left at the table and balanced precariously on a tiny stool as someone put a teacup into hands that would have held a pumpkin more comfortably. He sat there, stiff and awkward, afraid to move, when pastries were passed around; as so often in the life of Charles de Gaulle, destiny walked by, jiggled his arm and sent his hot cup of tea in one scalding wave into the lap of Yvonne Vendroux, the girl he wanted to meet.

The next day the gallant captain called at the Vendroux' hotel to renew his apologies for his clumsiness. Two weeks later he called on the family again, this time at their home in Charleville, still apologizing. A few weeks later, without apology, he proposed, was accepted and on April 7, 1920, shortly before his return to action in Poland, Charles and Yvonne were married. Yvonne Vendroux has been his constant companion for almost a half-century.

* * *

Madame de Gaulle was always shy, retiring, living in the shadow cast by her giant husband. A devout Catholic, she devoted herself to church and charity work, but always with complete discretion, keeping far in the background. As wife of the President of the Republic, she was obliged to participate in public events as the First Lady of France. Although she kept her participation in public ceremonies to a minimum, Madame de Gaulle did not mind in the least being seen informally in public. Like any French matron, she went to the market in the morning with her shopping bag, not to prepare meals, of course—she had the entire elaborate apparatus of the presidential palace at her disposal—but rather to select something that she knew her husband liked, to maintain at least the illusion of an individual, private life. She was respected by the majority of the people of France as a good Christian mother with all the old-fashioned virtues. But Paris wits, who respect nothing, nicknamed her "Tante Yvonne," and caricaturists depicted her as the typical provincial "Aunty Yvonne," a rather dowdy bourgeoise matron.

Madame de Gaulle was certainly a matron and a bourgeoise, but when she became First Lady she was not permitted to be dowdy. The fashion industry is important to France, and the obligations of office require that the First Lady be dressed by the famous couturiers of Paris, particularly on ceremonial occasions. No rival of the Duchess of Windsor, she was rather more chic than the Queen of England. Cartoonists, however, depicted her as looking like England's Queen Mother, to whom she did indeed bear a physical resemblance and whose rigid moral standards she emulated. Jokes that cannot be printed were common cocktail chatter in Paris, and one could hear sharp criticism of her even in some governmental circles among those whose friends were dismissed, they claim, because "Tante Yvonne" had learned they were divorced. She was known to be the unofficial but powerful moral censor of the Elysée Palace.

Several French magazines have printed stories attempting to portray Madame de Gaulle. None had the ring of authenticity nor any significant, illuminating glimpses of the de Gaulles' private life. In fact, this private life was always kept very private. Back in the early days of the Free French movement in London, Madame de Gaulle was hardly ever seen at all. The General had an apartment in the Hotel Connaught in London, but Madame de Gaulle remained at their house in the country outside London. As a reporter I saw General de Gaulle almost weekly through most of that period, but I never saw Madame de Gaulle for the first three years; then I met her only to shake hands at a formal reception. I have had dozens of conversations with the General, but not one with his wife, and I know no one other than a very few intimates who claim any knowledge of her, and those who do will not discuss her.

It is not that there is anything secret or to be hidden, but simply that General de Gaulle, President of the French Republic, is a personage, not a person. Charles de Gaulle, the man, is something quite apart, and he has never permitted the two to be confused. To an American—who grew up with the Roosevelt family and the President's dog Fala, Margaret Truman, the Eisenhower children, grandchildren and golf scores, John-John, Caroline and Macaroni, Luci, Him and Her—it is astonishing to know little or nothing about de Gaulle's children (a daughter, Anne, who was retarded and died in her youth; a second daughter, Elisabeth, married to an army officer; his son, Philippe, a naval officer), his hobbies (television viewing) or his wife.

* * *

In the early years of their marriage Charles and Yvonne de Gaulle settled down to what promised to be the tranquil life of a peacetime officer serving as a history professor at his old school. But Charles de Gaulle is a man of tempests, not of tranquillity, and even without war he found enough conflicts to keep him fighting with his superiors in the absence of more martial enemies.

He left St. Cyr to enter the Staff College in November 1922 and immediately began lecturing his teachers in his own inimitable style. This was his opportunity at the staff level to put into words the theories he had been formulating through all the long years of reading, playing, fighting, observing, from childhood reenactments of Agincourt through exercises at Arras to the battlefields from Verdun to Novo-Georgievsk to Warsaw.

Before Verdun, de Gaulle had criticized the high command for preparing to fight on the principles of the war of 1870, without taking into account the need to change tactics because of the cannon rifle and the machine gun. He and Pétain had agreed that the coming war with Germany would be a semistatic war, accurately foreseeing the trench warfare which evolved in 1915.

De Gaulle was therefore all the more appalled to find the Staff College leading theorist, General Moyrand, accepting the trench warfare of the battle just concluded as the new rule of war, once again preparing for the future by codifying the experiences of the past. De Gaulle, who had as much or more respect for and knowledge of the past as any man, argued that the major lesson of the past was the demonstration of constant change in military tactics. He violently denounced Moyrand's theory, known as the "méthode a priori," insisting that only disaster would befall the army that selected any rigid a priori universal system of strategy, for conditions that might prevail in a future war might very well be completely different from the conditions on which the a priori method had been based.

De Gaulle, analyzing the errors of this thinking in *Le Fil de l'épée,* wrote: "It seems that the French military mind simply refuses to recognize the essentially empiric nature of war action. It tries ceaselessly to construct doctrines which would permit it, a priori, to orient action, to conceive its form in advance, without taking into account the circumstances on which it might have to be based." De Gaulle went on to comment: "To believe that one is capable of avoiding all perils and surprises, through a system that dominates all eventualities, is undoubtedly a way to win a peace of mind, but it is an illusion to think that anyone has the power to ignore the mystery of the unknown."

Sentiments of this nature, expressed with the conciseness and acidity of de Gaulle's style, soon made him the most unpopular student-officer at the Staff College. For once de Gaulle did not have a commanding officer who understood and appreciated his genius and shared his views. The bitterness of his quarrels with General Moyrand, the denseness of the hierarchy, the lack of sympathy of fellow students who resented de Gaulle's superior manner only served to harden de Gaulle's heart and sharpen his tongue. He retreated more and more into himself, his personal penchant for solitude finding a rationalization in the hostility and incomprehension of those around him. It was the beginning of his long isolation in the army, growing more bitter through the years until the final tragic climax in the fall of France under an enemy who employed the tactics de Gaulle had tried in vain to have accepted by his own army.

Nothing embittered de Gaulle more than the tragicomic graduation exercise at the Staff College, in which General Moyrand gave de Gaulle command of the Blue Force, while he himself, the instructor and chief theorist, took command of the Red Force to teach his brash young pupil a real lesson and humiliate him in front of all the other officers.

The war game was fought in the foothills of the Alps. De Gaulle had personally reconnoitered the positions in advance and drawn up his battle plan to conform to the mountainous, tree-covered terrain. The difficulty of penetrating heavily wooded areas in the face of the firepower available to the defense suggested to de Gaulle that his troops should be organized into small, highly mobile, almost autonomous units for flanking and infiltration movements, taking advantage of the natural concealment that the terrain offered. This was the very opposite of Moyrand's theory of establishing a fixed front and concentrating on it devastating fire-power which could not be penetrated. De Gaulle believed that the answer to that was: "If you can't penetrate, infiltrate; if you can't go through the line, go around it."

As expected, General Moyrand had set up a closely knit defensive front for the Red Force, which his artillery covered so thoroughly that the Blue Force would not be able to gain an inch.

Blue Force Commander de Gaulle did not attempt to gain an inch through the impenetrable Red lines. He simply sent his units scuttling around the flanks while small commandos feigned a frontal attack, drawing Moyrand's fire until the mobile Blue forces had sped around the ends and then wheeled around to hit the Reds with stunning force in their backs, cutting them up and defeating them with ease, to the mortification of General Moyrand and the intense embarrassment of the senior Staff officers acting as observers and referees.

What enraged de Gaulle most was the fact that his decisive victory not only failed to shake Moyrand's conviction that his theory was correct but, even worse, that de Gaulle was accused of being lucky and was demoted in position as a result of having defeated his instructor in the graduation exercise. The stupidity and pettiness of his superiors so shook de Gaulle's confidence in the army that it required only one more act to destroy it completely and to set him on the road to rebellion to which events would inevitably lead him.

The final rupture was not long in coming.

Word of de Gaulle's spectacular defeat of Moyrand and his absurd punishment reached the ears of the Commander-in-Chief of the French Army, de Gaulle's old friend and leader, General Pétain, who promptly sent for de Gaulle, asking him to write a full detailed report on the entire incident.

Encouraged, Charles de Gaulle put himself to the report, summoning up all his military and literary skills, for he realized the

great opportunity that had been given to him, not only for
personal vindication but to impress the Commander-in-Chief
himself with the folly of the prevailing theory before it was too
late.

It seemed as though de Gaulle had won his point when Pétain
congratulated him on his report, telling everyone that it was one of
the most brilliant military essays he had ever seen, predicting a
leadership career for de Gaulle. To show that these were not
merely soothing words, Pétain appointed Charles de Gaulle instructor in military theory in the very same Superior Staff College,
with authority to expound his own doctrines. De Gaulle was
completely justified, returning in triumph.

He plunged back into work, determined to change the static
thinking of the current theorists and put into practice his own
developing ideas on mobile mechanized warfare, buoyed by the
approval of the Supreme Commander. At the end of his term of
teaching he was further honored by a call from Pétain appointing
de Gaulle to his general staff, where he served happily, with
growing confidence, until the termination of Pétain's own chair-
manship of the general staff. Pétain was succeeded by another
friend of de Gaulle, his commander in Poland, Maximilien Weygand.

De Gaulle, moving up in grade from captain to major, was
assigned to the General Staff of the Army of the Rhine for field
duty and intelligence on the German frontier, a post for which he
was ideally suited. He was happy, waiting for his friend General
Weygand to begin to put into effect his new theories, abandoning
the a priori doctrine which he had exploded and which he knew
Pétain disapproved. It was, therefore, just a matter of time before
his report would become a directive from Weygand, for Pétain
had surely taken this question up with him when transferring
supreme command and responsibility to him.

From his watch on the Rhine, Charles de Gaulle saw with
dismay the growing strength of Germany and the corresponding
inertia of France. Nothing had been done, nothing at all. Pétain
had not himself taken any steps to bring de Gaulle's theories to the
fore other than passing his report on in the mass of staff documents. Weygand went through all the routine motions of the
routine staff officer, making no attempt to repudiate the old
theories or institute any new training methods.

De Gaulle meanwhile had set himself the task of writing his first book, impelled both by his own literary appetite and family tradition and by the feeling that if he was to make any headway toward adoption of his ideas he would have to get more public attention, for, obviously, he could not count upon the torpid, unimaginative, tradition-blinded General Staff.

His first essay was about the German people and the German General Staff, entitled *La Discorde chez l'ennemi,* published in 1924 by his former prisonmate at Ingolstadt, Berger-Levrault. General Pétain made the public presentation of the book, saying, "One day a grateful France will call upon this man"—a prophecy all too sadly true for the aging hero of Verdun.

The main theme of the essay centered on de Gaulle's conviction that there is no universal system applicable to warfare but that war is waged and decided by personalities and circumstances of the moment. The only basic principles that hold true for all circumstances are the principles that apply to all national affairs, the determination of a people to succeed, a willingness to die for an ideal and a realistic assessment of all the factors that make a nation stronger or weaker than its neighbors.

The Germans had lost in 1918 although they were materially stronger, de Gaulle wrote, because of discord in their own ranks and because they were blinded by their own philosophy. He did not believe the French had won the battle of the Marne by superior tactics or strength, but rather because von Kluck had failed to follow orders and had gone his own way. De Gaulle found the Germans weakened by the long struggle of von Tirpitz against Bethmann-Hollweg to force him to declare unrestricted submarine warfare and by the governmental crisis of 1917, set off by the intrigues of Ludendorff.

Above all de Gaulle, himself a scholar of German philosophy and an avid, although critical, reader of Nietzsche, blamed the German General Staff for blind, fanatic adherence to the Nietzschean theories of the superman. He called the German generals "ambitious fanatics" who thought they must attain the qualities of superman "with his exceptional character, his will to power, his love of risk, his contempt of others," to the point of confusing their own personal glory with service to the general interest of the nation. De Gaulle sharply denounced the Master Race concept which the German General Staff evolved out of the writings of

Nietzsche and warned his fellow Frenchmen to be faithful to the
"rules of classic order and harmony" based upon a just balance of
forces, with no one quality developed to excess.

> This study will have achieved its purpose if it contrib-
> utes in a modest way to persuading our military chiefs of
> tomorrow to penetrate their minds and souls with the
> rules of classic order. It is in those basic rules that they
> will find a sense of balance, of what is possible, and just,
> which alone can render durable and fertile all of the
> creative energies.

As an example of what he meant, de Gaulle showed evidence of
his developing literary style in a little gem of a passage in which he
described a classic French royal garden:

> In a French-style garden no tree seeks to suffocate the
> others with its shade. The flower-beds are laid out harmo-
> niously in geometric designs, the tranquil pond does not
> aspire to become a waterfall, the statues do not clamor for
> attention. A kind of noble melancholy sometimes seems
> to pervade the air. Perhaps it comes from the belief that
> each individual element might, alone, have been able to
> shine more brilliantly. But that would have spoiled the
> over-all design, and the stroller can only be thankful for
> the classic rule that imposed upon the garden its
> magnificent harmony.

There is more in that description than the artistry of de Gaulle's
prose style. It contains, in embryo, his concept of government, his
design for the organization of the state. The royal garden of de
Gaulle was his ideal for France—a classic, royalist, harmonious
France, so different from the disorderly democracy of French
parliamentarianism or the slave superstate that neo-Roman te-
trarchs sought to mold out of the ancient German and Russian
lands. The individual statue that does not clamor for exclusive
attention but, at the same time, has its own beauty and is not
merely a duplicate of all the other statues was de Gaulle's ideal of
the talented, individual Frenchman, part of a cooperating society.
The tall trees that do not suffocate the others with their shadow,
but which obviously stand out above the bushes, are the wise
leaders of society. It is typical of de Gaulle that he felt—indeed,
enjoyed—the melancholy that would from time to time break

through this harmonious beauty, for this man who reveled in heroism could not but regret the rejection of heroism for those who live in a classic, controlled garden of life. One might add that it is even more regrettable that he refused to admit, during his own leadership of France, that he was a tall tree suffocating all others by his shade.

It is the very essence of de Gaulle that the "magnificent harmony" of his garden is enjoyed by a single solitary stroller. In his image, only one man walks through the garden and congratulates himself upon the "rule that imposed upon the garden its magnificent harmony." It is hard to resist the thought that the solitary figure is de Gaulle himself, the lonely leader, contemplating the beauty of his creation. Just as he hated the cold cruelty of Prussian despotism and of Communist collectivism, Charles de Gaulle abhorred the hearty team play of democratic republicanism. He would have been equally miserable in Valhalla, in a kolkhoz or in Disneyland.

It is no mere coincidence that Khrushchev, when asked what he particularly wanted to see during his tour of America, put Disneyland high on his list, whereas Charles de Gaulle's requests included the battlefield at Gettysburg.

This reporter will never forget a Sunday on the Eisenhower farm in Gettysburg, in May 1960, when French and American journalists and diplomats embarrassedly witnessed a dialogue of deaf men as Eisenhower proudly toured his stables and herds with a puzzled, bored de Gaulle until at the end of the day the French General asked the American to take him to the historic battleground just beyond the bullpens. De Gaulle came alive in the graveyard of the Civil War. Gettysburg was for him a classic garden pervaded with a noble melancholy, for it was there that unity was imposed in a collective effort that was made up of individual feats, where so many brave Americans had died so that the United States might live harmoniously and free, except of each other, in one nation, indivisible.

France has rarely known harmony, although it has enjoyed a magnificence just as rarely equaled by others. It was the ironic fate of Charles de Gaulle to yearn all his life for harmony while playing the role of the stormy petrel in all the unharmonious tempests of our times.

He was cast from the start in the role of the unhonored prophet shouting in the wilderness—a role which he was particularly fitted

to play by temperament and training. There was much of the
brooding, black Irishman, the Daniel O'Connell, in Charles de
Gaulle, and he had much to brood about, convinced as he was in
his observation post on the Rhine that the German generals,
blaming the politicians for their defeat, were more arrogant than
ever and plotting revenge, while the French generals, incorrectly
congratulating themselves on a victory that de Gaulle felt was less
due to their strategy than to the enemy's errors, were resting
contentedly on their laurels. It was de Gaulle's self-appointed
mission to be the thorn in their sides. He succeeded in that limited
mission, but, in the larger sense, he failed, for his was a voice
echoing emptily in the wilderness of French politics.

His essay *La Discorde chez l'ennemi* became a best-seller in
Germany, where the leaders carefully noted the errors that the
French analyst had so usefully brought to their attention. In
France the book had very little circulation—just enough to bring
de Gaulle into disfavor with his superior officers. Pétain as usual
praised it highly and introduced it as a text in the War College,
admonishing students to read it with the greatest care, while
blithely ignoring all of its warning on the highest command
level.

Pétain, however, did call de Gaulle to the War Council, where
the Marshal held the chair of vice-president, congratulated him on
his work and gave him the assignment of writing a history of the
French Army. In the course of writing this official history, de
Gaulle increased his readership among the officers and at the same
time sharpened the conflicts with officialdom, for his views ran
counter to prevailing theory. Inevitably he was drawn into politics,
for civilian leaders were carefully following what was becoming a
great debate inside the army.

De Gaulle's official work provided the basis for his own
unofficial essays, *La France et son armée* and *Vers une Armée de
métier*. Working prodigiously, Charles de Gaulle turned out
articles, lectures, books in a frenzied attempt to change the course
of events. It was during this period that he wrote a discourse on
leadership, *Le Fil de l'épée—The Edge of the Sword*—which is an
invaluable guide to his thinking and character. Fortunately for
historians and for his contemporaries, de Gaulle had a double
personality, the writer in him constantly betraying the mystery in
which the statesman tried to cloak himself.

In *Le Fil de l'épée* Charles de Gaulle attempted to rationalize his constant conflicts with higher authority, giving example after example of great patriots and leaders who saved their armies or their nation by refusing to carry out incompetent orders, great men who would not blindly accept prevailing theory as holy writ. Columbus and Galileo are among the heroes whose inspiring rejection of official dogma was invoked by de Gaulle. One of the most revealing passages is an anecdote in which de Gaulle recounts the story of Admiral Fisher, who, when he heard that Jellicoe had not moved on to destroy the German fleet after the Battle of Jutland, said, "He has all the qualities of Nelson save one; he does not know how to disobey."

In a recent conversation with General de Gaulle, the writer asked him if *Le Fil de l'épée* was still a reliable guide to his present-day thinking. President de Gaulle said that it was, insofar as fundamental military doctrine was concerned, but that if he were to rewrite it one day he would revise certain views on the leadership principle.

> I have learned in practice that a chief must be closer to the people than I had thought at the time. To move masses of people to accept the general interest over and above the individual egoism it is necessary to be at one and the same time above the crowd, pointing out the higher, wider horizons, and yet close in among the people, infusing them with one's own faith and drawing strength from them. A chief must be farsighted, but if he is too distant from the people he risks marching all alone. Decisions must be taken alone, but there must be followers close by, ready to understand and willing to march ahead.

President de Gaulle concluded:

> It would not be quite correct merely to say that I have revised my concepts in this manner. It is rather that times have changed, and my concepts change with changing circumstances. Universal education at higher and higher levels has produced a higher class of citizen, who requires and is worthy of more explanation, persuasion and association with the leaders of the nation.

To the question, "And what are your present views on obedience to the Chief?" President de Gaulle smilingly replied, "They, too, have changed, for I am now the Chief."

Charles de Gaulle knew how to disobey when he was not the Chief, and he would set one of the most stirring examples of patriotic dissidence in French history. But before events forced him to the final break with his leaders, he made every possible attempt to save them and his country from the disaster to which they were dooming themselves by willful, almost criminal, blindness, for the French leaders alone failed to see what de Gaulle and many other informed, clear-eyed men perceived.

In France as early as 1917 General Estienne speculated on the utility of an independent armored striking force. A man who became a close friend—one of the very rare friends of de Gaulle—Lieutenant-Colonel Emile Mayer, a brilliant Polytechnician, concurred with such strategists as Liddell Hart and Fuller in England, von Seeckt and Guderian in Germany, Tukhachevsky and Zhukov in Russia, all of whom were studying, analyzing, debating, developing the theory of a war of movement in the new age of the machine. And all were conversant with the brilliant theses of Charles de Gaulle. De Gaulle was not the sole world oracle of mechanized warfare, as his official mythologists claim, but he was certainly one of the original and most effective advocates.

Philippe Barrès, son of Maurice, as fervent a nationalist as his famous father, wrote of the day when he first heard the name Charles de Gaulle. He was in Berlin in early 1934, writing a series of articles on the Nazis' first year in power. As a well-known French journalist, Barrès was invited by Abetz to have dinner with Ribbentrop. At the end of the dinner an argument developed over the Versailles Treaty, and Ribbentrop, flushed with rage, shouted, "Versailles is dead!"

Barrès, just as angry but icily cold in the French manner, commented that if this was true, then war was inevitable.

Ribbentrop sneered and said that Germany had no intention of remaining enslaved by the Versailles Treaty or imprisoned by France's Maginot complex. And when Barrès sarcastically asked whether French fortifications were at all bothersome, Ribbentrop snorted in contempt and said, "No, no! We will easily pierce your Maginot Line with our tanks. That's no problem. Our specialist in those matters, Guderian, has told us he can do that. And, if I am not mistaken, your best technician holds the same view——"

Barrès, now puzzled, interjected, "Our best technician? Who is that?"

"A man named Gaulle," Ribbentrop replied. "He is a colonel. Colonel de Gaulle, I think, is his correct name."

Barrès was astonished to find an important Nazi leader familiar with the work of a French officer whose name he, one of France's leading journalists, did not know.

Barrès, who was to become one of the first and most fervent lieutenants of de Gaulle in the Free French resistance movement, might have forgotten the name and the incident, for he had much on his mind as he watched with growing fear the war preparations, strength and confidence of the Nazis. He was, however, to hear the name again, in dramatic circumstances, only a few weeks later.

Barrès went to Nuremberg in September of that year, to watch the Nazis stage one of their awesomely grotesque pageants in honor of Hitler, and the Führer himself invited Barrès to visit him in the medieval castle at which he was staying. Barrès describes with horror his conversations with the Nazi leaders around Hitler, particularly the talk of Streicher, who, holding his stomach as he roared with laughter, denied that he had killed 3000 Jews. "The correct figure is thirty thousand," he howled as he slapped the back of his friend Huenhlein, chief of the Army Motorized Corps.

Huenhlein, worried about the impression that Hitler and Streicher were making on the French journalist, came over and pulled Barrès aside, engaging him in a more innocuous technical dicussion of mechanized warfare, Huenhlein's specialty.

Barrès was in a state of shock, barely reacting to Huenhlein's rapid statements and questions about his motorized divisions. Suddenly he heard the Nazi General say, "And what is my great French colleague doing to develop these techniques?" Seeing the puzzled look on Barrès' face, the Nazi continued, "I mean your great specialist of motorization, your Colonel de Gaulle."

On his return to Paris a month later Barrès lunched with some friends, among whom were several cabinet ministers. He found himself sitting next to Paul Reynaud, the tough little bantam whose unjust fate it was a few years later to preside over the fall of France after having done all he could to save his country from disaster. Barrès told Reynaud of his Berlin and Nuremberg experiences and asked why the Germans knew so much about a man named de Gaulle.

"Why?" said Reynaud. "Why, because the Germans are well

informed of our affairs through their diligent military attaché here
in Paris, General von Kuehlenthal. Do you mean to say you don't
know the most brilliant innovator of our army, de Gaulle? That's
a bright young fellow who may save France one day!"

* * *

Charles de Gaulle was certain that France could not be saved—
indeed, could only perish—inside an isolated Maginot Line. In
that same year, 1934, when German and Russian specialists were
carefully studying his analyses and prophecies, de Gaulle was
urging the French to get outside the defensive shell of the Maginot
psychology and put their faith in alliances throughout Europe
while creating a mobile striking force which could take the
offensive at the first sign of danger, either to France or to her
allies.

In *L'Armée de métier* de Gaulle warned prophetically: "What
happens to Denmark, Belgium, the Saar, affects us vitally." Aware
of German threats in the Rhineland and of Nazi plots to destroy
Czechoslovakia, de Gaulle pleaded for a system of security alliances: "Under pain of finding ourselves here, there, everywhere
paralyzed in the face of accomplished facts, being one day all
alone, without allies or friends, surrounded only by our neighbors'
contempt, before an adversary bolstered up by his success, we must
be ready to act beyond our own frontiers, at any moment, in any
contingency."

De Gaulle, who loved and respected his country as much as any
Frenchman, refused to be blinded by his love, as were so many
other nationalists, and continually reminded his countrymen that
they were inferior in numbers and in resources while handicapped
geographically in relation to Germany.

Germany, he warned, produced twice as much steel, four times
as much coke, seven times as many machine tools, ten times as
much cellulose, twelve times as much nitrogen as France. Thus, he
argued, when a Frenchman says that his country is stronger,
greater than Germany, he must understand that this superior
strength and grandeur of France is not a superiority of brute force,
since quantitatively the German is materially stronger, but rather a
superiority of quality, brains, imagination, concept, if it is to exist
at all.

How, asked de Gaulle, in lectures, articles and books, can France
realize its potential for greatness, its qualitative superiority, when

it restricts itself to mass conscription of a numerically inferior population, rather than encouraging the creation of a highly skilled, trained corps of specialists of quality, an "armée de métier" which, using the machine skillfully, can overcome Germany's greater brute force? How can France stand off Germany alone, behind a defensive line which covers only France's own frontiers but leaves a gaping hole between the Belgian forests and the sea, along the traditional invasion route of northern Europe?

> The aggressor, his movements hidden by the screen of forests along the Rhine, the Moselle and in the Ardennes, finding everywhere a terrain which is easily penetrated, can pick at will the time and place of his attack. The defense, if it remains static and passive, will always be caught by surprise, pinned down and outflanked, and once again we will relive the defeat of Villeroy at Ramillies, the blockade of Bazaine inside Metz. . . . For the Germans, the route to France passes through Belgium.

Any major breakthrough and France would be finished, de Gaulle warned. "Paris is only 120 miles from foreign lands, only six days of march for an invading infantry, only three hours for a tank, only one hour for an attacking plane. One single setback on the Oise and the Louvre is within cannon-shot." And, asked de Gaulle, what is France without Paris?

> That agglomeration, a mere three leagues in radius, regulates the entire existence of the nation. Out of every seven Frenchmen one lives in Paris, and the existence of the other six depends upon what is thought and done there. . . . Each time in the last century that Paris was taken, the resistance of the rest of France did not last an hour.

The only answer to France's double handicap of geography and demography, de Gaulle insisted, was an armored, mobile, protective screen against aggression. "France cannot depend upon hastily recruited mass formations to support the first shock of assault. The moment has come to add to its mass of reserves and recruits—which is the principal element of national resistance, but one that is slow to assemble, too ponderous to put in action swiftly and useful only to fulfill the gigantic effort needed for the ultimate struggle—to add to this mass an instrument of maneuverability capable of acting without delay, permanently in being, coherent and superbly trained."

De Gaulle, never a theorist of generalities, worked out a detailed specific plan for the composition of this mobile striking and covering force of professional career technicians. It became with only the very slightest variation the basic organization plan, not of the French, but of the German Army, as designed by Guderian, who gave credit to de Gaulle's analysis in his own essay, *Achtung Panzer,* in 1937, three years after de Gaulle's original study.

Paul Reynaud, one of the leaders of parliament, frequently a cabinet minister during the recurrent crises of government, had been won over by de Gaulle's plans and had taken his warnings to heart. He greatly admired the drive, energy and courage of this officer who defied authority and risked his career by criticizing official theory. Reynaud recently told this reporter of the day when de Gaulle came to see him to beg Reynaud to put his plan for armored divisions before the chamber. At the time Reynaud was deeply involved in a critical debate on devaluation and general financial policy. He told de Gaulle that other men were able to espouse his cause. He reached for his parliamentary membership book on his desk, saying to de Gaulle that he would check off for him suitable names of men to see. Reynaud's shrewd old mandarin mask of a face crinkled in smiles as he recalled how de Gaulle stopped him and pulled out his own well-worn copy of the chamber list, smiling bleakly as he said, "No use, I have already seen them all. You are my man. You will do this."

Paul Reynaud did do as de Gaulle asked, many times, beginning with the debate of March 15, 1935, in which he prophetically warned the chamber that if war broke out Belgium might be invaded and the Belgian troops driven back to the sea, leaving 350 kilometers of French frontier unguarded. De Gaulle was sitting in the gallery with Reynaud's chief administrative assistant, Gaston Palewski, listening to Reynaud put forward his arguments. None of them knew, of course, that within five years Reynaud would be the prime minister of a France which would fall exactly under the predicted circumstances and that while Reynaud went to a German prison, Palewski would flee to London to become the chief assistant to the colonel sitting with him in the gallery that day. On that day the chamber ignored Reynaud's warning and cheered a rebuttal by the defense minister, General Maurin, who told the deputies that millions had been spent on building unconquerable defenses and that it would be folly to "go beyond our lines in pursuit of who knows what mad adventure."

General Maurin's rebuttal told the deputies exactly what they wanted to hear, and they heard it over and over again from every official military spokesman. The politicians were gratified to hear from the army chief-of-staff, General Debeney, who in the *Revue des deux mondes* argued that de Gaulle's armored divisions were obviously designed for offensive action, contrary to the intentions of France's peace-loving leaders. Flattering and gratifying words from a militarist, the deputies thought.

Socialist leader Léon Blum was particularly pleased to hear such outstanding authorities as Debeney, Maurin, Pétain and Weygand denounce the plans of young Colonel de Gaulle, for the socialist and humanist in Blum, while admitting the seeming logic of de Gaulle's brilliant argumentation, could not but feel uneasy when confronted with a plan for a specialized career force which, whatever its military worth, resembled most dangerously a praetorian guard. Blum told de Gaulle of his fears, pointing out that a professional corps such as de Gaulle proposed would be an excellent instrument for a military coup d'état and seemed much more like the motorized storm troopers that Hitler had already used in Germany. Blum admitted many years later in his memoirs that he had been wrong and de Gaulle had been right. History is filled with many fascinating ifs, but of all the ifs of history one of the most tantalizing to play with is the speculation on what might have happened if Blum's hindsight had been a foresight and if he had adopted de Gaulle's proposals when there was still time, during his presidency of the Popular Front in 1936.

Events moved, however, with the fatality of a Greek tragedy, in the essential meaning of true tragedy, which is the evitability of the inevitable. There was no mystery about the Nazi plans, no lack of knowledge of their tactics and strategy. The superior officers and deputies of France knew exactly what was coming. Most historians agree with de Gaulle's view that his superiors did not even believe their own reasons for rejecting his proposals for mechanized warfare preparations. They were not merely guilty of blindness and stupidity. They saw clearly what he was pointing out and understood it. They were not stupid men, they were tired, dispirited men wanting to buy peace at any price, deluding themselves into thinking it could be bought.

The "victory" of Verdun in the last war had gutted the French nation, killing many of the best young men, who did not live to produce the sons who would have come of age, perhaps in time to bolster the failing strength of their aging fathers, to give support to the few, like Reynaud and de Gaulle, who were so alone at the moment of decision. The role of Charles de Gaulle was to offer his advice, and then, in extremis, his great dissent.

CHAPTER THREE

THE DEATH-DEPARTURE

Yes, you can do this and Free France would die, as you warn. Well, then, Free France will die, but it will not live in your dominion.

CHARLES DE GAULLE *to Winston Churchill*

NO CRUELER FATE can befall a man than to predict correctly, without power to prevent, the death of someone he loves dearly. Charles de Gaulle loved France as much as a man can love, and it was his fate to predict correctly and impotently the disaster that befell her. Fate granted him only one small, bitter-sweet favor: he was given the briefest chance to fight for what he believed, in the way he had begged for a chance to fight.

In December 1938 the war council decided at last to create two armored divisions on the de Gaulle design. It was far too late to save France—de Gaulle looked upon the plan as a glass of water offered to a feverish man dying of a stomach wound. He raged at anyone foolish enough to congratulate him on the decree creating the two new divisions, for he had just seen the latest intelligence on Guderian's creation of twelve powerful, fully equipped panzers, with cadres and technicians who had an average of three years' intensive training.

In face of this massive power, France's two new divisions were puny. The equipment was lighter and more sparsely armed and, above all, there was an almost complete lack of the highly trained technicians needed for armored tactics, as de Gaulle had warned a thousand times. At that stage of development it took almost three times longer to train a tankman than an infantryman. In fact, the first of the two armored divisions whose creation was decreed on December 2, 1938, was not activated as a fighting unit until January 1940, and the second not until March, just in time to be destroyed by the overwhelming superiority of the Nazi assault on France.

Colonel de Gaulle had been given command of the Fiftieth Tank Regiment at Metz after completing his work at the General Staff Strategic Center in Paris, where he had tried in vain to persuade the high command to develop specialized divisions for mechanized warfare. He sat in Metz, his tanks immobilized, as the high command gave its top priority to strengthening the fortifications of the Maginot Line. The most powerful armored divisions—which the French did not have—would have been useless anyway in the static defensive concepts of the Maginot mentality. Yet it was the static fortresses that received top priority in France at the very moment that Guderian's fast-moving tanks were deploying across Europe, fanning out at the frontiers of Czechoslovakia and Austria.

In March 1938 Hitler swallowed up Austria in the Anschluss. In September it was Czechoslovakia's turn to be raped, even more shamefully, as the French and British delegations to the Munich Conference delivered her into Hitler's arms with the hope that the annexation of the Sudetenland would appease the dictator. Within six months Hitler forced the abdication of the Czech president, marched into Prague and took over the entire country. On September 1, 1939, the Nazis struck at Poland with all the power of the mechanized force that the French high command had told de Gaulle was not practicable and would never be used. All through this period France, in de Gaulle's words, "played the part of the victim that awaits its turn," while he himself "watched these events without surprise, but not without pain."

By the time of the Nazi invasion of Poland, Colonel de Gaulle was the commander of the tanks of the French Fifth Army in Alsace. French Intelligence was receiving daily reports indicating that almost all the Nazi offensive units were engaged in the Battle of Poland, striking all-out for a quick victory. Germany's own frontiers in the West, on the French border, were wide open and virtually unprotected. Hitler staked everything on his conviction that France was paralyzed behind its Maginot Line and by its defensive defeatist policies.

Colonel de Gaulle pleaded for orders to move at least up to the Albert Canal, to close the gaping breach in the defenses north of the Maginot Line and fill in the gap to Belgium. But the high command and the government refused to move. When the Presi-

dent of the French Republic, Albert Lebrun, came to Alsace to
review the troops, de Gaulle presented his tanks for inspection and
was told by the President, "I am familiar with your ideas. But it
does seem too late for the enemy to apply them."

Colonel de Gaulle knew it was too late for France to save herself,
but he felt it was his duty to make one last attempt. He drafted a
memorandum to warn the authorities that "the enemy would take
the offensive with a very powerful mechanized force, on the
ground and in the air." He argued that "our front might be broken
through at any moment" and that the French forces would be
annihilated unless they had their own powerful and highly mobile
counterforce to meet the blitzkrieg assault wherever it might
strike. He called for top priority for the manufacture of fast
armored vehicles but above all for a change in tactics that would
"gather into one mechanized reserve those units already existing
or in course of formation."

The memorandum was addressed to eighty of the top officials in
the government, the high command and the political parties. The
language of its conclusion revealed that it was also addressed,
through the eighty, to the French public, and perhaps to the record
of history. It is one of the documents that have earned for de
Gaulle a justified reputation as one of the most brilliant, farsighted analysts of military history. These were the concluding
words of the "Memorandum to the Eighty":

> The French people should not at any price fall into the
> illusion that the present military immobility might be in
> harmony with the nature of the present war. The oppo-
> site is the truth. The internal-combustion engine endows
> modern means of destruction with such force, speed, and
> range that the present conflict will be marked, sooner or
> later, by movements, surprises, breakthroughs and pur-
> suits the scale and rapidity of which will infinitely exceed
> those of the most lightning events of the past. . . . Let us
> make no mistake about it! The conflict which has begun
> might well be the most extended, the most complex, the
> most violent of all those that have ravaged the earth. The
> political, economic, social and moral crisis from which it
> has issued is so profound and so ubiquitous that it is
> bound to end in a complete upheaval of both the condi-
> tion of the peoples and the structure of states. And the

obscure harmony of things is providing this revolution with the military instrument—the army of machines— exactly proportioned to its colossal dimensions. It is high time for France to draw the conclusion.

The appeal went virtually unnoticed. As de Gaulle commented dryly in his memoirs, "My memorandum produced no shock." The French leaders and public were so numbed by the Maginot delusion of defense that they were shock-proof. De Gaulle was sharply reprimanded by high command officers for having circulated his memorandum out of channels and for not appreciating the tank command he had been given or the two new armored divisions that were being activated. De Gaulle countercriticized his superiors in additional memoranda, pointing out that the new tanks were thirty-ton type B models, some fifteen years old in design, lacking the firepower and mobility required and unavailable in sufficient number.

As the Tank Commander of the Fifth Army he had put in a requisition for 500 tanks and had been granted 120. He had proposed that the division be allocated seven support battalions of motorized infantry mounted on caterpillar vehicles; the high command had approved one battalion. His request for seven groups of all-angle artillery pieces was cut back to two groups. He was refused even the minimum of one air-reconnaissance group that he had requested; the Division got none. Finally, the coup de grâce that killed even his faintest hopes was the refusal to give the armored division any autonomous initiative of deployment. All mechanized divisions, the new with the old, were assigned to Army Corps, to be used at the discretion of the Army Commander in his own sector, with no tactical discretion at all to the mechanized commanders; there would be no mechanized reserve at the disposal of the high command to send swiftly to meet any major threat wherever it might occur on any front.

De Gaulle's constant conflicts with his military superiors and his rebellious appeals to civilian authorities had created enemies for him in high political circles as well as in the high command. When one of his few admiring supporters, Paul Reynaud, became prime minister, he was unable to appoint de Gaulle to a position in his cabinet, as he would have liked, because of powerful opposition, mainly from ex-Premier Daladier, the "man of Munich." Reynaud had been obliged to take Daladier into his government as

Minister of National Defense in order to obtain the votes of Daladier's Radical Party for Reynaud's government. When Daladier heard that Reynaud was planning to bring de Gaulle into the ministry, he told Reynaud's messenger, "If de Gaulle comes here, I shall leave this office, go downstairs and telephone Paul Reynaud to put him in my place."

Reynaud personally would have far preferred to have had Colonel de Gaulle in the place of the appeaser Daladier, but unfortunately de Gaulle did not have the votes of parliament that could replace the votes of the Daladier-pledged deputies. Reynaud had to postpone his plan to bring de Gaulle into his cabinet, but he was determined to do so as soon as the situation worsened, as he knew it would. Meanwhile he asked de Gaulle to continue to carry on his crusade for modernization and mechanization of the army.

De Gaulle was then summoned by General Gamelin, who had been promoted to Commander-in-Chief. The generalissimo told the colonel that he was going to increase the newly planned armored divisions from two to four and had decided to give de Gaulle command of the new Fourth Armored Division. It was a prodigious, unparalleled promotion from a specialized-unit colonel to major-general and divisional commander. De Gaulle expressed his appreciation and pride at the trust and honor bestowed upon him by the Commander-in-Chief. But his pleasure was promptly crushed when Gamelin replied, "I understand your satisfaction. As for your misgivings, I don't believe they are justified." Nothing could have been more typical of the high-command mentality of that time than this contradictory promotion of the outstanding advocate of a new policy while assuring him that his policy was not justified.

Within five weeks of de Gaulle's promotion to division commander the static "phoney war" of the winter of 1940 came to an end when the Nazis struck with full fury all along the Western Front. First Denmark, then Norway went the way of Poland, crushed under the treads of the panzers. Seven of the ten panzer divisions then swept through the Ardennes and reached the Meuse River in only three days of a lightning thrust. By May 14, only four days after the jump-off of the offensive, they crossed the Meuse, going from Dinant to Sedan, their armored advance supported by four big motorized units—the same kind of unit de Gaulle had pleaded for—while from overhead Stukas screamed down and slashed a clear way for the tanks. Big bombers blasted railways and road junctions behind the French lines but avoided the path in front of the advancing panzers which moved down the roads more freely than citizens out for a Sunday picnic.

By the end of only the first week of the attack no less than seven panzer divisions at full strength—more than twice the total armored strength mobilized for action in France—were regrouped around Saint Quentin, in positions to swoop on Paris or on Dunkirk. They had swept around and crashed through the weakest links in the Maginot Line, along the Belgian border, exactly where de Gaulle had warned that they would attack. The remaining three of the ten panzers attacked the Dutch, Belgian, British and French units spread out in loosely coordinated positions across the Low Countries and the fields of Brabant. Almost 800,000 allied men were caught in the panzer pincers. In those eight days in May 1940 the fate of the allied armies was decided and Hitler had won the battle of France all but for cleaning up the debris. It was the swiftest, greatest military victory in history—or perhaps more accurately, as de Gaulle insists, it was the swiftest, most terrible military defeat in history, for he firmly believes that it was the failure of the French high command to prepare for modern warfare rather than the success of the Nazis that accounted for the result.

It was only on May 11, the day after the Nazi offensive had started, that Colonel de Gaulle was informed that the Fourth Armored Division, which Gamelin had assigned to him, was at last ready to be activated under his command. He discovered, however, when he went to the assigned command post at Vesinet that his division did not in fact yet exist. The units that would constitute it were scattered at distant points throughout the commands. Only on May 15, when the panzers had already smashed through on the northern frontiers, did de Gaulle get summoned to headquarters to receive his divisional orders and battle instructions. He was assigned to the sector of General Georges, commander-in-chief on the northeast front, and instructed to get his detailed orders directly from him.

De Gaulle sped off to see Georges while his deputies were putting his division together. When de Gaulle arrived at headquarters, General Georges greeted him with the words, "Here you are, de Gaulle! For you who have so long held the ideas which the enemy is putting into practice, here is the chance to act."

* * *

Charles de Gaulle threw himself into action with the fanaticism of the conscious defender of a lost cause. When all is lost but honor, honor requires that all be given and he gave to the battle all the pent-up energy of his long-frustrated career. He hastily pinned his two new stars to his tunic and rushed out of headquarters to take command of his armored division.

General Georges' orders were to delay the enemy before Laon, in order to permit the army to set up a new defensive line on the Aisne and the Ailette to block the road to Paris. De Gaulle threw himself into the assignment as though the fate of France depended on him and his men, although he knew its fate had already been decided. Wearing a tank driver's helmet and black leather jacket, General de Gaulle set up an advanced command post at Bruyères and began trying to forge a fighting force out of the untrained, uncoordinated, freshly activated paper division.

He had barely visited the units of the division and shown himself to his men when a deadly combat began with Hitler's finest fighting men. With no infantry, no artillery, no aviation or antiaircraft cover, de Gaulle decided that the only thing to do was to attack the Germans. Foolhardy and quixotic as this sounds, it was nonetheless the only solution open to him. Any attempt at defense with his makeshift forces would be blasted out of the way by the advancing panzers and Stukas, and the Germans would instantly be made aware of the weakness of the raw division in their path. An attack would have the advantage of surprise and would almost certainly fool the Germans, who, fighting men though they were, were drill-book soldiers who would never believe that an enemy daring to attack them could possibly be so weak and untrained as de Gaulle's units happened to be. De Gaulle reenacted the famous command of Marshal Foch, who, in the first battle of the Marne in 1914, ordered his Ninth Army to take the offensive with the explanation to headquarters: "My center is giving way, my right is falling back—in short, the situation is excellent for an attack."

De Gaulle's right, left and center were just about nonexistent when he attacked with two battalions of heavy and one of light Renault tanks against a German force that outgunned and outarmored him at least three to one on the ground, with complete control of the air. Yet de Gaulle sent his tanks stabbing out through the forest to clear a vital canal and penetrate the German positions in depth. He caught the Germans completely by surprise.

They had been driving through France like tourists on holiday
and were psychologically unprepared for an attack by French
tanks, as de Gaulle had hoped.

De Gaulle had no illusions about being able to hold any ground
for long against superior German units and power. But his mission
was to gain time, to delay and harass the enemy, and this he did,
although at great cost to his lightly armed, untrained division. The
Germans, recovering from the initial surprise, regrouped and
poured a devastating fire on the French tank units, destroying
many of the light tanks in the battalion. De Gaulle was forced to
pull his spearheads back and regroup in the woods, not very far
from a famous field he knew so well, Agincourt.

De Gaulle had only begun to fight. When reconnaissance
reported sighting a long German convoy of thirty infantry-
carrying trucks, General de Gaulle rallied his tired, wounded, torn
tank units for another attack and came driving out of the woods,
intercepting and destroying the entire German convoy. The Germans, now stung badly, threw the full force of divisional and army
firepower and dive bombers against the French Fourth Armored,
inflicting grievous casualties on de Gaulle's green troops, trying to
drive de Gaulle back to his original lines and wipe out his
penetrating, harassing forces.

De Gaulle, fighting desperately, proud of his success and of his
men, sent messages to fellow commanders on his flanks telling
them what had been accomplished, informing them that he was
now drawing the full fire of the enemy forces opposite them,
begging them to take this excellent opportunity to attack and
outflank the Germans who were concentrating on de Gaulle's
front. But, as always, de Gaulle's messages and proposals went
unanswered. The French commanders on either side of de Gaulle
were imbued with the defensive spirit of the high command,
blindly putting their faith in fixed positions, afraid to attack, not
trained to attack. They made no move either to help de Gaulle or
to exploit his initial success. He had finally to fall back behind the
canal from which he had launched his offensive.

De Gaulle could take some pride in having captured 130 prisoners and inflicting heavy losses and delays upon the enemy,
although at a very great expense, for he had lost some 200 men and
many tanks. Yet he had given the Germans a taste of French steel
and had personally avenged the humiliation he had felt before
taking command, on a day when he had seen French soldiers

plodding down the roads as refugees, their guns thrown away on orders from the Germans, who had sneeringly commanded: "Throw away your arms and walk home. We have no time to take prisoners." On that day de Gaulle had felt himself "borne up by a limitless fury," as he noted in his memoirs. It was on that day that he vowed: "If I live, I will fight, wherever I must, as long as I must, until the enemy is defeated and the national stain washed clean." He began to carry out that vow in his desperately heroic attack on the very first day he assumed command of the Fourth Armored Division.

For that unique exploit Charles de Gaulle won his fourth major citation for valor and outstanding service. This one, on the army level, was issued by General Weygand, dated May 19, 1940:

> An officer with admirable daring and courage. Attacked, with his division, the bridgehead at Abbeville, very solidly held by the enemy. Broke German resistance and progressed 14 kilometers through the enemy lines, taking hundreds of prisoners and considerable matériel.

During the two weeks that followed, General de Gaulle fought as though he were a human tiger tank, clawing his way through German positions, constantly harrying the enemy, exhorting his tired men to superhuman efforts while remaining outwardly calm and confident. The only signs of his inner stress were the cloud of tobacco smoke floating constantly over his head and the chain of cigarette butts in the forest which told couriers where to find their divisional chief. So outstanding was the record of his division that he won his fifth citation, again on the army level, in this same battle which raged for two weeks. The citation was dated June 1, 1940:

> An officer of great value, who gives of himself with faith to his chosen profession and who applies himself to the vast problems of military organization. Commander of army tanks, imbued with resourcefulness, action, devotion, inspired by new and bold concepts, he is a leader who inspires confidence.
> Named to command the Fourth Armored Division, he has given new proof of his decision-making abilities, of his judgment and coolness in the most difficult circumstances and of his great intelligence, particularly during

the attack on the German bridgehead at Abbeville, from
May 18 to May 30.

The recognition of de Gaulle's "new and bold concepts," of his
great intelligence and confidence-inspiring leadership qualities, all
came too late. Within only thirty days of the combat which began
at the Abbeville bridgehead on May 18, 1940, the devoted and
faithful officer of the citation had fled France after learning that
his old chief and once loved friend, Marshal Pétain, by then a
doddering octogenarian, had decided to capitulate to the Nazis. A
man as brave, physically and morally, as Charles de Gaulle, with
five citations to attest to his valor and patriotism, could risk being
called a coward or a traitor, as he was after his flight to England.
But only a man as impersonally and singlemindedly dedicated as
de Gaulle, a veritable monk in uniform, could in the last moments
pass within a few miles of the house in which his beloved mother
lay dying and, refusing any divergence from his mission, go
straight on without stopping at her bedside. This is what de Gaulle
did.

De Gaulle knew that the end was coming rapidly, both for his
mother and his motherland. There was nothing that he could do
to save his mother—he never saw her again, she died while he was
in England—but there was still much he could do to save his
motherland and it was this which drove him on, fighting and
pleading with his superiors, arguing for a last-ditch military stand
in the northwest peninsula, the so-called Brittany redoubt, which
he had charted in the mission which brought him near his
mother's deathbed at Paimpont.

De Gaulle and Reynaud both thought that the ultimate wisdom
would be for the government to flee to North Africa, with the fleet
and with as many officers and cadres as could be rescued, to rebuild
the fighting forces in the empire, escaping under cover of the
army's last-ditch resistance on the Continent. But the defensive
passivity responsible for the high command's failure to understand
the nature of mechanized warfare had been only the outward
manifestation of a far deeper inner defeatism which now poured
through the gaping wounds in the body and the soul of the deathly
sick French Republic.

Reynaud, intelligent and courageous, lacked the weight to
impose his will. He vacillated at critical moments and compro-

mised with the cunning and skill of an old parliamentary fox when the situation required the force and the roar of a lion. Reynaud, in the last days of battle, recalled General de Gaulle from the front and brought him into his cabinet as under-secretary of war, but made this decision null and void by recalling at the same time old Marshal Pétain, whom he appointed vice-premier of the government.

From a historical perspective, however, Reynaud's appointment of de Gaulle to his cabinet, after years of espousing his theories, was perhaps the greatest accomplishment of his presidency. For if it was immediately nullified by the Pétain designation, it nonetheless gave de Gaulle the opportunity to save the honor of France by continuing the resistance to the enemy. It also enabled de Gaulle to save the face of grandeur for France while achieving greatness for himself. Had Reynaud not recalled him from the Abbeville front, de Gaulle would almost certainly have been either killed in action or taken prisoner at the surrender. De Gaulle would have had almost no chance to escape to London, and if he had, he would not have had any governmental title and not the slightest pretext or prestige to play the role he did. As it was, he had little enough to give him or his cause much hope or standing. That little, however, Reynaud granted him by appointing him under-secretary and, much more importantly, by sending him to London on the ninth of June—less than two weeks before the final collapse—to see Winston Churchill. And that small, late decision was of huge, momentous import, for Churchill, himself a giant, was instantly and profoundly impressed by the giant Frenchman who walked into his office at 10 Downing Street that historic Sunday in June, coolly confident and unconquerable in spirit as his country tottered on the brink of defeat.

Churchill, convinced of the impending French collapse, would hear nothing of Reynaud's request, relayed by de Gaulle, to send part of the gallant RAF to France. Churchill knew he would need every plane for the battle of Britain and he told de Gaulle bluntly that what he had seen and knew of defeatism in France and the disorganization of the forces in the field meant that the battle of France was already a lost cause. Flight to North Africa by the government and, above all, a speedy departure to safe ports by the French fleet would alone enable France to continue the war and keep her promise to Britain never to sign a separate peace. But

Churchill would not sacrifice the RAF to a lost cause.

Thus the very first meeting of Charles de Gaulle and Winston Churchill ended, as did so many of their meetings during the course of the war, in a policy disagreement but with mutual respect and admiration.

While de Gaulle was in London, Churchill's personal representative, General Edward Spears, was in Paris trying to bolster the sagging morale of Marshal Pétain, with little success. Pétain told Spears, "The country has been rotted by politics"; as for the soldiers: "They are fighting one against two and many of their weapons have been lost." Pétain went on to add, "This appointment of de Gaulle is not going to help matters." Spears, seeking a more cheerful note, said, "I thought he was highly spoken of. Has he not done very well in command of the armored division at Abbeville?"

Pétain angrily replied, "He thinks he knows all about the mechanics of warfare. His vanity leads him to think the art of war has no secrets for him. He might have invented it." Pétain claimed to have written the outline of de Gaulle's treatise on mechanized warfare and to have corrected the text, without de Gaulle's having acknowledged his contribution: "Not only is he vain, he is ungrateful. He has few friends in the army. No wonder, for he gives the impression of looking down on everybody. They called him 'The Constable' at St. Cyr."

The final break between de Gaulle and Pétain was only days away, as was the fall of France. The very day that de Gaulle was asking Churchill in London to send more help, the cabinet in Paris was deciding to declare Paris an open city, a sure sign of the defeatism which had led to the collapse. On June 10 General Weygand publicly proclaimed that Paris was an open city, and what was left of the crumbling Reynaud cabinet departed from the capital. That very night, General Ismay, on Churchill's instructions, called his aide in Vincennes and told him to try to find Premier Reynaud and arrange for a meeting of the war council for the next day. It took the British many hours to find Premier Reynaud in a small hotel near Orléans, to tell him that Churchill was flying over for a critical war conference.

General Spears movingly described this climactic meeting of the French and British leaders before the final fall of France in his colorful, personal history of that period, *Assignment to Catastrophe:*

The Frenchmen sat with set white faces, their eyes on the table. They looked for all the world like prisoners hauled up from some deep dungeon to hear an inevitable verdict.

For relief, I turned to de Gaulle whose bearing alone among his compatriots matched the calm, healthy phlegm of the British. A strange-looking man, enormously tall; sitting at the table he dominated everyone else by his height, as he had done when walking into the room. No chin, a long, drooping elephantine nose over a closely cut mustache, a shadow over a small mouth whose thick lips tended to protrude as if in a pout before speaking, a high receding forehead and pointed head surmounted by sparse black hair lying flat and neatly parted. His heavily-hooded eyes were very shrewd.

General Spears remembered and at once understood the meaning of the nickname "The Constable": "It was easy to imagine that head on a ruff, that secret face at Catherine de Medici's Council Chamber." Churchill, too, noted in his memoirs the striking resemblance of de Gaulle to the historic image of the "Constable of France." At the very last meeting of Churchill and the French leaders on June 13, Churchill, walking past de Gaulle in the courtyard, whispered to him as he passed by, "Man of destiny."

The British knew that the Battle of France was all but ended, although the magnificent warrior Churchill was to try once more, just before the surrender, to keep the French fighting by offering to merge the two nations into one Franco-British Union of Peoples. The declaration, drafted by Jean Monnet, who was then a delegate to the Franco-British Armaments Board, was handed to de Gaulle, who had returned again to London on another mission for Reynaud. Monnet and de Gaulle would clash for the next twenty-five years on the issue of merging French sovereignty into a supranational Europe, but on that day of despair de Gaulle approved the concept as a possible morale booster and telephoned it to Premier Reynaud, who saw in it a last-minute miracle. But the defeatists in his own cabinet and the high command wanted no miracles, particularly British-inspired miracles, and the cabinet majority refused to endorse Reynaud's recommendation to accept the British proposal. Reynaud was beaten and decided to resign that very day.

General Spears saw Reynaud the next morning and begged him to carry on the fight. Late that night Spears returned to see Reynaud for what he knew would be a futile last-minute plea. As he walked past an entrance column of the premier's residence he was "startled to see a tall figure flat against it, shrouded in its shadow." The hiding figure was Charles de Gaulle, who had just flown back from London in a plane which Churchill had given him.

De Gaulle called to Spears in a loud whisper, "I must speak to you, it is extremely urgent . . . I have very good reason to believe that Weygand intends to arrest me."

Spears felt he could not interrupt his visit to Reynaud. He told de Gaulle to wait where he was until he, Spears, came out again. Moving back into the shadows, trying to conceal his huge frame behind the column, de Gaulle took up a long, lonely, nerve-twisting vigil while Spears argued valiantly but vainly with Reynaud, who informed him that he had already resigned and that the President had already asked Marshal Pétain to form a new cabinet. Reynaud had the proposed list of ministers in his pocket, and Spears knew that the end had come at last when he saw that Weygand was minister of defense and that, in Spears' opinion, the cabinet "was composed entirely of abject defeatists."

"On leaving Reynaud's study I at once looked for de Gaulle," noted Spears in his memoirs. "He was standing bolt upright where we had left him, his back to the same column, in such a position as not to be seen from the entrance. The wait had evidently strained him still further. He was very white."

General Spears and British Ambassador Sir Ronald Campbell, who had accompanied him to the meeting with Reynaud, told de Gaulle it would be unwise for him to be seen in a British official car and suggested that he must take his chances on getting to the Ambassador's room at the Hotel Montre on foot, through side streets. De Gaulle agreed, moved silently away through the darkness, and rejoined them at the hotel after enough of a delay to worry the British diplomats.

In the privacy of the ambassadorial suite, de Gaulle said that he was determined to get away, for the fate of the French Empire was now at stake and there was no one in the defeatist Pétain cabinet who could rally the empire. A call to continue resistance must be made, de Gaulle said, before Pétain put out a call to lay down arms. If North Africa and the French Empire were to be saved, de

Gaulle argued, it could only be from England, and he was ready to make this call to resistance. Spears noted that "de Gaulle was plainly overwrought" by the shock of flying from London to Bordeaux—believing that Reynaud had accepted the offer of Franco-British Union to continue the war—only to find that Reynaud had resigned and that Pétain, the new premier, was planning to sue for an armistice and a separate peace. It was the intensity of this sudden emotional reversal, from the courageous optimism of London to the cowardly defeatism of Bordeaux, which impelled de Gaulle to his great decision to break with his superior officers, with all the noble and terrible consequences of that act, whose effects twenty-five years later are still shaking France and the French Army.

General Spears listened to de Gaulle, agreed with his exposé, put through a call to Churchill and obtained the Prime Minister's authorization to return to London the next day bringing General de Gaulle with him. Thus one of the most dramatic decisions of the war, with historic consequences for France, was quickly taken. Even more dramatic in terms of de Gaulle's personal future were the decisions of Paul Reynaud and his interior minister Georges Mandel to stay behind, at least for a short time. The time proved very short indeed before they were both arrested and imprisoned, leaving de Gaulle, a young brigadier-general who had been only briefly a junior minister, without a rival as the leader of the Free French in London. Destiny cared lovingly for Charles de Gaulle. Not only did he make the right moves at the right time, but other men had to make a series of errors to enable him to achieve his greatness.

The protection of the fates covered de Gaulle that last tense night of June 16 in Bordeaux. Despite his justified fears, no police came to arrest him. According to Spears, he was still nervous the next morning as he went through an elaborate bluff to throw the authorities off the track he had decided to take. De Gaulle went to his office and gave his secretary a list of names of officials with whom he wanted appointments later that day, to cover up any hint of his plan to flee France. It was agreed between him and the British that he would make his way to the airport with the ostensible purpose of saying farewell to General Spears, an official function in keeping with his concluding mission as undersecretary of war and liaison with the British war cabinet.

At the airport Spears nervously waited for de Gaulle and was relieved to see the tall figure making his way toward the plane accompanied by his aide, Lieutenant Geoffroy de Courcel. No one could know that day that de Courcel would be a constant companion of Charles de Gaulle for the next two decades, the very first of the "Gaullists" and the only man to remain in de Gaulle's service in a high position for most of the next quarter-century. On the morning of June 17, 1940, de Courcel was only a very young and very disturbed lieutenant, desperately searching for a few feet of strong cord on which the fate of France hung for a tense ten minutes.

De Gaulle had brought to the airport heavy valises and one large trunk with important documents, and the pilot of the British plane refused to take off if the trunk were not lashed down. De Courcel scurried around the airport looking for a length of rope while Spears and de Gaulle tried to look calm and cool, making small talk in front of a number of suspicious French police and military men gathered around the plane. Finally de Courcel came running breathlessly to the plane with the precious cord, and the pilot began to lash down the trunk.

At last the plane was ready, the blocks pulled away, the propellers whirling. Spears got in after shaking hands in farewell with de Gaulle. The plane began to taxi slowly, with the door still open, and then, just as it was ready to pick up speed, Charles de Gaulle took a giant step forward and threw his huge body in an arc up and into the plane, with Spears clutching at his jacket and hauling him in. The younger and more agile de Courcel vaulted in behind de Gaulle in a running dive. The door slammed shut and the plane sped off down the runway, leaving behind a gaping group of astonished French officials who had watched this extraordinary scene.

Inside the plane de Gaulle regained his composure. He sat silently thinking of the road ahead. Down below them, in the sea, the *Champlain* was lying on her side, sinking, with two thousand British troops on board. Spears watched helplessly as hundreds of tiny figures struggled in the water. The plane veered north and cut across Brittany, where Charles de Gaulle's mother lay dying. Somewhere down below, his wife and daughter were preparing to get passage to England on the very last freighter from Brest.

The plane, which did not have enough fuel to reach the British coast, had to stop on the Island of Jersey to refuel and just barely made it in time. General Spears asked de Gaulle during the refueling whether he would like a warming cup of coffee, and when it was given to him, de Gaulle sipped it slowly and then, in his deep grave voice, solemnly told Spears that "without implying criticism he must nevertheless proclaim the truth, that this was tea and he had asked for coffee." Spears noted wryly in his memoirs, "It was his first introduction to the tepid liquid which, in England, passes for either one or the other. His Martyrdom had begun."

In his own memoirs de Gaulle curtly dismissed the Spears version of events with the dry comment, "There was nothing romantic or difficult about the departure." The only other eyewitness still available today, de Courcel, naturally supports de Gaulle's denial of Spears' "romantic" account.

Future historians will find it difficult to determine which version is correct unless other witnesses eventually write their own memoirs. This writer is obliged by reasons of courtesy to President de Gaulle to accept his denial, but with the respectful reservation that it seems to hinge upon an interpretation of the words "romantic" and "difficult." Conceivably the scene may have been played basically in the manner recounted by Spears but was perhaps exaggerated by him; conceivably, too, the Spears version might have seemed romanticized to a de Gaulle and yet be basically accurate. Each man, therefore, would be seeing the truth in his own manner. Whatever the truth, the Spears version is simply too good a yarn not to spin and enjoy.

General de Gaulle acknowledged the valuable services that Spears rendered to the cause of France at a moment when France most needed help. However, they began to quarrel soon after de Gaulle set about creating Free France in London. The quarrel was inevitable, for General Spears was the kind of Francophile who would do anything for France except take orders from the French. He had adopted France as his second country, as so many foreigners do, but he expected France to behave like a grateful ward. When de Gaulle refused to be the ward of Britain—and, more pertinently, of Spears—chill set in. De Gaulle stated in his memoirs: "In spite of all that he did to help us at the start, General Spears was destined one day to turn away from our enterprise and to begin fighting against it. In the passion he brought to this, was there not regret at not having been able to lead it and sadness at having left it?"

In view of this relationship between the two men, it is not surprising that Spears would write an account of de Gaulle's flight from Bordeaux that would depict himself as a rescuer and de Gaulle as the nervous refugee. It was also in keeping with de Gaulle's proud temperament and his dignity as President of the Republic that he would have to deny Spears' version but would dismiss it without detailed debate. It was further typical of de Gaulle that he made almost no reference to his personal conduct or feelings. He must have had a very difficult time during his last day in France, but if he did not go slinking around in the shadows or diving into planes as Spears says, he did not himself throw any light upon his real movements on the night that he went to see Reynaud and during the flight the next morning.

It is hard to believe completely de Gaulle's own claim that there was nothing "difficult" about his departure. It was a very tense moment. The government, of which de Gaulle was a high official and a highly controversial one, had fallen. De Gaulle's bitterest enemies had taken power. They were planning to sue for an armistice and knew that he was planning to continue the fight. It is inconceivable that de Gaulle could have walked around in the open, conferring with the fallen Premier Reynaud, collecting large sums of secret funds and then, without difficulty, could have walked through security and customs control to fly off to London in a foreign plane. Something more "romantic" must have happened.

De Gaulle refused to discuss it. His refusal added to the mystery, and the whole story took its place in the mythology of Gaullism even more effectively than if de Gaulle had given his own version. In any case de Gaulle did not need to argue about the personal circumstances of the flight; the political significance was what counted. The final judgment of history will most likely endorse the sentiment expressed in the memoirs of Winston Churchill, who wrote: "He carried with him in this small airplane the honour of France." Churchill's words were a fitting epitaph to the death-departure of Charles de Gaulle, soldier of the Third Republic, who later acknowledged, "I felt within myself a life coming to an end."

PART TWO

THE SAVIOR

The hero saves us. Praise the hero! Now, who will rise to save us from the hero?

CATO THE ELDER *to the Senate of Rome*

No good deed ever goes unpunished.

ANCIENT ADAGE

The shepherd drives the wolf from the sheep's throat, for which the sheep thanks the shepherd, while the wolf denounces him for the same act, as the destroyer of liberty.

ABRAHAM LINCOLN, *Baltimore speech, April 18, 1864*

PART TWO

THE SAVIOR

CHAPTER FOUR

I, GENERAL DE GAULLE

I knew I would have to reckon with this man, this General de Gaulle. I became almost his prisoner.
PRESIDENT DE GAULLE, *interview with David Schoenbrun, Saturday Review, May 16, 1959*

THE SOUND ENGINEER sat in his cubicle in studio B 2, nervously chewing on his mustache, tugging at his frayed cuffs and wishing he were home, with a comforting cup of tea, listening to the Home Service instead of waiting here to shepherd the French news bulletin for the Continental Service of the BBC.

The studio door flew open and in rushed a breathless, harried woman escorting a giant of a French officer. The Frenchman's shiny black hair almost reached the ceiling. His polished boots gleamed against the shabby carpeting of the studio. Leaning over the console to watch the scene, the engineer recognized the woman as Elizabeth Barker of the BBC diplomatic escort service. She introduced the tall officer to Maurice Thierry, the French announcer, and then effaced herself, disappearing into a corner of the studio. Thierry seated the officer at the studio table, adjusted the microphone upward, turned to the technician and gave the thumbs-up ready signal. The engineer flashed the "on-the-air" red light and nodded at Thierry, who then began the bulletin with these words: "This is London, the BBC, calling France. Here in the studio tonight is General de Gaulle, Under-Secretary of National Defense in the government of Premier Paul Reynaud . . ."

As Thierry began the introduction, General de Gaulle hunched himself forward, leaning toward the microphone, poised for his signal to speak. As soon as he heard the words, "And here, now, is General de Gaulle," he squared his shoulders, raised his head and delivered his opening line in a voice so powerful that the startled engineer jumped out of his seat and clutched at the dials to try to bring the sound level down to normal. He twisted the dial with one hand and waved the other up and down in a signal to de Gaulle to lower his voice. General de Gaulle paid no attention; he continued to speak in the same strong voice, staring straight ahead, right through Thierry opposite him, seeing nothing but the unseen audience in France to whom he was addressing this desperate, passionate appeal to come to join him to carry on the fight against the Nazis.

It was there in studio B 2, in that 6 p.m. news broadcast of June 18, 1940, in the French Service of the BBC, that Charles de Gaulle felt within himself "a life coming to an end—the life I had lived within the framework of a solid France and an indivisible army." And it was there that he was reborn out of the ashes of defeat as he pronounced these words: "I, General de Gaulle, presently in London, call on all French officers and men who are at present on British soil, or may be in the future, with or without arms, I call on all engineers and skilled workmen from the armaments factories who are at present on British soil, or may be in the future, to get in touch with me.

"Whatever happens, the flame of French resistance must not and shall not die."

Of the unknown numbers of people who may have heard that now legendary "call to honor," and the hundreds of millions throughout the world who eventually heard about it, only one witness is still alive who was present in studio B 2 with General de Gaulle that night: Elizabeth Barker of the diplomatic escort service of the BBC. Today, a quarter-century later, she is still faithfully carrying on her duties as a producer of radio programs for the world's greatest broadcasting organization, the voice of London, that lonely but unstillable voice of freedom in the silence of the night that fell upon Europe in the summer of 1940.

Without the BBC, General de Gaulle would not have arisen out of the ashes of the death of Charles de Gaulle's France. Studio B 2 was the delivery room in which General de Gaulle was born on the air. He was created on radio, which became and has remained an integral part of his personality and his practice of power from then on, into the age of television, which played an essential role later in the birth and ascension of President de Gaulle. Other statesmen have learned to use the radio and television with great skill—

Roosevelt, Churchill and Kennedy were masters of electronic communication with masses of citizens—but none rose to power, none achieved his recognition solely on the air as did General de Gaulle, who for four years, from June 1940 through June 1944, did not set foot on French soil and was never seen by the French people, but who, as a voice alone, became their hero and unchallenged leader. There is no parallel in history, and there is not likely ever to be again, to the phenomenon of the radionic birth and career of General de Gaulle.

The sole living witness to that birth, Elizabeth Barker, admitted recently to this writer, with British candor and honesty, that she had no idea at the time that she was present at a historic moment. "I had been assigned to the French Service but was rather new at it. We had heard little about General de Gaulle and had no idea, of course, that his speech would become so important in history. I had never seen de Gaulle and had no idea what he was like until I went to greet him at the entrance to Broadcast House and escort him to B 2. I rather expected to find a dominating military man—you know, the big, jutting-chin type. He certainly was big, a huge man, but he had a surprisingly small head, a tiny absurd mustache over rather pouty lips, and virtually no chin at all. He was, above all, icily contained within himself. Not at all what one imagines a Frenchman to be. There was something different about him, different from other men. One could sense that straight away. Oh, I don't mean the 'man of destiny' bit. But he was most remarkably self-possessed."

Elizabeth Barker confirms the fact that no recording was made of the talk. She attributes it simply to the nature of the occasion. "You see, his talk was scheduled at the last moment, to be broadcast in a regular news program that was not normally recorded. Had we known sufficiently in advance that a very important statement was going to be made, we would certainly have laid on recording arrangements. But it was a time of fast-moving, unscheduled events, everything was in a state of confusion, so there was no opportunity to schedule a recording. In the days that followed, of course, when de Gaulle became the officially recognized spokesman of Free France, his talks were recorded, and we have many in our library today. But not the talk of June 18, 1940."

The failure to record the historic talk led to an incident that gives us special insight into the character of General de Gaulle.

Only a minor footnote to history, it nevertheless tells us much about the purist in de Gaulle as seen in his austere sense of historical responsibility. The incident occurred a few days after the June 18 broadcast, when BBC editors, producing a news-review-of-the-week program, discovered that there was no recording of the talk. A request was put through official channels for de Gaulle to make a recording when he came to the studio for his next broadcast. It was a routine request, a practice that is still occasionally followed today when, by accident or negligence, an important broadcast has not been recorded. However, General de Gaulle refused to make a recording of the June 18 broadcast. No explanation of the refusal was given at the time.

I came across this unexplained incident many years later, when my friend and colleague at CBS News, Edward R. Murrow, who was then putting together his record album of history called "I Can Hear It Now," asked me to obtain a recording of de Gaulle's radio broadcast of June 18. When BBC officials explained to me why it did not exist, I went to see General de Gaulle, explained the interest of the album to him and requested that he "reenact" the speech, with the understanding, of course, that it would be labeled a reenactment rather than the original. I advanced the argument that even so it would still have great value as being in de Gaulle's own voice.

General de Gaulle refused courteously but quite firmly, saying, "I refused originally because I was certain that, despite every precaution, sooner or later the recording would be used as though it were de Gaulle actually speaking on June 18, 1940. Whatever slight value a recording might have, it does not justify the risk of falsification or even an accidental misuse. Thus, although I do not doubt that you would handle this with every proper precaution, there is still an evident risk, no matter how slight, that the recording somehow would eventually be misused as an original." De Gaulle reflected silently for a moment and concluded, "Finally, I do not believe in reenactments of history. I could not possibly read those words today with the same voice, in the same rhythm, measure and feeling as I did on June 18, 1940. It is difficult enough to recollect the past; it would be quite impossible to reenact it accurately and honestly. I cannot do so, therefore I will not do this."

One could argue that de Gaulle's refusal was less purism than pettifoggery. He spoke almost daily over the BBC for the two weeks after his first call to resistance on June 18, repeating substantially the same arguments in the same vein and mood. He could have repeated the text of June 18 without substantial or significant change of any kind. Whatever differences might have occurred would have been of little importance compared with the great value of having a record of that historic address. Over the next twenty-five years, and particularly on the twenty-fifth anniversary of the event on June 18, 1965, radio producers and editors have been frustrated by the lack of the record, which has weakened the dramatic productions of historical programs.

This reporter does not subscribe to that argument, but believes on the contrary that General de Gaulle's refusal to reenact the broadcast does him credit. In the early and great days of radio broadcasting there used to be very severe restrictions on the practice of recording programs. All broadcasts were expected to be made "live"—that is, with the speaker actually in the studio and on the air—unless it were impossible—as in the case, for example, of Ed Murrow's magnificent eyewitness reports inside a bomber over Berlin, where there were no "live" broadcasting facilities. Even in such cases, however, Murrow was in effect broadcasting directly into the recorder during the bombing run and not writing and recording his script after the event, back at the base. And when he put the recording on the air, he was in the studio presenting it and identifying it as a recording made in a bomber.

This strict procedure ruled out any possibility of artificial dramatization or other kinds of trickery that are possible with the use of recordings. The uncompromising honesty of the Murrow school of reporting conferred dignity upon and confirmed the integrity of radio journalism and made it one of the most respected as well as most effective means of communication. General de Gaulle sensed this vital role of radio in the public affairs of that day. He himself was peculiarly dependent on radio to make himself known and to win the confidence of the people in occupied France, who were subjected to the most intense and skillful Nazi propaganda. Certainly he was justified—indeed compelled—to set the very highest standards upon the use of his public statements.

His refusal to accept the slightest compromise on this question served a double purpose for General de Gaulle. It projected the image of an unchallengeable integrity, without which his attempt to create Free France would have failed in its early stages, when defeatism, doubt, suspicion and cynicism were undermining the morale of the most patriotic Frenchmen. It also projected an image that de Gaulle esteemed as the most essential quality of his leadership, the image of a man totally dedicated and immovably intransigent on all that involved the honor and the independence of France. Intransigence was and is the fundamental quality of Gaullism; it is his concept of the immovable object that can stand up to the most irresistible force.

Recalling the early days of Free France in London in the first volume of his memoirs, de Gaulle described his situation as that of a man "starting from scratch," with no organization, no following, no reputation, no credit or standing, all of which indicated to him that his only possible "line of conduct" was to adopt "without compromise the cause of national recovery" in order to "acquire authority." He felt he had to act as the "inflexible champion of the nation and of the state." He was, therefore, deliberately intransigent. He justified it in these words: "Those who, all through the drama, were offended by this intransigence were unwilling to see that for me, intent as I was on beating back innumerable competing pressures, the slightest wavering would have brought collapse. In short, limited and alone though I was, and precisely because I was so, I had to climb to the heights and then never come down."

General de Gaulle has stated and restated this doctrine in many ways all through his long climb to the heights and ever since. In the course of a heated dispute with Churchill over the British plans to land forces in the French colony of Madagascar, General de Gaulle demanded that Free French troops be included in the landing forces. Churchill indicated that Roosevelt was opposed to de Gaulle's petition, and he urged de Gaulle to be patient and flexible in his relations with Roosevelt. "Don't rush things," said Churchill. "Look at the way I yield and rise up again, turn and turn about." De Gaulle shook his head in disagreement as he replied, "You can, because you are seated on a solid state, an assembled nation, a united Empire, large armies. But I! Where are my resources? And yet I, as you know, am responsible for the interests and the destiny of France. It is too heavy a burden and I am too poor to be able to bow."

Although de Gaulle thus justified the way of intransigence as the strength required to overcome the fundamental weakness of his means, he also equated the quality of intransigence with the quality of greatness, as evidenced in his exchange on this issue with Anthony Eden. Eden, as the revelation of secret documents has since demonstrated, was de Gaulle's staunchest friend and supporter in the allied camp. Often, unbeknownst to de Gaulle, Eden fought with Churchill on de Gaulle's behalf. He frequently defied Churchill's directions, going so far upon occasion as to destroy an order, to fight for time to cool off Churchill. Nonetheless, Eden also chided de Gaulle for his stubbornness and for his frequent deliberate provocation of controversy. On the day that de Gaulle, preparing to leave London to set up his headquarters in Algiers, came to bid farewell to Eden, the Foreign Secretary smilingly said he would not soon forget de Gaulle, for of all the allied governments-in-exile, Free France, Eden could not help but say, was the most difficult to deal with. To which de Gaulle dryly replied, "I don't doubt it. France is a great power."

De Gaulle evolved this doctrine of intransigence and controversy over some thirty years, from the publication of his self-revealing essay on leadership, *The Edge of the Sword,* to his confessional three-volume memoirs. Rarely in history has the leader of a great nation told his people and the world so much about himself while he was still in the full exercise of his leadership. Not only by his words but also by his deeds Charles de Gaulle lived by the precept he quoted in the foreword of *The Edge of the Sword:*

> Rightly to be great
> Is not to stir without great argument.
>
> HAMLET

It is odd that de Gaulle should open his book of essays on leadership with a citation from *Hamlet,* for the gloomy Prince was essentially a man who could not make up his mind, whereas Charles de Gaulle, who was a blend of many different kinds of man, was above all else a man of decision. For Charles de Gaulle the only imaginable formula was to live or to die, but never the Hamletian alternative "to be or not to be." For de Gaulle, to be is to live, to live is to decide, to decide is to act; not to be is not to live, rather than merely not to do. De Gaulle's personal philosophy was closer to that of La Bruyère, who argued that freedom is not the right to do nothing but rather the right to choose freely what one will do.

De Gaulle was especially impregnated with the philosophy of

his father's friend Henri Bergson and his thoughts on the basic
trinity of decisive qualities; instinct, intuition and intelligence. De
Gaulle repeatedly cited Bergson in the five essays collected as *The
Edge of the Sword*. Anyone who wants to understand de Gaulle
would be well rewarded by reading and rereading those essays,
written when de Gaulle was in his forties at full intellectual and
emotional maturity.

The Edge of the Sword is almost as up-to-date a guide to Charles
de Gaulle today as it was on the day it was written.* His memoirs,
published almost three decades after the essays, can be read, as a
sequel to *The Edge of the Sword*, with almost no break in the
continuity of the ideas expressed, despite the great gap in the years
of composition. However shifting de Gaulle's policies were—and
the unfolding record shows they were as inconstant as the swirling
winds of his destiny—his fundamental beliefs were as fixed as his
own faith in eternal France.

Of all the constants of human existence none is more basic than
war, as de Gaulle views the aggressive nature of man. "Its history
is the history of the human race," he stated in the essay entitled "Of
Prestige," which is one of the clearest of the windows to the mind
and soul of Charles de Gaulle. He acknowledges the evil of war:
"War stirs in men's hearts the mud of their worst instincts. It puts
a premium on violence, nourishes hatred and gives free run to
cupidity. It crushes the weak, exalts the unworthy, bolsters tyranny . . . time and time again it has destroyed all ordered living,
has devastated hope and put the prophets to death."

No pacifist could condemn the horrors of war more sternly than
does General de Gaulle, but he is no pacifist, as he demonstrates
when he sees the other face of war as the face of an angel. "But
though Lucifer has used it for his purposes, so, sometimes, has the
Archangel. With what virtues has it not enriched the moral capital
of mankind! Because of it, courage, devotion and nobility have
scaled the peaks. It has conferred greatness of spirit on the poor,
brought pardon to the guilty, revealed the possibilities of self-
sacrifice to the commonplace, restored honor to the rogue and
given dignity to the slave." De Gaulle surely merits the golden-
broomstick award for sweeping statements with this perorative
sentence: "Had not innumerable soldiers shed their blood, there
would have been no hellenism, no Roman civilization, no Chris-

---

* All the following quotes in this chapter are from *The Edge of the Sword*
unless specifically attributed to some other work or source.

tianity, no Rights of Man and no modern developments."

What is a reader to think when he realizes that the man who wrote this passage became the President of one of the world's great powers? In the Gaullist balance of the evils and virtues of war, is it not war's virtue which weighs heavier on his scale? Was this not a chilling thought to come from the leader of a great power in the thermonuclear age?

It is true that the thought was expressed by de Gaulle in the prenuclear period of the thirties, but everything he said as President of France thirty years later corresponded to that same doctrine of yesteryear. The best that can be said about this view of de Gaulle is that it was frankly exposed, more candid than the doctrines espoused but not admitted by other statesmen, who did not eschew war in the nuclear age. De Gaulle could point to French Premier Guy Mollet, British Prime Minister Anthony Eden, Israel's modern prophet Ben-Gurion, all good men, all humanitarians, who risked a nuclear holocaust in their reenactment of ancient history at Suez. What is one to think, moreover, of Kennedy's ill-conceived endorsement and poorly executed action of the Bay of Pigs operation? Or of Lyndon Johnson, who sent out his bombers over North Vietnam in the name of freedom while citing passages from Deuteronomy? Were these not acts carried out in the terms of Charles de Gaulle's vision of war as the purpose of the Archangel against the Lucifers of aggressive Arabism and Communism, as Mollet, Eden, Kennedy and Johnson did in turn proclaim?

Most honest men would answer positively, agreeing with de Gaulle that war can be the staff of an Archangel as well as the fork of a Lucifer. Only a very rare few sincere pacifists and conscientious objectors would judge war to be wholly evil. Yet there was something deeply wrong, something unwholesome, in de Gaulle's glorification of war's historic "virtues."

Whatever the justice of the case may be, one cannot read de Gaulle's essays without engaging in this kind of silent but intense argument between the reader and the writer. His was the essential artistry of the most talented writers, the ability to engage the reader in a dialogue, to make him feel what the writer feels, like it or loathe it. In his writings, as in his speeches and in his execution of policy, Charles de Gaulle always stirred with great argument.

Just as France is the microcosm of the world of nation-states, whose agonies and achievements reflect in miniature those of all others, so is Charles de Gaulle an almost perfect laboratory specimen of the universal leader type, in the most exaggerated form possible within the bounds of rationality. He asks in the foreword to his essays, "How can we understand Greece without Salamis, Rome without legions, Christianity without the sword, Islam without the scimitar?" In the same spirit, we might ask how one can understand Charles de Gaulle without his words, or the kind of men who wield power in the world unless we understand Charles de Gaulle.

One finds in the essays of the soldier sentences that reappear in the speeches and the directives of the statesman thirty years later. For example, in 1963 President de Gaulle rejected the atomic-test-ban treaty with the words: "There is no rule of law without the force necessary to defend and impose the law; since there is no world government and no world army or police force, each nation must be responsible for its own defense and can count only upon itself, in the final analysis, for the eventual arbitrament of arms." These were the identical words penned by Major de Gaulle in 1932 in *The Edge of the Sword:* "In whatever direction the world may move, it will never be able to do without the final arbitrament of arms."

The past explains the present, spanning the gap of three decades as though they were a week end. Which de Gaulle, for example, said this—the soldier or the statesman? "Is it really likely that the present balance of power will remain unchanged so long as the small want to become great, the strong to dominate the weak, the old to live on?" Answer: both de Gaulles posed this problem, Major de Gaulle in 1932 and President de Gaulle in 1962. De Gaulle's repeated denunciations of the Russian-American-sponsored atomic-test-ban treaty grew directly out of his long-held conviction that the strong seek to dominate the weak and impose their own balance of power upon the world. As President he was the champion of a small nation that wanted to be great again, of an old nation that wanted to live on, of the weak who meant to have at least enough power to resist domination by the strong.

De Gaulle pointed out a dozen times that the so-called test-ban treaty was only a partial ban on tests in the atmosphere but did not ban the underground testing that permitted the advanced powers to improve their weapons, while it denied by the atmospheric ban an opportunity to others to advance to the point where they could have the basic nuclear force that would permit them to advance to the more sophisticated stage. De Gaulle boycotted the disarmament talks and challenged the great powers to agree to discuss total disarmament, including not only conventional arms controls but also liquidation or strict controls of nuclear stocks, missiles and launching pads.

Whatever one may think of de Gaulle's nuclear-striking-force program, his cherished and highly controversial "force de frappe"—and this writer believes that it was an unsound, wasteful program—one might agree that if de Gaulle's program was wrong, the others were not necessarily right. De Gaulle at least based his program on principles that have been proved too unfortunately true and have at least the virtues of clarity and consistency.

Any citizen who was familiar with the style of Gaullist leadership in the Fifth Republic would easily find his own examples of presidential conduct faithfully reflecting these thirty-year-old precepts of the soldier-writer:

> A chief must stand apart, for authority is not possible without prestige, or prestige without aloofness.

> That is why great men of action have always been of the meditative type. They have, without exception, possessed to a very high degree the faculty of withdrawing into themselves.

> It is not enough for a chief to bind his men into a whole through the medium of impersonal obedience. It is on their inner selves that he must leave the imprint of his personality . . . intelligence, instinct, and the leader's authority combine to make the conduct of war what it is. But what are these faculties if not the expression of a powerful and resourceful personality?

> Strong characters are, as a rule, rough, disagreeable and aggressive.

> Faced by action the mob feels fear, the apprehension of each individual multiplying infinitely through the apprehensions of all the others . . . that is why the energy of a chief bolsters the morale of his subordinates like the sight of a life jacket that reassures the passengers on a ship.

From each such personages there radiates a magnetism of confidence and even of illusion. For those who follow them they personify the goal and incarnate hope itself.

There are those who declare that success can only grow out of favorable circumstances. They overlook that it was necessary, however, to bring those circumstances about.

Great leaders were always conscious of the role and value of instinct. What Alexander called his "hope," Caesar his "luck," Napoleon his "star," is this not the certainty of a gift that brings them into close contact with reality so that they can always dominate it?

De Gaulle was constantly pictured as a "man of mystery" whose sibylline pronouncements were pondered by editorialists and official analysts. There was in almost every major capital a school of trained "Gaullologists," similar to the "Kremlinologists" who pore over the speeches and texts of the masters of Moscow, looking for hints and guides to the realities hidden behind the wall of secrecy that surrounds the Kremlin. In fact de Gaulle was not so much a mystery man as he was a deliberate mystifier, less mysterious than mystical. His secrets were not hidden behind closely guarded walls, nor was he as inaccessible as the masters of the Kremlin. The reality of life in Paris in the reign of Charles de Gaulle was the planned mystification and confusionism practiced by him. He delighted in private audiences in which he stated his views oracularly and frequently contradictorily, saying different things to successive visitors.

De Gaulle's masterstroke of mystification was achieved early in April 1965, when he received six members of the National Assembly to discuss the nature of constitutional reforms he had in mind. All six were present together at the same talk, and each of the six, on emerging from the meeting, gave reporters a different version of what de Gaulle had said and intended to do.

The confusion among the six deputies was a triumphant application by President de Gaulle of this old Gaullist principle: "First and foremost there can be no prestige without mystery, for familiarity breeds contempt." And this addendum: "In the design, the demeanor and the mental operations of a leader there must always be a 'something' which others cannot altogether fathom, which puzzles them, stirs them, and rivets their attention . . . to hold in reserve some piece of secret knowledge which may at any moment intervene, and the more effectively from being in the nature of a surprise. The latent faith of the masses will do the rest. Once the leader has been judged capable of adding the weight of his personality to the known factors of any situation, the ensuing hope and confidence will add immensely to the faith reposed in him."

In the same manner, his so-called press conferences, whose careful staging prompted editorialists to describe them as "press performances," were faithful to this doctrine: "The great leaders have always carefully stage-managed their effects. . . . Every page of the Commentaries provides us with evidence of the studied manner in which Caesar moved and held himself in public. We know how much thought Napoleon gave to showing himself in such a manner as to impress his audience." The fact that these "press spectaculars" and his similarly stage-managed radio-television addresses to the nation were spaced far apart—a winter and a summer press conference, a spring and a fall electronic address—is explained in these citations:

> Sobriety of speech supplies a useful contrast to theatricality of manner. Nothing more enhances authority than silence. It is the crowning virtue of the strong, the refuge of the weak, the modesty of the proud, the pride of the humble, the prudence of the wise and the wit of fools.

> To speak is to dilute one's thoughts, to give vent to one's ardor—in short, to dissipate one's strength—whereas what action demands is concentration. . . . "Imperatoris brevitas," said the Romans. Who could be more taciturn than Bonaparte? He did, it is true, when Emperor, occasionally unbosom himself in words, but only when he was debating on political matters.

Why was de Gaulle so haughty? What was the reason for his obsession with grandeur? Why did he behave in so kingly a manner, almost at times as a divinity above all other men, disdainful even of the normal need to protect a president? These were the answers supplied by the writer Charles de Gaulle:

> It is essential that the plan on which the leader has concentrated all his faculties shall bear the mark of grandeur.

Conscious of their own limitations, each measuring his own littleness, men accept the need for collective action on the condition that it will contribute to an end which is, itself, great. No leader will ever succeed in asserting himself unless he can touch that spring.

Whatever orders the leader may give, they must be swathed in the robes of nobility. He must aim high, show that he has vision, act on the grand scale. . . .

Every man of action has a strong dose of egotism, pride, hardness and cunning. But all those things will be forgiven him, indeed will be regarded as high qualities, if he can make of them the means to achieve great ends. [Great men] are later remembered less for the usefulness of what they have achieved than for the sweep of their endeavors. In the concourse of great men, Napoleon will always rank higher than Parmentier.

The price paid for leadership is unceasing self-discipline, the constant taking of risks and a perpetual inner struggle. The degree of suffering involved varies according to the temperament of the individual; but it is bound to be no less tormenting than the hair shirt of the penitent.

Winston Churchill perceived in de Gaulle this capacity for suffering, this hair-shirt syndrome. He noted in his memoirs, after his meeting with de Gaulle in London on June 16, 1940, in the last hours before the fall of France: "Under an impassive, imperturbable demeanour he seemed to me to have a remarkable capacity for feeling pain. I preserved the impression, in contact with this very tall, phlegmatic man, 'Here is the Constable of France.' " Whether or not de Gaulle truly had a capacity for feeling the pain of leadership, or whether it was, as he himself said, a "harsh joy," a "bitter satisfaction," no one but de Gaulle himself could state with certainty. What is sure is that de Gaulle did give the impression to such shrewd and hard-minded observers as Churchill, as well as to many others who worked closely with him, that he was a sensitive, emotional man underneath the mask of his "impassive, imperturbable demeanour."

Statesmen who dealt often with de Gaulle learned to take good note of the Churchillian view of de Gaulle and of the Gaullist self-revelations. Some discovered the mistake in thinking of him as a mere actor, although he was always, as the French say, "un grand comédien." Even his severest critics concede that his "acting" was performed in the service of his policies and not merely for the sake of the performance itself. If de Gaulle was a great actor, it was because he believed that acting was an integral part of governing and not because he was a mere showman, "all voice and gestures, prating the lines of the playwright." De Gaulle was the playwright and the producer as well as the performer.

However much his performance in the role of the great man was acting or genuine, or a combination of both, there is little doubt that it corresponded to the basic principles of his reasoning and was in tune with his spirit and emotions. He said as clearly as he could, over and over again, that he enjoyed challenges and welcomed difficulties. The record of his acts bears out his words, for he often stirred up trouble quite deliberately.

This addiction to difficulty, even where it could be avoided, is part of de Gaulle's personality but it is also part of his belief in the value of difficulty as a measure of leadership, as expressed in this formula from his essays: "The man of character finds a special attractiveness in difficulty, for it is only by coming to grips with difficulty that he can fully realize his potential." And he added, "The passion for self-reliance is obviously accompanied by some roughness in method. . . . Whatever happens, he seeks only the harsh joy of bearing full responsibility."

Charles de Gaulle viewed greatness as a blend of inner forces and external challenges that gave these forces an outlet and a crucible in which they would be poured and then molded by the great man:

All he asks is that he shall be given a task to do, and then be left alone to do it.

"Arrogant and undisciplined" is what the mediocrities say of him, treating the thoroughbred, who has a tender mouth, as they would a donkey which refuses to move.

Resolute and inconvenient men are to be preferred to easy-going natures without initiative.

The deep root of action by the best and strongest of men is the desire to acquire power.

[The man of character] lends nobility to action; without him there is but the dreary task of a slave; thanks to him it becomes the divine sport of the hero.

The trust of little people exalts the man of character. . . . His firmness increases proportionately but so, too, does his benevolence, for he is a born protector.

. . . For nothing great is ever achieved without that passion and that confidence which is to be found only in the man of character . . . nothing great will ever be achieved without great men, and men are great only if they are determined to be so.

One of the most fascinating insights among the many provided by the essays is the conclusion that de Gaulle draws from his thesis that the price of leadership is the pain that the leader must suffer. He wrote: "This helps to explain those cases of withdrawal which, otherwise, are so hard to understand. It constantly happens that men with an unbroken record of success and public applause suddenly lay the burden down."

In this sentence, written in 1932, one finds an answer to a question that has been asked ever since the "mystery" of de Gaulle's sudden resignation as prime minister in January 1946, less than a year after the victory in the war, at the height of his postwar powers. Few observers were aware of the statement in *The Edge of the Sword,* and even those few were reluctant to believe that a phrase in an essay written some fourteen years earlier by a soldier could be accepted as the reason for the resignation of the prime minister that the soldier had finally become. It sounds too fantastic, too literary an interpretation. And yet, strange as it may sound, it is an explanation that is consistent with de Gaulle's character and with the circumstances of his resignation.

Throughout 1945 Premier de Gaulle found the frustrations of parliamentary democracy an intolerable hair shirt. This is not inconsistent with his love of challenge and difficulty. He would never have resigned under fire, never have laid the burden down if any clear difficulties had menaced France. Indeed, he went to considerable pains to explain in his resignation message that he had put France back on the rails again and it was time to let another engineer take over the controls. Although his claim that the situation was stable enough for him to resign was highly disputable, he had to insist upon it, for he could not permit himself to lay down the burden unless he could claim he had made it light enough for others to bear. The truth was that he himself was bored with peacetime problems, uninterested in economics and finance, impatient with the give and take of parliamentary democracy. He was willing to rule but unwilling to govern France. Thus, despite his "unbroken record of success and public applause," he suddenly withdrew into "the loneliness that is the wretchedness of superior beings," exactly as he had foretold in *The Edge of the Sword* in his comment on the sudden resignation of a leader.

Throughout the lives and times of Charles de Gaulle the evidence piled up overwhelmingly on the side of the accuracy and reliability of his writings as a guide to his actions, explaining them better than most official documents which themselves become much more valuable when overlaid on de Gaulle's essays and memoirs. In a quarter-century of study of de Gaulle, of close association with, and upon occasion participation in, the events of his career, I found that any act or official document that did not conform to the principles and self-revelations of his writings was probably not reliable evidence of his real policy, but that any such act which conformed exactly with his written principles was not only genuine and reliable but instantly comprehensible, no matter how mysterious, irrational or inexplicable it might otherwise seem. Any serious historian of modern France must not only know de Gaulle's essays and memoirs by rote, but must also keep them ever in mind as he examines the record of events.

The memoirs contain more specific details of policy than the essays, which concentrate rather on the enunciation of general principles, but all the cases cited in the memoirs are faithful to and grow out of the basic principles. His writings are not the conventional platitudes written for statesmen by "ghosts." The essays, above all, were not the self-justifying afterthoughts of a great public figure, but rather the utterly uninhibited expostulations of an almost unknown and very angry young man, fearless and seeking no favor, but on the contrary risking his entire career in a polemic assault on orthodox thinking.

In addition to providing a guide to the policies and actions of his presidency, these writings also provided an even more precious guide to the personality and character of the man inside the statesman, although not separate from the statesman, for de Gaulle did not really exist other than as a statesman. His early

written views on statesmanship could be strictly applied to his own
conduct of the affairs of the French State:

> The statesman must concentrate all his efforts on capti-
> vating men's minds. He must know when to dissemble,
> when to be frank. He must pose as the servant of the
> public in order to become its master. He must outbid his
> rivals in self-confidence, and only after a thousand in-
> trigues and solemn undertakings, will he find himself
> entrusted with full power.

De Gaulle has no illusions about public gratitude or con-
stancy.

> Public opinion, that inconstant mistress, follows his
> lead with a capricious step, ready to stop dead when he
> should race too far ahead or to take giant strides when he
> thinks it advisable to move with caution.

Decades later President de Gaulle would put those principles to
the test in practice. One of the most remarkable examples in
history of a leader's ability alternately to dissemble and to be frank
was de Gaulle's handling of the Algerian crisis. For the entire year
of 1958 and well through 1959 he so hid his hand that neither the
"Algérie Française" forces that had brought him back to power
nor the pro-independence forces of the opposition knew where he
stood.

At the outset, in 1958, both pro- and anti-Algérie Française
leaders joined de Gaulle's government, with neither side knowing
which was cast for the role of the dupe. No public servant
operating in a republican framework was ever more the master of
the people than President de Gaulle. He had no "rivals in self-
confidence" and was the mastermind of "a thousand intrigues,"
skillfully blended with "solemn undertakings" as he made his way
toward being "entrusted with full powers." Never once did de
Gaulle fully trust himself to his "inconstant mistress." He imposed
the most complete controls on public opinion, just short of outright censorship, converting the national radio and television
networks into an almost totally exclusive government domain. He
virtually won the struggle of Algeria on the radio in the historic
"Battle of the Transistors," while he dominated public opinion in
France on television in a spectacular demonstration of "captivating
men's minds."

The belief expressed in his essay that the capricious public can stop dead when the leader wants to race ahead or can demand giant strides when he thinks caution advisable was borne out in two important issues of his presidency: national defense and European policy. On national defense President de Gaulle insisted upon racing ahead to become a nuclear power while the French public in overwhelming majority opposed his program. Despite his powerful personality and control of parliament, he had the most difficult time obtaining the necessary budget and the cooperation of scientists to carry out his atomic plans. On the issue of European unity, however, the majority of the nation's leaders wanted to "take giant strides" toward the construction of Europe and fretted irritably under President de Gaulle's constraints and caution, in a manner that Major de Gaulle had foreseen in his soldierly meditations on statesmanship.

President de Gaulle, in his mid-seventies, with a dazzling record of prescience behind him, inevitably loomed over the scene not as a statesman but as a kind of superman. He carefully cultivated this image, but he himself had no such personal illusions. He once admitted to this writer: "I have never achieved any of the major goals I set myself. Although I led Fighting France to the liberation of the country, the Fourth Republic was not the kind of state I had hoped to construct after liberation. The Fifth Republic is not yet perfected or solidly rooted. The French Army is not yet the professional army I want it to be, with all the modern weapons that it needs. We have made progress in our economy, but it is still not stable nor growing fast enough. Wherever I look, in Europe, in Africa, to the world councils, there remains more to be done than has been done." De Gaulle did not often indulge in such confessional self-critiques, but in occasional private confidence and a few public flashes of self-examination in his memoirs and public speeches, he sometimes showed us the real man under the mask of the superman.

Even the hidden "real man" was not like ordinary men. It is not possible to live the extraordinary lives that he lived and retain many ordinary human qualities. The rigid constraints upon human emotions that he saw as necessary for the conduct of a chief eventually eradicate normal emotions. His belief in the necessary loneliness of a leader led him to reject normal friendships. In an interview in the spring of 1959 I asked de Gaulle about his wartime friendship with Eisenhower and suggested that it was a happy accident of history that two comrades-in-arms had become presidents of their countries. De Gaulle said, "I do have the most friendly feelings for General Eisenhower. He is a good and honest man." Then with a deep sigh and sincere sadness in his voice, he added, "Men can have friends. Statesmen cannot."

Every man or woman who ever worked closely with him suffered sooner or later a banishment based upon de Gaulle's refusal to allow anyone to stay close to him long enough to have a lien upon his affections. Geoffroy de Courcel, his first aide-de-camp in London, faithful servant over the years, who would willingly have remained at de Gaulle's side, was granted an ambassadorship by the President. Captain Guy loved de Gaulle so passionately that he was sent away. De Gaulle believed that a chief cannot accept love. This was not because he was a cold man, as he has been inaccurately described by some he froze out of his heart, but rather because he was a very passionate man himself, as Churchill perceived, and did not trust himself to be exposed to human affections. When I asked him about friendship and fidelity, de Gaulle replied, "A leader can only be faithful to the nation and not to any particular citizens or class of citizens. As for love, it is a two-way street or it becomes a dead-end alley, cluttered with the ugly debris of unrequited emotions. A leader cannot give love, therefore he must not accept it, for love unrequited turns to hate."

These were not the words or sentiments of a cold man, but rather those of a passionate man who packed his heart in dry ice because he felt he must. Nor was Charles de Gaulle naturally the solemn man of few words that he trained himself to be, in accordance with his precepts of silence and sobriety as necessary qualities of leadership. In private upon occasion he could be exhaustingly loquacious, as many a visitor to his office discovered. He could become a torrent of words and launch into one of his discourses upon the historical origins of contemporary world politics. He rarely indulged in personal reminiscences and never in ordinary small talk, but he did upon occasion indulge in talk itself, and when he did, it rushed and gushed forth like water long pent up in a dam that suddenly breaks through a breach in the wall and pours forth in a great flood.

More often, however, the man inside de Gaulle showed himself in flashes of wit as electric, illuminating and quick as a bolt of lightning. Like lightning, it was gone as swiftly as it had come, and the dark clouds of solemnity would close in again upon the

chieftain's brow. De Gaulle would not allow the somber image of
the chief to be lightened for long. He did not tolerate or indulge in
anything so vulgar as mere humor. His wit was not genial or
amiable. It was sharp, often cruelly cutting, always ironic, but
nonetheless it could be very funny and, as such, a revelation of a
carefully controlled, hidden charm that he unquestionably possessed and that would not be squelched completely, no matter how
long and deeply buried.

One cannot vouch for the authenticity of all the anecdotes and
quips attributed to de Gaulle. Therefore, I cannot vouch for the
reliability of some of the following examples of Gaullist wit in
action other than those personally heard and witnessed. However,
these have been selected out of the hundreds that could be cited
because they are most likely to be true and, if not, are at least true
to the spirit and nature of de Gaulle. I would testify that, if he did
not actually say what these anecdotes quote him as saying, he could
have said it, for each of these tales is characteristic of this man of
character.

My own favorite personal Gaullist anecdote is one in which I
was a victim of his sharp wit. It stung me at the time, but in
retrospect the sting is gone and the wit of the rebuke remains. The
incident occurred early in de Gaulle's return to power. At the time
there were many serious problems of press relations between the
new regime and the foreign correspondents. Most of the problems
fell on my head because it was my unfortunate privilege to be the
president of the Anglo-American Press Association. One day, in
that capacity, I called upon President de Gaulle at the Elysée
Palace. The usher who led guests into the President's office had a
sense of humor of his own. He knew me well, for I had come often
to the Elysée over the years, and there was never any official
protocol involved. However, that day he decided that I was an
official and so, as he opened the door to de Gaulle's office, he drew
himself up to parade posture, swelled his chest so that the heavy
heraldic chain of silver draped around his neck bounced and
jingled on the starched, full-dress bosom of his shirt and bellowed
like an imperial majordomo: "MONSIEUR LE PRÉSIDENT DE LA
PRESSE ANGLO-AMÉRICAINE DE PARIS!"

I had just crossed the threshold as he began to trumpet out this
pompous introduction, and I tripped and almost fell flat on my
face under the sardonic smile of a watching de Gaulle. Somehow I
gathered myself up and managed to walk the long distance, some

twenty endless feet of carpeting, from the door to de Gaulle's desk in the ornate Napoleonic office of the French President. De Gaulle bowed gravely to me and said, "Good morning, Mr. President." Red with embarrassment, I flushed even more at being addressed as "Mr. President."

As I sat down I managed to acknowledge his greeting, and then blurted out, "Mr. President, may I address you as General, as in the past?" I meant no offense, of course. The informal "Mon Général" was often used by those who were in the army with de Gaulle and had a special wartime relationship with him. I was trying to break the ice and recover from my own confusion, not thinking of the fact that in an official call it is not proper to use the more familiar address. He knew perfectly well, too, that I did not take myself seriously as an official. Yet with a diabolical grin he nodded affirmatively at me and in his deep, grave voice said, "Yes, of course . . . Mr. President." It was nothing less than a most elegant rebuke to grant me permission to call him "General" while he continued to call me "Mr. President." It stung like a slap in the face, putting me in my place with a punctilious courtesy more wounding than an open rebuke would have been.

Our talk was stiff and painful, for I never could recover my equilibrium. I kept calling him "Mr. President" several times in every sentence, refusing to use his permission to call him General. He knew he had wounded me and I could sense that he regretted it, for he had not meant to be deliberately unkind. It was just one of those quick lunges of a rapier that a Frenchman cannot resist making when a target presents itself. At the end of the talk, to make amends, de Gaulle arose, accompanied me to the door and took my proffered hand in his two huge hands in a very unusually affectionate gesture and said how pleased he had been to see me and that I must promise to come soon again. I looked up at him, grinned and said, "I would be pleased to do so . . . General." I then walked quickly away, as fast as I could. As the door closed I heard him laughing, a sound one rarely hears in the Elysée.

It was during the same period that I kept trying, as did all journalists, to obtain an on-the-record interview with de Gaulle. His press chief at the time, Baron Olivier Guichard, held out no hope at all. The President of the French Republic, he said, does not grant press interviews. He is the Chief of State and cannot be interviewed, particularly not by foreigners. Guichard refused even to relay the request, saying it was quite out of order.

Some weeks later Max Shuster, the American publisher, came to see de Gaulle to complete arrangements for the American edition of de Gaulle's memoirs. Max was an old friend of mine and he asked me to be available to help his translator, Richard Howard, who might need some assistance on checking out the exact equivalents of certain unusual military or political terms not found in conventional dictionaries. He also suggested that I review the American edition of de Gaulle's memoirs and offered to make the necessary arrangements for me to do so for *Saturday Review*.

I saw in this an opening to get the interview I sought, and promptly agreed. As soon as *Saturday Review* made its request, I wrote to General de Gaulle requesting an interview for the purpose of clarifying certain points raised in the memoirs. I knew how important the memoirs were to de Gaulle, for he has a love of the written word and a sense of his own role in history as recorded in books. To strengthen my request I wrote to de Gaulle on my personal stationery, not on the CBS letterhead, and I wrote, under my name, "author of *As France Goes.*"

Within two days of sending my letter, I received a phone call from Baron Guichard. In his dry, highly sophisticated style, Guichard said, "If the author of *As France Goes* would care to interview the author of *The Memoirs of Charles de Gaulle,* he may come to the Elysée Friday at ten." He then paused and added, "Needless to say, this is not an interview with the President. It is merely a literary interview between authors. President de Gaulle wants this clearly understood."

Guichard himself tells a wonderful story of de Gaulle's wit at his expense. He had spent a trying morning on the telephone, one of those mornings of telephone frustration that only busy Parisians suffer, when there is no dial tone or when connections are broken off in the middle of a conversation or when anybody you get through to seems to have lost his senses. Finally, in total frustration and exasperation, Guichard slammed down the phone and shouted "Death to all fools," using a particular French word for fools that cannot properly be translated into English. Behind his back, unbeknownst to him, General de Gaulle had come walking by, on the way to his private office. De Gaulle walked by Guichard at the very moment that he shouted "Death to all fools" and, without breaking stride, in perfect timing, de Gaulle leaned over and, in his most sepulchral tone, said, "What a vast program, my friend!"

Another presidential staffer close to de Gaulle, who prefers not to be named, has told me of his experience with his leader. He had worked for de Gaulle for almost ten years and had never once heard de Gaulle address a single remark to him other than routine business. Suddenly one day, as he brought a report to the President, de Gaulle looked at him and said, "You're looking thinner." The aide, startled, was struck dumb by the unexpected personal comment after all the long impersonal years. De Gaulle stared at him, awaiting a reply, and then said, "You're not a very talkative fellow, are you?" The aide staggered out of the office and has been waiting three years since then for de Gaulle to address another remark to him so that he might continue the "conversation."

One day, shortly after the coup d'état in Algiers that had brought down the Fourth Republic and brought de Gaulle back to power, one of the Gaullist plotters in the coup, Léon Delbecque, came to see him in great distress. "General," he lamented, "all of my friends say you are deserting us. They want me to get you to change your Algerian policy. What should I do?" De Gaulle snapped back, "Change your friends."

"Conversations" with de Gaulle were apt to be brief and embarrassing, as one unhappy deputy learned to his sorrow. The man in question had run for parliament on an extremely conservative anti-Gaullist platform and was one of the few avowed opponents of de Gaulle to get elected. When de Gaulle held the traditional presidential reception for the new parliamentarians, the anti-Gaullist debated with himself whether or not to attend. He decided to brazen it out but got more and more nervous as he got nearer to de Gaulle on the reception line, wondering what he would say to de Gaulle. The moment arrived, and, red-faced and nervous, the deputy stammered out the words, "Uh, General, you know that my wife is a Gaullist." De Gaulle unsmilingly shook his hand, nodded slowly, and said, "What a coincidence, my wife is too."

His humor sometimes twists a different way. In Oran one day an aide told him that a delegation of war veterans was waiting eagerly to have an audience with him before he flew back to Paris. De Gaulle, busy, annoyed, told his aide to have the group wait. Time went on and the aide twice stuck his head into the office to see if de Gaulle was still so busy. Finally, with many apologies, he came in and said, "General, they are very upset now. They ask me to tell you please to receive them. After all, they are fervent Gaullists." De Gaulle, blazing with anger at the importunity, growled, "Well, I'm not. Let the Gaullists wait."

He did not spare his bravest comrades from the bite of his tongue. At the liberation of France, de Gaulle flew down to Toulouse, to inspect the maquisards of southwestern France who had fought bravely against the German occupants and were carrying out an essential and dangerous mission still, for neither the French nor the allied armies were going to be sent to southwest France. They were too busy fighting the Germans and trying to drive them east.

At the airfield an honor guard of the resistance was lined up waiting for the "First Resistant of France." De Gaulle walked up to the honor guard, to review them, and with the distaste of a professional officer of St. Cyr scowled at their homemade bizarre uniforms. As he walked down the reviewing line, he inspected each man in turn, with a darkening frown twisting his thick eyebrows. The first man wore a handknit sweater on which he had sewn the insignia of a captain. The second man in line had a Sten gun slung around his neck and wore a major's stripes sewn on his rakish beret. Each and every man had an officer's stripes embroidered somewhere on a makeshift uniform, until finally de Gaulle stopped in astonishment in front of one unmarked and sturdy fellow, broad of chest, wide of shoulder, his head high as he stood proudly for inspection by his chief. De Gaulle plucked at his sleeve to see if any insignia were sewn in the folds. He looked at the maquisard's cap—no insignia of any kind. De Gaulle shook his head sadly and said, "So, you are not an officer, eh? What's the matter, young man, don't you know how to sew?"

A wartime resistance agent and peacetime critic of de Gaulle, Emanuel d'Astier de la Vigerie, a brilliant journalist who has written many excellent essays on de Gaulle, told me that he had tried to verify some of these Gaullist anecdotes, in particular the one about the soldier who was a private because he could not sew. He asked de Gaulle about it and the General replied that the scene described at Toulouse never took place. "However," said de Gaulle, "I have been told by aides, and vaguely remember, that I made a remark of this kind on some other occasion. I think it was at a military review in England." D'Astier is convinced that the anecdote is essentially correct, whatever the precise geographical details or exact timing and phrasing may have been.

Like myself, d'Astier de la Vigerie believes that the best de Gaulle anecdotes "are true or could be true." He gave me one of his own, a bright gem for any collector. In the course of researching a new book he recently went to see an old friend who had become one of the highest officials in de Gaulle's personal cabinet, Etienne Burin des Roziers. Burin had told him he would have time to talk because de Gaulle was awaiting a meeting with his state guest, the King of Denmark, and it was a quiet morning at the presidential palace.

D'Astier was chatting with a relaxed Burin, when suddenly a series of musical notes sounded from the inside of Burin's desk—the kind of musical "indicatif" used by the telephone company's new automatic dialing system: "beep-beep-bop-bop-beep-beep-beep," loud and clear as though played on a fife, and emitting mysteriously from inside a closed desk. D'Astier was astounded and Burin was blushingly embarrassed as he explained, "It's a new system. The General does not like telephones or messengers. When he wants one of us quickly, he now presses a button that makes this musical beeper go off inside the desk." Burin then groaned and added, "We each have a different tune the General selected for us. We really do dance to his commands, you see."

The fantasy of the presidential beeper, the flashes of mordant wit, the fondness for French cheeses and wines that have given de Gaulle the silhouette of a huge kangaroo, his addiction to nicotine (thirty cigarettes a day up to his late fifties, when his doctor and his wife forced him to give up smoking), a little-known but verified reputation as a dashing Lothario in his salad days, a rare ribald remark from time to time to a close aide—all these are signs that inside the solemn statesman, the intractable, intransigent knight-errant of France, the dour soldier and austere essayist that history will immortalize as the legendary General de Gaulle, there is a very human being. These human faults and foibles are his saving grace. At best a most difficult man, he would be an intolerable monster if he were entirely and only what he had trained himself to be.

Perhaps the most remarkable and fascinating human quality of the man was revealed to me in the course of the "literary conversation between authors" that we had in April 1959. Among the questions raised by his memoirs that I put to him for clarification was his habit of referring to himself in the third person. Students of French affairs and biographers of de Gaulle have long been intrigued by this and have speculated on its meaning. Some have argued that this is the royal form of address. Others insist that when he says, "de Gaulle" he means France and when he means de Gaulle himself he says "I." The best authority, of course, is de Gaulle, and I asked him if he would explain this stylistic puzzle so that the record could be set straight. This was his reply:

> There are two reasons for this. One, purely for purposes of style. It is repetitive and immodest always to be saying "I" or "me." For style alone I chose, according to the rhythm of the sentence and the context, to say "de Gaulle" in some places. However, the more important reason was my discovery that there was a person named de Gaulle who existed in other people's minds and was really a separate personality from myself.
>
> I made this discovery at Douala, which was my first contact with the French people after my call to resistance. I landed there after the expedition to Dakar had failed. There were thousands of people and they began to shout, "De Gaulle! De Gaulle! De Gaulle!" I was taken aback. Until then, in London, my contacts had all been personal and individual, with ministers, soldiers, attachés, and so forth. But here was the people, the voice of the crowds. And I suddenly realized for the first time what a heavy burden I bore, what a responsibility I had to all these people who were counting upon a man named de Gaulle to liberate them, to give them back their freedom and independence. I realized then that General de Gaulle had become a living legend, that they had formed a certain image of him, that they expected many things of him, that they thought of him as behaving in a certain way.
>
> From that day on I knew I would have to reckon with this man, this General de Gaulle. I became almost his prisoner. Before I made a speech or reached a major decision I had to ask myself, "Will de Gaulle approve of this? Is this the way people expect de Gaulle to act? Is this right for de Gaulle and the role he plays?" There were many things I would have liked to do but could not, for they would not have been fitting for General de Gaulle.

After Douala the limits of what was fitting for General de Gaulle were immutably fixed. As he later noted in his memoirs, it imposed "upon my personality an attitude I could never again change. For me this meant, without respite, a stubborn self-supervision as well as an extremely heavy yoke." Here again one finds the singleminded consistency of the Gaullist character, for these words, written in the mid-fifties, are identical in spirit with the formula expressed decades earlier in *The Edge of the Sword*. The "stubborn self-supervision" of the memoirs is none other than the "unceasing self-discipline" which he had stated to be the price of leadership. The "extremely heavy yoke" he felt after Douala was the familiar "hair shirt" that symbolized his "perpetual inner struggle" or, as he rephrased it in his memoirs, the "perpetual bondage" of General de Gaulle.

The self-forged chains of bondage were made of metals fused in the flames of war and frozen into an inflexible mold by defeat. From the fall of France and the flight to London to the disastrous failure by an expedition to Dakar, the character and career of General de Gaulle were finally cast, as were the form and substance of his relations with the British and the Americans or, as he calls them, the "Anglo-Saxons." From June 18 in London to October 8 in Douala the Anglo-Saxons were to become, with his fellow Gauls, his principal allies but also his principal adversaries. De Gaulle could not come to grips directly with the Germans or with their satellite, the Vichy Government of France; he had first to cope closely and urgently with the parallel tasks of imposing his will upon the hesitant and doubtful Free French while opposing his will to the dynamic and determined allies.

The twin struggle of de Gaulle against the Anglo-Saxons and de Gaulle among the Gauls began in 1940 and for the next quarter of a century was extended in ever-widening circles of conflict, from London to Africa, to France, to Europe, to South America and to Asia. Throughout the entire world, in every theater of action, the man of June 18, 1940, "I, General de Gaulle," kept the pledge that "whatever happens, the flame of French resistance must not and shall not die."

Resistance can be one of the noblest qualities of man, but, if self-feeding, it can become self-consuming. The noble and base characteristics of resistance were all present in the systematic Gaullist struggle inside and outside France. What the final balance will be can only be judged by future historians.

The contemporaries of Charles de Gaulle could be certain only that French resistance would not die so long as he lived and that he could not live without a resistance that continued to stoke his own internal fires. The spirit of resistance provided the fuel for the flame of hope that he lighted in London on June 18, 1940. What an extraordinary day of destiny is June 18! How ironic that it should have been on that day, and in London of all places, that a General de Gaulle should have arisen to say that nothing had been lost in the Battle of France, for it was on June 18, 125 years earlier, that Napoleon went down to defeat at Waterloo.

General de Gaulle did not know that he was making his appeal for resistance on the anniversary of Waterloo. He did not choose the date for his radio appeal. Destiny chose it for him—the same historical accident, if accident it is, that one finds throughout the lives of the man who bears the name of Gaul.

CHAPTER FIVE

DE GAULLE AGAINST THE ANGLO-SAXONS

> *There was a great crowd to welcome Charles de Gaulle; one might say that after centuries leading to immense trials, the ancestral soul of the Gauls and the Franks lived again in those who were there.*
>
> CHARLES DE GAULLE, *describing his visit to Mainz, Germany*

ARRIVING IN LONDON, lonely and destitute, Charles de Gaulle felt "like a man standing in front of an ocean that he would try to cross by swimming." His aide, Geoffroy de Courcel, had checked in at the French Embassy and, he reported to de Gaulle, had found a chilly reception. Shipwrecked and friendless, de Gaulle was rescued and befriended by Winston Churchill. In his memoirs he admits before the bar of history his debt to the greatest of the Anglo-Saxons: "Swept in desolation by the shipwreck on to the shores of England, what could I have done without his help? He gave it to me at once."

How de Gaulle admired and envied the British—almost as much as he came to spurn and resent them! From the start he had a love-hate relationship with the British element of the Anglo-Saxon races; for America he had and still has little love, as the record will testify. But the British: they were the people he would have liked the French to be. "In England itself, the Free French were surrounded by esteem and sympathy. The King, first of all, was quick to give proof of these. . . . But it would be impossible to imagine the generous kindness which the English people everywhere showed toward us. . . . When the London papers announced that Vichy was condemning me to death and confiscating my property, quantities of jewelry were left at Carlton Gardens anonymously and dozens of unknown widows sent their wedding rings in order that the gold might serve the work of General de Gaulle."

Even more than by their kindness, the British won the heart of General de Gaulle by their unity, civic responsibility and courage. "It was a truly admirable sight to see each Englishman behaving as if the safety of the country depended on his own conduct. . . . The British as a whole were getting ready to fight. Each man and woman joined in the network of defense." Despite his austerity of style and economy of words, author Charles de Gaulle took space in his memoirs to describe a newspaper cartoon which, for him, illustrated the magnificent spirit of the British:

> One newspaper cartoon showed the formidable German army already in Great Britain, but held up on the road, with its tanks, its guns, its regiments, and its generals, in front of a wooden barrier. A notice indicated, in fact, that to pass it one must pay a penny. Not having received from the Germans all the required pennies, the Englishman in charge of the toll gate, a little old man, courteous but inflexible, was refusing to raise the barrier, in spite of the indignation which ran the whole length of the invaders' monstrous column.

All through his conflicts with the British, which broke out very soon, parallel to their kindness and aid to Free France, General de Gaulle kept in mind their great spirit. The British were different from the French, their national interests were competitive and dangerous, but they were different members of the same great family of Europeans, whereas America was always alien to de Gaulle. The British played in the same league as the French and by the same rules. Not America. As de Gaulle noted in his memoirs: "When all is said and done, Great Britain is an island, France the cape of a continent, America another world."

In June 1940 America was very far away, still living in isolation, officially neutral, sympathetic to the plight of the British but still far from ready to go to their rescue. De Gaulle clearly saw all the dangers ahead. "What I know of men and conditions left me no illusions on the obstacles to surmount." He knew better than most men the power of the enemy. He foresaw "moral and material difficulties that a long, bloody struggle would bring forth for those who would have to fight it as pariahs without means." De Gaulle had no illusions about his allies either. He believed that allied intelligence services would exploit the divisions among Frenchmen in order to dispose of France. "Finally there would be the tendency of the great states to profit from our weakness in order to push their own interests to the detriment of France."

Although he had unlimited faith in his country and in himself, de Gaulle never fooled himself about the reality of his country's weakness and his own loneliness. "I was nothing at the start. At my side not the shadow of a force, nor of an organization. Inside France no response to my call, no wide attention. In foreign lands, no credit, no justification. But this very nudity dictated to me my line of conduct. It would be by espousing without reserve the cause of national salvation that I would at last achieve authority."

The immediate objective that de Gaulle set himself was "to serve and save the nation and the state." This was to him even more important than victory over the enemy in the war, for he never wavered in his belief that the allies would win. What was important to de Gaulle was that France, as France, and not the French mercenaries of foreign armies, should participate in that victory. If one understands this imperative of de Gaulle one understands why he fought his allies with even more passion than he fought the Germans and why he has continued to do so from 1940 through 1965. Roosevelt and Churchill were for de Gaulle more dangerous enemies than Hitler. De Gaulle did not fear Hitler's victory, which he was certain was impossible. What de Gaulle feared was the victory of Britain and America, with the spoils of victory leaving them the dominant postwar powers in Europe at the expense of a humiliated, powerless France.

"I thought that honor, independence and unity would be finished if it should come about that, in this world war, France, alone, would have capitulated and remained in that state." No matter what happened after that, whether France remained in slavery or was one day freed of the oppressor, "the disgust that she would feel for herself and that she would evoke in others would poison her soul and her life for long generations." It would not be enough, de Gaulle noted in his memoirs, to furnish "auxiliaries for another power.* No! For our effort to be of value, it had to bring back into the war not merely Frenchmen, but France."

In the first weeks and even months of his call to resistance it seemed as though de Gaulle would fail to bring back into the war many Frenchmen, let alone France herself. Not only did his call inspire little response inside France, but many of the early responses were negative. His broadcast on June 18 was not even heard by most of the French forces stationed in London and the British countryside. There had been no advance publicity, and few of the officials or officers knew Charles de Gaulle, a temporary brigadier-general, only very recently appointed under-secretary of war in the last days of a falling government.

The French ambassador to London, Charles Corbin, a career diplomat, was too old, too used to obeying orders from Paris, to commit so grave an act of insubordination as to reject his government's decision in favor of an armistice and to follow the lead of a junior, dissident cabinet official. Corbin and others also noted that in his broadcast de Gaulle addressed his appeal to "soldiers, engineers and skilled workers of the armaments industries"—not to diplomats, government officials or citizens.

The refusal of the senior French diplomat in London to join or support de Gaulle was a serious setback to the dissident's hopes. Even men concerned with armaments and industry disapproved of the nature of his plan for resistance. Jean Monnet, who was to play a major role in the future of his country and of all Europe, and who may yet have the last word on the shape of Europe's future, was critical of de Gaulle's concept of resistance. Monnet wrote de Gaulle a long letter disapproving the plan to set up resistance headquarters in London. "You are wrong to set up an organization which might appear in France to be under the tutelage of England," Monnet wrote. Monnet said that he shared de Gaulle's determination to keep France fighting, but: "It is not from London that the effort of reconstruction can be launched."

Just as de Gaulle never forgot Churchill's initial help and faith, so did he never forget Monnet's initial rejection of him. Although Monnet eventually joined de Gaulle's Free France and served in

---

* Here again is a phrase and attitude of the past that is still alive and current in the present. In his radio-television address to the nation on April 27, 1965, President de Gaulle stated that "France does not accept the role of a subordinate auxiliary in the Atlantic system."

his postliberation administration, Jean Monnet and Charles de Gaulle became engaged in a historic struggle to plot the future course of French history. De Gaulle appealed to the heart of Frenchmen for a supreme effort to regain grandeur in national independence while Monnet worked quietly on the minds of Frenchmen and their European neighbors to abandon dream fantasies of the past and seek new greatness and leadership in the international independent communities of Europe and the Atlantic world. The conflict between de Gaulle and Monnet grew naturally out of conflicting philosophies, and this disagreement was to increase through the years, having taken root in the very first days of the defeat of France.

De Gaulle wanted to restore the glory of the past and cast the future in the same mold, if a bigger one. Monnet wanted to wipe out the past and build a completely new and, in his view, greater future in a different mold. This quarrel between de Gaulle and Monnet was obscured by the more urgent and dramatic issues of the war and the fall of France, but it is as important to understand as is de Gaulle's determination that France over and above Frenchmen must participate in the war, for it is the essence of Gaullism today, as it was twenty-five years ago. As the community of Europe grows, as ground is being broken for the first common institutions linking Europe and America, the outcome of the contest between the aims of de Gaulle and the views of Jean Monnet is of paramount importance to the United States and the nature of Western society.

Western society at the time that General de Gaulle emerged as leader of Free France was a hostile world for his aspirations. Not only did few men rally to de Gaulle's broadcast, but most men, Frenchmen and Western diplomats together, remained in direct contact with Paris and the defeatist regime of Marshal Pétain. The Consul-General of Canada, M. Dupuis, and the representative of South Africa failed to maintain Commonwealth solidarity with Churchill and stayed with Marshal Pétain. Pétain was, indeed, the legal chief of government, for his powers had been invested in him by the parliament in a free, legal, constitutional vote on July 9 and 10.

Pétain and the government he set up in Vichy were recognized as the legal authority of France by the world's greatest powers, as de Gaulle dryly noted in his memoirs: "Above all, one could see assembling in Vichy, gathered around Monsignor Valerio Valeri, the Papal Nuncio, Mr. Bogomolov, the Soviet Ambassador, soon to be joined by Admiral Leahy, the American Ambassador—an imposing diplomatic corps. It was enough to chill the ardor of those whose first inclination might have been to hold up the Cross of Lorraine."

The awfulness of the tragedy, the vast nothingness that was France, inspired Charles de Gaulle. This was the moment he had been waiting for all his life, the moment to render France "the signal service" he had dreamed of as a young boy. There is something strangely joyous rather than tragic in de Gaulle's description of how he reacted to the early failures of his appeal for resistance: "In the frightening emptiness of the general renunciation, my mission appeared to me in one clear and terrible flash. At this moment, the worst of her history, it was up to me to take France upon myself."

The essence of de Gaulle is found in that phrase: "to take France upon myself." It is even stronger in the original French than in translation. The French phrase is: 'C'était à moi d'assumer la France." Most ordinary men would have said that it was up to them to assume *the responsibility* for France. That extraordinary man Charles de Gaulle assumed France directly in a kind of personal transmogrification through which he assumed the country itself rather than the responsibility for it.* France and de Gaulle became the single emanation of one spirit in which the man, the soldier, the citizen, the leader, the state, the nation were no longer component parts but rather one entity, so that one could say, interchangeably, France or de Gaulle. In that sense a correct translation of the phrase "C'était à moi d'assumer la France" might well be: it was up to me to become France. Even that most arrogant figure of history, Louis XIV, seems modest when compared with Charles de Gaulle. The Sun King declared: "I am the state." Charles de Gaulle declared: "I am the nation."

From the moment that this clear and terrible vision appeared to him, Charles de Gaulle became the spirit of France. It was this spirit that sustained him through the lonely weeks and months,

---

* In the American edition of his memoirs, the phrase is translated as "to assume the burden." It could be argued that this is an accurate interpretation of the more elliptical phrase "assumer la France." In the opinion of this writer, however, de Gaulle was not being deliberately elliptical for reasons of literary style, but literally meant that he had "to assume France," exactly as he wrote.

enabling him to persevere through many grievous tribulations and
to overcome the opposition to his cause among his own fellow
exiles and his closest allies, who insisted upon making a distinction
between de Gaulle and France.

The earliest test of this issue came when the British sought to
recruit French troops for the allied armies rather than for independent forces under de Gaulle. Every time that de Gaulle tried to
rally the French troops to his banner, the British officers would
come along after him to try to dissuade the Frenchmen from
following him. A typical example of this conflict of interests
occurred on June 29, when de Gaulle visited the men of a
mountain division to appeal to them to sign up for Free France.
The commanding general of the division told de Gaulle that he
was determined to return to France. Only a few young officers,
among them some who would become famous and infamous
names in the years to come, stepped forward to salute Charles de
Gaulle and join his ranks. One was young Captain Koenig, who
would become commander-in-chief of French forces in the liberation campaign. Another was Captain de Wavrin, who was to
become one of the most controversial figures of the Gaullist
movement when he took the resistance pseudonym Colonel Passy
and created de Gaulle's secret service, which was later accused of
all sorts of nefarious intrigues, including torture of French citizens
opposed to de Gaulle. Along with these young officers there were a
few hundred Alpine troopers, two battalions of the Foreign
Legion, two-thirds of a tank company and some scattered artillery-
men, engineers, signalmen and staff officers to compose the pitifully small band of men that Charles de Gaulle managed to rally
as the microscopic nucleus of a Free French force in the grim
summer of 1940.

It was astonishing that even these few answered his call, for no
sooner had de Gaulle left the camp of the mountain division than
two British colonels, sent by the war office, appeared on the scene
and told the troops, "You have a free option to serve under the
order of General de Gaulle. But we must tell you, speaking man to
man, that if you so decide, you will be considered as rebels by your
own government." The colonels then pointed out that the French
could enlist in the British forces and receive all the protection of
His Majesty's Government while still being able to fight the
common foe.

The war office and the British general staff tried to block de

Gaulle at every turn and tried literally to steal recruits from him and lure them from the Cross of Lorraine into the ranks of the Union Jack. The admiral commanding the naval station at Liverpool turned de Gaulle away at the gate when he came there to speak to French sailors, and de Gaulle had to rush off to other camps to seek recruits before the British could buy them or frighten them away. Because de Gaulle could not be everywhere at once, could not spend all of his time recruiting, many a patriotic Frenchman, wanting to continue the fight, joined up with the British, who had the only effective fighting force left to oppose Hitler.

Claude Bouchinet-Serreulles told this writer of his own experience in Liverpool when he arrived there in mid-July:

> British officers were everywhere on the docks talking to the Frenchmen as they disembarked, offering to help them carry on the fight or to work in war industries, pointing out that the British had not and never would surrender. Against the visible strength of material and spirit that the British presented there was only one lonely young French naval officer on the dock, trying futilely to tell the men about de Gaulle and Free France. He came over to me and I asked him who was with de Gaulle in London. The names he mentioned meant nothing to me. Obviously de Gaulle had failed to win support from any of the leaders or high-ranking officers of my country. I was dispirited and on the point of walking off when suddenly, among the names he was citing, I heard the name "de Courcel." It is not an uncommon family name in France and I doubted that it could be the same de Courcel who had been the friend of my schooldays, Geoffroy. But, just to be sure, I asked him to describe him. When he said he was tall and thin, with a long nose curving down to a pointed chin, I grinned with delight. It was my Geoffroy all right. A good omen! So, off I went to London, with no better reason than that. That was how I came to rally to the call of Charles de Gaulle.

Serreulles' story illustrates perfectly the haphazard and often unheroic manner in which chance determined the early enrollments in de Gaulle's movement. Some men found a friend in London, others had friends or relatives in Canada or the United

States. A few, inspired by de Gaulle's radio address and by the brilliant propaganda work of a young Gaullist team composed of Raymond Aron, André Labarthe and Maurice Schumann, rallied enthusiastically to his side. But they were very few, and mostly young, inexperienced men, and it is doubtful that Free France would have lasted long or progressed far without the personal support of Winston Churchill.

Churchill's support was not, of course, without self-interest. No chief of state, particularly in time of war, can afford any emotion other than complete devotion to his own nation's cause. The comradeship of Churchill and de Gaulle was effective but not affective. When they met it was as statesmen, not as men, and their personal feelings were set aside.

Neither de Gaulle nor Churchill had any illusions about the nature of their future relationship. On the very first day of his arrival in London, de Gaulle told Churchill that it was his intention to form a "national committee" to direct the war efforts of France. Churchill's staff advisors would far have preferred to enlist individual Frenchmen in British ranks. But Churchill, with his greater vision of the future, as well as with his better understanding of the present, knew that Pétain would not only conclude an armistice but would yield more and more to the Nazis, thus making it imperative to create a pro-allied resistance movement.

A passionate nationalist himself, Churchill sensed that a French resistance movement, both inside France and in the empire, would be more likely to grow into an effective instrument for the allied cause than a mere recruitment of French mercenaries in allied ranks. Churchill alone of the Western leaders believed this and espoused the cause of de Gaulle for this purpose. But Churchill the politician also knew that the price would be the elevation of the leader of the French movement to a position of power; and, knowing de Gaulle, Churchill knew the price would be high. He was prepared to pay any price, however, for no cost was high weighed against the need to defeat the Nazis.

On June 23, the day that Pétain concluded the armistice with Hitler, the British issued a communiqué announcing that England no longer considered the French government in Bordeaux to be independent. The communiqué also announced that a group of Frenchmen in London intended to form a National Committee of Resistance. Two days later the British government announced that it was ready to aid independent Frenchmen anywhere in the empire who might be planning to organize a resistance movement. Churchill was not, however, prepared to recognize de Gaulle without evidence that he was the only man available. For three more days Churchill waited anxiously for some sign, for any sign, from a French government official or high-ranking officer responding to his offer of aid. Finally, a full ten days after de Gaulle's call of June 18, Churchill accepted the fact that Charles de Gaulle was the only man ready and able to form a French resistance movement. On June 28 the British government officially recognized Charles de Gaulle as the "Chief of all the Free French, wherever they are, who rally to him for the defense of the allied cause." De Gaulle had won the first round, not only by his own aggressive action, but mainly by the default of all potential rivals for leadership.

It was, however, only the first round of what was to be a very long fight for recognition of the greater authority to be accorded to Free France if the name of the movement was to have any validity. The British recognition of de Gaulle had been very carefully qualified and minimized. It recognized de Gaulle only as chief of those "who rallied to him." Frenchmen who did not wish to rally to de Gaulle personally could enlist in the British forces or get jobs in British industry. The recognition was, therefore, not all-embracing, not a closed-shop contract. Furthermore, de Gaulle was recognized only as chief of men fighting "in the allied cause." The official recognition said nothing of Free France as a state or government organization but mentioned only a group of men united for the purpose of fighting a common enemy.

In the earlier communiqué of June 25, offering aid to Frenchmen in the empire who would organize a resistance movement, the British government had stated that "the aim of Great Britain is the complete restoration of the French colonial and metropolitan territory." De Gaulle had taken good note of that promise and sensed that it was a vital opportunity to obtain an immediate commitment to a postwar settlement. It was evident that the only hope of France to retain its empire was an allied victory, but that this hope itself depended upon French participation in the allied effort from the start. Moreover, a clear obligation on the part of the allies to support restoration of French territory would have to be formally extracted from Churchill if the promise was to become a pledge.

This was de Gaulle's position from the first. He knew at once what was at stake for his country. But Mr. Churchill had no reason to make such a commitment to de Gaulle, for de Gaulle was not in a position to rally the French Empire's resources to the allied war effort. Only General Noguès, in North Africa, could do so. This is why de Gaulle promptly offered to serve under the orders of Noguès and why Churchill offered this precious guarantee, hoping to win over Noguès or any other high-ranking leader who could deliver the colonies. But Noguès did not respond, and Churchill had to turn to Charles de Gaulle.

Since de Gaulle, however, was not able to deliver the resources of the French Empire, which had not yet rallied to his call, Churchill felt he did not have to pay any high price at the start to the National Committee headed by de Gaulle with so few followers. After much argument, the terms of recognition and collaboration were finally spelled out in a letter of agreement on August 7, in which Churchill said that His Majesty's Government would "assure the integral restoration of the independence and grandeur of France." Significantly, there was no mention of any restoration of French territory, only the vague words "independence" and "grandeur"—abstract concepts rather than measurable areas. Just to be certain that there was no misunderstanding on this vitally important issue, Churchill sent de Gaulle on that same day a second but secret letter * in which he pointed out that the phrase "integral restoration of the independence and grandeur of France" should not be considered to apply strictly to the "territorial boundaries" of France. The absence of any commitment on territory in the first letter was thus made explicitly negative in the second, secret communication. Churchill requested written confirmation of this understanding.

In a secret reply of the same day de Gaulle promptly acknowledged receipt of Churchill's letters and cited in quotations the pertinent passages to show that he had read them and *understood* them. But—and this was a big but—de Gaulle certified only his *understanding* of Churchill's intent and commitment. He did not confirm his *agreement* on this point, as Churchill had sought in his request for confirmation. Instead, de Gaulle limited himself to saying, "I take note of the fact that such is the interpretation that the British government puts upon the statement cited above." And

* This secret letter, as well as de Gaulle's secret reply, which were not released for publication at the time, were published after the war and were included in an appendix to de Gaulle's memoirs.

de Gaulle dryly added, "I hope that circumstances will one day permit the British government to reconsider these questions with less reservations."

This very first negotiation between Churchill and de Gaulle set the pattern for the many conflicts of interest that were to mark the stormy relations among the allies throughout the war, into the postliberation era and right through to this very day. De Gaulle's reaction confirmed Churchill's fears about the troublesome ally he had taken on, whereas the imperialist Churchill's refusal to guarantee the integrity of the French Empire confirmed de Gaulle's conviction that his allies were ultimately more dangerous than the common enemy.

Within less than a month of this mutually mistrustful "agreement" establishing uneasy official relations between the British government and the Free France committee a major event occurred that came close to breaking the relations altogether and destroying de Gaulle's resistance movement before it had even gotten started. It demonstrated how fragile and complex relations were going to be and illustrated tragically the central conflict between the differing interpretations of the two letters, between restoration of independence and restoration of territory, between the allied cause in general and French or British interests in particular. It was the fratricidal battle of Mers-el-Kebir.

On the night of July 3, 1940, only two weeks after de Gaulle had broadcast his appeal for continued resistance to the Germans, the British fleet without warning attacked the French squadron at anchor in the harbor of the military base at Mers-el-Kebir, in Algeria. Simultaneously, British raiding parties boarded all French vessels in British ports, forcibly disembarked and interned on shore the command staffs and officers. This action was decided on unilaterally by Churchill because of intelligence reports that led him to fear that Pétain was preparing to turn the French fleet over to the Germans or would not effectively resist a takeover.

General de Gaulle denounced the British assault as "a terrible hatchet-blow to our hopes." It was an unjustified attack, whose main result would be to turn Frenchmen away from the alliance and even back into the camp of Pétain. De Gaulle requested permission to use the BBC radio channel to broadcast a comment on the "lamentable affair" of Mers-el-Kebir. His grief and his fears were frankly evoked in that address on July 8, but they were nonetheless held in check by his stern self-discipline and realistic appreciation of his position and that of his British allies. He said, "There is not one Frenchman who has not learned with grief and anger that ships of the French fleet have been sunk by our allies." He characterized the attack as "an odious tragedy," and he solemnly adjured the British not to represent it as "a direct naval success." After describing the assault as a kind of sneak attack on unprepared and anchored vessels, de Gaulle then went on to say, "Addressing myself to Frenchmen, I ask them to consider the basic situation from the only viewpoint that counts in the end, that is to say the ultimate viewpoint of victory and liberation." With courageous candor de Gaulle bluntly told his compatriots, "There is not the slightest doubt that, in principle and through necessity, the enemy would have used them [the ships] some day against England or against our own empire. Well, then! I say to you without evasion that it is better that they should have been destroyed!"

De Gaulle castigated the Pétain government for exploiting the incident and attempting to turn Frenchmen against the British, "our betrayed allies." He insisted that the highest act of patriotism for Frenchmen and Englishmen alike was to recognize the drama for "what it is, a deplorable and detestable affair," but to prevent it from having any result that might lead to the division of the allied peoples. "Whatever happens, even if one of them is for a time under the enemy yoke, our two peoples, our two great peoples, remain linked one to the other. They will both succumb or they will win together."

This speech cost de Gaulle many recruits and gave Pétain and the Germans a valuable propaganda weapon to use against de Gaulle, "the lackey of the British," "Churchill's French butler." Head high, outwardly unmoved by these insults that made his heart ache, Charles de Gaulle pressed on with his plans for resistance. He insisted upon reviewing his pitifully small troops on the French national holiday, July 14, and on July 21 persuaded the general staff to let a few French planes participate in a bombing raid on the Ruhr. On August 24 King George VI reviewed the Free French forces. De Gaulle noted in his diary the resolution of his men and wrote, "The edge of the sword would bite deep." And then, in a very rare moment of despair, de Gaulle added, "But, my God, how short it was!"

The armed forces hardly totaled 7000 effectives, ill-assorted and weakly armed. The navy consisted of only a few ships, while many more French vessels than de Gaulle had under his command were sailing under British command. "It was heartbreaking," de Gaulle confessed, "to see them navigate under a foreign flag." Nothing could have been more painful to this passionate French nationalist than to see Frenchmen and the French arms under foreign orders. De Gaulle never forgot those early days. These events influenced his thinking and his policy throughout the war and again two decades later, when he returned to power at the head of the Fifth Republic. In February 1959 President de Gaulle took the decision to withdraw the French fleet in the Mediterranean from NATO command, partly because the commanding admiral was an Englishman and the supreme commander an American, but mainly because he had been traumatized by his wartime experiences to fear integrated commands under Anglo-Saxon directives. De Gaulle noted that he accepted "the general directives of the British High Command" but that "in all cases I reserved for myself the supreme command of the French forces," thus establishing their "purely national character."

For de Gaulle, the military might of a nation was inseparable from the very notion of the nation itself. "There is no France without a sword," he wrote in his memoirs, and more specifically, "France could not be France without a navy." Any understanding of the policy of President de Gaulle must take into account this fundamental policy, which, even more than a policy, was an article of faith, almost a religion. De Gaulle the politician, the realist and virtually the provisional bondsman of Churchill at the outset, might forgive the British their attack on the fleet at Mers-el-Kebir, but he could not forgive any Frenchman, and less so any ally, who attempted to subordinate French national forces or in any way to diminish the sovereignty of France.

In his original accord with Churchill, de Gaulle specified that "in no case could the volunteer forces bear arms against France." In a typically Gaullist distinction that reveals the true character of the man, de Gaulle added that "This did not mean that they must never fight against Frenchmen." France exists over and above Frenchmen in the Gaullist vision. There are both good and bad Frenchmen, but France is only good. Frenchmen are mere mortals, but France is immortal. The state is a passing manifestation of a system of government, but the nation is the emanation of an eternal spirit. In that sense it was quite conceivable—indeed, necessary—to envisage Frenchmen fighting Frenchmen and Free

France fighting Vichy France. "Vichy, being what it was and not at all France," would have to be fought. But—and this is the essence of Gaullist thinking—allied military action "when applied against the forces of official France would not be used against the real France."

De Gaulle's concept of the false and the real France eventually led him into conflict with the United States even more than with the British. The British had officially declared that in their view the Pétain regime was not an independent government, and they had recognized de Gaulle's Free France movement, if not as a government, at least as the sole organization empowered to speak for French interests. However, from 1940 to 1943 the United States granted no recognition of any kind to Free France or to de Gaulle but, on the contrary, recognized Pétain as the legal government of France and accredited an official American diplomatic mission to his capital at Vichy, and even after breaking with Vichy the United States continued to recruit and support Vichyites in North Africa.

The American people, shocked by the fall of France and the abject surrender of Pétain, may have been thrilled by the defiant courage of the patriotic Charles de Gaulle, but the American government, perhaps sharing the same general sentiments, felt it could not afford the luxury of shaping policy for sentimental reasons. Roosevelt and Hull, aware of America's unpreparedness for war, struggling to change a public opinion blinded by the illusion of neutralism, carefully weighed the advantages and disadvantages of a break with the legal Vichy government. The disadvantages seemed to them far greater in the summer of 1940. They were concerned about the terms of the French-German armistice as it affected the French fleet and the armed forces and territories of French Africa, which remained somewhat uncertainly under French command. It was, in the view of Secretary of State Cordell Hull and of the chiefs of staff, vital to keep the African ports—particularly Dakar, the African base nearest to the Americas—out of Nazi hands. It was equally important to keep the Germans out of French possessions in the Caribbean, where they might directly menace the United States. An endorsement of de Gaulle and a break with Vichy might have led Pétain to grant the Germans submarine and air bases right off the shores of the United States. This was a prime consideration of what Professor

William Langer called, in the title of his history of this period, *Our Vichy Gamble*.

The architects of the state department's Vichy policy also argued that Pétain, defeatist though he was, remained a symbol for the people of occupied France and that even Hitler, unless highly provoked, would not infringe any more than he already had upon the integrity and authority of the Pétain administration. It was thought, therefore, that Pétain would keep France out of the war from then on, rather than let its remaining forces be used for Nazi purposes. It was also believed that Admiral Darlan, regarded as a fervent nationalist and passionate champion of the French Navy, would never let the fleet fall under Nazi command. General de Gaulle himself admitted that he, too, believed this to be a fair calculation, insofar as Darlan was concerned. "A feudal lord does not deliver over his fiefdom," de Gaulle said contemptuously of Darlan. De Gaulle, however, challenged the thesis that Pétain could defend French integrity and independence, and he hotly denounced America's continuing Vichy policy after Laval had been named foreign minister in the summer of 1940, for Laval, he insisted, was a lackey of the Nazis.

The Free French in London were dismayed and furious when Roosevelt sent Admiral Leahy as Ambassador to Vichy after the Laval appointment had already demonstrated the pro-Hitler orientation of the Vichy regime. De Gaulle did not believe the official explanation that Leahy's mission was strictly limited to contacts with high officials, particularly in the navy, to keep the French fleet immobilized. From his own experiences in London, de Gaulle knew that one could not so separate out the military from the political and psychological consequences of an embassy's existence. America's recognition of Vichy was a terrible blow to Free France. And the choice of Leahy as ambassador was particularly unfortunate. Leahy had virtually no political or diplomatic experience and was not temperamentally suited for such an assignment.

Strictly a military man, Admiral Leahy cultivated military men and cabinet officials and had little knowledge or understanding of the state of mind and aspirations of the people of occupied France, nor was he able to assess the strength of Gaullist sentiment in the country. Leahy, impressed by flatteringly favorable reactions of Vichy officials to his pleas to keep the French fleet out of German

control, became convinced that there was a subtle underground
resistance movement inside the Vichy government and that
Vichy itself was secretly sympathetic to the allied cause. Therefore he felt there was no reason to support an external resistance
movement like de Gaulle's. In fact, Admiral Leahy became convinced that any support for de Gaulle might alienate Vichy and
push it into Hitler's camp. This was the burden of his reports to
Secretary Hull and resident Roosevelt.

When in 1942 Admiral Leahy was recalled from Vichy and
appointed military attaché in the White House, his views, already
solidified, became official policy, with disastrous results. One of
America's most authoritative historians of that period of history,
Arthur Layton Funk, in his book *The Crucial Years 1943–1944*,
wrote:

> Leahy's inflexible and conservative temperament pro-
> duced in him a disinclination to alter his opinion readily,
> and in 1943 and 1944 he would tend to assume that
> conditions in France remained as they had been when he
> was there in 1941. This lag in current intelligence would
> cause him to argue that de Gaulle had no support in
> France at a time when the major underground networks
> had clearly demonstrated their willingness to affiliate
> with Fighting France.

Leahy's reports, and particularly the concern he expressed about
Dakar's threat to American security, led Roosevelt not only to
support Vichy, but also to veto a British plan to blockade North
Africa, which he thought would be provocative and ineffective.
On advice of his leading counselors, Roosevelt sent Robert
Murphy to North Africa to work out an alternative deal with
General Weygand. The idea was to ship economic aid to the
French colonial territories in order to build up good will among
the population as well as among the soldiers, so as to strengthen
their ability and their readiness to resist a German takeover. The
theory also held that American invasion troops, when they finally
came, would thus be welcomed as friends and liberators. This
theory was contested not only by de Gaulle but also by the British,
who told the Americans that Weygand was totally loyal to the old
Marshal and could not be won over. Washington decided nonetheless to push on with the Murphy mission and send aid to Weygand.

De Gaulle, outraged at the unilateral action by America, appalled by the lack of knowledge and judgment of the Americans, never forgave Roosevelt or Murphy. His feelings about Murphy grew more bitter as the years went on and reached a new height in 1958, during Murphy's "good-offices" mission to North Africa, shortly before the uprising in Algiers on May 13, 1958, that brought de Gaulle back to power. De Gaulle has quarreled with many men, and the list of his adversaries is long and distinguished. But Robert Murphy was one of the few men whom de Gaulle despised personally to the point of hatred. This hatred for Murphy further poisoned French-American relations in 1958 and 1959 when President Eisenhower, who had the highest regard for his friend "Bob," as did many people in Washington, retained Murphy as a special assistant and appointed him to an allied three-power consultative council. This appointment of his personal enemy to a consultative post with France embittered de Gaulle and soured his otherwise excellent relations with Eisenhower.

In the greater scheme of things Murphy was only a small pebble among the many boulders on the rocky road of French-American relations. But it was the kind of small pebble which gets inside a man's shoe and causes a pain and a stumbling out of all proportion to its size and importance. It is astonishing how often some little pebble like this caused irritations of a major order, as though some evil genie were assigned to wrecking the long friendship of France and the United States.

Few territories were less important than the stony little islands of Saint-Pierre and Miquelon off the coast of Newfoundland, yet these little North Atlantic pebbles exploded like giant oceanic volcanoes and came very close to breaking relations completely between Free France and the United States in the first days of America's entry into the war. Saint-Pierre and Miquelon are twin islands of little strategic importance aside from possessing a weather station and radio transmitter which could conceivably be used to give information to German submarines, a likelihood no one seriously considered. The inhabitants were patriotic French citizens and, because of their proximity to the coast, were familiar and friendly with the Canadians and Americans. Nothing indicated that these innocent, unimportant islands were to become storm centers.

De Gaulle's sympathizers had won support among the islanders, who were ready to rally to the Free French. Churchill concurred and sent a message to this effect to the Canadian government, which added its endorsement to such a move. However, the Canadians and the British both felt that they ought to get Washington's approval before the Cross of Lorraine was hoisted so near America's coast. At the time, Washington was still in a state of shock following the sneak attack on Pearl Harbor and was peculiarly sensitive to any question involving offshore islands.

Under the influence of Leahy's thinking, officials were unwilling to take on the extra burden of a break with Pétain that might occur if the United States approved a transfer of sovereignty of the French islands. Negotiations were undertaken, and on December 13, 1941, less than a week after Pearl Harbor, Roosevelt informed Pétain that the United States would not abrogate the Havana Convention of 1940 which provided for maintenance of the status quo in the Western Hemisphere.

De Gaulle's representative at the time, Admiral Muselier, was preparing for a landing on the twin islands. He had three corvettes and a submarine standing by awaiting orders to go in and hoist the flag of Free France. When he was informed of the Roosevelt-Pétain agreement he promptly sent a signal to de Gaulle, asking for new instructions. On December 17 de Gaulle sent him orders to take no further action because of allied opposition to the plan.

Secretary of State Cordell Hull, pleased at having avoided additional difficulties at this anxious moment of American history, was shocked and enraged to learn only a week later, on Christmas Eve, that Admiral Muselier had nonetheless gone ahead and landed because de Gaulle had changed his mind. It was, to Cordell Hull, a clear case of treachery by a friend. There could be no argument about it; in his view, de Gaulle had given his word that he would not land his forces on Saint-Pierre and Miquelon and had then broken his word.

Cordell Hull, a model of rectitude, was so outraged by this act that he wrote off de Gaulle as a liar and a cheat and declared that he would no longer grant him any consideration. He issued a communiqué in which he dismissed the National Committee as "the so-called Free French." Churchill, in turn, was sharply critical of Cordell Hull for losing his temper and endangering allied unity over what was essentially a minor affair.

De Gaulle was as enraged by Hull's communiqué as Hull had been by the Gaullist landings. De Gaulle, clearly off-base in the affair, had tried to justify it by saying he had been informed by the foreign office that Canada, at American instigation, had decided to land forces on the island. He argued that this canceled out previous agreements on the status quo and that he had to act quickly to safeguard French interests. The explanation would not have carried much weight, nor won much sympathy for de Gaulle, if Hull had not exceeded the bounds of reason in his furious attack upon the Free French and his badgering of Churchill, who had flown to Washington just before Christmas to confer with Roosevelt.

According to historian Funk, who had access to the official documents of this period,

> Hull proved himself pettish to a degree which at first amused but finally irritated the President, who saw that his Secretary of State had lost his sense of proportion to the point of nearly producing a rupture between himself and the Prime Minister over a relatively minor problem. Thereafter Roosevelt became more and more inclined to eliminate Hull from top-level discussions when French matters were raised. He came to consider the State Department's Robert Murphy as his own personal emissary in North Africa, and he tended to handle French political matters through the Joint Chiefs of Staff. . . . While the responsibility for the Saint-Pierre–Miquelon incident is indisputably de Gaulle's, Hull, by his uncontrolled irritation and irascibility, contributed to the cross-purposes and overlapping which were to characterize American policy toward the French.

The cross-purposes of American policy were more than matched by the swirling, whirlpoollike cross-purposes of de Gaulle's policy. At the outset, as evidenced in his historic call for resistance on June 18, 1940, Charles de Gaulle, a military man, thought essentially in military terms of building up an effective armed force in the overseas territories with the aid and supplies of the British and Americans. His only thought then was the war against the Nazis and France's participation in the final victory and, therefore, in the shape and form of the postwar world. Very soon, however, de Gaulle discovered that this was a proper long-range objective but that it overlooked vital immediate problems that would necessitate a shift in orientation from the military to the political.

The quarrel with Hull, the influence of Leahy, the failure of

Gaullist agents to rally top-level support and sympathy in Washington, even among French émigrés, convinced de Gaulle that he could not count on full American support for Free France as an organization or a movement in general or for himself in particular. Although Churchill was a constant, loyal friend, de Gaulle understood that Churchill put the alliance with America over and above all else, even above British interests at times, for Churchill knew that victory could only come through American power and that Britain's future depended upon becoming the partner, albeit a junior partner, of an Anglo-American alliance. In any major conflict Churchill would, whether it was right or wrong, support the United States against de Gaulle, and he so told de Gaulle in exactly those terms. Thus the alliance with the British and Americans, while still vitally necessary for ultimate victory and the peace settlement, could no longer be counted on as the prime pillar of immediate support for Free France.

As de Gaulle became increasingly aware of the need to seek other means of building his movement, he also became aware of interesting developments inside France which coincided exactly with his need for another lever of power. The relatively small flow of men from France to England to join de Gaulle was a constant discouragement throughout 1940. The spirit of the Free French was sustained mainly by de Gaulle's personal exaltation and also by the few successes in the empire, where a handful of patriots rallied to the flag of Free France in scattered colonies if not in the principal power bases of North Africa. However, de Gaulle learned to his relief that resistance inside France was developing powerful groups which had endorsed de Gaulle's objectives and that the Cross of Lorraine was being raised right under the noses of the Nazis. This, then, was the answer de Gaulle had been seeking—the new lever of power to replace his sole dependence on British and American support.

This was the ideal instrument for a nationalist like Charles de Gaulle. He had never been comfortable in the posture of a dependent upon the British nor as a supplicant of the Americans. As the leader of a French resistance actively fighting the Nazis inside France and rallying the colonies overseas, Charles de Gaulle was in his element. He could now truly present himself as the champion of fighting France. It was for this reason that he decided to change the name of his movement from Free France to Fighting France. This was a more inspiring and logical name for his movement. It accurately described the resistance networks inside France and linked them to the external forces in the empire which were beginning to engage the enemy in combat, such as the French air-force bombers and fighter pilots and the colonial troops who bloodied themselves and won praise and honor in the battle of Bir Hakeim and the Leclerc column that marched north from Lake Chad. Above all, the existence of these resistance forces inside France provided de Gaulle with a strong card to play in his game of diplomatic poker with Churchill and with Roosevelt.

So long as he was their ward, with little to offer them in return, he was condemned to a subordinate auxiliary role. However, the relationship changed when the supreme command perceived the combat potential of the internal resistance as a harassing force in the rear of the Nazi lines, which could make an important contribution—as it eventually did—to the allied invasion troops. General Eisenhower in his own memoirs and speeches has attested to the important role of the French underground in the famous "Battle of the Rails," in which the resistance fighters disrupted the German railway and communications system before and during the landings in Normandy. Eisenhower understood sooner than Washington how valuable a source of intelligence information and harassment of the enemy could be provided by the pro-de Gaulle resistance inside France, and de Gaulle, knowing how Eisenhower valued it, used it to fullest advantage in his conflicts with London and Washington.

The Black Knight of France seemed to revel in the thunder and lightning of the storms that swept around the allied camps, first in London and in Washington, then in Algiers. Prominent French exiles, quarreling with the state department and the White House staffs, fighting among themselves for control of the exile movement, went back and forth among America, Britain and North Africa to consult both Churchill and de Gaulle, and they were constantly amazed at de Gaulle's truculence and intransigence. Etienne Boegner, son of the President of Protestant Churches in France, later to serve on de Gaulle's presidential staff, was the victim of one of de Gaulle's tonguelashings and reported to a friend that de Gaulle was "a phenomenon of patriotism which, whenever you touch on anything French, electrocutes you instantly with a violent discharge."

De Gaulle exploded into "violent discharges" against Churchill on a number of occasions, notably upon the British decision to publish a declaration of independence for Syria and Lebanon, territories that were then under French mandate. Nothing that Churchill did, however, so enraged de Gaulle as did the actions of Roosevelt and his agent Robert Murphy. De Gaulle was in a fury when he learned of the deal with Admiral Darlan after the American invasion of North Africa. He sent a note to Admiral Stark in which he wrote, "I understand that the United States buys the treachery of traitors, if this appears profitable, but payment must not be made against the honor of France." Stark, appalled at the violence and the unforgivable insult in this note, avoided a major diplomatic incident by refusing to accept it. He simply returned it to the French with a memo suggesting that it must have been sent in error. De Gaulle's aides, horrified at what their chief had done, tore up the note, and de Gaulle's chief assistant, Gaston Palewski, hurried over to see Admiral Stark to apologize.

Not all of the clashes could be headed off by intelligent and tactful diplomats. Other men were at work stoking the fires. Jacques Soustelle, Minister of Information for Fighting France, saw to it that journalists in London knew about these incidents and the story of de Gaulle's note to Stark soon appeared in the press, to the dismay and anger of Admiral Stark, who, like Hull, lost confidence in de Gaulle and the Gaullists as men of honor. The Gaullists, writing off the chance to win over the state department or the joint chiefs of staff, based their hopes on public opinion as a lever on Roosevelt. They knew that liberals in Britain and in America had been shocked by the appointment of Admiral Darlan as high commissioner in North Africa and equally dismayed by the appointment of General Henri Giraud as Roosevelt's foil against de Gaulle. Soustelle and other Gaullists concentrated upon inflaming public opinion by any and all means, at the costly expense of angering men like Stark and Hull.

One of several low points was plumbed on Christmas Eve, 1942, when Admiral Darlan was assassinated in Algiers.

The Americans were immediately suspicious of the Gaullists, and these suspicions were strengthened when Henri d'Astier, a fervent Gaullist, was arrested by the police on suspicion of murder. The Gaullists, enraged by the accusations, not only denied them, but went so far as to whisper that American intelligence agents had engineered the assassination to get rid of Darlan, whom they had found to be a bad card to play. Incredible as it may sound,

General de Gaulle has told certain visitors that Murphy must be blamed for the Darlan assassination. He did not go so far as to accuse him personally of ordering it, but he has made it clear that he feels the responsibility for the assassination can be charged against Murphy.

Among those of us who were in Algiers at the time, some believed that extremist Gaullists had incited Bonnier de la Chappelle, an unstable young man, to kill Darlan, not necessarily as an organized official plot, but rather as a violent act typical of those violent times. The Gaullists, however, point out that French officials in Algiers, under American control, held the trial of de la Chappelle in secret, condemned and executed him without a public hearing. This suggests to the Gaullists that the officials did not dare reveal the real plot behind the assassination.

Roosevelt, shaken and angered by the assassination, decided to force the French National Committee to appoint General Giraud in place of Darlan, to keep power out of de Gaulle's hands. On New Year's Day, 1943, a week after Darlan's assassination, President Roosevelt confirmed in a telegram to Churchill his insistence on Giraud's assumption of the role of high commissioner for North Africa and Commander-in-Chief of French forces, referring contemptuously to de Gaulle in the telegram with the question: "Why doesn't de Gaulle go to war?" Roosevelt added derisively, "Why doesn't he start North by West half West from Brazen-ville? It would take him a long time to get to the Oasis of Somewhere." This is extraordinary language and unseemly flippancy for a chief of state to use in a wartime telegram on a matter of great importance to the war effort, but Roosevelt could not menton de Gaulle's name without a jeer or a jibe.

All through the preparations for the Casablanca conference, called to deal with the crisis of North Africa, Roosevelt kept referring to de Gaulle in his telegrams to Churchill as the "reluctant bride" whom he was trying to bring into the arms of Roosevelt's chosen "bridegroom," General Giraud. It was at that Casablanca conference that Giraud and de Gaulle did finally meet and agree to cooperate, under pressure from Roosevelt and Churchill. And it was that pressure which sowed new seeds of bitterness between de Gaulle and Roosevelt and traumatized de Gaulle against any alliance in which the Americans had a dominant voice.

Churchill, nettled by de Gaulle's intransigence, which made his task more difficult, nevertheless thoroughly disapproved of Roosevelt's attitude and policies. The Prime Minister told the Americans that it was wrong to set Giraud up against de Gaulle, and when it was suggested to him that de Gaulle be relegated to a secondary role, Churchill flatly rejected the proposal, saying, "No, you can't do that. De Gaulle is more than a man. He is a movement and a symbol."

Although an agreement to cooperate was drafted at the Casablanca conference, the bad feelings engendered were never forgotten, particularly Roosevelt's constant mocking of de Gaulle. Before the conference de Gaulle had talked at length with Admiral Stark, explaining to him the background of French history, pointing out how many times France had risen like a phoenix from her ashes to go ahead under new leadership to a new destiny. De Gaulle had talked passionately of the greatness of the French nation and the reservoir of human strength which produced new leaders and new strength in the midst of crisis itself, arguing that it was a grave error to write France off as finished or decadent only because of the Pétain surrender. De Gaulle talked of Joan of Arc and Napoleon and other leaders risen from the ranks, even from the illiterate peasant classes, to world prominence.

Admiral Stark, very impressed by de Gaulle's exposition, by his fervor and faith in France, suggested that de Gaulle explain this to Roosevelt, hoping that Roosevelt, who believed France to be decadent, might see her in a new light and understand the role and character of a de Gaulle.

Unfortunately when Roosevelt and de Gaulle met, the President, vainly proud of his French, which was weak at best, insisted on conducting the conversation in French. It was frequently interrupted by the need to translate and explain. De Gaulle struggled to explain his country to the President and to counter Roosevelt's argument that he would not recognize the de Gaulle movement even as a provisional government because de Gaulle had not been elected or invested. De Gaulle pointed out, as he had to Stark, that in time of war patriots arose—as had Joan of Arc, for example—without elections or investiture, to fight for their country. Roosevelt, confused by the intricacies of French grammar, particularly the complex style of de Gaulle, which became almost incomprehensible because of interruptions and inaccurate translation, conceived the notion that de Gaulle was comparing himself with Joan of Arc. The President knew, of course, perfectly well, as Harry Hopkins testified in his diaries, that de Gaulle did not have a Joan of Arc complex, but the idea tickled his humor and provided rich material for dinner jokes with White House cronies on his return to Washington.

Roosevelt took a special delight in poking fun at the overly solemn troublesome Frenchman and gave the lead to others to follow suit. Wendell Willkie angered de Gaulle by repeating a conversation in which he insisted that de Gaulle thought he was Louis XIV. Even Churchill, who respected de Gaulle, could not resist joining in the fun when he was irritated with de Gaulle. To an aide who told him that Roosevelt said de Gaulle thought he was Joan of Arc, Churchill growled in reply, "Yes, I know. But the trouble is my bloody bishops won't let me burn him." These quips deeply offended de Gaulle, who was a tough fighter but not a mudslinger. It offended, above all, his sense of dignity and of good taste. He once told me, during this period, in explanation of his contempt for these attacks, "A man fights with a sword, not with spittle."

Neither sword nor spittle was spared in the savage struggle inside the allied camps even while the allies were engaged in deadly, crucial combat with the Nazi forces. Three wars were fought simultaneously on the same battlefields, from North Africa to Italy to the landings in France, through the final campaign deep into Germany, up to and after the victory itself. The three wars were: the allied war against the Axis; the war inside the alliance, between de Gaulle and the Anglo-Saxons; and the struggle for power among the French. The first inter-French battle was between Vichy and Free France. Then there ensued the struggle for power and leadership inside Free France, and finally the ultimate battle for France itself after the liberation. The struggle for power among the French was a full-scale civil war, a shooting war with Frenchmen combating Frenchmen both inside France, in the resistance movement, and in the landings in North Africa. It was also a political civil war between Gaullists and anti-Gaullist agents, intelligence services, military recruiting staffs and administrative officials. The following chapter will deal in detail with this French civil war.

The conflicts between de Gaulle and the Anglo-Saxons might be characterized as an uncivil war, in all the meanings of the word uncivil. It was uncivil first in the sense that it featured constantly uncivil exchanges, characterized by rudeness, name-calling and sabotage. Secondly, the range and intensity of incivilities among the allies stopped only just short of actual combat and, upon occasion, even included armed hostilities in Italy and Germany. Therefore, it had the characteristics of a civil war if one regards the alliance as a union of nations. One cannot doubt the extremely divisive nature of the allied conflicts. Nor can one doubt that, if not actually a shooting war, it was a political war that was fought furiously and at times viciously. If the conflicts between East and West in the past two decades can properly be called a cold war, then the conflicts between de Gaulle and the Anglo-Saxons can properly be called an uncivil war.

Quite apart from the difficult personalities of the principal protagonists, there would have been serious conflicts among the allies by the very nature of the world war itself. The global war involved a fundamental and violent shift in the world's balance of power, thus affecting the vital interests, imperial and ideological, of all the parties, both between and inside the Axis and the alliance. The conflict of interests need not, however, have been magnified into an allied uncivil war if Roosevelt had had the same understanding of and sympathy for the cause of France and of de Gaulle as had Churchill, the unhappy man in the middle.

Upon occasion Churchill feared and fought de Gaulle as intensely as did Roosevelt, but he never despised him and never made Roosevelt's mistake of underestimating him. Churchill sensed de Gaulle's potential for greatness almost as soon as he met him. As early as June 13, 1940, in the last days before the fall of France, Churchill was impressed by de Gaulle's courage. As Churchill noted in his memoirs: "I saw General de Gaulle standing stolid and expressionless at the doorway. Greeting him, I said in a low tone, in French: 'l'homme du destin.' He remained impassive."

Winston Churchill understood and felt, more than Franklin Roosevelt ever could, the frightful misery of the French defeat, and consequently he appreciated more than Roosevelt the noble splendor of de Gaulle's "impassivity" and its concomitants, the intransigence, intrepidity and total independence of mind and action. Churchill had no illusions about de Gaulle. "I knew he was no friend of England," he wrote in his memoirs. But he added, with the generous spirit of the truly great: "I understood and admired, even while I resented his arrogant demeanor. Here he was—a refugee, an exile from his country, under the sentence of death, entirely dependent upon the good will of the British Government and then of the United States. The Germans had conquered his country. He had no real foothold anywhere. Never mind, he defied them all!"

Roosevelt never appreciated, as did Churchill, de Gaulle's vital psychological need to hold the French flag high and de Gaulle's compulsion at times to hit his allies over the head with it. After all, the French flag was the only weapon and the only shield of his very own that de Gaulle had; all the other weapons or matériel, all finances of substance were provided by the allies. The allies—above all, the Americans—knew how vital was their aid to Fighting France and did not hesitate to use it as a lever of power. They threatened constantly to cut off supplies and support to the French whenever de Gaulle opposed their policies.

Although Roosevelt, Murphy and the official American apologists for this policy attempted to justify their high-handed treatment of Fighting France on the grounds of military necessity and political expediency, there were a number of actions taken and orders cabled that were very remotely removed from any military justification, and, indeed, the policies were continued in North Africa *after* the Axis forces had been defeated there and the territory transferred to civilian administrative controls. Of the mass of official evidence now available to historians the following few examples are representative and tell the story, out of the American files, more damningly than de Gaulle himself could argue his case:

** *State Department File Number 851.01/983. Washington, January 7, 1943*

[AUTHOR'S NOTE: *the following document was a telegram from London delivered by the British Embassy in Washington to the state department in answer to a complaint by Secretary of State Cordell Hull about British press and political support for General de Gaulle and criticism of American policy. Mr. Hull had requested that steps be taken to suppress the "emotional views of little men on political matters." Churchill and Eden, shocked and angered by this undemocratic request for censorship of nonmilitary matters, sent the following acid reply*]

Under our present constitution and war-time procedure we have been ceaselessly exposed to "emotional views of

little men on political matters" and to check this entirely
would involve His Majesty's Government in a direct attack on freedom of Parliament and Press. There is a deep
loathing in this country, particularly strong among working classes, against anything which savors to them of intrigues with Darlan and Vichy which are held to be
contrary to the broad simple loyalties which unite the
masses throughout the world against the common foe. It
took the Prime Minister all his time and all his influence
to smooth things out with House of Commons in secret
session. You should warn Mr. Hull that there is almost a
passion on this subject. . . . Prime Minister can no more
embark on an effective muzzling of Press and Parliament
than State Department could gag Willkie, Luce and company when they say things which give profound offense
here.

[*Anyone familiar with Churchill's policy of avoiding a
quarrel with the Americans and his almost obsessive
feeling of dependence on Washington will appreciate
how deeply offended he was by American policy in this
matter to have used such strong language in a formal
intergovernmental communication. The full record
shows that Churchill was frequently critical of de
Gaulle's arrogant opposition to America's Vichy policy
and attempts to support anti-Gaullist rivals for leadership
of the Fighting French movement, but Churchill was
appalled himself by both American policies and practices.
Roosevelt's mistrust and dislike of de Gaulle led him to
send Churchill some of the most undiplomatic telegrams
in diplomatic history. The raw record of those wartime exchanges was published in June 1964 by the Department of
State in* Diplomatic Papers 1943—Volume II—Europe. *The
following excerpts reveal the embittered nature of the uncivil-war relationship between de Gaulle and the Anglo-
Saxons.*]

** *May 8, 1943. Roosevelt to Churchill*

I am sorry, *but* the conduct of the Bride continues to be
more and more aggravated. His course and attitude is
well nigh intolerable. . . . De Gaulle is, without ques-

tion, taking his vicious propaganda staff down to Algiers to stir up strife between the various elements, including the Arabs and the Jews . . . he has the messianic complex. . . . I am inclined to think that when we get to France itself we will have to regard it as a military occupation run by British and American generals. . . . I think that this may be necessary for six months or even a year after we get into France, thus giving time to build up for an election and a new form of government. . . . I do not know what to do with de Gaulle. Possibly you would like to make him Governor of Madagascar.

** *May 13, 1943. Memorandum of conversation, Secretary Hull with Churchill*

I said that if this de Gaulle matter is allowed to go forward as it has been, it will undoubtedly bring about serious friction between our two governments. . . . I wished to point out with emphasis the poisonous propaganda activities of the de Gaulle organization. . . . I then suggested that there were numerous ways for the British to get away from the build-up of de Gaulle.

** *May 18, 1943. U.S. Ambassador Winant to Secretary of State*

Winant reported a conversation with Maurice Dejean, a French National Committee staff official, who, according to Winant, said that de Gaulle was taking measures "to prepare for his dictatorship after the liberation of France." Dejean reportedly was distressed at de Gaulle's moves to exercise "full political control" of the National Committee. Winant added his comment, "This admission from within Carlton Gardens itself [*de Gaulle's headquarters*] seems not without interest." [*A high Gaullist official, upon reading this telegram in the summer of 1964, pointed out that Maurice Dejean, the official quoted twenty years earlier, had now become de Gaulle's ambassador to Russia. He commented: "The embarrassment to high French officials and to President de Gaulle, himself, provoked by these allegations, this unedited, unverified rumormongering in guise of history, is not, itself, without interest."*]

** *May 30, 1943. U.S. Consul General Wiley at Algiers to Secretary of State*

British financial subsidy, which I am told [*by the Prime Minister*] approximates about 20 million pounds annually will cease during the month of June . . . the Prime Minister says that the facilities of the BBC in London will no longer be available to de Gaulle.

** *June 1, 1943. Consul General in Algiers to Secretary of State*

He [*Eden*] was fed up with de Gaulle and had no desire to see him. The Prime Minister again warned that de Gaulle was capable of a coup d'état and asked whether Giraud was taking all necessary police measures.

** *June 10, 1943. Roosevelt to Eisenhower in Algiers [On hearing that de Gaulle was planning to dismiss former Vichyite Governor General Boisson from his post in West Africa, Roosevelt asked Eisenhower to deliver the following message to de Gaulle:]*

In view of Governor General Boisson's ability as an able French Administrator such action would be contrary to the aims we have in view.

[*F.D.R.'s intervention on behalf of a French civil administrator and his personal comments on his ability were quite inadmissible interferences in French affairs. De Gaulle not only did dismiss Boisson, but he later had him arrested, an act that infuriated Roosevelt, who felt personally responsible for Boisson, whom he had backed, and this fact, in turn, further enraged de Gaulle, and so forth and so on, back and forth in the most absurdly vicious of circles.*]

** *June 10, 1943. Roosevelt to Churchill [Referring to de Gaulle's move to dismiss Boisson and appoint a loyal Gaullist to Dakar]*

Neither you nor I know where de Gaulle will end up. Therefore I find it impossible to consider any de Gaulle domination of French West Africa. This is so serious that I should have to consider sending several regiments to

Dakar and also naval vessels if there were any sign that de Gaulle proposes to take things over in West Africa.

** *June 16, 1943. Robert Murphy to President and Secretary of State*
[*On learning that the French Committee of 7 had increased its membership to 14*]

The membership in our opinion insures supremacy to de Gaulle. . . . General Giraud informed me this morning that in his opinion Monnet has betrayed him. . . . It is obvious to us that things have gone to Monnet's head and that he feels strongly like de Gaulle that French rights and sovereignty must be more aggressively asserted in respect of the Allies. . . . In the light of recent developments it is necessary for the U.S.A. to review its present policy of rearmament of French Forces.

[*The full force of Roosevelt's anger and the contrasting patience and diplomatic resiliency of Churchill are illustrated in the remarkable exchanges of telegrams that took place from June 17 through June 23, 1943.*]

TELEGRAM NUMBER 288, OF JUNE 17, 1943—3:30 P.M.
WASHINGTON—PRESIDENT TO PRIME MINISTER
I am fed up with de Gaulle, and the secret personal and political machinations of that Committee in the last few days indicates that there is no possibility of our working with de Gaulle. . . . I am absolutely convinced that he has been and is now injuring our war effort and that he is a very dangerous threat to us. . . . The time has arrived when we must break with him. It is an intolerable situation. . . . We must have someone whom we completely and wholly trust. We would under no circumstances continue the arming of a force without being completely confident in their willingness to cooperate in our military operations; we are not interested, moreover, in the formation of any government or committee which presumes in any way to indicate that, until such time as the French people select a government for themselves, it will govern in France. When we get into France, the allies will have a civil government plan. . . . I want to state for your exclusive information

(secret and personal copy from the President to General
Eisenhower) that at this time we will not permit de
Gaulle to direct, himself, or to control, through partisans
on any committee, the African French army, either in the
field of supplies, training or operations.

** *File number 851.01/6–1943. Prime Minister Churchill to
President Roosevelt, London, June 18, 1943*

I agree with you that no confidence can be placed in de
Gaulle's friendship for the allies . . . [but] I am not in
favour at this moment of breaking up the Committee of 7
or forbidding it to meet. I should prefer that General
Eisenhower should take your instructions as his directive
and that Murphy and Macmillan should work towards
its fulfillment. [*Churchill went on at some length describing the possible steps that could be taken to make
de Gaulle fall in line, suggesting that, before any break,
"it would be wise to try this first." He even went so far as
to say that he had ordered Macmillan to notify the French
that he was stopping all payments from British funds to
the French National Committee and that no further
payments would be made unless the Committee agreed to
act by majority vote—a device to cut down de Gaulle's
power, to divide the Committee and thus conquer de
Gaulle. But the entire telegram, despite all of the clever
Churchillian proposals, added up to a rejection of the
essential Roosevelt demand to break with de Gaulle.
Churchill was ready to do anything to mollify Roosevelt,
anything but breaking with de Gaulle. His policy was to
try to bend de Gaulle, not break him. De Gaulle knew
this and appreciated it, although he could not but take
note of the extent to which Churchill was prepared to go
to bend him to his will. Anyone who heard or read de
Gaulle's radio-television address to the French nation on
April 27, 1965, in which de Gaulle said that France
could maintain her independence only by avoiding debts
to others and counting only on herself will find the origin
of that Gaullist obsession in Churchill's threat to cut off
all funds to the French National Committee.*]

** *File number 851.10/6–1943. The Prime Minister to the President, June 18, 1943*

[AUTHOR'S NOTE: *the following telegram was sent on the same day, as an addendum to the telegram quoted above. Roosevelt's telegram had deeply disturbed Churchill, and he brooded for several hours after his first wire, particularly about a phrase in Roosevelt's telegram which showed that Roosevelt believed that Churchill had earlier suggested the time had come to break with de Gaulle. This was Churchill's added comment to clarify his position.*]

Further to your 288. Some of my colleagues have questioned your sentence "I agree with you that the time has arrived when we break with him." As you will remember I sent a telegram from the White House when we were together, but as I told you at the time, the Cabinet did not accept this view because, inter alia, de Gaulle was just starting for Algiers to meet Giraud. This was a new fact to me and we were all inclined to give the meeting a fair chance. Since then we have been watching their manoeuvres with growing dissatisfaction. It would not however be right to say that we have decided "that the time has arrived when we must break with him." This may come but it would come as the result of his refusing to accept the necessary military conditions to ensure that the French army remains in trustworthy hands on which full agreement exists between our two governments. Would you very kindly read this message in conjunction with my earlier message 316 of today.

[*It is obvious from the exchange that Churchill, in private conversation with Roosevelt, cigar in one hand and brandy glass in the other, had indulged in some verbally extreme anti-Gaullism but had been dismayed by Roosevelt's taking him seriously about breaking with de Gaulle. It is a measure of the grandeur of Winston Churchill and British democracy that he was prepared to eat his words in his cable to Roosevelt and admit that he had been overruled by his cabinet. What is most fascinat-*

*ing and significant, however, is to watch Churchill walk
his tightrope, with Roosevelt and de Gaulle pulling on it
from opposite ends. He was determined not to break with
either or to permit either to break with the other. It is also
most instructive to note that Churchill kept his arguments within the limits of "necessary military conditions"
while Roosevelt, although always invoking military
justification, extended his conflicts with de Gaulle to the
full gamut of political, civilian and administrative issues
in an effort to control totally the entire French movement. The following exchange of telegrams illustrates
this beyond question and, as all the documents do, explains the traumatic experience that de Gaulle underwent
which tells us so much about his policies more than two
decades later.]*

** *File number 851.01/6–1943. The President to the Prime
Minister, Washington D.C., June 21, 1943*

It would appear that the Committee now stands as overwhelmingly de Gaullist. Full authority over all the war
effort of French territory and the French is claimed by
this augmented Committee. I am sure you agree that the
jeopardizing of our military position in North Africa by
an antagonistic element in such control cannot be
accepted by us.

** *File number 851.01/6–1943. The Prime Minister to the
President, London, June 23, 1943*

[AUTHOR'S NOTE: *Churchill again tells Roosevelt that he
will "deal only with the Committee of 7 in its collective
capacity expressed by a majority of the seven; otherwise
no payments will be made." But he goes on at length to
tell Roosevelt how much money the Committee has in
reserve and can get from French sources and loans from
admirers, warning, "It is therefore likely that the Committee may be able to get on without payments hitherto
made to de Gaulle from the British Exchequer." With
great skill and patience Churchill puts himself into the
posture of sympathizing with Roosevelt's desire to break*

with de Gaulle while subtly making it evident that a break is impossible.]

We have also made trade arrangements with various French colonies, who joined de Gaulle, which are serviceable to us and vital to them and in addition we have guaranteed pay and pensions of all French officials who renounced Vichy and gave us their allegiance in these places. Should de Gaulle break with the Committee of 7 and go off into the wilderness I should consider that discharge of these obligations would depend on our relations not with him any more but only with majority of Committee of 7. This would be a very much more powerful lever of control. . . . On quite a different plane is the question of recognition of this Committee of 7 which they will certainly demand as representative of France in some degree or other. Here I feel with you that it would be most unwise to commit ourselves until we know much more clearly than we do now how they are going to behave. In this connexion I send you a paraphrase of message which is being sent to Stalin. The United Nations must certainly try to act together on this larger question also.

[*One sees here how Churchill keeps reminding Roosevelt of allied commitments to the French, not lightly to be broken, while defining conditions he knows are unlikely to occur. Churchill proved himself to be a master diplomat as well as an indomitable warrior.*]

The Roosevelt-Churchill exchanges were duplicated on lower levels of government, and, in each case, it is apparent that Roosevelt's advisers adopted his attitudes as well as his policies on de Gaulle. Some of the language used and charges made go far beyond not only proper diplomatic usage but simple common sense, as in the following:

** *July 7, 1943. Assistant Secretary Berle to Secretary of State*
[*Quoting a conversation with Etienne Boegner, who had resigned from the de Gaulle delegation*]

He is convinced that General de Gaulle, despite his

protestations, is now merely the promoter of a French Nazi movement with himself as Fuehrer and that both the French and the allied cause are in grave danger if it gets out of hand.

** *Secretary of State to the Consul General in Algiers. December 22, 1943*
[Relaying an order from President Roosevelt to General Eisenhower to be delivered to the French Committee]

In view of the assistance given to the allied armies during the campaign in Africa by Boisson, Peyrouton and Flandin, you are directed to take no action against these individuals at the present time.

[Of all the unusual language used in the many exchanges this is unique. In the phrase "you are directed to take no action," in actually issuing an American presidential order to a French Committee on a nonmilitary issue, Roosevelt was far off base; he had no right to do this and he would never have dared use force to make this order effective, as de Gaulle well knew. It provided de Gaulle with documentary evidence of what he never ceased to describe as "America's will to dominate."

[The Roosevelt message sent by Hull to Algiers was also sent to London to inform Churchill. In that London message, No. 423 of December 21, 1943, Roosevelt expressed the hope that Churchill would agree with this directive, and concluded with this final sentence: "It seems to me that this is the proper time effectively to eliminate the Jeanne d'Arc complex and return to realism." Churchill once again evaded replying to Roosevelt's demand to get rid of de Gaulle but sought to mollify him by promptly wiring his agreement with the directive to the French Committee to take no action against the three men. De Gaulle nevertheless went right ahead and arrested them, but did, as Churchill later proposed, put them under house arrest rather than in prison. Roosevelt, frustrated, continued to fume and fret and prepare for the next round with de Gaulle.]

These few documents cited above are only a handful among the hundreds published by the state department's historical section, which themselves are only a small percentage of the many thousands of documents and citations that appear in memoirs of the principal actors in this uncivil war between de Gaulle and the Anglo-Saxons. I have seen most of the evidence published and some that has still been kept secret, as well as having participated personally in many of these battles in the course of liaison work between General Eisenhower's headquarters and the French National Committee in Algiers. In intelligence service liaison with Jacques Soustelle, then chief of de Gaulle's intelligence bureau, and then as an American soldier assigned to the French First Army, I watched the concentric circles of hot, cold and uncivil wars spinning around together, crossing and criss-crossing battle lines so that it was often difficult to tell friend from foe.

It was not difficult to know who was wrong, for practically everyone was. There was no doubt in my mind that many of the Murphy-Hull-Roosevelt policies were ill-conceived and poorly executed. As for de Gaulle, he missed no opportunity to make the worst of a bad thing. Disaster was averted only by the strength and wisdom of Churchill, who was himself guilty of a few almost disastrous aberrations. The only men who kept their heads and constantly saved the day time and time again were Anthony Eden and, above all others, General Eisenhower, who was at his very best as a peacemaker among his warring chiefs.

A full account of all snarls and tangles would fill several volumes. The major overriding issues of the uncivil war can, however, be grouped under five general headings: (1) the territorial integrity of the French Empire; (2) the extent of authority and recognition to be granted to Fighting France by the Anglo-Americans; (3) the right of the French to work out themselves the leadership rules inside the French movement; (4) the role the French were to be assigned in the planning of and participation in the liberation of France and Europe; (5) the role of the French in the postwar settlements in Europe, Africa and Asia.

Territorial integrity became an issue at the very start of the de Gaulle–Churchill relationship, as is shown in their exchange of secret letters in the summer of 1940. It was a constant factor of friction all through the war, particularly in the incidents of Madagascar and of Syria and Lebanon, where French and British imperial interests clashed. In the Levant the uncivil war between de Gaulle and the Anglo-Saxons broke out into armed combat when British troops intervened against the French when they

landed in Syria in May 1945, marring the celebration of their joint
victory over the Nazis. One cannot read without a chill even today
the words pronounced by General de Gaulle to the British ambassador in Paris, on June 4, 1945: "We are not, I acknowledge, in a
position to make war upon you at present. But you have outraged
France and betrayed the Occident. This cannot be forgotten."

These ominous words were underlined and given new importance when they were reprinted in the memoirs of Charles de
Gaulle, in the third volume published in 1959, when the man who
swore not to forget was back in power as president of France. This
menacing threat will be referred to again in the discussion of the
outbreak of the second uncivil war between de Gaulle and the
Anglo-Saxons, which was waged as furiously as the first, from 1958
through 1965, in the first seven-year term of President de Gaulle.
The territorial integrity of the French Empire as menaced by
the British is no longer the same issue today, since neither empire
exists any longer, but the issue is not dead even though the empires are. It has simply been sown and has taken root in other
fields, notably in the rivalry between the Common Market Six and
the British-created Seven, the organization known as EFTA, as
well as in a series of uncivil wars being fought on many fronts
from the western Atlantic to the lands east of Suez and the jungles
of Asia.

On the second issue, recognition and authority, de Gaulle won a
total victory over Roosevelt, who, as was predictable very early in
the campaign, had to end by recognizing de Gaulle's French
Committee of National Liberty as a provisional government. Roosevelt was as proud and stubborn as de Gaulle, and he
would not yield until after the landings in France, so late that it
endangered the landings themselves. Formal recognition of the
National Committee as the provisional government of France was
not accorded by the Anglo-Americans until October 25, 1944,
almost five months after the landings in Normandy. It came so
late that it was less a recognition than a resignation of allied policy.
It caused no joy, healed no wounds.

De Gaulle himself, in answer to a press-conference request for a
comment, icily remarked, "The French government is satisfied to
note that it is being called by its name." It had taken three years for
Roosevelt to recognize the fact that de Gaulle did represent France
in fact if not yet in law. Thereafter, de Gaulle looked with
scornful eyes at America's hasty recognitions of reactionary mili-

tary juntas from Brazil to Saigon, passing through Santo Domingo, without free elections, or elections of any kind, except a ballot by bullets. The seeds of the first uncivil war were to bear bitter fruit in a second uncivil war.

The third category of conflict, the right of the French to choose their own leaders in their own way, rightly or wrongly, also left sensitive scars that never healed. This issue will be reported in detail in the following chapter, on the civil strife between de Gaulle and the Gauls.

The role of the French in planning and participating in the elaboration of allied strategy was certainly the major source of conflict among the Western allies from 1958 to 1965. It is the issue that the writer has himself followed most closely and on which will be presented a number of secret documents and confidential citations that will be revealed here for the first time. As for the past, a massive record is available in official publications and the memoirs of the leaders in the struggle. In the briefest summary form, these are the most important and representative examples of the fighting on this front of the uncivil war:

1. THE BATTLE OF TUNISIA AND LIBYA. The Anglo-American high command refused to assign French troops to combat in the liberation of Tunisia and of Libya. By threatening to pull his troops out of North Africa and send them to join the Red Army on the Eastern Front, de Gaulle forced the high command to let the French participate in the liberation of this area, in which France had a long traditional interest and influence. It was the first of many similar conflicts that led de Gaulle to the conclusion that nothing less than a totally independent, national defense force could assure French security and the support needed for French diplomacy. In this area, above all, the record of yesterday reads like the headlines of this morning's papers.

2. THE STRUGGLE FOR STRASBOURG. The most dramatic of all these incidents was the Eisenhower order to evacuate Strasbourg, to tighten allied communications against the last, desperate Nazi offensive at the end of 1944. General de Gaulle agreed with the military needs on which Eisenhower based his decision but argued that war was not just a military affair. Strasbourg was an essential psychological and political symbol of French sovereignty in Alsace and Lorraine, sentimentally of the greatest emotional importance. De Gaulle refused to obey the supreme commander's evacuation order, was unmoved by all threats and stated France was willing to

die with Strasbourg if America pulled out supporting troops. Eisenhower was so impressed and moved by de Gaulle's suicidal courage that he rescinded his order, left his troops and took the risk of being cut off by the German offensive. De Gaulle has never forgotten Eisenhower's own courage and fairness.

Ugly scars were left by two instances of de Gaulle's intransigence as applied not to a noble cause like Strasbourg but to two petty, unworthy objects of arrogance—Stuttgart, Germany, and the Val d'Aosta, Italy—where French soldiers were ordered to resist by arms the transfer of those occupation-zone territories from their forces to the Americans.

These incidents occurred after Roosevelt's death and brought de Gaulle into conflict with Harry Truman, a no-holds-barred fighter himself. Truman, enraged, ordered Eisenhower to cut off supplies to the French Army and to go in and take the zones by force if de Gaulle did not back down. De Gaulle did back down promptly— these were rare instances in which he yielded under pressure. He is a realist who will yield if the stakes are not worth the game, just as he is a romantic quite prepared—indeed, almost eager—to die gloriously if, as in the case of Strasbourg, honor and glory are at stake.

De Gaulle went too far for too little in his test of Truman, and little Truman cut the French Goliath down to size. De Gaulle never forgave him. When, on Truman's seventy-fifth birthday, a national committee was formed to collect signatures from great men on a plaque to be given him as a present, de Gaulle refused to sign. *

Finally, on this important issue of sharing in strategy, de Gaulle was outraged by and has never forgiven the "Anglo-Saxons" for not keeping him informed of French invasion plans, for cutting off his own communications with France at that moment, for printing allied occupation money and setting up an allied military government for France. This was the main reason why de Gaulle refused to attend personally or take much notice of the twentieth-anniversary celebrations of the Normandy landings, on June 6, 1964.

The fifth great area of uncivil warfare, the issue of French participation in the postwar settlements, is, of all the traumatic

---

* I was the committee delegate for France and pleaded earnestly with de Gaulle and de Gaulle's closest associates, trying to persuade him to relent, but in vain. De Gaulle is "wild about Harry" but not in the affective sense.

conflicts, the deepest, most permanent, most acute: the exclusion of France from the allied conferences at Yalta and at Potsdam. For de Gaulle, Yalta is the living symbol of Anglo-American duplicity and of the ambition of the Anglo-Saxons and the Russians to divide the world between them.

The need for the allied powers to confer on a postwar settlement became apparent in the fall of 1944. On Armistice Day in Paris, Churchill and Eden lunched with de Gaulle and then had a two-hour conference, in the course of which de Gaulle urged the British to pressure Roosevelt into giving them modern equipment for eight additional divisions so that they could make a greater contribution to the final offensive against the Nazis. Churchill reported this to Roosevelt in a telegram on November 15, on his return to London. He told Roosevelt, "I sympathize with the French wish to take over more of the line, to have the best share they can in the fighting." He added that this would justify France's taking part in the postwar occupation of Germany, which "we should certainly favour." Churchill then proposed that these questions be discussed "at an inter-allied table," in at least a tripartite conference if Stalin refused to come or a "quadruple meeting if he will."

In this and subsequent telegrams in the last weeks of 1944 Churchill fought to include France in the decisive postwar settlement that was being prepared. Knowing that Roosevelt would not like this, he attempted, as always, to anticipate and work his way around Roosevelt's prejudices against both de Gaulle, whom the President distrusted and disliked, and the French nation, which he believed decadent and impotent. Roosevelt's telegrams and memoranda document his view that France needed radical reforms in the structure and nature of her government and society and that she would not be able to play a great role for many years in the future. Churchill thoroughly disagreed. In his telegram of November 15 he predicted to Roosevelt that "before five years are out a French Army must be made to take on the main task of holding down Germany."

Churchill was acutely aware of Britain's war weariness and weakness and was haunted by the nightmare of a prostrate Europe at the mercy of the triumphant Red Army as soon as the Americans withdrew, which Roosevelt had already advised him they would do soon after victory. He had none of the Americans' naïve faith in "good old Uncle Joe" Stalin, nor did he trust Roosevelt's

anticolonial views, which, he foresaw, might seriously endanger
the British and French hopes to hold their empires in the postwar
world. Like de Gaulle, Churchill was frightened by the specter of
the two colossi, Russia and America, astride the world, in all their
immense power, self-righteousness and almost total inexperience
in world affairs. It was clear to Churchill that England and France
had to stand together to hold off the Russians and educate the
Americans to the new realities of the world balance of power.

This was his long-term view, but it was buttressed and made
urgent by the immediate necessity of preparing to move into the
vacuum that would be left by the final collapse of Hitler's crumbling defenses. Roosevelt had stated that there was no need to keep
an American army three thousand miles away from home after
the war and had promised a rapid evacuation of Europe and
demobilization of the armed forces. Great Britain did not have the
troops to replace the Americans while maintaining imperial communications. Unless France stepped in to take over an occupation
zone and step into the breach, there would be nothing but Red
Army troops in the heart of Europe. Thus Churchill pleaded for
inclusion of France "at the inter-allied table" and for a place for
France in the Allied Control Commission for the occupation of
Germany.

Stalin suspected what Churchill was up to, but he was not
unduly concerned. Like Roosevelt, he felt that France was decadent and not to be taken seriously; unlike Roosevelt, he felt no
personal animus for de Gaulle and even saw some advantage in
having him present as a possible pawn to use against Roosevelt and
Churchill. He dispatched a reply to Churchill on November 20,
accepting his proposal to include de Gaulle "provided that the
President agrees with this," but laying down the condition that "it
is necessary first to settle definitely the time and place of the
meeting between us three." At the same time Stalin was preparing
to invite de Gaulle to Moscow to negotiate a Franco-Soviet Pact
which de Gaulle had proposed.

Roosevelt would have nothing to do with de Gaulle. He wired
Churchill his approval of an interallied conference, but only of the
"Big Three," without de Gaulle. Churchill, fighting hard, sent off
another plan to Stalin on December 5: "As you have seen, the
President does not expect de Gaulle to come to the meeting of the
three. I would hope this could be modified to his coming in later
on, when decisions especially affecting France were under discus-

sion." But Roosevelt dug in his heels stubbornly. He wired Stalin on December 6 recommending that the Soviets turn down de Gaulle's request to settle the postwar frontier with Germany at that time, proposing instead "that its settlement subsequent to the collapse of Germany is preferable." He also sent off another message to Churchill that same day: "I still adhere to my position that any attempt to include de Gaulle in the meeting of the three of us would merely introduce a complicating and undesirable factor." This was Roosevelt's last word and Churchill could not budge him further.

The Yalta Conference began at 3:45 P.M. on the afternoon of February 5, 1945, with France absent by exclusion. But it was the absentee, Charles de Gaulle, who had the last word to say in terms of history. Exactly twenty years later, almost to the exact hour, at 3:00 P.M. on February 5, 1965, President de Gaulle, only living survivor of the leaders of the Yalta period of history, seated himself alone on the thronelike dais in the great banquet hall of the Elysée Palace, to tell the world's press that, in the present view of France, the German problem should be settled only by Germany's neighbors. Thus de Gaulle sought to avenge Yalta by excluding the Yalta powers from Europe as they had excluded him exactly twenty years earlier.

The fact that de Gaulle's attempted exclusion was obviously as futile and unrealistically absurd a policy as that of Roosevelt and Stalin was undoubtedly known to de Gaulle, who is a realist, no matter how unrealistic he may often seem to be. He had no illusions about excluding America from European settlements, but he had a surrealistic view of the value of attitudes over and above substance. As he had written in *The Edge of the Sword,* "great leaders are remembered less for the usefulness of what they have achieved than for the sweep of their endeavors." His Yalta anniversary proclamation was the kind of sweeping statement designed not literally to sweep America out of Europe, but to be a master stroke in the grand sweep of Gaullist endeavor.

After his return to power in 1958 President de Gaulle tried by every means possible—by sweeping statements in public, by pleas and threats in private, by secret letters and memoranda, by barnstorming trips through Europe, Africa and South America— to form alliances within the alliance, to play ally off against adversary or neutral, to convert, counter or otherwise obliterate the memory of Yalta and to make any form of a new Yalta impossible.

This is the trauma that motivated his intensive negotiations with Eisenhower, Kennedy and Macmillan to elaborate a three-power strategic directorate of the Western world in which France might have an equal voice in the world power struggle. He finally abandoned all hope after Kennedy turned him down as had Eisenhower and Macmillan. After that he devoted himself to leading the medium-sized and small nations of the world in a challenge to the great powers.

This struggle for world power and the search for a new balance of forces among the big and small nations is the most fascinating and meaningful politico-diplomatic story of our times. It began in the forties and may well continue to dominate world affairs for the rest of this century. It was the most important motivating force in the third life of Charles de Gaulle, in his incarnation of France as President of the Republic, just as it was one of the most important elements in the life of General de Gaulle, wartime leader of the Fighting French.

Although the uncivil war between de Gaulle and the Anglo-Saxons was a separate war in itself, it paralleled the civil war among the Fighting French. The Fighting French were aptly named: they fought against everyone and most of all among themselves. It is to that peculiarly French battlefront that we now turn: the story of de Gaulle and the Gauls.

CHAPTER SIX

DE GAULLE AGAINST
THE GAULS

---

*The Gauls are a warring people; when they are
not fighting the Germans, their neighbors across
the Rhine, they are fighting among themselves.*

JULIUS CAESAR, *Gallic Commentaries*

THERE IS NO WAR SO cruel as civil war, as Americans know more
than most peoples. More Americans were killed by Americans in
the War between the States than in all the foreign wars that
America has fought.

The French, too, have killed each other in greater numbers than
the toll of death inflicted upon them by foreign enemies, although
the deadly superiority of civil over foreign war is less apparent in
French history. France, unlike America, never fought one big,
bloody and decisive civil war whose total casualties stand out in
huge black figures. Instead, all of French history is a never-ending
series of fratricidal battles, a history of a continuous civil war.

From Gaul to de Gaulle, the French nation as we know it today
was forged in war. The descendants of Hughes Capet, Count of
Paris, and of Clovis, King of the Franks, carved out France with
their swords, united it by force and faith and baptized it in blood.
More Bretons, Normands, Flemings, Lotharingians, Alsatians,
Savoyards, Burgundians, Aquitainians, Arvernians and Albigen-
sians died in the French wars of national unification than ever fell
under the slings, arrows, bolts, bullets and bombs of the recurring
invasions of Phoenicians, Vikings, Romans, Goths, Huns, Saracens, Slavs or Anglo-Saxons or in the corresponding French
invasions of their lands. However, no historian has ever attempted
to calculate the total casualties of France's millennia of civil wars.

It is difficult enough merely to keep track of France's regimes that rise and fall as regularly as the tides.

France is the land of the living past, where old quarrels never die because they were never fully resolved either by decisive victory or by mutual compromise.

The French Revolution was aborted in its early years, setting off a chain reaction of revolutions and counterrevolutions that is still splitting French society today. The constitutional monarchy of 1789 had its head chopped off by the guillotine in 1793; the First Republic did not live longer than two years, falling under the Terror which led to the Directory, to the Consulate and to the First Empire of Napoleon in 1799. This decade of revolution, 1789–1799, was followed by a century of recurrent revolutions in France: the fall of Napoleon and the restoration of the Bourbons in 1814; the revolt of 1830 and the subsequent ascension of the Orléans monarchy; the revolution of 1848 and the creation of the Second Republic; the usurpation of power by Prince Louis Napoleon and his erection of the Second Empire in 1852; the collapse of the second Napoleonic regime in the Franco-Prussian War of 1870–1871; and the creation of the Third Republic in 1875.

In this century the Third Republic went down to defeat in 1940, to be succeeded by the French state of Marshal Pétain, which lived as a Nazi satellite for four years and then gave way to the postliberation Fourth Republic, which in turn was overthrown by the coup d'état of Algiers little more than a decade after its founding. The Fifth Republic created by Charles de Gaulle is only seven years old at this writing. It has not known a day of security or tranquillity since its inception and is not an odds-on favorite to last longer than the lifetime of its founding father.

General de Gaulle himself was not an odds-on bet to live very long when he began his new life in London on June 18, 1940. Within a few days of his call to resistance he was condemned to death for desertion and treason by the Vichy government of France. Wounded in body and soul, he was, at the age of forty-nine, a middle-aged man, worn and torn by a lifetime of strife, friendless and lonely. Although he had exhorted the French people in his June 18 broadcast to believe that France was not alone, not alone, not alone, General de Gaulle was himself terrifyingly alone.

His aide, Lieutenant Geoffroy de Courcel, was his only staff officer. A young French girl, Elisabeth de Miribel, who had volunteered to work at the French Embassy, was his secretarial staff. The embassy itself did not rally to his call. Ambassador Charles Corbin, a veteran diplomat, could not bring himself to break with old habits and traditions to join forces with a soldier who had broken his oath of allegiance and was proposing to lead an insurrection.

General de Gaulle did not try hard to win over the Ambassador. His basic appeal was addressed to soldiers, officers, armaments workers and those directly or closely connected with the war effort. He was, therefore, more particularly disappointed by the refusal of Jean Monnet, for Monnet was closely connected with the most influential industrial and political groups of England and the United States. De Gaulle knew it would be very difficult to win support for a resistance movement in America without men of Monnet's stature to lead the way.

Disappointing, too, was the failure or refusal of prominent French politicians to support de Gaulle or heed his call. René Mayer, who was to become an important leader of postliberation France, reluctantly rejected de Gaulle's appeal, although he endorsed its sentiments. "I must return to France," Mayer wrote in a message to de Gaulle because, he explained, he was a prominent Jewish leader and he felt that he "must not separate my fate from the trials of my people who are going to be persecuted." Many other leaders of French society similarly turned down de Gaulle. "We are going to America," said André Maurois, Henri Bonnet and Henri de Kerilles, "where we can be most useful." Others returned to France or stayed on in England, working in British industry or in the war organizations.

Only one well-known politician of the dying Third Republic, Pierre Cot, rallied to the standard raised by Charles de Gaulle, telling the General that he would do anything to help: "I'll even sweep the stairs," said that scholarly deputy of the National Assembly. Cot almost had to sweep the stairs, so thin were the ranks of the Gaullists as they set up headquarters temporarily at St. Stephen's Place and then in Carlton Gardens.

One of the early volunteers, a young man in his twenties, Claude Bouchinet-Serreulles, who became de Gaulle's delegate to the resistance movement in Paris, still recalls today the nakedness and poverty of the Free French organization at its start. Serreulles, now a Companion of the Liberation and a banker in Paris, told me recently, "Without Charles de Gaulle's religious faith in himself, which he was able to transmit to others, and without the sympathetic support of Winston Churchill, who understood de Gaulle's dour nature and truculence, we would have failed as we waited with heavy hearts for the wave of resistants that came as the smallest trickle to our doors."

Serreulles himself arrived in England, at Liverpool, a full month after de Gaulle's broadcast of June 18. He had fled Bordeaux after first calling a friend, Major Ely (who became chairman of the joint chiefs of staff in the postwar years), to ask him whether a patriot had the right to refuse to surrender and a duty to escape in order to continue the fight. "The flame of French resistance must be kept burning," Ely and Serreulles agreed after a long talk on the evening of June 17, not knowing, of course, that the very next day this sentiment would be expressed by General de Gaulle from London.

Many other Frenchmen, like Serreulles and the young army officer Ely, were that day talking of ways and means to carry on the fight. A young Catholic politician, Edmond Michelet, later to become a minister in de Gaulle's governments, both at the liberation and in the return to power in 1958, was that day distributing tracts in his home town, calling on the people to resist the imminent fall and surrender of the armies. De Gaulle was certainly not alone, although he could not know this at the time of his decision. There were millions of Frenchmen thinking the same thing, wondering whether, and some preparing, to fight on.

Of all Frenchmen, Charles de Gaulle was the one who moved fastest, at the most important level, and the only man of cabinet rank to take the vital first step. All the others held back and hesitated or refused to act at the critical moment. The history of France and the personal history of Charles de Gaulle might have been very different had any one of dozens of men—such as Reynaud, Herriot, Blum or Mandel—gone to London to tell Churchill that they wanted to set up a French government in exile or a dissident movement.

To de Gaulle's credit, the historian must note that he tried hard to persuade such men to come and that he offered over and over again to step down himself and to serve under any prominent personality of the government or the army who would choose to come and lead. The records do not bear out the charges, spread by the detractors of de Gaulle, that he was a self-seeking apprentice dictator who had created Free France in order to seize power for himself. This calumny had wide circulation in the United States and contributed to poisoning American-Gaullist relations from the start and indeed continues to do so to this very day.

No modern dictator ever acted the way Charles de Gaulle did. From the very first moment of his call of June 18, 1940, to the pinnacle of his fame and power in postliberation France, de Gaulle acted in the name of France and for France, refusing to seize and hold power without the consent of the French who were free to state their choice. The fact that he also acted as though he were France and, indeed, fused his personality with his ideals to the point that France and de Gaulle often became one and indistinguishable, should not be permitted to confuse the fundamental fact that he first gave others their chance and then won majority support from those free to choose, defeating in a fair fight every rival for power.

On the very day of de Gaulle's arrival in London on June 17, 1940, he sent a telegram to General Weygand, his superior officer, offering to carry on under Weygand's orders the mission of seeking supplies from America and arranging for transport of French troops to Africa. When Weygand promptly telegraphed back contrary orders to return at once to France, de Gaulle wrote him a letter, cited in his memoirs, "to entreat him to put himself at the head of the resistance and to assure him, if he did so, of my complete obedience."

Without even waiting for Weygand's reply, which he knew would be negative, de Gaulle also sent a telegram to General Noguès, Resident-General in Morocco and Commander-in-Chief for North Africa, offering to put himself immediately under the orders of Noguès "if he would reject the armistice." On June 24 General de Gaulle dispatched yet another appeal to Noguès and sent similar messages to General Mittelhauser and High Commissioner Puaux in Lebanon, as well as to General Catroux, High Commissioner in Indochina. With the single exception of Catroux, who sent a message to his son telling him to carry on the fight and to give de Gaulle his "sympathetic approval," all the others turned down de Gaulle's appeal to them to take over leadership of Free France. None of the top men of the army or of the parliament came to London to take command, nor did anyone attempt to set up a resistance movement anywhere in the French Empire or in allied territories. De Gaulle seized and held leader-

ship by a combination of his own foresight and patriotism and the
default of all other potential leaders.

* * *

The very few Frenchmen who rallied to de Gaulle in those early
days in the summer of 1940 were all impressed by his massive self-
confidence and the impersonal, almost inhuman calm with which
he confronted crises. One of the most interesting descriptions of de
Gaulle in those days of trial appears in a brief biography written by
one of his first adherents, Philippe Barrès. Barrès was the journalist
who had first heard de Gaulle's name pronounced with admiration by the Nazi officers who had studied his military treatises—
the same Barrès whose father, Maurice, had been the most fervent of French nationalists during the childhood of Charles de
Gaulle. This is his description of de Gaulle in London, in June
1940:

> The General was seated behind his desk and he offered
> me a cigarette and took one himself, one of the forty
> Players a day that he chain-smoked. He took his time
> about speaking to me. His eyes, somewhat veiled, peering
> out of a stern face, watched me with a kind of calm
> curiosity. This man does not look like a man of our times;
> there is something elemental in him, which gives him
> power, the look of a soldier and of a man of the
> soil. . . . As excitable as he seems in his public speeches
> and acts, particularly when France is at stake, de Gaulle
> is, by nature, the most phlegmatic man in the world.
> When he was a little boy his parents and brothers used to
> say teasingly, "Charles must have been born in the ice-
> box."

Philippe Barrès tells the story of what happened on June 18
while de Gaulle was preparing his speech of that day. He had
given orders not to be disturbed and his aide, de Courcel, took all
his calls. One of the calls made de Courcel jump out of his seat
with joy: it was from Madame de Gaulle, who had made her way
out of France on the last boat from Brittany with her daughters,
Elisabeth and Anne, and her son, Philippe. De Courcel passed the
phone immediately to the General and heard him say, "Ah! It is
you," in a calm, unexcitable tone of voice, like any husband getting

a casual call from his wife during a busy session of work. De Gaulle gave his wife instructions on how to get to London. He then rang off and without another word to anyone turned back to his work. His wife and children were safe, but France was not, and there was much to do. "Such a man is Charles de Gaulle," wrote Philippe Barrès.

Another early Gaullist, less in awe of de Gaulle than most, was the writer Félix Garras. He agreed with Barrès that de Gaulle was "phlegmatic" but attributed it rather to the fact that "the ordinary routine of life simply bored him," as Garras put it in his book, *De Gaulle seul contre les pouvoirs*. Garras wrote:

> That is why we see these sudden outbursts when he indulges in his thirst for the sublime that is second nature to him. His mind is classic but his heart is romantic. It is only in action that he achieves the unity of his personality. . . . the 18th of June liberated the nonconformist in de Gaulle that had been suffocating under the carapace of military discipline. In revolt he at last became himself.

Garras saw de Gaulle clearly and correctly. De Gaulle is an essentially restless, negative man who comes alive only in action and is at his best when the action is motivated by resistance rather than by creation. Charles de Gaulle has always fought hardest and most successfully against something or somebody, rarely for something and never for anybody but France, and by himself. He never constructed anything that lasted for any time after he himself had left it: the Fighting French organization that he created as a war instrument disappeared as soon as the war ended. Its members had quarreled among themselves and with de Gaulle all through the war itself. Although it was normal for an organization like Fighting France to disband as soon as liberation permitted the formation of a government, one might have expected a certain camaraderie to continue and some fraternal clubs to be formed and to live on. Such was not the case.

Half-hearted attempts to form veterans' clubs were made after the liberation by some sentimentalists, but they did not last more than a few months. Perhaps fraternal organizations are un-French, more fit for sentimental Anglo-Saxons; in any case, they are certainly un-Gaullist. Brotherhood, fidelity to friends, personal loyalties and sentiments, these are conspicuously absent from the history of Gaullism, as is any consistency or cohesion of doctrine, dogma and political organization.

The liberation of France opened the floodgates to the dammed-up frustrations and rivalries of the wartime coalition. Former Gaullists rushed into print with their own versions of the fight for liberation, many of them attacking de Gaulle as viciously as the Gaullists had attacked them earlier. Typical of the opposition attempts to discredit de Gaulle was the book of Admiral Muselier, the "liberator" of Saint-Pierre and Miquelon, who had broken with de Gaulle early in the campaign and had become one of his mortal enemies. The title of his book reflects exactly the complex contradictory emotions of the warring Gauls. It is called *De Gaulle Against Gaullism*.

Admiral Muselier, like many other disenchanted Gaullists, believed that only he represented true Gaullism and that de Gaulle was a traitor to himself. The charge was absurd, for it was based on the primary fallacy that there was such a thing as "Gaullism" to begin with. "Gaullism" is not a doctrine or an ideology; it is only the peculiarly personal style of the man de Gaulle, which he could not betray if he wanted to do so, for it is his own personality that makes it what it is, and this could not be represented by anyone else, any more than de Gaulle could become something other than what he was. This slightly mad kind of polemic over Gaullism is still being argued today by those who call themselves Gaullists and who have split into left, right and center factions, as well as a hard core of "unconditional" Gaullists who continued to follow de Gaulle blindly and pathetically long after he refused to lead them or even recognize them.

* * *

From the start of the Free French movement the armed forces split into pro- and anti-de Gaulle factions, with the "antis" very much in the majority. De Gaulle had never been popular in the army, neither with his superior officers, against whose hidebound doctrines he railed, nor with his own classmates, from whom he kept his distance.

General Eisenhower, a man as different from de Gaulle as the open fields of Kansas are from the sheltered cloisters of Flanders, was fascinated by de Gaulle's aloofness and self-imposed loneliness. He kept searching for explanations and kept hoping to find a formula that would end the factional fighting among the French military men. In his account of the war, *Crusade in Europe*,

Eisenhower put down his own estimate of the division among the Gauls:

> It is possible to understand why de Gaulle was disliked within the ranks of the French Army. At the time of France's surrender in 1940 the officers who remained in the Army had accepted the position and the orders of their Government and had given up the fight. From their viewpoint, if the course chosen by de Gaulle was correct, then every French officer who obeyed the orders of this Government was a poltroon. If de Gaulle was a loyal Frenchman they had to regard themselves as cowards. Naturally the officers did not choose to think of themselves in this light: rather they considered themselves as loyal Frenchmen carrying out the orders of constituted civilian authority, and it followed that they officially and personally regarded de Gaulle as a deserter.

For the first few months of his organizing efforts General de Gaulle was able to recruit mainly young officers under field rank. In retrospect, what then seemed tragically difficult, almost hopeless, proved to be only another manifestation of the power of de Gaulle's personal lucky star, for he himself was only a brigadier-general, of temporary rank, and he would have had great difficulty exercising authority over older, higher-ranking officers had they joined him early in the campaign. Later, when his fame had spread and the laurel leaves of the Grand Resistant had been placed upon his head, he would be able to command the respect of all men, including those who wore many stars and laurels of rank. He was thus able to stand up to such prestigious soldiers as General Giraud and General Georges when, in 1943, they were backed by all the power and stubbornness of Roosevelt.

De Gaulle dominated them all mainly by the force of his personality but also by his superior intellectual capacities and his skill at high-level in-fighting and political maneuvering. Roosevelt always underestimated de Gaulle, as did his principal advisor, Robert Murphy. They were ever ready to believe those who reported that de Gaulle was not the man whom the internal resistance regarded as their leader or who insisted that most army officers would not follow him or preferred a different chief.

The real test came after the Casablanca conference of January 1943, when Roosevelt and Churchill forced de Gaulle to accept

coleadership of Fighting France with General Giraud, operating
through a seven-member French National Committee of Liberation. In a few months' time General de Gaulle outmaneuvered
Giraud, a good soldier but a limited man with no sense of high
politics. The battle was won finally when de Gaulle forced the
issue of an enlargement of the Committee, from seven to fourteen
members, in which he would have a clear majority loyal to him.
He deliberately created a crisis by tendering his resignation to the
Committee of 7, threatening to split Fighting France into two
hostile forces at a critical point in the war. He had also assured
himself of the support of the key man in the contest, Jean Monnet,
who was highly regarded by Murphy and by Roosevelt. Monnet
held the swing vote among the seven, who were split three for
Giraud and three for de Gaulle.

Jean Monnet was not particularly fond of de Gaulle and had
gone to Washington after having refused to join de Gaulle in
London three years earlier. Then, as today, Jean Monnet believed
that France's future depended upon maintaining the closest possible relations with the Anglo-Saxon powers. But Murphy and
Roosevelt both overlooked the basic fact that Jean Monnet, internationalist though he was all his life, was also a loyal Frenchman
and, above all, a man of the most rigorous intellectual honesty and
keenest political judgment. Monnet quickly came to the decision
that Giraud was a poor organizer and a weak leader, lacking
political judgment and skill, whereas de Gaulle was far and away
the best leader that could be found for the Free French. Once this
became clear, Monnet devoted himself to persuading Giraud to
enlarge the Committee, thus clearing the way for de Gaulle's
subsequent emergence as the undisputed leader.

Jean Monnet had no illusions about de Gaulle's ambitions for
power and he was not unconcerned about the dangers, but he
knew, as did other leading personalities who were not dedicated
Gaullists, that Fighting France needed to be unified under a
dynamic chief, and no one but Charles de Gaulle could do the job.
Although Monnet has been engaged in a tense struggle of his own
against de Gaulle's policies on Europe ever since 1958, he does not
regret having served de Gaulle during the war and in his postliberation administration. He told the writer recently: "First things
come first. Before a united Europe and an Atlantic partnership
there had to be a united France, strong, modernized and able to
assume a leading role among the Western allies. Without de

Gaulle or against de Gaulle, we could not have liberated or reconstructed France. There was no one but de Gaulle. Whatever his faults, he was a tower of strength and inspiration."

* * *

One of the principal causes of friction between de Gaulle and the Gauls was the primordial Gallic fear and mistrust of strong men. Charges that de Gaulle was an apprentice dictator, seeking personal political power more than any other objective, were made against him by enemies and rivals very early in the struggle. Even some of his own supporters and admirers felt that he should devote himself exclusively to the participation of Fighting France in the war effort and not get involved in complex, suspicion-breeding maneuvers in political affairs. They were naïve and did not understand the nature of a world war as de Gaulle did. Politics and postwar settlements cannot be separated out from military efforts as though the war were only a military affair. Whatever his personal ambitions may have been, General de Gaulle was correct in insisting upon fighting for political recognition of Fighting France, and he was compelled to set up an authority to compete with the French state of Pétain for the right to be considered the head of at least the provisional government of Free France.

De Gaulle began to force this issue as early as October 1940, only four months after his first call to resistance. He moved to dispute the Vichy title as the government of France right after Pétain met with Hitler at the Montoire conference and made a number of concessions to Nazi control of France, virtually surrendering the northern occupied half of the country to outright Nazi administration. General de Gaulle insisted that the Pétain government had thereby abandoned the independence of France and could no longer be considered as the French government. He made his views known by issuing a "Charter" of Free France, in a manifesto drawn up at a conference that he convened in Brazzaville, in the French Congo.

The Brazzaville "Manifesto" of October 27, 1940, provoked immediate controversy among the French and between de Gaulle and the allies; it also had consequences that could not be foreseen that day but were to haunt de Gaulle twenty years later, when French generals rebelled against de Gaulle's Fifth Republic and cited his own Brazzaville Manifesto as justification.

The Manifesto laid down principles without precedent in international law, in language that was more poetic than legal:

> France is undergoing the most terrible crisis of her history. Her frontiers, her empire, her independence, and even her soul are threatened by destruction.

No one but a de Gaulle would dream of invoking the "soul" of a nation in a document seeking to establish political claims to representativeness. De Gaulle then went on to claim that the Vichy subservience to Hitler, which had brought about the destruction of all that was France, nullified Vichy's title to govern France:

> Now a truly French government no longer exists. In effect, the organism at Vichy, which assumes this name, is unconstitutional and subject to the invader.

One notes that de Gaulle had to prefix the words "in effect" to this remarkable interpretation of the basis of constitutional government. In fact and in law the French state was constitutional, deriving its powers from the duly elected representatives of the French people in parliament assembled. The parliamentarians were certainly under great pressure, were craven at worst, mistaken at best, but unquestionably they had acted legally. This compelled de Gaulle to find extralegal arguments to justify his contention that the Vichy government was no longer representative. He sought this argument in Vichy's "state of servitude":

> In its state of servitude this organism cannot be, and is not, other than an instrument used by the enemies of France against the honor and the interest of the country. It is thus necessary that a new power assume the charge of directing the French war effort. Events have imposed this sacred duty upon me. I will not fail.

De Gaulle concluded the Manifesto with this pledge:

> I make a solemn commitment to render an account of my acts to the representatives of the French people when it will be possible for them to judge freely.

De Gaulle's pledge to render account to the French people later did not remove the suspicion that he would in the interim conduct himself not only as the military leader of the French resistance but also as the political leader in the name of the "new power" he invoked in the Manifesto. As a political leader de Gaulle demanded more and more recognition as guardian of the French sovereignty, and this led him to make further demands to participate in the allied war councils and not merely to contribute to the allied war effort.

The Americans wanted de Gaulle's forces to contribute to the war effort but not to participate in the elaboration of war strategy, for they did not trust the Gaullists. As for de Gaulle's argument that the legal government of Vichy was really unconstitutional because of its servitude to the Nazis, the allies considered this a very dangerous theory because of the precedent it might set in regard to all the other countries and territories around the world where power might be seized and justified in this manner by all sorts of personal adventurers or Communist agents.

De Gaulle in fact had laid down a strange, dangerous distinction between legal and illegal governments, which frightened both French and allied jurists. His proposal to judge legality by an interpretation of the government's ability to serve the "honor and interest" of the country was ethically and emotionally satisfying but logically and legally undefinable. It recalled all the subversive intrigues during the thirties when a number of Fascist leagues and so-called patriotic societies attempted to set up ideological standards for civil obedience or disobedience.

De Gaulle's argument seemed like an application of the old Maurrasian distinction between "le pays réel" and "le pays légal," a distinction that had been used time and time again by the enemies of parliamentary democracy in France. This theory holds that the legal government becomes unreal when the members of the executive and the parliament become confused and corrupt and quarrel among themselves to the point that they no longer can govern the country effectively or defend its independence as a state. At that point the "legal country" becomes a mere fiction and it is the "real country" of workers, farmers, businessmen, career civil servants and other groups of loyal citizens who truly represent the nation and serve its interests.

De Gaulle's version of the doctrine of Maurras was to draw a distinction between the legality and the legitimacy of governments. He did not dispute, because he could not, Vichy's claim to legality, but he claimed, with justification, that the legality had become unreal because in practice there was no representative government functioning in occupied France and that the governmental sovereignty had in practice been transferred to the Nazi overseers of the French state. Thus de Gaulle considered that his call to resistance was not an act of dissidence but rather the continuity of the "legitimate" government of a free France. Under this line of reasoning the legal government of Pétain was illegitimate and dissident, for it did not serve the interests of the French nation. It was not de Gaulle, therefore, who broke his oath of allegiance by refusing to obey his superior officer, Pétain, but rather it was Pétain who betrayed the higher oath of allegiance to France by refusing to fight for freedom and independence.

The Gaullist doctrine of legitimacy versus legality would be invoked by both de Gaulle and his enemies a quarter of a century later in an ironic twist of history, when army officers rose up in revolt against President de Gaulle, citing the principles and the example of General de Gaulle to justify their dissidence. They claimed that by refusing to fight to keep Algeria French, and by offering independence to that land which had been French territory for a century and a half, President de Gaulle, like Pétain before him, was surrendering a part of French sovereignty to an enemy. They argued that the "honor and interest" of France dictated the patriotic necessity to defend Algeria against the defeatist state of President de Gaulle.

President de Gaulle, rising to the challenge, put on the old wartime uniform of General de Gaulle and, addressing the nation on radio and television, began his appeal with the words: "I, who represent twenty years of French legitimacy . . ." Thus President de Gaulle and the anti-de Gaulle forces confronted each other in 1960 on the basis of the principle laid down by General de Gaulle in 1940. It is no mere fantasy of writers to note that France is a country where nothing is ever forgotten or forgiven and little is ever learned. The frictions and fragmentations of French society are demonstrated over and over again in the recurrent cycles of internecine conflicts. De Gaulle is a true Gaul in his own incarnations of the Gallic spirit and his detestation of Gallic factionalism among his fellow Gauls.

* * *

Although the necessity for a common front against the Nazis and the powerful Anglo-Saxon allies served to keep the warring Gauls from a complete rupture, that restraint began to give way as liberation of the French territory proceeded. As the foreign war began to recede, the civil war among the French increased in intensity. Gaullist agents, moving along with the allied armies, occupied public buildings and began systematically to get rid of Communists as well as of Vichy collaborators and, indeed, of any forces suspected of something less than complete loyalty to de Gaulle.

General de Gaulle himself set in motion long-planned measures to break up the resistance committees and to disband and draft the F.F.I. underground forces into the regular French Army. He was keenly aware of the power of the Communists, and despite his constant conflicts with the allies and his jealous defense of French independence, he was not too proud to seek help from Eisenhower to make a show of strength. De Gaulle did not admit in his memoirs that he asked Eisenhower for help to take over control of his own resistance forces—there is a limit to the remarkable candor of even his memoirs. However, in *Crusade in Europe* Eisenhower states that de Gaulle did request American troops to open up and protect Leclerc's entry into Paris and additional troops in a military parade to put on a show of strength and American support for de Gaulle.

The full story of that extraordinary event had never been recorded officially, but I heard it in detail from General Eisenhower at a private talk at his farm in Gettysburg in the summer of 1964. I had called upon the General on August 25, on the twentieth anniversary of the liberation of Paris, a sentimental moment for all of us who had been there on that marvelous day.

Eisenhower was in a reminiscent mood as he thought back to August 25, 1944. He talked for hours about the war and also about the postwar period, when he and de Gaulle, after having both retired, were called back to public life and became presidents of their countries. In reporting on the second uncivil war between de Gaulle and the Anglo-Saxons, I will cite in full Eisenhower's explanations of his major policy conflicts with de Gaulle during their parallel presidencies—conflicts which were the roots of the virtual rupture of the Atlantic alliance. This is the moment in the chronology to present Eisenhower's testimony on the civil war among the Gauls, and to fill in an important page in French history that de Gaulle left blank in his own record of events.

On the problem of liberating Paris, well, our troops got to the outskirts of Paris on August 25 and I was anxious to have French troops as the spearhead. That's what de Gaulle wanted most of all. It was also my hope that it would help create French unity. So I decided to give the honors of liberating Paris to the Leclerc Division. . . . I went to see our Fifth Corps Commander, General Girow, and I said, "Where is General de Gaulle? I hear he's set up somewhere in Paris." Well, Girow said he was over in the War Office . . . not in the presidential Elysée Palace.

I went over to call on him promptly and I did this very deliberately as a kind of de facto recognition of de Gaulle as the provisional president of France and he was very grateful—he never forgot that. It was really something. After all, I was commanding everything on the Continent—all the troops—and all that de Gaulle could count on, troops, equipment, everything supplied by America and under my recommendations and orders. And so he looked upon it as what it was, and that is a very definite recognition of his high political position and his place, and that was, of course, what he wanted and what Roosevelt had never given him.

I got to Paris about eleven o'clock on the 27th, and I called on de Gaulle, as I recall, at two o'clock in the afternoon—anyway, as soon as I could. . . . General de Gaulle needed something that day to show to the populace that he was quite a fellow, and another thing that was bothering him was the armaments that the maquis had. Some of them were of a doubtful loyalty, you know, and some were dedicated Communists. So de Gaulle wanted some help from us. So, I said, well, the first thing we'll do is this. We'll give you a review of allied troops. You know, this is as strange an incident probably in all military history because I got General Bradley and I said, "Now, Brad, you go down and stand with General de Gaulle on the reviewing stand of the Champs-Elysées and remember that the review is for him as the provisional President of France."

Now, those troops that he reviewed were American troops actually deploying for battle, but they first put on a military parade on the way to combat and that was a very unusual thing. I proved to de Gaulle that we would support him and his efforts to disarm the people he wanted to disarm—the doubtful ones and the Communists. And so he knew he could go ahead and take over the maquis irregulars and put them into units if he could, and we would do what was necessary in arming them, but only *after* they were inside the regular army.

General Eisenhower, like General de Gaulle, respected and appreciated the valor of the individual Frenchman who had fought so courageously in the resistance movements. But both the American and the Frenchman mistrusted the organized politically oriented groups inside the resistance movement. As a Frenchman, Charles de Gaulle may have personally admired and appreciated the underground fighters as patriots, but General de Gaulle, as leader of France, feared and mistrusted the resistance organizations and their chiefs. He knew that they would try to maintain their military networks for peacetime political purposes and would demand a major voice in postwar France as a reward for their contribution to the liberation. He understood only too well how the links of solidarity forged in the underground would become chains on his own freedom to maneuver as the leader of the nation. Above all, he feared the power and political skill of the Communists. He would not defeat them or outmaneuver them as easily as he had outmaneuvered rivals like General Giraud or the disorganized politicians who had joined him in exile.

De Gaulle wasted no time in taking on the challenge of the internal resistance. He had to use his full power and fame as the liberator while he had it to use. That is why he asked Eisenhower to put on a big show for him, and that is why he deliberately set about controlling the resistance on the very day of the liberation, as he himself admitted in his memoirs, when he wrote this comment on the resistance: "I found in it, at the crucial moment, a valuable instrument in the struggle against the enemy, and, in relation to the allies, an essential prop for my policy of independence and unity." For de Gaulle, therefore, the "glorious resistance" was basically an "instrument" and a "prop," discarded when it no longer served his purpose or what he considered to be the purpose of France.

At the liberation of Paris he snubbed the resistance delegates who were waiting for him at the Hotel de Ville. Before paying his respects to the resistance fighters, he stopped off to review and honor the Paris police, even though that corps had made little if any contribution to the resistance. Then he ordered the dissolution of the COMAC resistance committees and the incorporation of the F.F.I. into the ranks of the regular army.

De Gaulle was determined to prevent Communist subversion of France. He knew the Communists had heavily infiltrated the resistance networks, and he knew that even among non-Communist elements there were many radical and revolutionary forces loose in the resistance. He had no compunctions about crushing them, for he believed they would be as harmful to peacetime France as they were valuable in the war.

The traditional political party leaders and the new men who had arisen in the resistance had no more illusions about de Gaulle than he had about them. The struggle for power in France began while enemy troops were still on French soil. The civil war among the French reached a paroxysm of passion at the height of the liberation campaign, as resistants and collaborators fought in the streets in a national settlement of accounts. De Gaulle himself was a prime target for snipers and assassins, whose true origins were never discovered. At the end of his triumphal march down the Champs-Elysées he was greeted not only by the cheers of the people massed in the Place de la Concorde, but also by a hail of bullets from surrounding rooftops. Another fusillade exploded as General de Gaulle arrived at Notre Dame Cathedral, and in the middle of the ceremony assassins began shooting at de Gaulle inside the church. He stood upright facing the altar, his deep voice intoning the Te Deum, as bullets whined and echoed through the Cathedral.

The battle of the ballots was due to follow close on the bullets that were fired at de Gaulle on the day of liberation. The first cabinet of the provisional government, formed on September 5, lasted only four days. The resistance delegates had protested the predominance of the "men of the exterior" and demanded a bigger, fairer share in the government for the "men of the interior" resistance. On September 9, therefore, de Gaulle as provisional president reshuffled his cabinet. He named veteran politician Jules Jeanneney, President of the Senate, as minister of state, and appointed the chief of the interior resistance council, Georges Bidault, as his foreign minister.

De Gaulle kept Communist participation down to the very minimum possible, giving them such empty portfolios as the post office (Augustin Laurent) and the air ministry (Charles Tillon). These were fairly impotent posts, since the air force remained under the control of the Allied supreme commander and the postal, telephone and telegraph services were virtually nonexistent outside of the military communications. Of the full cabinet of twenty-two men, only two were Communists—a percentage not exactly in proportion to the Communist forces in the country and the war effort.

The Communist Party held a mass rally at the Vélodrome d'Hiver that same September 9 as a demonstration of its real strength in the country as contrasted to the share it was given of the legal power—a familiar echo of the old Maurrasian–de Gaulle theory of "le pays réel" and "le pays légal." The Communists, like the devil, know how to quote scripture. It was only the first of many times that de Gaulle's words and theories would be used against him by his rivals and enemies.

De Gaulle, unimpressed by the demonstrations, knowing that his popularity was not challengeable and that he had the allies, particularly the Communist-sensitive Americans, behind him, moved rapidly to break the power of the Communists. On October 28, immediately after the United States and Great Britain had at last granted formal recognition to his provisional government, Premier de Gaulle obtained majority support from his cabinet for a decree disbanding and disarming the "patriotic guards" and the "national militia." These were armed civilians under nominal control of the C.N.R., the National Council of Resistance, through its military committee, COMAC. It was the nucleus of a danger-ous, revolutionary force, for its hard core was Communist or Communist-infiltrated. However, most of its men were loyal Frenchmen and resistance heroes, and they bitterly resented the order to disband and the suggestion that they should volunteer for the regular army as individuals. They wanted to remain as units and to be granted a special statute to enter the army with their own unit flags and honors.

De Gaulle would have no part of any special statute for the resistance fighters. The French Republic and its army were one and indivisible, he said. He would not yield on this issue, and he promptly gave orders to the police to disarm all unauthorized civilians. Resistance leaders, most particularly the Communists but not only the Communists, held protest meetings. Communist poet Louis Aragon and his wife, Elsa Triolet, and Paul Eluard rallied non-Communist writers and artists and resistance heroes such as Vercors, Salacrou, Pierre Emmanuel and many others, to join them in protest meetings and articles published in the Communist paper *L'Humanité*.

On November 2 the Communist Party political bureau issued a communiqué denouncing de Gaulle for the first time publicly: "Once again the Premier has shown his disdain for the resistance, treating it as a negligible quantity in the national effort. This attitude will be cruelly resented, not only by the National Council of the Resistance, but also by the departmental and local committees of liberation."

The reference to the resentment of the liberation committees was a thinly veiled warning to de Gaulle that the Communists might stir up trouble, perhaps even an insurrection, by sending out the word to their local leaders throughout the nation. It was no idle threat, for the government had not yet been able to establish reliable communications or security control through the still war-torn land and there were large areas in the south and southwest, very distant from allied troops, where the Communists were strong.

It is a somewhat ironic footnote to history to record the fact that only a year and a half earlier, on May 10, 1943, Secretary of State Cordell Hull in a then secret memorandum to President Roosevelt warned that de Gaulle had opened up his movement to Communists who were "the most highly organized political force" in France. Hull told Roosevelt of the Communists' "insistence that de Gaulle be their leader" and suggested that "the remedy for this situation is in our hands today, but if not used, may not be tomorrow." The secret memo of May 10, 1943, was made public in the historical documents issued by the Department of State in 1964 and was undoubtedly seen by President de Gaulle. It may possibly have influenced his sharp denunciation of the United States when a similar accusation was made against the Santo Domingo revolutionaries in the spring of 1965.

De Gaulle was never at any moment deceived by or unaware of the Communist threat, nor did he have any intention of letting the Communists have any levers of real power in the government of France. It was this very determination that led to the biggest crisis of the postliberation government, followed shortly thereafter by de Gaulle's resignation as prime minister.

The Communists and the Gaullists fought for power all

through the last months of the war, each side strengthening its own position without making a dent in the other's. The Communists' stronghold was the working class, almost solidly behind them, with equally powerful, if less numerous, support from the intellectual community of France. General de Gaulle drew his strength from almost every social class across a very wide spectrum but less deeply implanted in key sectors, such as the Communist bastions in the coal mines, the docks and the Paris "Red Belt" of industrial suburbs.

The first test of electoral strength came on October 21, 1945, in a national election to a constituent assembly whose members were given a seven-month mandate to draft the constitution of a new Fourth Republic of France. The election results confirmed the fact that the Communists were the strongest political party of postwar France:

Communists	5,005,000
Catholics (MRP)	4,780,000
Socialists	4,561,000

These "Big Three" parties were the ones that had been most active in the resistance, but the overwhelming majority of nine and a half million went to the inner group of Marxist parties, the Communists and Socialists. Fortunately for de Gaulle, the top Socialist leaders, Léon Blum and Vincent Auriol, were social-democratic and anti-Communist. However, the Socialist voters included a large percentage who favored an alliance with the Communists and who would not willingly go along with a rupture of the resistance comradeship. De Gaulle knew he was in for a very tough fight for control of the new republic, for he could not be sure of forcing this Marxist bloc to draft the kind of constitution that would give him the powers he felt the executive office had to have.

The Communists knew that their majority voice in the Constituent Assembly was a trump card, held in reserve. They had no fears about voting de Gaulle into office provisionally, thus avoiding too early a showdown with him. On November 13 the assembly elected de Gaulle premier by the unanimous ballot of the 555 deputies present and voting. But both sides were merely wheeling their big guns into position and entrenching their armies for the battle about to erupt.

De Gaulle opened hostilities when he called in political leaders to discuss the formation of his cabinet and informed them that he would not give the Communists any one of the three top ministries: interior, foreign affairs, national defense. The Communists had claimed these posts as their right as the first party of France. De Gaulle stated that, as chief executive, he had to direct his administration as he saw fit. The basic clash of French political life, between the executive and the legislative, provided the issue for the opening attack that would split the wartime coalition hopelessly apart.

The Communists stalked out of the meeting, refusing to accept any minor portfolios. They had suffered this humiliation a year earlier while the war was still on, but they said they did not have to accept that kind of second-class citizenship after they had won a free national election.

De Gaulle promptly sent a letter of resignation to the speaker of the assembly, saying that he could not form a government without the support of the first party of France, but that he was unwilling to entrust that party, which he considered to be an agent of a foreign power, with ministerial authority over the police, the diplomacy or the armed forces of France.

The Communist Party immediately announced its readiness to form a government without de Gaulle.

The Catholics opened their own barrage with a blast at the Communists and a declaration of allegiance to General de Gaulle, vowing to bar any government other than one headed by the liberator of France.

The Socialists, caught in the crossfire on their left and on their right, announced that they were ready to form a government without de Gaulle but only if the three resistance parties joined it. This was, as usual with the French Socialists, a big blank shell, since the Catholics had already said they would not support a government without de Gaulle at the head.

While all the politicians were firing off their blasts at each other, General de Gaulle, without consulting anyone, did as he always had done in a time of national crisis, ever since June 18: he went on the air to address the French people in a nationwide broadcast. De Gaulle told the French people that he was ready to cooperate with the Communist Party but that he absolutely refused to entrust them with "the three levers that control the foreign policy of a nation: the diplomacy that expresses it, the army that supports it, the police that covers it." The policy of France, he said, requires "a balance between the two great political powers of the world, in the interests of the nation and of peace itself." With this oblique but crystal-clear reference to America and Russia, de Gaulle went on to say that France must not take sides between the great powers, in substance or shadow, and that he therefore could not grant a key ministry to a party whose leaders were pro-Soviet.

Thus, as early as November 1945, de Gaulle adopted a neutralist "Third Force" position for France, between the Soviet and the American "blocs," and stressed the need for an independent national French posture in world affairs. He concluded his radio address by saying that he would consider himself "unworthy of being chief of government of France if I failed, for reasons of political expediency, to give full consideration to this issue of supreme national interest."

The Communists screamed insults at de Gaulle, denouncing him as a dictator, a new Napoleon, a throwback to Caesar. The Socialists were almost as violent in their reaction and were particularly angry at his use of the radio as a means of going over the heads of the deputies directly to the people after having resigned as premier. They, too, muttered about demagogues and dictators. The Catholics, no less alarmed at de Gaulle's use of plebiscitary techniques, nonetheless rose to his defense. At the same time they appealed to the Communists and the Socialists not to break the resistance coalition and to seek a compromise solution. They sent delegates to talk in secret to the Socialist leaders, warning them that they would be gobbled up by the more powerful Communists if they broke away from the Catholics and de Gaulle.

The Socialists did not need much prodding or warning from the Catholics. They were more fearful of the Communists than any other group could be. They feared de Gaulle, too, if somewhat less. Above all, the Socialists agreed with the Catholics that the only hope of true democrats was to seek a compromise and prevent a break with the Communists and de Gaulle, each of whom would dominate the forces in their own camps, on the left and on the right. Thus Socialist André Philip and Catholic Robert Schuman jointly proposed a motion expressing confidence in de Gaulle, rejecting his resignation and asking him to make an attempt to negotiate a solution with the Communists. They had already gone to see the Communist Chief, Maurice Thorez, warning him that a civil war would break out if he did not come to terms and that the Communists would not have a chance in a civil war against de Gaulle.

The Communists knew this to be true. Thorez and his deputy Jacques Duclos both told this writer at the time that "Frenchmen are essentially negative. The only majority possible in this country is a majority against something. The only way to win a civil war in France is to let the other side start it and then fight against it." This may have been their real reason for backing down, or they may have anticipated that they would have the last word in drafting the constitution. Whatever the reason, they agreed to seek a compromise. De Gaulle, too, realized that a test of strength would tear the still war-weary country apart. He knew he would win, but he also knew it would be at great cost, and he felt it would be better to make some kind of face-saving gesture at that time.

The ingenious Gauls, who are always brilliant at finding face-saving formulae that do not solve the basic issue, came up with a Solomonlike decision. They cut the ministry of national defense into two parts: a ministry of the armed forces and a ministry of armaments. De Gaulle gave armed forces to Catholic Edmond Michelet and armaments to Communist Charles Tillon. Thus the army was kept out of Communist control, but the Communists were given a hand in an area of national defense. The compromise solved nothing, but it saved faces and gained time to prepare for the battles ahead.

The next and final battle came a month later when the Socialists, with Communist support, proposed a 20 per cent cut in the military budget. The debate began on New Year's Eve, continuing through New Year's Day. Premier de Gaulle had to go to the assembly and demand that the cuts be restored immediately. He warned the deputies:

> I want to tell you now: if you do not respect the necessary conditions for responsible and dignified government, you are heading for a time when you will bitterly regret the path you have chosen. . . . The government alone bears the responsibility of executive power. If this confidence is withdrawn, even partially, the government will resign.

The deputies were once again outraged by de Gaulle's concept of power and responsibility. They pointed out that in a democratic republic, like America, the division of power gave the congress the authority to approve budgets and authorize funds for executive programs. They claimed that de Gaulle saw himself as a monarch or a dictator, reducing parliament to a rubber-stamp role. Once again, however, the Catholics prevailed upon the Socialists not to join the Communists in a move to overthrow de Gaulle. The Socialists accepted a subamendment which in effect postponed the decision for three months.

De Gaulle had had just about enough. His "victories" gave him no satisfaction, for they were never definitive. He had nothing but contempt for his opponents and loathed the political fighting, which he described as mud-slinging contests in an infested swamp. It was quite clear to de Gaulle, as it was to the parties, that the majority of the delegates to the Constituent Assembly favored a parliamentary system of government, with the executive power subject to the legislative. De Gaulle could not, and would not even attempt to, govern France under such a system. He had won the battle of the budget but not the war against the parties.

* * *

Parliament recessed for a New Year's holiday, and General de Gaulle decided to leave Paris for a holiday on the Riviera. He went to the Cap d'Antibes for "rest and reflection." On January 9 reporters received word that the Premier would receive them at a press conference.

The conference was a relaxed and informal affair. De Gaulle looked well and was in good humor. He refused to talk politics and, instead, delivered to us a rhapsodic lecture on the beauties of the Côte d'Azur and its qualities as a tourist center that would bring important revenues and prestige to France. He stayed on for another five days before returning to Paris. There was no hint of any emergency or pending crisis.

Reporters returned to Paris with de Gaulle and settled down for the new political season following the parliamentary recess. Nothing very important was on the calendar in January, and I was surprised to receive a call from Jacques Menachem, a spokesman in the Premier's office, inviting me to a "small, confidential luncheon session" with the minister of information, André Malraux, France's famous writer, a close "companion" of General de Gaulle.

The luncheon took place at one of the great four-star restaurants

of France, in a private salon. Accompanying M. Malraux were
Menachem and Malraux's chief administrative assistant at the
time, Raymond Aron, one of the early members of the Free
French team in London, then a fervent Gaullist, who has since
become an independent and often critical commentator of French
affairs. Aron is now a professor of sociology and an internationally
respected columnist and author, sometimes described as a French
Walter Lippmann. The other men present were American foreign
correspondents.*

Malraux discussed everything but politics during the excellent
meal. He put on one of his brilliant performances, ranging from
an analysis of the theater of Giraudoux to a critique of Bergson
and Bachalard through a series of anecdotes about Molière and
Balzac to a history of French Canada, all in the most complicated
prose that exploded out of him in snorts, sniffs and whistles, like a
locomotive pulling out of a station. It was all terribly Parisian,
titillating, delightful and apparently without other purpose than
"getting together" with the press.

But suddenly we discovered the real purpose. Malraux put it to
us simply but dramatically: "Gentlemen, you were present at the
year-end debate on the budget. You are familiar with the serious
problems we have been facing at home and in the world. It is
necessary that you American correspondents understand the issues
and the thinking of General de Gaulle. I must tell you quite
frankly that the General is, to put it bluntly, appalled by the chaos
of politics and the anarchy of world affairs. He has no intention of
tolerating the situation as it now prevails. He believes, indeed, that
it is very dangerous."

Under questioning, and without much reluctance or fencing,
Malraux drew a picture of Russia and America driving a collision
course over the prostrate body of Europe while competing for
imperial dominion in Asia. As for France, politicians were falling
into all the vicious old habits that had undermined the Third
Republic while the Communists, "a highly organized revolutionary force, were plotting to undermine the Republic until it
collapsed into their arms." At one point Malraux, in answer to a
question, snapped back with a question of his own: "Would you

* Harold Callendar, *The New York Times;* William J. Humphrey, *New
York Herald Tribune;* Relman Morin, Associated Press; Joseph Grigg,
United Press; Henry Cassidy, NBC. I recall that there were one or two
more whose names did not show up in the notes I wrote after the session.
I was representing CBS Radio and the Overseas News Agency at the time.

Americans like to see the Russians in Paris?" He went on to say, "For that is what you will see if you do not support General de Gaulle and the true France when the crisis comes, as it soon may." He warned, "Do not think that General de Gaulle will necessarily care to carry this burden much longer." *

Malraux's warnings about Russian-American tension were not remarkably novel, although he stated them more sharply than most cabinet ministers would normally dare. Very remarkable, however, and in fact startling, was Malraux's suggestion that there was a Communist plot to subvert the republic that might open up the gates to a Russian takeover of France. More than startling was the very strong hint that General de Gaulle might be planning to resign, which was the only conclusion to be drawn from the remark about his not being willing to "carry this burden much longer."

Malraux was as close to de Gaulle as any man; as minister of information he must have known what he was talking about, particularly in a talk with foreign correspondents. Yet we all found it impossible to take his statements at face value for several reasons. In the first place, it was unprecedented for a minister of information, and a minister of de Gaulle above all, to reveal to foreigners a national secret as important as the fact that the premier was considering resignation. Had Malraux clearly stated this, we would have believed it, but we could not dare trust his oblique suggestions, particularly when they were delivered in his rapid, complex syntax. Malraux also had a reputation as both a firebrand and a very clever propagandist. No group of reporters was more wary of being "used" by a top Gaullist official than the American press corps of Paris. Every man at the table had his

* When I recently asked Aron to verify my notes and recollections of what turned out to be a memorable luncheon, he said that he does not keep notes himself but remembered the luncheon well although more than twenty years have now passed since that January 18, 1945. Aron recalled that just after New Year's Day he had helped Malraux plan and schedule a series of meetings with the "Anglo-Saxon" and other foreign correspondents. "We did not know when we scheduled your lunch that an important change in French politics was pending," Aron said. Aron told me that he does not recall today the specific statements made by Malraux but that my notes correspond to his recollection of the basic situation. He said that Malraux and he knew on that day that de Gaulle had decided to resign. He also said that Malraux's reference to "the Russians in Paris," as I noted it down, "sounds very much like Malraux and the views he expressed."

strongest defenses up, particularly when a de Gaulle minister began talking of Soviet-American tensions and playing upon the Americans' well-known anti-Communism. For all these reasons the top veteran correspondents—men like "Pat" Morin of the AP and Harold Callendar of the *Times*—decided against writing any stories, not even the most careful "think pieces," until they had "checked out" Malraux's hints with several other sources.*

The "check-out" period did not last long. Less than forty-eight hours after our confidential luncheon with Malraux, we were called urgently by Gaston Palewski, de Gaulle's official spokesman, who, when we arrived at his office, announced that General de Gaulle had called in the cabinet that morning and had announced his "irrevocable" decision to resign. Palewski said that the formal letter of resignation would be delivered to the President of the Constituent Assembly later in the day. Much later that night, at about 10 P.M. Palewski held a press conference in which he stated, "This is not just the tender of a resignation. De Gaulle is leaving office irrevocably." We were then told that de Gaulle would explain his decision to the people in a radio address the next day, Monday, January 21.

No radio address was made. Socialist Party leader Vincent Auriol, who later would become the first president of the Fourth Republic, persuaded de Gaulle to abandon his plan to take to the air again, as he had done in the November crisis. Having quit his post, he no longer had the authority to commandeer the national radio network. It would have been not only illegal and unethical but would, said Auriol, take on the characteristics of a Caesarean or Napoleonic plebiscite, if not the appearance of encouragement to insurrection. General de Gaulle finally decided to accept Auriol's warnings and cancel his planned broadcast.

The circumstances and manner of de Gaulle's departure shocked, stunned and frightened the nation. At first the people could hardly believe the news, and in fact it took some time before most of the citizens even knew that de Gaulle had resigned, for he had chosen to walk out on a Sunday and at a moment when the parliament was in recess. Also, no papers were published on Sunday or on Monday in postliberation France because of mate-

---

* There was no way of knowing at that time just why Malraux had taken this line with us and why he was preparing us for de Gaulle's resignation. I discovered the reason very much later, as explained on page 194.

rial shortages. A few papers brought out one-sheet extras, but most of the country did not know exactly what had happened until Tuesday, January 22. In the absence of papers rumors spread wildly throughout France; in the absence of any explanation other than the unbelievable official letter saying that France no longer needed him, there was, among political leaders, bewilderment and uneasiness about de Gaulle's true reasons and future intentions. Nobody believed that "all was well," as the letter stated, and no one believed that de Gaulle, at the age of fifty-five, was going to retire from public life at the height of his powers.

The bewilderment and disbelief of the official letter was best expressed by prewar Premier Léon Blum in the Socialist Party paper *Le Populaire:*

> In the absence of the assembly, after consistently unanimous confidence votes, without any difficulty inside his cabinet, with no specific dispute between his government and any of the majority parties supporting him, in a word without any immediate, understandable cause—what reaction other than stupor and shock could such a sudden, brusk decision cause?

The stupor and shock were only increased by de Gaulle's disappearance from the scene. He first spent a few days resting at the presidential hunting lodge at Marly, then locked himself away from all contacts at the country estate of his brother-in-law. After six years of dominating French affairs, from his first appeal to resistance in 1940 through the strife-ridden but hope-infused illuminations of the long fight back to liberate France, General de Gaulle had suddenly and completely dropped out of sight. It was like an eclipse of the sun or the silence after a terrible battle, all dark and broodingly ominous. Had he fallen ill or dead, the shock could not have been greater, but, in a strange way, the fears would have been less. A great nation and people can survive the loss of any man no matter how dominant he is or how much he is needed. What made the French nervous in the year 1946 was the uncertainty surrounding de Gaulle's mysterious resignation and retreat at a moment when none of the fundamental challenges to France's future had been met.

The highways, bridges and communication networks had not been completely restored, nor had the productive machinery been rebuilt. Economic recovery was only limping along, not marching ahead, as de Gaulle had claimed in his official letter of resignation.

The reconquest of French imperial territories had not been solidly won. There had been serious riots in Tunisia on V-E Day itself. The resistance leader of Indochina, Ho Chi Minh, had emerged from the underground in the wake of the Japanese collapse and had proclaimed the freedom and independence of Vietnam. There were ominous rumblings of revolt throughout the entire French Empire, which were soon to erupt into the terrible war of Indochina.

The assembly had not completed its work on a draft constitution. Politically France still had only an embryonic state. There was no republic, no agreed form of government. The threat of Communist subversion of France was greater than ever, with the Communist Party able to boast of its first position at the polling booths and its absolute domination of the strongest unions of France. Most of its resistance fighters had not handed over their guns, as de Gaulle had demanded. France was an armed camp, and the constant menace of civil war still hung over the land. De Gaulle's letter of resignation blithely ignored these grim realities. As a farewell address, it was not one of his better efforts.

* * *

Until his decision to quit his post and disappear broodingly into the countryside, General de Gaulle's quarrels and conflicts with his fellow Gauls had taken place in the framework of a united front against the enemies of France. After January 20, 1946, the conflict between de Gaulle and the Gauls would become direct, open civil strife that could only end in total victory or total defeat for one side or the other.

The mistress of a king of France once said, with supreme disdain for the consequences of her lover's acts: "After us, the deluge." General de Gaulle was destined to give a new twist to those words in the deluge that followed after him, a deluge that eventually engulfed all the contending forces in the civil war between de Gaulle and the Gauls.

CHAPTER SEVEN

AFTER THE DELUGE, DE GAULLE

On the surface, I would have been within my rights to prolong the kind of monarchy that I had assumed not so long ago and that finally had been confirmed by the general will.

* * *

The momentary dictatorship that I exercised in the course of the tempest, and that I would not hesitate to prolong or revive if the country were again in danger, I did not wish to cling to when the public safety was once again an accomplished fact.

CHARLES DE GAULLE, *Memoirs, Volume III, 1959*

AFTER THE FIRST SHOCK of de Gaulle's abrupt departure, the majority parties rose to the challenge and moved swiftly to demonstrate that they could govern France without the great man.

Only three days after de Gaulle's resignation the leaders of the "Big Three" parties—the Communists, Socialists and Catholics— agreed to elect a man from their own ranks to replace the General. In a night session at the assembly, Socialist Félix Gouin was voted in as premier of the provisional government. The election was a shadow of coming events, accurately reflecting the kind of republic that France would live under for most of the next decade: a government of coalition headed by a relatively obscure politician whom no one feared, thus leaving real power in the hands of rival party leaders who canceled each other out. It was not a balance of powers but a paralysis of power.

Jealous and mistrustful of each other, the three major parties carefully divided the government among themselves in a three-way division of the spoils. Socialist Premier Gouin was flanked on his right and left by Catholic Francisque Gay and Communist leader Maurice Thorez as vice-premiers. Ministry portfolios were dealt around the table like playing cards in a three-handed game: one for the Socialists, one for the Catholics and one for the Communists. There was only one significant restriction on the deal: the deck was stacked against the Communists exactly as de Gaulle had marked the cards two months earlier. The Communists did not get the police, the diplomacy or the army. The interior ministry that controlled the national police forces went to Socialist André Le Trocquer, the foreign ministry to Catholic Georges Bidault and the national defense ministry was split in two, as de Gaulle had split it, between Catholic Michelet, in charge of the armed forces, and Communist Tillon, in charge of armaments.

The very same editorialists who had denounced de Gaulle for insulting the Communists, "our comrades of the resistance," were strangely silent when the resistance comrades all agreed among themselves to do exactly as de Gaulle had done. No one trusted the Communists any more than de Gaulle did, but no one, including the Communists, protested this mistrust as they had protested against de Gaulle.

Having agreed upon a provisional government, the parties set about the urgent task of making it permanent by drafting the constitution of a new republic. With de Gaulle safely and silently out of the way they had a clear field on which to build their dream house of the people—that is, a highly centralized republic with sovereign power in a single house of parliament, the national assembly. It was a modern re-creation of the revolutionary assembly of 1793 and would surely have been as unworkable an experiment in government-by-assembly as had the first attempt. It was not, fortunately, put to the test, for the draft constitution—to everyone's astonishment—was rejected by the French people.

The vote took place in the national referendum of May 5, 1946. The people were asked to vote "Oui" or "Non" on the draft constitution that had been prepared by the majority parties and this was the result:

Oui	9,454,000
Non	10,585,000

The songwriters had been wrong again. Paris is not lovely in the spring and, in France, they do not say oui, oui. In the springtime of 1946 it was cold and rained constantly, and in France they said non, non, loud and clear. General de Gaulle had had the last laugh. Even in silent retreat he had defeated the parties, for the French people remembered his warnings about the abuse of power by the absolute sovereignty of parliament.

The rejection of the draft ended the life of the constituent assembly, and new elections had to be held for a second constituent group. The decisions took place on June 2, and the results confirmed the swing away from the Communist-Socialist bloc that had tried to force its "people's democracy" on the French nation. The Catholic Party, M.R.P., displaced the Communists from the position of first party of France:

Catholics	5,589,000
Communists	5,199,000
Socialists	4,188,000

This represented a big shift since the elections of the first constituent assembly on October 21, 1945, only some six months earlier. The Catholics had jumped from 4,780,000 to 5,589,000—a gain of 800,000 votes. They had picked up half of those gains from the Socialists, who dropped by 400,000, and half from the center and right-wing voters. These were citizens who, frightened by the Communist menace, sought to strengthen the Catholics who had campaigned as the "party of fidelity" to de Gaulle, although de Gaulle, still silent, had not endorsed them. Thus the Communists were faced with a powerful rival inside the tripartite coalition. They were not unduly disturbed, for they had held their strength and had even increased their total by 100,000. They were not at all unhappy to see the Socialists getting squeezed out of position.

The new "first party" won the premiership for its most prestigious member, Georges Bidault, wartime President of the Resistance Council, postliberation foreign minister of General de Gaulle's first cabinet. Bidault ordered full speed ahead for a new draft constitution, knowing that France's prestige in the world as well as her internal security depended on establishing a legal republic. Confident of his strength as leader of the first party, aware that the Communists and the Socialists above all would be less rigid in their demands, he proposed to them that the tripartite coalition be maintained, that it preserve the principle of parliamentary democracy but modify the extreme form of legislative power that had been rejected by the people in the referendum.

General de Gaulle had kept total silence ever since his resignation in January. He broke his self-imposed silence on June 16 at the moment that the new government was being formed, following the elections of June 2 to the second constituent assembly. Although the country had voted against the Socialist-Communist first draft, General de Gaulle wanted to make sure that the second assembly, with a strong pro-Gaullist, Catholic element, would draw up the kind of constitution that would give France a stable and efficient executive, able to withstand the power of parliament.

He chose the historic Norman city of Bayeux, the first major city liberated in the landings, as the site to consecrate his vision of a new France. On a beautiful sunny summer Sunday flags were flying from every rooftop and were draped on every balcony. There were flowers everywhere—the whole city was a garden. At the street corners were erected miniature Arcs de Triomphe, decorated with flowers and fruit and all bearing blue, white and red banners inscribed with the words, "General de Gaulle, premier résistant de France."

Accompanying the First Resistant were some of the first men who answered his call to resistance: General Koenig, Admiral Thierry d'Argenlieu, Gaston Palewski, Jacques Soustelle, René Capitant and the man who had been his spokesman from London on the nightly broadcasts "Les français parlent aux français," Maurice Schumann. With de Gaulle at the head of the procession, they made their way through cheering, laughing, crying crowds to the cathedral to celebrate a high mass and a Te Deum. Then they lunched and thereupon marched to the liberation monument through crowds that had begun to chant, "De Gaulle au pouvoir! Au pouvoir! Au pouvoir!" reaching a peak of frenzy when the Liberator walked up to the rostrum and lifted his huge arms in the giant V sign into which he transformed his body. The crowd had become a mob screaming its demand that de Gaulle come back to power. For a full five minutes he could not speak over the chanted screams of "Au pouvoir!"

Finally the people, worn out by their own delirium, quieted down, and General de Gaulle began to speak, his first words since his abrupt farewell at the start of the year. "The public powers have no validity, in fact or in law, unless they are in accord with the superior interests of the country and repose on the confident approval of the citizens," said General de Gaulle. Once again he was laying down his fundamental concept of government, based on the idea of legitimacy over and above legality. It was a dangerous concept, for it was indefinable. Who is to say with infallibility what constitutes the "superior interests of the country" and how can one measure reliably the "confidence" of the citizens' approval of the public powers? Few men have de Gaulle's own massive self-confidence in his unique ability to answer those questions without hesitation.

De Gaulle stated that he had served this superior interest of the country, had reestablished the public powers after breaking the bonds of France's slavery and had therefore been able to resign "once the train was back on the rails." He had resigned, he said, because he did not want to engage in a direct power contest with the political parties which would have forced him to bring into the fight the special qualities that he "symbolized" and that "belong to the nation as a whole." He did not, that is, "want the constitution to be made for or against himself" because of what he represented. Therefore he had resigned, retired and retreated into silence.

De Gaulle then stated that his faith in his decision and in the French people had been justified and confirmed by the rejection of the draft constitution the month before, without his having personally interfered or having influenced the decision in any way. Now, he said, it was proper for him to speak out and tell the people what kind of institutions they needed for a strong France. Above all, said de Gaulle, "we must guarantee the authority and prestige of the state," particularly in the light of the narrow views but profound appetite for power of the parties.

General de Gaulle called for a constitution broad enough to include all the French territories in the world, "on a scale of a French Union of peoples," including metropolitan France, the Saar and all the overseas lands of the old empire. He proposed that it be flexible enough to evolve in step with the progressive advances of the peoples in education and political maturity, toward a vast worldwide "federation" of France. De Gaulle used the word "federation" in the particular French sense for which the closest American equivalent would be "confederation," or the British, "commonwealth."

The French Republic would be founded on the twin principles

of Montesquieu: separation of powers and balance of powers. General de Gaulle warned particularly against the dangers not only of an all-powerful single house as proposed in the draft constitution just rejected, but even of a too powerful assembly, as had existed in the prewar Third Republic. De Gaulle proposed a bicameral system, something midway between the British system of Commons and Lords and the American House and Senate. In the Gaullist concept, the people's assembly would be less powerful than the Commons but more powerful than the House. In order to guarantee a further separation and balance, the chief of state would have considerable powers, more than in any previous French republic, but less than the power of the American presidency. The true chief of the executive power, he would designate personally all of his ministers, including the prime minister. This would be a radical departure from past French history, for the prime minister had traditionally been designated by the national assembly, rather than by the president of the republic. The president, as de Gaulle saw the office, would play the role of the arbiter of the nation, above the parties, above the parliament. He would have the unconditional power to dissolve the parliament.

De Gaulle argued that he was proposing a "marriage" of the British and American systems: in Britain, a prime minister can dissolve parliament by handing in the resignation of his party to the sovereign; an American president is elected by the direct suffrage of the entire nation and is not chosen by the parliament. He called this "marriage" a form of "presidential democracy." De Gaulle's thinking was influenced by the fact that in 1940 there was no single national authority vested in one man who could have gone to London to continue the fight. The power was vested in a huge, unwieldy parliament, totaling almost one thousand members, which could not move in a crisis and which abdicated its sovereignty when the enemy armies invaded and overwhelmed the country. He was also undoubtedly thinking of how he had had his hands tied by the postliberation assembly despite all his personal authority.

All the major parties, with the single exception of the Catholics, "the party of fidelity to General de Gaulle," reacted unfavorably to the "Bayeux Constitution." The Communists immediately denounced it as a step toward dictatorship: "This chief of state could not help but dream of Caesarism with such power in his hands," said the Communist Party parliamentary leader, Jacques Duclos.

The Socialists, too, raised the red flag of warning against Caesarism. Léon Blum wrote in the *Populaire,* "The Assembly alone, directly elected by all the people, must be collectively responsible to the people and must have the first and last word. A presidential power of dissolution would be a tyrant's dagger poised over the heart of parliament." The moderates and conservatives approved those proposals which put some brakes on the assembly but not the proposal that "would give the president the power to blow up the assembly." "Dissolution is a dangerous bomb in any man's hands," said the spokesman of the Radical Party.

Although the Catholics were the first party of France and "the party of fidelity," their leader, Georges Bidault, knew they could not govern without the consent of the other parties, and they were, in the crucial test ahead, more faithful to the parliamentary republic and to their own personal aspirations than to the person of General de Gaulle. Bidault met with Communist leader Thorez and Socialists Blum and Auriol and in a series of intense conferences worked out a tripartite compromise that gave the real power to the national assembly but dressed up the measure and covered it up with a number of devices that made it look as though the senate had a significant share in the legislative power, while the façade of a worldwide "French Union" was to be erected.

The "Union" would prove to be a global Potemkin village, and the national assembly would toss off its loose dressings rapidly to emerge as the central power of the republic, with the executive its prisoner. But the truth would be proved only in the application of the constitution; it was not clearly perceived in the draft—or, if it was, the people were wearied of debate and fearful of prolonging the dangerous and embarrassing absence of a legal state. Despite de Gaulle's opposition and despite the deep doubts of millions of Frenchmen, the second draft constitution proposed by the major parties was approved in the national referendum of October 13, 1946.

General de Gaulle did not like the second draft any more than the first. On September 22, when the constituent assembly was voting to adopt the final draft for presentation to the people, General de Gaulle spoke out against it. At Epinal, on the anniversary of its liberation, he denounced the draft and called upon the French people to vote no a second time. De Gaulle charged that the draft did not respect "the principles of separation of powers" in such a manner as to "assure an established equilibrium so that one might not be able to crush the other." He predicted that such a constitution could only lead to anarchy first and then to tyranny either by a man, by a group of men, by a party or by a group of parties. This was indeed the evidence of history from 1793 to 1799, when the all-powerful first assembly degenerated into chaos, to be followed by the tyranny of Robespierre, Danton, the Terror, the Convention, the Directory and, finally, Napoleon.

De Gaulle's criticism was based upon principles which he had long espoused publicly: a strong executive, a president of the republic "above parties" as the arbiter of the nation and guardian of its independence, all of which he would put into practice himself very much later in the Fifth Republic. The only surprise in the Epinal speech was his anger and the violence of his words, particularly in his denial of charges that the parties had made against him as a political dictator. He said that he viewed with "an ironclad disdain the devisory imputations of dictatorial ambitions that certain people are spreading against me today."

It was not like de Gaulle to betray anger, and extremely unusual for him to rage against charges of dictatorial ambitions. These had been made often enough in the past six years, and he either laughed them off or disdained to reply at all. Rarely if ever had he angrily denied such charges in a major public address.

It was not possible to find out at that time just why de Gaulle was so stung by charges which he had shrugged off a hundred times, just as it had been impossible to understand Malraux's motives in warning us of de Gaulle's impending resignation. Ever since 1946 these curious incidents had been part of the unsolved mystery of de Gaulle's abrupt resignation and full year of inactivity before his return to the political wars early in 1947.

The mystery was still a subject of speculation in 1965, revived by a new piece of "evidence" presented in a book called *La République des illusions* by Georgette Elbey, a French journalist and chronicler of contemporary history. She spent several years digging through the records of the Fourth Republic and interviewing hundreds of the leading actors in its drama. Among the men she interviewed was Francisque Gay, the Catholic Party minister in the early postliberation cabinets. According to Gay, he had gone to see de Gaulle to plead with him not to resign. De Gaulle told him not to worry because the party leaders would be so frightened that in a short time they would beg him to come back and he would be able to set his own terms that would permit him to govern France efficiently.

If we are to accept Georgette Elbey's report on the event, de Gaulle's decision was not really as "irrevocable" as he had pretended but was a carefully calculated scare thrown at the party leaders to make them yield to de Gaulle's will. This version was given considerable prominence in the press in April 1965, when the Elbey book was published.

Francisque Gay had died before the publication and there was no other witness or corroborating evidence to his version of the resignation. There is no reason to doubt that he was sincere and truthful in his statements to Georgette Elbey. I knew Francisque Gay well and believe that he told the exact truth—that de Gaulle did indeed tell him that he expected to be called back. But that does not mean that de Gaulle was sincere in what he told Francisque Gay. On the contrary, I am convinced by all the evidence I have gathered since, and by a knowledge of de Gaulle's own politics and character, that he did not expect to be called back and would not have come back even if the politicians had begged him to.

In the first place, de Gaulle had never derived his power and authority of office from the politicians and would never accept such an investiture except as the most superficial formality. He despised the political system and most of the politicians. He had been self-invested, by rising to the challenge of history, as he had explained so many times to Churchill, Admiral Stark, Roosevelt and many others, just as Joan of Arc and Clemenceau had arisen to save France. At the liberation he had accepted the formality of political endorsement, for he did not want to govern except under democratic and republican procedures, but he always felt that he represented the nation and was responsible directly to all the people and not to the politicians. This is so basically de Gaulle that it cannot be doubted.

It is not logical to believe that de Gaulle would go through a grotesque charade such as Francisque Gay described. It is true that he had several times before played the game of tendering a resignation and then letting himself be persuaded to take it back. But never before had he gone all the way through the game to the point of actually quitting, announcing that his decision was irrevocable and then going into seclusion. His departure in January 1946 was no game. He simply slammed the door shut and ended the story. Knowing how much the parties feared and disliked him, he would have had to be a wild gambler and a dreamer to count on their calling him back at that point. He would also have little respect for the French people or himself if he thought he could go back on such an "irrevocable" decision and still be taken seriously by anybody thereafter.

The evidence points in a completely different direction. De Gaulle did not expect to be called back, he planned to come back on his own, in a coup d'état, as soon as the necessary conditions for a coup came about, as he felt *almost* certain they would. The key word that explains what finally happened is "almost." For the first and only time in his life, Charles de Gaulle was not sure of himself. He hesitated and wavered at a critical moment.

The first sign of hesitation was his decision to cancel the radio address to the nation that he had planned to make the day after his resignation. Aside from de Gaulle himself, only two men knew why he changed his mind then. One of these men, Léon Blum, is dead; the other, Vincent Auriol, is a very old and sick man. Neither ever revealed his secret. However, there is reason to believe that they did have an important secret to keep.

There is something very unreal about the official explanation of their insistence to de Gaulle that he not make that radio address. The argument that it would enrage the parties and revive the old charges of going over their heads to the people in a Caesarlike manner is not convincing. The old charges were based, very properly, on his going to the people in a dispute with the parties on a critical issue of substance, but this is completely different from the intention simply to deliver a farewell address. After all, his letter of resignation had denied that there was any crisis. All was sweetness and light, he said. France was on the rails again and rolling. France did not need de Gaulle, so he was relinquishing the heavy burden he had so long borne.

What was so terrible about that explanation which would motivate Blum and Auriol to plead with him not to go on the air? Obviously nothing. Therefore there must have been something other than the innocent farewell address of the official version.

A hint of something else can be found in the French annual almanac called *L'Année politique* for the year 1946.* In it de Gaulle is reported to have planned a radio speech "in which he

---

* Published at that time by the Editions du Grand Siècle, the series has since been taken over by Presses Universitaires de France, 49 Boulevard St. Michel, Paris.

would explain to the French the *true reasons* for his brusque decision." The editor of *L'Année politique* went on to add that an alleged copy of the radio text was "circulated" in Paris a few weeks later. The text was an attack on the political party system, denouncing particularly the "compact and disciplined parties" which made it impossible to get any true representation of public opinion. The editor added that General de Gaulle "has never disavowed or affirmed the authenticity of the text" and that therefore he could not vouch for its reliability.

Although it is impossible to prove definitely, there is no reason not to believe that the text was authentic. It fits all the facts. The views expressed are genuine, for de Gaulle had said the same thing before and he repeated the same attack on the parties and the "system" ad infinitum thereafter. It would explain why Blum and Auriol begged him not to go on the air, for he was planning to deliver, not a peaceful farewell address, but rather one designed as a declaration of political warfare against the constituent assembly. It could well have led to an outbreak of civil war between the paramilitary, well-armed clandestine forces that existed throughout France, with the country split between the Gaullists and Communists. That would exactly fit the situation which prevailed in France at that time.

A planned de Gaulle radio appeal to the people would also explain why Malraux had quite suddenly decided to warn Americans about an impending resignation and the threat of seeing the Russians in Paris. If there were going to be a test of strength and a possible outbreak of civil hostilities, it would be imperative for de Gaulle to prepare and to win over world public opinion and, above all, the sympathy of foreign troops not very far away in the occupation zone of Germany. De Gaulle knew perfectly well that he was extremely unpopular in Washington. Truman had less use for him than even Roosevelt had. The only sure way to win American support would be to wave the red flag of a Communist peril. Examined from this viewpoint, the Malraux luncheon becomes very understandable.

All of this is deduction—very persuasive deduction, but not proof. It is, however, an explanation that fits all the facts better than any official or other version so far known. There is, moreover, documentary evidence that fits into this analysis so perfectly that it leaves little room for doubt. De Gaulle himself has testified, both in his writings and in public speeches, that he was considering a coup d'état to seize power at that time.

The admissions came several years later, but they apply chrono-
logically to the year 1946, during which a number of Gaullists
urged the General to lead a coup or to give them the green light to
go ahead and act for him. This not only suggests a fascinating
drama in itself, but also throws new light on the coup that was
actually engineered in 1958, the coup d'état of Algiers, which
brought de Gaulle back to the office that he quit in 1946, on
his own terms at last. I have long believed that the coup d'état of
May 13, 1958, was set off by a delayed-reaction time-bomb whose
fuse was first lighted in 1946.

De Gaulle struck the match that lighted it publicly in his Epinal
speech in September 1946, when he appealed to the French people
to reject the draft constitution. When the people failed to heed him
and approved the constitution, he held up a big torch in April
1947, emerging from frustrated retirement to announce the formation of a new national movement. He called it "le Rassemblement
du Peuple Français," deliberately choosing the word "rassemblement" or "rally" to avoid calling it a political party.

This was and remains today one of the basic contradictions and
confusions in de Gaulle's thinking. There are only two ways to
come to power: by free elections or by a coup d'état. To win power
freely at the polls, it is necessary to participate in the political
system and to operate through an organized, orthodox political
party. This Charles de Gaulle refused to do. The alternative is a
coup d'état. That alternative was rejected by Charles de Gaulle
after long reflection throughout the year 1946. It was not until
1958 that he felt the time for a coup was ripe.

General de Gaulle publicly hinted at the use of force on a
number of occasions. For example, at the R.P.F. national convention in Lille on February 12, 1949:

> If by adventure or by misfortune those who are abusing
> their power should come to the point of strangling
> democracy by suppressing a consultation with the people,
> then there would be only one course to follow: to drive
> out the usurpers.

A roar of applause from 3,000 delegates acclaimed this unmistakable threat. A storm of controversy broke over the country when
de Gaulle followed this up the next day by appearing on the
balcony of the town hall of Lille, his native city, and shouting,

"We are France, we are the future." A barrage of editorials blasted de Gaulle as an apprentice dictator. Socialist leader Jules Moch, the minister of the interior who had broken the Communist nation-wide strikes a year earlier, stated that the republic was ready and able to defend itself against an insurrection from the right as well as from the left. He called de Gaulle a would-be Caesar.

De Gaulle, unabashed, continued to make similar threats: at the R.P.F. rally in the Vélodrome d'Hiver, in February 1950; again at Levallois-Perret, in March 1951. Finally, in July 1952, at a meeting in Saint-Maur, General de Gaulle delivered a discourse on French politics to explain why he had definitely decided against the use of force. He explained that it was his conviction that the requisite conditions for a successful seizure of power did not prevail.*

The final proof of de Gaulle's thinking on this issue was provided beyond any possible doubt by General de Gaulle in his memoirs. He pinpointed the key conditions of a successful coup in these words: "beyond the period of public danger there can be no lasting dictatorship." He added the thought that dictatorship can only thrive "on a great national ambition or the fear of a menaced people." In this view the key conditions, "public danger," "fear" and "national ambition," did prevail during the liberation campaign, permitting him, thus, to exercise "a kind of monarchy."

In January 1946, however, there was no clear and present danger that would, in de Gaulle's opinion, justify the French people's acceptance of a monarchy or a dictatorship. He resigned irrevocably, therefore, because he could not govern efficiently and because the conditions were not ripe for a coup d'état at that time. Lest there be any doubt that he meant this, he went on to state that he had kept himself ready to strike a coup if circumstances should bring about the necessary conditions. He put it, in his memoirs, in these completely unabashed terms:

> The momentary dictatorship that I exercised in the course of the tempest, and that I would not hesitate to prolong or revive if the country were again in danger, I

* The Lille speech is reprinted in full in *L'Année politique 1949.* The Vélodrome d'Hiver and Levallois-Perret speeches are found in the collection *La France sera la France,* containing his speeches and statements from 1946 through 1951, published by the R. P. F. The Saint-Maur speech appears in the July 11, 1952, edition of the R. P. F. journal, *Le Rassemblement.*

did not wish to cling to when the public safety was once
again an established fact.

It seems to this observer that these documentary attestations,
read along with the deductive and circumstantial evidence, provide the solution to the mysterious case of the General's strange
behavior. If one lists the clues, one by one, in logical sequence, in
Sherlock Holmes' time-honored style of reconstruction, the barest
summary is overwhelming:

1. De Gaulle's statement in *The Edge of the Sword* that the
price of leadership is painful and that "it constantly happens that
men with an unbroken record of success and public applause
suddenly lay the burden down."

2. De Gaulle suddenly lays the burden down on January 20,
1946, after the painful suffering of the year-end budget debate.

3. De Gaulle ponders the conditions for dictatorship and con-
cludes that it is possible in France only in times of national danger
and fear. Meanwhile, his minister of information and confidant,
André Malraux, spreads the word that there is a great danger of a
Sovietization of France.

4. De Gaulle is not certain whether this is sufficient to justify a
coup d'état. In his letter of resignation he admits that there is no
clear and present danger, but he sees a hidden cancer in the
political system and he plans to warn the French against it in a
radio appeal to the people.

5. De Gaulle cancels the radio appeal when Socialists Blum and
Auriol warn him that it would provoke charges of dictatorship
and would turn many people away from him.

6. De Gaulle goes into silent retreat and reflection to weigh the
imponderables of French politics and public emotions. Are Blum
and Auriol right? Would the people turn against him? Or would
a coup d'état succeed? Or is there some other way to govern
France?

7. De Gaulle decides that the conditions for a coup are not ripe.
He launches the R.P.F. as a political action movement to help him
win power at the polls.

8. De Gaulle admits in speeches to the R.P.F. activists that he
spent a long time considering the advisability of a coup d'état and
finally rejected it on the grounds that there was not a great enough
peril or national ambition for the French to pay the price of a
dictatorship.

9. De Gaulle confesses in his memoirs that he had imposed "a kind of monarchy" and a "momentary dictatorship" under war conditions and that he would not hesitate to revive it if France were again in danger and if circumstances called for such a move.

10. In May 1958 all the necessary conditions and circumstances come together: the war in Algeria; the recurrent cabinet crises that had led to the decline of government authority and cohesion in Paris; the fragmentation of French society; the anger and frustration of the army officers; the surrender of French sovereignty to the Americans in NATO and to European "technocrats"—in brief, a very clear menace to the nation.

* * *

This was the essence of the hot-and-cold civil war that was unceasingly fought between de Gaulle and the political leaders of France from the day of his resignation as premier in January 1946. It was a tortuous and complex battle, fought both out in the open and in the underground of French life, with plots within plots and an unholy, undeclared but real alliance of circumstance between the Gaullists and the Communists, strange fellow-travelers in a common contempt for the republic, with a jointly fought but separately held objective of power in France.

Both de Gaulle and the Communists denounced the final draft constitution of the Fourth Republic, which was narrowly approved by a small plurality, amounting to a minority of the French people. The total of the opposition votes and the nonvoting abstentionists among the confused citizens represented a majority of the electorate. The Fourth Republic was doomed at birth by the Gaullist-Communist twin opposition. It is astonishing that it lasted eleven years and achieved great progress for the country, squeezed as it was in the deadly right-left pincers of a disloyal opposition. As de Gaulle himself told visitors in moments of despair at ever coming back to power, "The Republic governs France badly but defends itself well."

The Fourth Republic defended itself so well in 1952 that General de Gaulle suffered a serious setback. His own R.P.F. movement was split and seduced by politician Antoine Pinay. Pinay appeared on the scene out of nowhere. He had not even been eligible for election to the first constituent assembly because he had been a wartime delegate to the Vichy national council. He was an obscure little businessman from central France, a leather merchant, a kind of conservative French Harry Truman if one can imagine Truman as a true conservative. He was the direct antithesis of de Gaulle, and he arrived on the scene at a moment when de Gaulle's star was dimming.

Six years had gone by since General de Gaulle had resigned. His R.P.F. had started off like a meteor, winning almost 40 per cent of the votes in the nationwide municipal elections in the fall of 1947 and reaching a peak in the parliamentary elections of 1951, when the Gaullist lists won a total of more than four million votes. This made the R.P.F. the second party of France electorally, just a million short of the Communist total, but it became the first party of France in terms of seats won in the assembly, for many of the Communist votes were wasted in big pluralities in working-class constituencies. The Gaullists won 118 seats against 104 for the Communists and 103 for the Socialists. The Catholics, who were briefly the first party of France in 1946 when de Gaulle was absent from the scene, had fallen by 1951 to 85 seats.

General de Gaulle admitted at a postelection press conference that his movement had won only a "limited success" by not surpassing the Communist votes, but he boasted that it nonetheless was "the first party of France in parliament," a strange contention coming from de Gaulle, who had so often said he would not govern except as the majority choice of the people. In 1951 he failed to win the majority. A year later, in 1952, his group, which had won first position in parliament, split apart when impatient and frustrated Gaullist deputies, hungry for a share of power, voted to invest Antoine Pinay as premier, against de Gaulle's orders.

Of the 118 Gaullist deputies, 27 were the first to break ranks in the investiture vote on March 6, 1952. By June the rebels had increased to 41. They had by then sent a letter to General de Gaulle telling him that his systematic opposition to the regime "was tiring his parliamentarians, discouraging his militants and driving away his voters." They warned him against the futility of his tactic of "awaiting an inevitable catastrophe" and begged him to let his group enter the majority and accept the rules of politics.

General de Gaulle released their letter to the press on June 10, along with his answer rejecting their plea. He said he had lost patience with their complaints and would dispose of the issue definitely at the national convention of the R.P.F. in July. At the

July meeting he forced through a motion imposing total discipline on the parliamentary group. Thereupon 26 of the dissidents instantly rebelled, resigned from the R.P.F. group and formed their own parliamentary unit. It was the opening wedge in the Gaullist ranks. The R.P.F. group, cut down to 89, fell into a virtual tie for fourth place with the Catholics. General de Gaulle had become the leader of a splinter faction in French politics.

The beginning of the end of General de Gaulle started with that first small dissident group that declared its independence in mid-1952. By January 1953 the R.P.F. dissidents went far down the road of the republic by agreeing to join the government after another break with de Gaulle. The original 27 dissidents were joined by another 81 R.P.F. deputies in a vote to invest René Mayer as premier, succeeding Antoine Pinay, who had inevitably fallen from grace, as did all the premiers of the Fourth Republic at an average of about two a year. Not only had virtually all the Gaullists voted for Mayer, but two of them accepted cabinet posts in the Mayer government. They had given up their long vigil in the wilderness, the hopeless waiting for the republic to collapse into de Gaulle's arms.

Events moved rapidly from then on. In April the Gaullists lost heavily in the municipal elections. In May General de Gaulle denounced the dissident Gaullist deputies and ruled them out of his movement. They shrugged him off and formed a new party of their own, U.R.A.S.—the Union of Republicans for Social Action. It had taken only five years, from de Gaulle's creation of the R.P.F. in April 1947 to the split of May 1952, for the great crusade to falter and founder in the political swamps far from the gates of the Promised Land.

General de Gaulle devoted less and less time to the R.P.F. in 1953 and began a series of trips through France and Africa. His interest perked up a bit in 1954 when Mendès-France, for whom he had a high regard, came into office to liquidate the Indochinese war. At an R.P.F. meeting he spoke warmly of the "ardor, the vigor and the value" of Mendès-France, but warned Mendès that "the regime is a minotaur that devours and will devour all men." As for his own role, General de Gaulle stated that he held himself "in reserve" as the nation's guide for the "grave crisis" that would have been "even by the use of force," as an extreme move; General de Gaulle said, he would be ready "to intervene directly by no matter what means, even by the electoral path."

The twist of irony at the end of that phrase was pure de Gaulle. It was both sardonic and sincere: sardonic because the usual phrase would have been "even by the use of force," as an extreme move; sincere because nothing could be more extreme, more a measure of the gravity of the crisis, than de Gaulle's willingness to come to power by elections, a means that had been tried too often and found failing.

General de Gaulle permitted himself this irony because he had already come to the conclusion that his long, tortuous and self-torturing campaign had completely failed. The R.P.F. experiment had fallen far short of his goals, and the movement had been fragmented by the frictions of French political life. The fervor had gone out of it. It had become a feeble caricature of itself. At the same time, the end of the war in Indochina had eliminated one of the greatest dangers to France. The war in Algeria had not yet really gotten under way in earnest, as it later would. De Gaulle was tired, bored, frustrated by public affairs in which he was reduced to the role of a hollow-voiced Cassandra whose dire warnings fell on deaf ears. It was time for a man approaching his sixty-fifth birthday to retire, with much to look back upon and little hope ahead.

* * *

The time for departure came in the summer of 1955. De Gaulle was almost a forgotten man by then. The curve of his decline can be read clearly in the index of the yearbook *L'Année politique*. In the year 1947, when he organized the R.P.F. and launched his campaign, the alphabetical listing under the name of de Gaulle is an inch deep and contains references to thirty-seven pages of text, totaling 1135 lines of citation. In 1948 de Gaulle is cited on thirty pages of the almanac, and long text pieces are appended in the annex. By 1954 the citations are down to only ten page references. In 1955 one finds a single stark line under the listing "Gaulle, de, General," followed by five page references in a volume of 800 pages.*

On July 2, 1955, General de Gaulle called a press conference to say farewell. The national radio was no longer at his disposal, nor

---

* In comparison, former Gaullist politician Jacques Soustelle rates more than fifty references in an inch-deep block of type, while America's Secretary of State John Foster Dulles gets a listing two inches deep, with the hundreds of lines of citations formerly accorded to de Gaulle.

had he at the time much experience with or access to French television. He looked old, tired and disenchanted, and he spoke in a heavy, slow voice: "More than a year has gone by since we last met. Everything points to the probability that a long time will pass before we meet again. My intention, in fact, is not to intervene in what one conventionally calls 'the conduct of public affairs.'"

General de Gaulle's tone of voice remained calm and almost ponderous as contrasted with the usual vigor and power of his press conferences. There was no cutting edge to his sword when he spoke of the regime. "It is incoherent and obsolete," he said wearily, with no snap and no spirit to his words. He said that he would have nothing further to do with politics: "I am totally disinterested in whatever may happen in the national elections next year."

Only at one point did the old spirit of de Gaulle manifest itself. He sat up straight and stiff, cleared his throat and, in his deepest baritone, struck this parting note of doom:

> The crises of the world are unleashing themselves on our shores. Without being able to foresee exactly which factor or what event will bring about the end of the regime, one must believe that the shockwave will strike.

The image was starkly clear. De Gaulle was predicting the collapse of France when the deluge of world crisis would strike its shores. It was his own very Gaullist twist on the famous last words of Madame de Pompadour to Louis XV: "After us, the deluge!" General de Gaulle had said, in effect, "After the deluge, de Gaulle."

General de Gaulle closed the conference with these words: "I bid you farewell—and perhaps for a very long time."

He retired into the shadows of his library at Colombey to write the memoirs that were to be his political testament. For two long years Charles de Gaulle remained entombed in the mausoleum of his memories and came to believe that the deluge would not arrive in time for him to render one last "signal service" to his beloved France.

The last pages of his memoirs read like an obituary, with only the very faintest hope still alive. As he contemplated himself, looking out of his lonely library to the classic garden of his home and the gloomy woods beyond, he penned these parting words:

Old Earth, eaten away by the ages, buffeted by rains
and winds, empty of life but ready, as always, to produce
again what is needed so that the living may follow on.

Old France, worn down by history, wracked by wars
and revolutions, rising and falling, without a pause, from
grandeur to decadence, yet always coming back, from
century to century, with your genius for rebirth.

Old man, perennial recruit of crisis, now removed from
enterprise, feeling the approach of the eternal cold, but
never weary of staring into the shadows, always looking
for the light of hope.

So end the confessions of Charles de Gaulle—with this image of
an old man peering into the abyss, kneeling, like his country, on
the brink, feeling the cold of eternity, almost welcoming it, never
doubting, whatever his own fate, the eventual renascence of his
beloved France.

For General de Gaulle, the years since his own reincarnation as
the resistant, far, far back on June 18, 1940, had been glorious but
long and, finally, disappointing. The great adventure had come to
an inglorious end. The resistant had been resisted, the savior
spurned, the liberator liberated of all responsibility. The prophet,
once again, was not honored in his own land. General de Gaulle
was dead.

But not Charles de Gaulle.

That stubborn old man, indomitable as ever, sat silently staring
into the shadows of the future, looking for the flash of lightning
that would signal the tempest, the deluge that would shake but
cleanse France, and infuse him, in his last years, with a new and
third life.

PART THREE
THE STATESMAN

States are as the men are; they grow out of human character.

PLATO, *The Republic VIII, c. 370 B.C.*

All governments face one great judge, an infallible judge, from whom there is no appeal, and do you know who that judge is? It is the event!

AUGUST THIERS *to the Senate, 1877*

A statesman who is ignorant of the way in which events originate is like a physician who does not know the causes of the disease he undertakes to cure.

POLYBIUS, *Histories III, c. 125 B.C.*

The State can serve its citizens only if the citizens render their services to the State.

CHARLES DE GAULLE *to the Paris Resistance Council,*

1944

CHAPTER EIGHT

TOO OLD TO BE
A DICTATOR

I am a man who belongs to no one and therefore who belongs to everybody. . . . Can anyone believe that at age sixty-seven I am going to begin the career of a dictator?

CHARLES DE GAULLE, *Press Conference, May 19, 1958*

AWAITING THE DELUGE, Charles de Gaulle was not altogether unhappy in the loneliness of his library. He had long grown accustomed to the cloak of solitude in which he had wrapped himself so many years before. Although he sensed the approaching cold of eternity, he had his faith and his loves to keep him warm: his faith in himself and in his destiny; his love of writing and his love of France, to which he was able to give himself completely for the first time in a life of constant struggle.

Never before had Charles de Gaulle been able to immerse himself totally in his twin loves. His retirement from active politics in the summer of 1955 left him with all his time free for the writing of his memoirs, whereas the demise of the career of General de Gaulle, and his own advanced age, freed Charles de Gaulle of any inhibitions. He was able to put down his innermost thoughts and to reveal himself with the total lack of shame or modesty achieved only by those who are about to die or those burning with a long-repressed passion.

The memoirs of most men seek principally to justify their public life. Charles de Gaulle, like other memorialists, did defend his own decisions; unlike those of other memorialists, however, his memoirs were not only self-justifying but also self-accusing. Charles de Gaulle confirmed the charges of his critics by stating that General de Gaulle had exercised "a kind of monarchy" and a "momentary dictatorship" which he would not hestitate, if need be, "to revive." These were not conventional memoirs; nor was his love for his country the conventional love of a patriot for his motherland. The love of Charles de Gaulle for France is the love of a man for a woman, a woman who is at one and the same time his mother and his mistress. It is a unique example of a quasi-sexual anthropomorphism by a leader whose nationalism, fiery as it is, is only a pale reflection of the hotter fires of love burning deep within him, a deeply sensual love for the nation-woman his imagination has created.

Charles de Gaulle did not hesitate to use the language of love, not merely of sublimated love, but of physical, sexual love, to describe the relations of a man with his country. There are surely few examples in literature that match the aberrational quality of his description of the relationship between Hitler and Germany:

> That man, who came out of nowhere, had offered himself to Germany at a moment when she felt a desire for a new lover. . . . She had given herself to this unknown passer-by who represented adventure, who promised domina-tion and whose passionate voice deeply stirred her secret instincts. . . . Hitler was strong but also skillful. He knew how to lure and to caress. Germany, seduced to her innermost depths, followed her Führer with joy. Right up to the end she gave herself to him, serving him with more zeal than any other people ever has offered to any chief.

The prime manifestation of this sexual anthropomorphism was a literary work, not of de Gaulle himself, but of France's re-nowned Catholic poet and playwright Paul Claudel. Claudel com-posed an ode to the General which may not win any poetry prizes, but which deserves some kind of special award, for there is nothing like it in contemporary literature. Of itself, it would have had no importance and would probably have been quickly forgot-ten as the temporary delirium of an overwrought patriot at a moment of exaltation. Its importance was given to it by General de Gaulle, who accorded the ode the very first place in the documen-tary appendix to the final volume of his memoirs, before all the important political, diplomatic and military papers of state.

The ode has never been translated into English, so far as I have been able to discover. The translation offered here is mine. Whatever its faults of style, it is exactly faithful, word for word, including punctuation and capitalization, to the original text. The ode is in the form of a dialogue between a man and a woman. The woman is France and the man is called "General." These brief excerpts accurately represent the full text:

"And now I care not what others think of me! . . ."

"Look into my eyes, which show no fear, look closely at me, and search carefully, and say whether I am afraid of your eyes, the eyes of a son and of a soldier!"

"And say whether this is enough for us, both of us, this that you are seeking in my eyes, and that very soon I will find in your arms! . . ."

"The rest, it means nothing to me! but thou, ask me for that thing which is not other than everything!"

"They thought to mock me by calling me woman! They will see the kind of woman that I am and what it is to have a soul and a body!"

"They have often enough asked me for my body, and thou, ask me for my soul!"

—And the General replies: "Woman, be quiet! And do not ask for anything other than what I am able to bring thee!"

—"What canst thou bring me then, O my son?"

—And the General, lifting his arms, replies:—"My will!"

This was not the first such ode that Claudel had written. Five years earlier he composed a poem to the glory of another military man whom he saw as the savior of France, Marshal Pétain. In December 1940, when General de Gaulle was in London trying to build a meaningful force out of the still pitifully small group of men who had answered his call to resistance, Paul Claudel, future eulogizer of de Gaulle, was writing a love poem to the old Marshal who had condemned de Gaulle to death. It was entitled "Paroles du Maréchal," and, as the title suggests, was written in free verse, a flow of words in a monologue by a woman named France. It

resembles in many ways the ode he later wrote to de Gaulle, with
the difference that Pétain was so doddering an old man that his
role was more of a father than that of son and lover. There are,
however, a number of sex sublimations in the ode and examples of
the exaltation that was to appear in more epic, heroic phrases in
the later ode to de Gaulle. The following lines are excerpts
translated by this writer:

"Mr. Marshal, here now is France in your arms, having
only you, slowly and quietly coming back to life . . .

"I have been stretched out full-length on the road and
even the most cowardly could dare insult me.

"But just the same I still have my body which is pure
and my soul which has not been dishonored! . . .

"And now you no longer need to deny this womb in
which was conceived Joan of Arc!

"Let me with piety cover up these naked limbs.

"Now I am alone with you, how good it is! And there is
no one to gaze upon us! . . .

"The secret that I share with thee, Mother, no one can
steal from us! . . .

"France, listen to this old man who is leaning over you
and who speaks to you like a father.

"Daughter of Saint Louis, listen to him! And say, have
you not at last had enough of politics?

"Listen to this voice of reason which proposes to you
and explains to you.

"Proposals soothing as oil and truth as bright as
gold!" *

* Paul Claudel included this ode to Pétain in a one-volume collection
of his poetry at the liberation. However, conscious of the contradiction
between his first adoration of the collaborator, Pétain, and the later adulation
of the resistant, de Gaulle, he added a footnote explaining that the ode to
Pétain was written after he learned that Pétain had dismissed his pro-Nazi
prime minister, Pierre Laval. Laval was brought to trial by de Gaulle after
the liberation, found guilty of treason and executed by a firing squad. This
may explain and justify Claudel, but it does not explain why de Gaulle was
willing to honor Claudel by taking the poem seriously and giving it his
personal imprimatur.

One wonders how a man of measure like de Gaulle, with a love of the classics and a talent for expressing himself in an austere prose, could possibly have endorsed so lurid an outburst as a Claudel ode, to the point of appending it to his own writings as an official document for historians. Perhaps the answer is that de Gaulle's love for France is greater than his love for classicism and that his passion knows no measure. One cannot doubt, however, what conclusions are to be drawn from his reprinting of the ode. He is so proud of his love that he flaunts it. He bears his love as a banner on his lance as he rides for France in the tournament of the world, against the Anglo-Saxons, against the Teutons and the Slavs and all the Orient, and even, perhaps foremost, against the Gauls, those unworthy native rivals for the hand and the heart of his own true love.

* * *

Whatever de Gaulle may have felt about his love affair with France in 1945, he knew by 1955 that France had spurned his hand and had turned to other suitors. Perhaps that is why he put the Claudel ode into the documents of his memoirs, as one presses into a diary a flower, as a remembrance of things past. The Fourth Republic was a wanton in his eyes, the eyes of a son and a lover and, above all, the eyes of a royalist. By most royalists, the republic had traditionally been seen as "la gueuse." The Fourth Republic certainly did play the field of lovers—as one Gaullist politician put it: "like a nymphomaniac in a barracks"—changing prime ministers every four or five months, wearing out a long line of ardent suitors for power, one after the other, in ten years of a wild political debauch.

General de Gaulle, however, was not systematically and emotionally antirepublican; he was rather an antiparliamentarian by conviction and practical experience. He felt that the excessive powers traditionally granted to the parliament encouraged the most extreme abuses of the governmental process. He regarded parliamentary government as the most inefficient form of democracy, doomed to decline into anarchy and then tyranny unless there were countervailing forces, and particularly a strong executive. The "Bayeux Constitution" remained his definitive concept of the only possible form of government for France. The constitution of the Fifth Republic, which he brought into being in 1958, was based upon the Bayeux principles and was almost identical to it in many respects. He spent long hours studying constitutional history during the years he was writing his memoirs. At the same time, as he sat in the shadows waiting for the thunderbolt to strike and shake France, he devoted himself to an intensive, detached observation and analysis of the situation in the crumbling French Empire and of a world in upheaval—a situation with which he would have to be ready to deal if and when he was again called to the rescue of France.

It was the extremely critical and deteriorating situation of the world's great powers, as much as the failure of the R.P.F. to win the elections in France, that induced de Gaulle to withdraw from the public scene in July 1955. However unreal his own world policies may seem, General de Gaulle is a realist in his appraisal of the force lines of current history. He rarely makes a mistake of appraisal, no matter how mistaken or inconsistent the policy conclusions that he draws from the appraisal. He has often said in private, "I may often make mistakes in policy but never in predictions."

This writer had many long talks with de Gaulle in the months immediately preceding his decision to leave the political arena, and frequent conversations during the years of his silent contemplation of the scene. At all times I found him following events closely, alert to every shift in the wind, predicting with extraordinary accuracy the trend of world affairs many weeks and months before the actual events, in some cases years before the end that he foresaw finally came about.

The most interesting illustration of the differences between Gaullist policies and predictions was the case of Algeria. As early as the winter of 1954, only a few weeks after the first outbreak of rebellion in the Aurès, General de Gaulle foresaw the eventual independence of Algeria. He told this writer that the process had begun many years earlier, as far back as the Japanese capture of Singapore early in World War II:

We can see now that the fall of Singapore was the beginning of the end of Western hegemony in Asia. The war hastened the deterioration: India, Pakistan, Indochina, now North Africa. The landings of the allied armies in North Africa in 1942 and the liberation campaign of 1943 lighted the fuse, and the fires were fanned by Roosevelt's concept of anticolonialism and the inevitable impact of thousands of American soldiers and the slogans of the Four Freedoms. It was a natural, inevitable process. The mistake and the misfortune was not decolonization but the hasty, ill-prepared destruction of the centuries-old order, with no coherent plan or structure to replace it. We shall now see years of suffering ahead before this Algerian drama plays itself out to what may be a tragic end.

General de Gaulle had made similar statements as early as 1944, in Algiers, at the time his National Committee promulgated citizenship for some 60,000 Algerian Moslems representing the country's intellectual and social élite. De Gaulle told his commissioner for African affairs that this was undoubtedly the first step in a process that would move "ineluctably to the independence of Algeria."

Normally reserved in his conversations, preferring to make his visitor do the talking, General de Gaulle occasionally would indulge himself in his favorite pastime, a discourse on history and a worldwide tour d'horizon of contemporary affairs. This was particularly true early in 1955 during the months when the desire to give up the political struggle was growing within him. He seemed to sense that the tides were swirling into a whirlpool that would "sweep away the rotted pilings of the old order." He felt, and told many visitors, that this was the time for him to retreat to safety, to high and dry ground, to keep himself free, clear, uncommitted and unstained by the mud that was sure to be churned up, the more so since he had no big base of political power from which to operate. "The thunderheads are forming everywhere over the world," he told this writer. "It is only a matter of time before the tempest unfurls itself upon the planet. All the great powers will be shaken, France the first and most severely."

General de Gaulle made similar predictions to his former "companions" of the wartime resistance, Edmond Michelet, Maurice Schumann and André Philip, and even to American authorities, such as Senator Margaret Chase Smith. I escorted Senator Smith to de Gaulle's office on the rue Solférino for an informal talk during her tour of Europe, and the General treated the Senator to an exhaustive but precise and lucid critique of the Atlantic Alliance and the misconceptions of American policies. He noted ironically America's failure to understand the positive aspect of nationalism in Europe although Americans themselves, he said, "are among the most nationalistic of all peoples." De Gaulle assured the Senator that he valued highly the Atlantic Alliance and the need for European unity but was unalterably opposed to "integration" and such "anomalies" as a European Army.

By the summer of 1955 General de Gaulle was more than convinced that there was nothing he could do to influence the course of events better than to step aside and hold himself in reserve for the crisis he had seen coming since the dawn of the new year. The chronology of events in that turning-point year of postwar history, as one looks back upon it today, shows the ominous approach of the thunderheads that de Gaulle saw forming over the world.

The year 1955 began with the rearmament of Germany in NATO. A tense, desperate Mendès-France had fought for his government's life all through Christmas week to win approval for Germany's entry into the Alliance as the natural consequence of the French refusal to create an integrated European Army in the debate on EDC in August 1954. Wearied by the fight in the assembly, nervous about Russia's reaction, Mendès-France had written to London and Washington to inform his allies that he was planning a trip to Moscow to talk with the Russians before attempting to put the German rearmament treaty to final ratification in the senate.

The allied reaction was violent. John Foster Dulles sent off a letter that an official described as the most strongly worded denunciation of an ally in the history of American diplomacy. It was reported by well-informed men that Dulles threatened severe reprisals against France and accused Mendès-France of trying to use the half-ratified treaty as a means of "selling out" to the Russians at a high price. The letter was so violent that no part of it, not even a paraphrased summary, has ever been released for publication.

An almost equally violent letter from Churchill was, however, made public weeks later, in March 1955, when Foreign Minister Pinay referred to it and cited parts of it in testimony to parliament. Churchill, like Dulles, said that if Mendès-France went to Moscow before completing ratification, it would look as though he were seeking terms from the Russians not to proceed with the treaty. The Russians had denounced German rearmament in NATO and were threatening to cancel the Soviet friendship treaties with

France and England—a threat they finally did carry out when Mendès canceled his trip. In his letter Churchill warned Mendès that, much as he personally opposed a "peripheral policy" for Western defense, he was prepared to proceed with Atlantic plans while leaving "an empty chair" for France—a clear threat to write France out of NATO, pull NATO out of France and reorganize Western defense "peripherally," that is, around, outside and without France. The Churchill threat was even more effective than the violence of Dulles, for its iciness was more solid than the steam of anger, and the French had a special feeling for Churchill that they did not have for Dulles.

General de Gaulle was most particularly impressed by the solid Anglo-Saxon front against France, with Germany's role in the Alliance as the object of the dispute. He felt that Mendès, whom he admired, had made two serious errors: the first was to let himself appear to be using Germany as a trading instrument; the second was to back down and not explore the trade once he had gotten himself into that position. He felt there was nothing worse than backing down publicly under allied pressures. De Gaulle was not concerned about the Anglo-Saxon threat to isolate France or about "peripheral defenses," which were geopolitically unrealistic. He felt that Mendès could overcome the weakness or the threatened isolation of France by playing off the great rival blocs of East and West against each other if need be. What appalled de Gaulle was the internal weakness of the Mendès-France government in a divided, faction-ridden parliament.

Shortly after the storm over Germany, new clouds appeared low in the sky over Asia, at Bandung, where at the end of April a new current that would swell to a torrent in world affairs flowed in from Africa. At Bandung was held the first major meeting of both the independent and the still-colonized peoples of the two continents that had so long lived under the rule of the Western powers. The world would never be quite the same again after the week of April 18–24, 1955.

It was at Bandung that Nehru proposed an Asian aid program for Africa, a proposal whose significance was not fully appreciated by the Western powers because Asia was hardly in a position to help itself, let alone furnish aid to others. The West failed to grasp the psychological value of the proposal: the smallest cup of rice from Asia meant more to Africans than all the wheat the granaries of the West could supply, for it meant that the poor were helping the poor, the ex-slaves the still-enslaved, and that by this spirit they would break all remaining chains and some day be strong as well as free. It was a dream of a distant dawn that was more meaningful than any present reality to the Afro-Asian peoples.

If any man understood this and began preparing for the day that he himself might have to meet this challenge head on, it was General de Gaulle. He had recently been on a tour of Africa, had seen the storm clouds building up, had heard the new beat in the drums and had sensed the throbbing in the pulse of the Africans. He was filled with foreboding of what was to come in Algeria, had watched with deepening concern the floundering of French policy in Tunisia and Morocco as successive French governments talked big but carried a small stick.

After July 1955 General de Gaulle sat in his library looking out at the gathering storm, searching for "the light of hope" that he then knew could come only as a bolt of lightning. The lightning began to strike in 1956, one of the most turbulent years of change in modern history. If 1955 was the turning-point year, 1956 was the year in which the turn took place. The disintegration of French positions in North Africa crashed into an almost complete collapse in 1956. Total independence was granted to Morocco and Tunisia, presaging the beginning of the end for the country that lies between them, Algeria. It was akin to madness to believe it would be possible to maintain a French enclave inside a free North Africa in a world of rapidly evolving liberation of colonial peoples. Yet a madness did seize the French and many other peoples in that year of crises, 1956.

At the end of January 1956, the "peace-loving" Khrushchev convoked his satellites to a meeting in Prague of the eight Warsaw Pact countries, which had been joined together on the same general lines as the NATO pact organization in Paris. The Warsaw Pact Organization had been constructed in May 1955 as an answer to the entry of Western Germany into NATO. At the end of the January 1956 meeting, Soviet General Antonov was named "Secretary-General" of the organization, a post corresponding to that occupied by Lord Ismay in NATO. At the same time it was decided that an East German "national, popular army would be created and its forces incorporated" into the Pact. An East German would be named one of the deputies to the Supreme Commander, Russia's General Koniev. East and West seemed to be squaring off for a fight, and the so-called "Geneva spirit" seemed more like a specter in the aftermath of the failure of the second Geneva conference in November 1955.

President Eisenhower, in his State of the Union message on January 5, had spoken of his keen disappointment at the decline of the high hopes that had arisen at the first Geneva summit conference in July 1955. He said that by November the Soviets had demonstrated the hollowness of their protestations of peace. He felt, however, that the cold-war tensions had eased a bit nonetheless. (This was two weeks before the new Warsaw Pact military decisions.) The favorable effect on world opinion of the Eisenhower optimism and his words of moderation were wiped out five days later by a new tough and glacial cold-war declaration by his Secretary of State, John Foster Dulles, in the form of an interview published by *Life* magazine.

Dulles revealed to *Life* that on three different occasions the world had dangled on the brink of atomic war. The first time was in June 1953, on the occasion of the escape of 27,000 North Korean war prisoners inadequately guarded by the South Koreans, an occasion that gave the Chinese Communists a chance to break off armistice negotiations. China was warned that if war broke out again, America would no longer deny herself the use of atomic arms. Again, in April 1954, an atomic war threatened when the French government asked the United States to intervene with its bombers at Dienbienphu, a request finally turned down by Eisenhower. The third critical moment arrived in the autumn of 1954, said Mr. Dulles, when the Congress voted by an overwhelming majority to authorize the President to use atomic weapons if the Chinese attacked Formosa. Mr. Dulles' revelations caused a worldwide uproar of protests, and even in the Congress of the United States sharp words were spoken, notably by Senator Hubert Humphrey.

Senator Humphrey attacked Dulles for his "brinkmanship" and demanded that the Secretary of State disavow his declaration to *Life*. Mr. Dulles did not back down, but he did back away by having his official spokesman say that the article was accurate on the substance of his thoughts but that he had not written it himself and had not read the text before publication, so that he could not vouch for every detail. Hardly anyone doubted for an instant that the very professional men of *Life* had edited the article efficiently and accurately and that it was a faithful reproduction of what Dulles had said. The text stood for what it had said and remained part of the record of that not so wonderful year 1956, which had gotten off to a dreadful start and was due to end in a twin tragedy at Suez and Budapest.

The deterioration of the world order continued at a rapid pace from the bad beginning of January. By July 1956 the Russians were in trouble at home and in their own Iron Curtain sector. In Moscow the Central Committee issued a declaration condemning the cult of personality. This was taken seriously in Poland and in Hungary. The Poles demanded that Soviet General Rokosoffsky, who had been imposed on them as defense minister, pack up and go back to Moscow. Rumbles of discontent echoed ominously along the Iron Curtain from East Germany down to the banks of the Danube in Hungary. Tension erupted in the Middle East as Arab and Israeli forces engaged in frontier skirmishes, and there were riots and fights between Greek and Turkish elements in Cyprus all through the summer. In July, Dulles turned down a bid from Nasser to finance the Aswan Dam, and the Soviets flew agents down from Moscow to see what kind of fishing they could do in the troubled waters of Egyptian politics. The whole world balance was tilting strangely as small nations that were hardly bigger than cities began to defy the world's greatest powers. Tiny Iceland began to quarrel with the United States, demanding that America close down its important NATO air bases and radar stations in that Arctic outpost.

From Reykjavik to Port Said the star of nationalism was rising in a clouded sky. Everywhere little men were standing up to the giants and screaming insults at them, waving bare, grimy and famine-wasted fists at tanks and atom bombs. 1956 was the year of the turning of the worm. The little countries were, however, peopled by men, not by worms, defiant men almost eager to die to prove their manhood and their independence. They had no real power, but they sensed their opportunity for self-expression and self-determination in the paralysis of power that had gripped the great nations of the world.

The centuries-old balance that had imposed a stable order on the world, broken only by the wars among the big powers, had been destroyed by the two world wars. France, Germany and Britain were all losers in the world wars, for they destroyed themselves in their power struggle. The two new world powers were inexperienced giants neither of whom had imperial outposts, neither of whom was able to replace or rebuild anything stable on the ruins of the old empires. The colossi stood astride the world, facing each other, bombs in hand, nervous, suspicious, confused and, above all, hypnotized by the terror that each would be able to inflict on the other if hostilities broke out.

The old balance of power was replaced, therefore, by a balance of terror which, in the year 1956, balanced only two countries and terrified only two countries, the two colossi themselves. America and Russia were like giant elephants towering over the jungle of the world, trumpet to trumpet, afraid to move, while far below, in the underbrush of Africa, Asia and South America, the warrior-ant nations, sensing the paralysis of the pachyderms, went on the march. The climactic hour struck in the month of November, when two crises erupted that were to change the course of history: the Anglo-French-Israeli drive to Suez and the insurrection of the people of Budapest.

Stirrings in the Soviet satellite states had begun long before November 1956. There had been an aborted insurrection in East Berlin three years earlier and a wide range of manifestations of discontent, from rumblings to riots, in almost every country chafing under the chains of Sovietization. But no uprising so violent and so total had broken out as erupted in Budapest. It was not a manifestation of discontent by angry slaves: it was a national revolution by men who were fighting to be free. The Freedom Fighters did not have a chance alone against the Russian tanks. They were savagely, brutally crushed. But the Russians had to come out into the open to carry out their savage repression, with the whole world watching, and never again would the Soviet claims to be the genuine champions of people seeking liberation be given credit anywhere in the world—not after November 6, 1956. Nor would the satellite system ever again bind the peoples of eastern Europe as closely or hopelessly. They had all seen what had happened at Budapest, and they remembered not only the brutal repression but, more importantly, the magnificent courage and the surge of hope.

What one could do, others could do; what some could do, all could do. The Russians saw and understood this, too. So did Communists and pro-Communists throughout western Europe and the rest of the world. The events in Budapest shook and split Communist parties, disillusioned many a fellow-traveler and sympathizer. Neither Russia nor the world Communist movement would ever be the same again after November 6, 1956. Within a short time the Poles, Rumanians and Bulgarians were showing signs of impatience and independence—not with violence, not against the Soviet, but quietly asserting their right to trade and travel and to pursue an increasingly independent course. Those currents are running swiftly today and without waterfalls or floods, flowing around rather than against obstacles. Russia is trying to channel the flow rather than to dam it up as she did at Budapest, opening up floodgates in the Iron Curtain to ease the pressures.

Foremost among those who saw a great opportunity in these new currents was General de Gaulle. He saw the tides change as he watched world affairs from the tranquillity of his study at Colombey. He maintained close contacts throughout that period with Soviet and eastern European diplomats in Paris. Ever since his service in Poland after World War I he had been interested in the eastern lands. The loosening of ties behind the Curtain gave him as President of France an opportunity to offer the friendship of France as an alternative to domination by the great powers and as a way out of the East-West rivalry. It was during the period that followed the uprising in Budapest that de Gaulle completed the elaboration of his foreign-policy doctrine: to restore France to her rank as one of the great powers of the world, either by creating a directorate of the West or by assuming the leadership of a Third Force between the West and the East. That policy evolved more completely after his return to power in France. At this point it is important to note only that it was the pattern of events in 1956 that made his later doctrines possible. The daily tides of 1965–1966 can be traced back to the changing currents of 1955–1956.

Of all the events of that watershed year a decade ago, the one that had the greatest impact on the life and times of Charles de Gaulle was the last of the traditional adventures of imperial history: the expedition to Suez. For centuries one of the major elements in Western domination in world affairs had been Britain's control of the waterways. The "imperial lifeline" ran from Gibraltar through Malta, Cyprus, Suez, Aden, Colombo and Singapore to Hong Kong. Suez sat astride the vital junction point of three continents—Europe, Africa and Asia. It was located in the middle of the giant pumping stations of Arabian oil and was of enormous economic and industrial importance as well as serving as the symbol of imperial eminence.

For the British, Suez was an emotional symbol of a glorious past that men of Eden's generation clung to desperately. For the French, too, it was a symbol evocative of the past: Napoleon, de Lesseps, the Suez Canal Company, created and presided over by a Frenchman; but even more cogently, a present-day symbol of the pan-Arabism that was aiding and abetting the Algerian rebels. More and more hard-pressed in Algeria in 1955 and 1956, the French leaders convinced themselves that they had to, and could, crush the rebellion by cutting off its principal support and supplies in Egypt. Finally the Israelis, surrounded by overwhelming numbers of hostile Arabs, whom Nasser was trying to unite for a holy war against the Jewish state, were themselves worked up by their fears to believe that Israel would be able to live only if Nasser's ambitions were crushed.

It is impossible to state with any certainty what the world equation would be like today if Anthony Eden had not yielded under American pressure to call off the expedition when it was in sight of Suez. The French and Israelis wanted to fight on despite American and Soviet threats to intervene. Nasser certainly was as good as dead. His troops had been badly beaten by the Israelis alone—in fact, no one seriously doubts that the Israelis would have swept away his last defenses and marched on to Cairo without the British and the French. The war with the Arabs would certainly not have ended there, but Nasser would have been through as the great man of Araby. The Russians might or might not have intervened at Suez had Eden stood firm. America might have had to intervene too, but the United States would not have tolerated Soviet control of that strategic region. Almost everyone today agrees that it was a mad adventure, ill-conceived, poorly executed, with no serious consideration in advance of the possible Soviet and American reactions. We do not know what might have happened had it not been aborted, but we do know the catastrophe that followed when it was.

Suez was almost a death blow to the Western alliance, which has never been the same since. Millions of Britons and Frenchmen will never forget that America turned upon them and joined with the Russians to humiliate them. Relations among people are not always judged by the rights and wrongs of a particular policy, but rather by the sentiments of loyalty and friendship. Ever since Suez it is impossible to discuss world affairs in France without the inevitable interjection: "Et Suez?" particularly when an American criticizes de Gaulle's unilateral actions and departures from allied solidarity. Nothing that de Gaulle has done—not the veto of Britain's entry into the Common Market, not the recognition of China—has had a greater impact on allied relations than America's application of power against Eden and Mollet to force them to retreat from Suez.

For General de Gaulle, "L'Affaire Suez" was simply another proof that France had to maintain an independent military establishment and refuse integration in an allied command. He said in private comments, "The French Army supply lines were entirely dependent upon the British Navy. When Eden pulled out of the line, Mollet could only order his forces to retreat, for they were totally cut off and would have been left stranded, as were Napoleon's troops when Nelson destroyed the French fleet off Alexandria."

The most significant testimony to the long-range effects of the Suez debacle came from General Jacques Massu, Commander of the French paratroopers. Massu told reporters, "When the order to retreat came through from Paris, I asked myself whether to obey or to drive on to Cairo. I thought of General de Gaulle in 1940, wanting to fight on, and his call to resistance when a defeated government capitulated. De Gaulle would have disobeyed the order to retreat, I thought. But then I realized it was hopeless. Even de Gaulle would have had to pull back if the navy and the supply lines were pulled out behind him." Then Massu added, "We will not be trapped like that again. First Indochina, now Suez—but never again! Never again will we let Paris fold up behind us! I give you my word on that!"

General Massu kept his word. Within a year of Suez he was commanding his paratroopers in Algiers, and along with fellow officers he had taken a vow to fight on there until death if necessary but never to retreat again. The army officers had little liking for the French colonials in Algeria, whom they regarded as rich, retrograde profiteers, but they gladly chanted one of the colonial slogans, "The coffin rather than the valise!" as their defiant reply to the rebels' challenge to pack up and get out or die.

The coffins piled up in Algeria all through the year that followed Suez. Total deaths on both sides mounted by the tens of thousands. Socialist Premier Guy Mollet, "the man of Suez," had become the hero of the colonialists and nationalists in the course of 1956. He had been elected at the start of the year in a swing to the left but had reversed the trend when he came under a barrage of rotten tomatoes thrown at him by the colonials on his first trip to Algiers, on February 6, 1956. He abandoned plans to attempt liberal reforms. Although he continued to pay lip service to the objective of a negotiated peace and equality for the Moslems, Mollet carried out a policy that transferred real power to the army, which, despite its contempt for the colonials, had little time to carry out reforms while fighting a war. Mollet's Socialist Party colleague Robert Lacoste handed his police powers over to the military in Algiers after Mollet had also taken the decision to permit draftees to be assigned to do their military training in the Algerian theater of war. Within a few months after Suez, Mollet had exhausted his leadership and abdicated virtually all civilian and governmental authority to the army.

While these events were moving to their inevitable denouement, General de Gaulle was becoming once again the focus of all those who saw the ultimate collapse of the declining regime. There was a parade of visitors to his office in the rue Solférino, where he held court once a week, and a smaller but far more important stream of callers whom he received at La Boisserie, his home at Colombey. De Gaulle still refrained from public appearances, accepting only rarely invitations to speak on commemorative occasions, such as the inauguration of a monument to the resistance at Cerdon, in June. There he attacked the "system" which, he said, was "doomed," but he assured the citizens that there was "solid reason to believe in a great future for France." De Gaulle's constant tactic—to condemn the rot that was destroying the republic but to maintain the people's faith in France—was not merely a device: it was his sincere conviction that the Fourth Republic was rotted through and his article of faith that France could rapidly recover her health and greatness under his leadership.

He spoke frankly of this to his visitors, particularly when his name began to be mentioned more and more often as the savior that France needed. The Gaullist party and the Gaullists in the assembly kept his name alive, calling upon the politicians to turn to de Gaulle to restore the nation. But they kept warning that he would not accept a bid to form a government under the present system. The Social Republican group issued a communiqué stating that "de Gaulle will not cover up the errors of a regime that he has never ceased to fight."

De Gaulle's name was officially put into the lists in the national assembly in speeches by Gaullists after the fall of the Mollet cabinet in June 1957, but in the same terms of unconditional surrender by the parliament. For the first time one heard a phrase that was to be the rallying cry of revolution a year later: "a government of public safety." The Gaullists were the first to pronounce the revolutionary slogan that recalled the Committee of Public Safety presided over by Robespierre during the period of the Terror after the regicide of 1793. The Social Republican group in the assembly called for the "creation of a Government of Public Safety presided over by a man whose prestige and authority is recognized by all the French."

The assembly paid little attention to the Gaullists. The deputies invested Maurice Bourgès-Maunoury with the premiership. In October the Bourgès-Maunoury government fell. The end of the Fourth Republic was not far away. In November the rabble-rousing, antiparliamentarian Poujade delivered an address in Strasbourg attacking the United States and calling for a return to power of General de Gaulle along with Marshal Juin "as the only men who could keep Algeria French and restore France to first rank in the world." In December, Poujade made a new appeal for de Gaulle.

De Gaulle despised Poujade and had little use for many of those using his name. He kept silent, still sitting in the shadows of his library but more alert not to miss the flash of lightning that would be the sign of the tempest that he knew would come, although he had almost abandoned hope of seeing it soon enough for him to act.

In January a secret meeting was held at the Avenue Victor Hugo apartment of a young lawyer, Jean-Baptiste Biaggi, a hot-headed extremist who had publicly and repeatedly called for a revolution. This meeting differed significantly from others that had been held in his apartment in that more important men were present than the rabble that normally infested the Biaggi premises. Among the men was Senator Michel Debré, just as hot-headed and fanatic as Biaggi, but a man of national stature, one of the wartime resistance leaders, a postliberation Commissioner of the Republic and a fervent Gaullist. Significantly, Michel Debré, not Biaggi, presided over the meeting. Also present was another famous resistant, Maxime Blocq-Mascart. Jacques Soustelle, Léon Del-becque, Olivier Guichard and many other well-known Gaullists had been contacted by Biaggi and invited to his apartment, where he pleaded for the creation of a new underground organization, a revival of the wartime C.N.R., the National Council of the Resistance. By the end of January 1957 a series of conspiratorial groups had been created and were preparing for operations. Code names had been devised for each of the members of the network, and plans had been laid for a seizure of power as soon as the situation was judged to be ripe for a coup.

General de Gaulle knew what was going on; he could not be ignorant, since some of his closest and most outspoken supporters, like Debré and Roger Frey, were deeply involved, as was his personal aide, Olivier Guichard. Debré had predicted the public approval of a coup in a book published in 1957, *Ces Princes qui nous gouvernent,* in which he wrote, "A revolt against the public powers is a grave act, but it could be a high moral act." He added, "If tomorrow a famous or even an unknown person would impose his authority by a kind of coup, by the use of force and, by making his intentions known in a nationwide broadcast, would win over the army, then who would protest?" No one had any doubt as to the identity of the person who might pull off this kind of coup or make the kind of radio address which Debré had "imagined."

De Gaulle himself did not hesitate to discuss the growing crisis and the use of his name by the partisans of revolution. He said to several visitors, "The Republic is agonizing. It will not live long, but only a fool would seek to come to power in France by a coup d'état. No power can exist in France now unless it is both legitimate and legal."

De Gaulle's words immediately rang a bell in my memory when I heard them. I recalled the day, a decade earlier, when I had asked Jacques Duclos and Maurice Thorez about a Communist seizure of power in France. I remembered how they had laughed and said that this was only an American nightmare. The Communists, they had said, knew France too well to attempt a coup d'état, because all France would unite against anyone who attempted to seize power by force. "The only revolution that can succeed in France is a counterrevolution," they insisted. I realized that de Gaulle was saying something very similar. He had not denied that he would come to power *after,* or as a *result* of, a coup d'état; he only denied that he would accept power at the head of a coup or in any *illegal* manner.

In all likelihood de Gaulle was sincere in saying, as he did to many visitors, that a coup would not succeed at all. He had very little faith in any of the plots and plotters, including the Gaullist conspirators, all of whom were planning separately, together and also at cross-purposes, to overthrow the Republic. He made it clear, however, that he himself would agree to be invested with power only by legal, constitutional procedures, no matter how illegally pressure was brought to bear upon the assembly to call him back in due legal form. When he had spoken of a "secousse"—a shaking up of the republic—in his farewell conference of July 1955, he had foreseen precisely the kind of situation that came to a head in May 1958: the shaking of the foundations of the regime that would force the politicians to call him to the rescue.

One of the most important and convincing documents testifying to de Gaulle's attitude in the weeks of the gathering storm is the text of the minutes of his meeting on March 27 with the group known as C.A.N.A.C.* This association of war veterans had sent a delegation to see de Gaulle to sound out his intentions on returning to power. The delegation leader, Alexandre Sanguinetti, reported back to the full association at a congress in Paris stating that de Gaulle "refuses to consider a return in the framework of the present regime, whatever might be the ways and means of such a return. He knows, moreover, that parliament will never recall him before the catastrophe is final." The delegate said that de Gaulle believed the situation could drag on unchanged for a long time, perhaps even thirty or forty years, "which is nothing in the history of a nation." De Gaulle is quoted as saying: "The mediocrity of our allies and of our enemies both permits the regime to survive." However, General de Gaulle had noted "a slight sign of an awakening of conscience" and had said that "if, under pressure of events, and progressive paralysis of the regime, this were to become irresistible, then the General, without really wanting to, would agree to face his responsibilities, and take into his hands again the reins of the nation." De Gaulle would insist, however, that the responsibility be his alone and that he would have nothing to do with the "political balance-of-power play" between the right

* The name CANAC is made up of the initials of one of the French war veteran associations: Conseil d'Action Nationale des Associations d'Anciens Combattants. Its secretary-general at the time, Alexandre Sanguinetti, became a high official of the ministry of the interior and was later elected as a deputy to the national assembly on the ticket of the Gaullist party, the U.N.R. The text referred to above was drafted by Sanguinetti and was published in the documents Annexe D, page 477 in *Secrets d'Etat* by J. R. Tournoux, Librairie Plon, Paris, 1960.

and the left. General de Gaulle condemned both sides: "The right, which ignores the necessity for generosity, and the left, which ignores the necessity for national power."

All de Gaulle's feelings and estimates of the situation in the springtime of 1958 are accurately reflected in the C.A.N.A.C. report: his fear that the crisis could remain chronic for many years; his hope that it would become rapidly acute, so that the fever would break and the patient could be cured; his refusal to be called in by parliament under the system of the Fourth Republic, but his readiness to go to parliament for a legal investiture after the catastrophe was "final," so that he could assume full and unchallenged responsibility to restore the republic. General de Gaulle was not an enthusiastic republican but, like Churchill, he had come to believe that parliamentary democracy was "the least bad form of government known to man." He was not a systematic antiparliamentarian, not a Bonaparte, not a Boulanger, not a Maurras. He shared many of their critical views on parliamentarianism and on the weaknesses of the republic, but not to the extent of thinking it possible to govern France under any other system. Emotionally he was a constitutional monarchist of the Louis-Philippe type; but he had come to the conclusion that the only possible form of state viable for France was the republic, with a separation and balance of powers between the executive office and the legislature, as he had laid it down in his "Bayeux Constitution" of 1946.

General de Gaulle was prepared to exercise a "momentary dictatorship" or a "kind of monarchy" in a moment of national peril, as he said in his memoirs, but he was not prepared to restore a true monarchy in any sense nor was he willing to stage and lead a coup to install himself as a dictator. De Gaulle willingly explained his views on the chances of a rule of personal power in France. Jacques Soustelle, in his book *Envers et contre tous,* quotes de Gaulle as telling him, "The French people by their very nature are the most opposed to personal power. At no moment was anyone able to impose himself for long." Many other writers can testify to the same words that de Gaulle pronounced to this writer: "France is not a South American-style republic. The French detest 'pronunciamentos,' fear men on horseback who would make themselves dictators. In today's world neither dictatorship nor monarchy is possible in France." He told publisher Emil Buré, "In France there is no point in overthrowing the republic, for as soon as it is overthrown, a new one has to be erected."

General de Gaulle held himself ready, he told all who asked him, to take whatever steps were necessary *"after* the tempest broke over the land" to restore republican law and order in a more efficient republic, with a more powerful executive serving a stronger state. He neither encouraged nor discouraged the conspirators acting in his name: Roger Frey, Michel Debré, Jacques Soustelle, to mention only a few of the leaders who later became cabinet ministers in his postrevolutionary government. But the leading plotter who most actively called the signals as the quarterback of the team, Léon Delbecque, understood clearly that he had the green light to go all the way. If the plot succeeded, de Gaulle would return, uncommitted to anyone, even to his own group of revolutionists; if the plot failed, de Gaulle would keep his silence and his innocence, for he felt himself to be a "national asset, not to be used except in the service of the nation."

Rarely has a coup d'état been so publicly discussed by the plotters as the coup that was being prepared in France. De Gaulle's recognized spokesmen did not hesitate to talk about the coming revolution while exercising parliamentary mandates in the Republic they had taken an oath to defend. Roger Frey, the present minister of the interior, in charge of the entire security apparatus in France today, was one of the leading and most outspoken of the apprentice rebels. In a report to the National Council of the Gaullist Social Republican Party on March 23, 1958, he said, "The gates of darkness are opening before the regime. One more step and France will be enveloped by the shades of night." He warned that unless proper measures were taken to pursue the war in Algeria, the Gaullists would have to "join the opposition to a regime whose continuance would be fatal for France."

Roger Frey pronounced the key words when he said, "While waiting for the government of national safety, we will become the opposition of national safety." This slogan, "national safety," was to become the battle cry of revolution. He went on to lay down the justification for the coup in terms of de Gaulle's doctrine of legitimacy: "This was the attitude of Charles de Gaulle vis-à-vis Vichy from 1940 to 1945. This could now be ours, for our opposition should be viewed in the perspective of Gaullism—that is, the call of June 18, the combats of Fighting France and of the Resistance."

Firebrand Michel Debré had already given the regime warning

of what was to come when he wrote in his paper, *Courier de la Colère,* on March 6 that the leaders of France were behaving like princes and dukes who once said, "After us, the deluge," and he warned, "If you do not take heed, you will see the deluge fall upon you sooner than you seek."

The Gaullists were not by any means the only plotters or the most outspoken. They were, indeed, a small minority among the "13 plots of May 13," as the revolutionary movements came to be described. Most of the revolutionaries, outside the Gaullist group, were found among three kinds of malcontents:

1. Professional army officers who still burned with the shame and despair of the Indochinese campaign and who had convinced themselves that the army had not been defeated in combat but had been betrayed by corrupt politicians and selfish, profit-seeking bourgeois back in France.

2. Frenchmen born and bred in Algeria, who considered Algeria to be French national soil, worked, planted, nourished by the sweat and blood of the forefathers. These native-born "French Algerians" called themselves "pieds noirs" in the same kind of local patriotic way that Carolinians in America call themselves "tarheels," a word that well translates "pieds noirs." Many of the French "tarheels" were sincere patriots and decent citizens, but, like many of their kind in the American South, they could not and would not come to terms with changing times and the inevitability of the "revolution of rising expectations" of the majority Arabic Moslem peoples of Algeria. The tarheels were, in effect, not so much revolutionaries as counterrevolutionaries. They were not primarily motivated by a desire to overthrow the republic in France for the purposes of a political change of regime, but rather because they suspected that the regime was too weak or too liberal to safeguard Algeria as French territory.

3. Men who were totally different from the proud crusaders of the army and the native-born fighters for their patrimony. They cared little about the army's crusading spirit, sought no Holy Grail and could not care less about the local problems of the French tarheels. This group hated the Republic, despised "la gueuse," regarded Marianne as a cheap little prostitute and Joan of Arc as a religious maniac. They were, for the most part, frustrated, frightened little shopkeepers, farmers fearful of dispossession, white-collar or unskilled workers ill-adapted to industrialization—all of

them disinherited, disenchanted, discontented unadjustables that exist in all the evolving modern societies. And, among them, there were just enough racists and rightists of all kinds to provide a fascist type of leadership and direction to this boiling lava of human fear and anger.

These were little men, not great men. They were enraged Lilliputians, not true revolutionaries. Sterilized by hatred, they could not become fathers of a country; they could only be patricides, murderers of their fatherland. General de Gaulle saw and sensed this Lilliputian quality of the plotters. He told writer J. R. Tournoux, "Power is not to be taken, it is to be picked up out of the ruins. Ah! Believe me, this is not an age for giants!"

While Gulliver sighed in his despair in Colombey, the Lilliputians went on the warpath in Algiers, surprising him as much as themselves. The most remarkable thing about that period of plotting and the culmination of the coup is that from start to finish hardly anyone really believed that what was happening would, in fact, happen. I recall today the dreamlike quality of those incredible days. The political leaders of the national assembly went about their ritual procedures like sleepwalkers, paying no heed to the words of treason being spoken in their midst by some of their fellow members. Governments rose and fell, without regard for the prosecution of the war in Algeria or the threats of civil war and coup d'état in France. Down went Mollet, up went Bourgès-Maunoury, down went Bourgès-Maunoury, up went Félix Gaillard, down went Félix Gaillard, all within the space of about six months.

Roger Frey shook his fist, Michel Debré screamed his rage, Jacques Soustelle muttered darkly, General Faure flew to Paris to seek support for a coup, Biaggi and his gang roved and rioted in the streets, a bazooka was fired into the office of General Salan, killing his aide while he narrowly escaped death by not walking into his office when he was supposed to; thieves broke into arsenals to steal weapons, students in Algiers printed revolutionary placards, convoys of cars suddenly started honking horns to the beat of al-gé-rie-FRAN-ÇAISE—three short beeps and two long ones, a pause, then again beep-beep-beep-BEEP-BEEP, al-gé-rie-FRAN-ÇAISE; or, in reverse, two long and three short notes, BEEP-BEEP-beep-beep-beep, meaning DE-GAULLE-au-pou-voir! And the police, like the politicians, did almost nothing. The leaders and officials of the Republic huddled together in a hutch like hypnotized rabbits watching in fascination the writhings of a band of snakes crawling under the netting and coiling up to strike.

* * *

France and Algeria were huge snakepits all through the winter and spring of 1958. The army, goaded beyond patience by the attacks of the Algerian rebel bands, which would then flee to a safe sanctuary across the Tunisian border, gave the air force the authority to conduct a "hot pursuit" of rebel forces. In February the air force struck, bombing the Tunisian village of Sakhiet and exploding the anger of the entire world at the brutality of its blow against a virtually defenseless village. Although the Algerian rebels had set up machine guns on rooftops inside the village and had fired on French planes, this was not accepted as justification for the savage bombing of the village. The allies of France, alarmed at the threat of an extension of the war, proposed the creation of an Anglo-American "Good Offices" mission, which was accepted by Tunisia and France.*

The United States unfortunately chose de Gaulle's old adversary Robert Murphy as its "Good Officer." The Gaullists howled with rage, and a wave of anti-Americanism swept over France. When Murphy came to Paris, he asked to be received by de Gaulle, but the General coldly declined to meet with him. Georges Bidault, Jacques Soustelle, Roger Duchet and André Morice joined together to call for the creation of a "Government of Public Safety" to replace the Gaillard cabinet. The civil service and the nationalized industries went on strike. On April 15 Premier Gaillard went to parliament to report on the results of the "Good Offices" mission and to ask for its approval. The assembly refused to endorse the mission, voted against Gaillard and toppled his government.

* It was at this time that a young U.S. Senator, John F. Kennedy, who had made a speech critical of France the year before, thought he might make a new address calling for Algerian independence. He asked CBS Washington correspondent Eric Sevareid to send me a message asking my views on such a move. I sent back a cable strongly advising against any public intervention by a senator during this tense period. I was certain that even the best-intentioned and most carefully worded speech would be twisted and turned against the senator and cause great harm to the United States. Any appeal by a senator on Algerian independence would have blown up a violent storm. Senator Kennedy decided finally to cancel the speech that was scheduled for May 8. Five days later the insurrection of Algiers erupted.

The government crisis provoked by the fall of the Gaillard cabinet turned out to be the last government crisis of the Fourth Republic, for it signaled the end of that republic. What almost everyone had come to believe would never finally happen finally did: the political cabinet makers could not put another government together. The carpenters had lost their touch, the wood was rotten and would not hold nails or glue. Everything had come unstuck. Day after day, week after week, the politicians paraded to the office of the President of the Republic, René Coty, conferred with him and separately among themselves, but the game of musical chairs was over because all the chairs and, indeed, all the furniture of the much-used and abused parliamentary system were thoroughly worn out.

By the second week in May, France had been without a government for a month. The opposition loosed its scorn on the system while the army watched nervously, and the colonials, exulting, called for an overthrow of the "rotten, defeatist, corrupt regime of Paris." On May 9 General Salan, commander-in-chief in Algiers, sent an urgent message to General Ely, head of the joint chiefs of staff, warning of the "unpredictable reaction of despair" of the troops if any government were formed that seemed to be considering negotiations with the Algerian rebels. He urged him to warn the President of the Republic of the danger. On May 12 Salan sent a message directly to President Coty, repeating his warnings. One of France's most respected political writers, Jacques Fauvet of *Le Monde,* commented in his book on the decline of the Fourth Republic that these telegrams "marked the official entry of the army into the political life of the nation."

The Gaullist group of revolutionists met at the Paris apartment of Roger Frey with Léon Delbecque, who brought with him from Algiers Alain de Sérigny, the director of the paper *Echo d'Alger,* one of the most powerful of the colonial voices. At the meeting were Michel Debré; de Gaulle's personal assistant, Olivier Guichard; and a general staff officer, General Petit. Delbecque has since said that the meeting gave him "the green light" to go ahead on the 13th.

The clandestine Gaullist high command met three times that day—twice at the apartment of Roger Frey, once at the home of "Bat" Biaggi—to discuss whether or not Jacques Soustelle should fly at once to Algiers to take over the leadership of a coup d'état for the Gaullists when the hour struck. They all agreed that the moment would come the next day, May 13, when Catholic politician Pierre Pflimlin, the latest candidate to try to form a government, was speaking to the assembly. Soustelle promised to deliver a speech in the course of the debate and then leave immediately for Algiers.

Pflimlin had spoken and written of his plans to call for a cease-fire in Algeria, and although in no way could he justifiably have been charged with planning a "sell-out" or a "surrender," these accusations were made in the overheated climate of the times. Pflimlin later admitted that he had been guilty of "indiscretion" and had failed to read the thermometer of the crisis carefully, but insisted that he was innocent of all the other charges leveled against him. Most observers now agree that any pretext would have served the impatient conspirators. Though it was Pflimlin's misfortune to give them the pretext they were looking for, in all likelihood another pretext would have been found. The hour of revolution had struck.

General de Gaulle was kept informed of every move, but he steadfastly refused to take any overt part in the preparations of the coup. When asked for his opinion on the advisability of Soustelle's departure, he curtly replied, "I have nothing to say on the subject." The Gaullists understood his reasons for keeping clean the "national patrimony named de Gaulle." He could not and would not risk dirtying or bloodying his hands or his prestige and his authority. He had waited a long time for the cleansing tempest to break over France, and he was not at the very last moment going to go out into the full fury of the storm.

De Gaulle was not the responsible captain on the bridge of the ship of state. He had left the ship twelve years before, disgusted with its mutinous crew, predicting it would run into reefs and be wrecked. He had become the lighthouse keeper, constantly pointing to perils, but no one would heed his signals. Now that the ship was floating rudderless and captainless in the storm, he would make no move to rescue it. It was his mission to build a new ship of state and guide it through safe channels out on to the high seas of the world.

Did de Gaulle do nothing more than listen to the sounds of rebellion, keeping his silence and freedom of maneuver? Or did he give secret instructions to the Gaullist conspirators through his staff men and agents? Is it credible that Guichard could have met constantly with the plotters, that de Gaulle himself could have received some of them, and yet that they were planning all the moves themselves without a word from de Gaulle? Was he not, in fact, the mastermind of the coup, keeping in the shadows but calling all the signals?

Ever since May 13, 1958, these questions have been hotly debated in France and among the world's observers. Future historians will have a mass of testimony, pro and con, to pore over. More evidence will be revealed each year as certain men decide to add their testimony to the already huge record, and as certain telegrams, letters and other documentary pieces of evidence are revealed. This writer, who lived through that period and who saw most of the principal actors before, during and after the coup of May 13, does not doubt for a moment that de Gaulle was in complete control of the Gaullists at all times. It could not—and should not—have been otherwise.

It was de Gaulle's duty as well as his opportunity to steer the coup his way. He would have been guilty of failing his responsibilities had he remained as uncommitted as the Gaullists reported him to have been. It was, after all, not de Gaulle who had created the situation leading to the insurrection. The Gaullists were neither the first nor the most important conspirators in the plot to overthrow the Fourth Republic. De Gaulle is nothing if not intelligent, and no intelligent man in those circumstances could have or should have refrained from guiding his troops to victory.

Those who say de Gaulle could have saved the Republic are seriously underestimating the violence of the passions that had broken loose. Had de Gaulle denounced the coup and tried to save the Fourth Republic, he would have gone down with it. His only chance, and the only chance for a new republic in France, was for de Gaulle to keep himself ready to take power after the Gaullist conspirators had outmaneuvered all the other plotters and steered the coup his way. That is exactly what happened, and nothing else could have happened, as all the leaders of the Fourth Republic have finally come to admit, even those who were most opposed to de Gaulle.

Pflimlin, Mollet, Pinay, Mendès-France, even the most strongly critical opponents of de Gaulle like Socialist Minister of the Interior Jules Moch, who wanted to distribute arms to the people to fight to the death for the Republic, have all told this writer that, upon reflection, the final outcome was the best way out of a hopeless situation. Had de Gaulle acted other than the way he did, either there would have been a terribly bloody civil war, as bad as or worse than the war in Spain, or a military dictatorship would have been imposed on a France that had failed to fight for freedom. De Gaulle saved what was still left to save of the honor, democracy and unity of a France on the brink of the abyss.

* * *

The "film of the affair," as the French press calls the record of a fast-moving crisis, is too well-known to need recounting here. The Gaullists, led by Léon Delbecque, joined later by Soustelle, succeeded in persuading the generals, principally Massu and Salan, to clear out the other groups and take over the coup in de Gaulle's name. At a moment of indecision, with civil war hanging in the balance, General de Gaulle broke his self-imposed silence and on May 15 issued a communiqué stating: "I hold myself ready to assume the powers of the republic."

It was this statement that led many observers to charge de Gaulle with pushing the regime over the brink and into the abyss at a moment when the army was wondering whether it had made a mistake and was considering turning against the coup. Certainly it was a departure from de Gaulle's previous "hands-off" policy. He had brought his hands into play and given the regime a big shove over the brink. Gaullist defenders, like Michel Debré, argued that this was the only thing he could do. If he had not expressed his willingness to come back to power, thus sanctioning the coup, civil war would have broken out among all the dissident groups. In any case, nothing could have saved the regime at that moment, even if de Gaulle had not said the word. Michel Debré was arrogant, pompous and often hysterical in the expression of his opinions, but on this issue it is difficult not to agree with his view. There was no other choice for de Gaulle but to avoid the violent rupture of French society that would have taken place if he had not intervened as he did at three critical moments in those seventeen days that shook France and the world from May 13 to May 29, 1958.*

The first intervention, the communiqué of May 15, was fol-

---

* The drama was acted out on two stages simultaneously, one in Paris, the other in Algiers, while the fifty-five million inhabitants of France and the overseas territories were anxious spectators and, at times, players in the drama. The following pages focus on the Paris stage. Events in Algiers and throughout overseas France will be recounted in the next chapter.

lowed four days later by the press conference of May 19, the first
time that de Gaulle had come out of the shadows in almost three
years since he had bid us farewell in July 1955. De Gaulle told us
on May 19 that he had made no declaration and exercised no
political action in three years because, as he had promised in 1955,
he had been holding himself in reserve for the coming tempest: "I
am a man who belongs to no one and who belongs to everybody."

General de Gaulle was then asked, in the question-and-answer
period that followed, what he had meant by saying that he held
himself ready "to assume the powers of the republic." He replied
that he had served the republic and France all his life, through two
world wars, and had restored the republic after the liberation and
the defeat of the totalitarian forces that had imposed a fascist state
in occupied France. De Gaulle disdainfully dismissed charges
against him of antirepublicanism by "those professional saviors,"
of whom he felt he had the right to ask, "What have they done
with liberated France and to its restored republic?" As for the
insurgents in Algiers, "One does not shout 'Vive de Gaulle' if one
is not for the nation."

De Gaulle did not deny that he might have revived the faltering
courage of the insurgents by his communiqué of May 15. He
stepped around the question and replied that he was ready to
encourage all Frenchmen "on both banks of the Mediterranean" if
they desired national unity. He said that one had to deal with facts.
And what had happened in Algiers was a fact. "Responsibilities
and blame will be studied and fixed later. Today we must deal
with a fact." He refused to say what kind of "arbitrage" role he
would play, since he had not yet been officially asked to play any
role. De Gaulle told us that no judge would give his verdict before
he was named or "before a hearing had been held, knowing,
moreover, that in the circumstances his advance judgment could
only end up as a dead letter."

At the close of the press conference a journalist asked him to
comment on rumors that if he came to power he would suppress
civil liberties. General de Gaulle raised his long arms, looked up in
the air as though invoking the heavens to bear witness to what he
had been asked and then, in his deepest voice, speaking slowly, and
moving his head from side to side, looking more than ever like an
angry old camel, he said, "Can anybody believe that at sixty-seven
years of age I am going to begin the career of a dictator?"

The tension broke in the crowded, hot, smoky conference room. Everyone roared with laughter and with relief, Gaullists and anti-Gaullists together. The truth is that quite a lot of people believed that de Gaulle was an apprentice dictator and that age was not necessarily a bar to such a career. Yet the moment after de Gaulle delivered this quip, the fears began to fade away. Dictators do not joke about being dictators. And when one thought of de Gaulle's entire career, everything he had ever said and done, it was not possible, except for those blinded with hate for him, to see him as a modern French Franco, Salazar or any other variety of modern dictator. A Louis Napoleon or a Louis-Philippe, in spirit and updated, perhaps, but not a dictator; it was laughable, and it was de Gaulle's political genius to understand the need to laugh at that grim moment and to be able to make us laugh. Then his equal sense of timing and theater led him to stand and bow as the laughs and the applause from his clique, planted in the conference room as usual, swelled up through the room.

General de Gaulle waited for the laughter to die down and then bid us good day: "I have said what I had to say. Now I will return to my village and there hold myself at the disposition of the country." He raised his arms in a farewell gesture, turned and walked off the stage. A better curtain line had never been written and no actor ever delivered one better than Charles de Gaulle, the greatest of all the actors among statesmen of the world.

Too old to be a dictator at sixty-seven? What an answer to all the agonizing questions that Frenchmen were facing! Restorer of the republic? What an answer to the charge that he was now cast in the role of its wrecker, or at least its dry-eyed pallbearer! Encouragement to those on both sides of the Mediterranean, in the name of national unity? What an answer at a moment when one side of the Mediterranean had risen in revolt against the other side in an uprising that split the nation! The most skillful, cynical, double-talking politicians and statesmen of modern history were nothing but clumsy amateurs compared with Charles de Gaulle. For sophistry and casuistry he is in a class by himself.

Only de Gaulle can surpass de Gaulle in cynicism and Machiavellism, not so much in the goals and objectives he sought—I am convinced that de Gaulle believed in the nobility of his cause and was never cynical about his purpose—but in the tactics he adopted to carry out his strategy.

De Gaulle's crowning achievement of Machiavellian maneuvers

was the third and decisive intervention of those seventeen world-shaking days in May. It followed a secret meeting with Premier Pierre Pflimlin, who had courageously insisted on going through with the empty, symbolic investiture of his government by the assembly. By the time of this meeting, the rebellion had spread from Algeria to Corsica, where Gaullist agents—some say on de Gaulle's own orders *—had seized power. Pflimlin demanded that de Gaulle denounce the unpardonable, treacherous insurrection in Corsica, where there was not the slightest excuse or justification for a seizure of power (in contrast to Algiers, where, whatever else one thought, there was a war against Arab rebels, which could be taken to be a reason for anxiety, no matter how deplorable). Pflimlin told de Gaulle that he could seriously envisage resigning and handing over the powers and responsibility of government to him, but only if he were to denounce the Corsican sedition. General de Gaulle insisted that an intervention by him in this sense would be completely useless unless he could at the same time say he was in the process of forming a government. Pflimlin told de Gaulle that he himself would not turn over power to de Gaulle and that he would not resign and abandon his responsibilities unless de Gaulle spoke out against the seditionists. They argued all through the night of May 27–28 and parted finally at dawn, at five in the morning, without reaching agreement and promising each other to keep their meeting and their exchange of views secret.†

At noon on May 28 Pflimlin was appalled and outraged when his aide handed him the copy of a communiqué just issued by de Gaulle. It was the statement of a virtual chief of government:

> I have undertaken the regular process necessary for the regular establishment of a republican government capable of assuring the unity and independence of the country. I expect that this procedure will continue and that the country will show, by its calm and its dignity, that it hopes it to be completed successfully. In these circumstances any action, from whatever quarter it may come, which imperils the public order may have grave

* For details, see the account in J. R. Tournoux, *Secrets d'Etat.*
† Pierre Pflimlin, in an interview at my apartment in Paris, and then a second time, for verification, at his office, has given me this version of the conversation. I have no reason to doubt its accuracy. De Gaulle and Pflimlin were alone; there are no other witnesses to the talk they had.

consequences. While understanding the circumstances, I would not be able to approve this. I expect that the land, air and naval forces of Algeria will remain exemplary in their conduct, under the orders of their chiefs, General Salan, Admiral Auboyneau and General Jouhard.

Pflimlin did not know what to think or what to do when he read de Gaulle's statement to the press. It was a clear breach of the word of honor given by de Gaulle to Pflimlin at dawn that morning. It was also untrue. He had not begun the "regular process" of setting up a "republican government." Pflimlin had not resigned. The President of the Republic had not called de Gaulle in, according to regular procedures, to designate him to "undertake the regular process." The whole statement was highly irregular, particularly the message to the armed forces, which de Gaulle had no authority to make as a private citizen.

However, the entire situation was highly irregular. Pflimlin himself, as premier, had delegated governmental powers to General Salan although Salan had endorsed the insurrection and shouted "Vive de Gaulle" from the balcony of the forum in Algiers. It was no time to quibble with de Gaulle's irregularity and inaccuracy of procedure, but rather to find out why he had apparently broken his word and what he had in mind by saying he had begun the process of taking power. Pflimlin was convinced that something grave had happened to force de Gaulle's hand. He went to see President Coty and told him that he believed de Gaulle must have received word that a paratroop assault on Paris was imminent and that de Gaulle had issued his communiqué to forestall such an attack, which would have led to civil war. Pflimlin did everything possible to find an excuse for de Gaulle's action, and President Coty agreed with him that it was essential to get in touch with de Gaulle at once to find out what he had in mind.

Meanwhile de Gaulle had dispatched an urgent message to Salan asking him to send a liaison officer immediately to Colombey to inform de Gaulle directly of events in Algiers. De Gaulle said he would send him back with a full report for Salan on de Gaulle's own plans. Salan promptly put General Dulac on a plane to Colombey. Dulac has since told several interrogators that his mission to de Gaulle prevented the attack upon the metropolis which had been prepared and which was ready to be launched. It is impossible to confirm beyond doubt whether this was true or whether the entire procedure was really an elaborate "intoxication" of the regime by psychological-warfare methods. Contemporary historians can only note that all of the Republic's leaders, including such last-ditch opponents of de Gaulle as Jules Moch,* refused to hold him responsible and turned to him to save the country from civil war and the republic from a totalitarian seizure of power by force.

The highest-ranking political leaders of the Fourth Republic sought out de Gaulle to try and commit him to a denunciation of the insurgents and a pledge to save the Republic. Leading the supplicants were two prominent Socialists, former Premier Guy Mollet and former President of the Republic Vincent Auriol. Auriol had told President Coty, his successor to the office of chief of state, that he himself "was now too old for an active mission" but he did agree to send a letter to General de Gaulle, appealing to him to denounce the rebellion. He sent his letter on May 26, and received the following reply from de Gaulle on May 28:

Dear President,

At this moment I am blocked by a determined opposition on the part of the parliamentary representatives. Moreover, I know that the temper of Algeria and of the army is such that, despite what I have said or could say today, a refusal of my proposals would break the last barriers and even bring down the high command.

Since I could not consent to receive power from any source but the people, or at least its representatives (as I did in 1944 and 1945), I fear that we are heading toward anarchy and civil war. In this case, those whose incredible sectarianism will have prevented me from saving the republic once again, when there was still time, will bear a heavy responsibility. As for me, there will be nothing left to do but to withdraw into my sorrow until the day I die.

General de Gaulle

* Pflimlin's minister of the interior, Jules Moch, a bitter-end anti-Gaullist, confirmed his belief that there was a real threat of an assault on France from Algiers on May 27. In an article published by *Le Midi libre* in June 1958, M. Moch said that de Gaulle's communiqué was not a personal maneuver, an act "which would have been unworthy of de Gaulle, whose sense of honor and of loyalty were beyond dispute."

De Gaulle did not denounce the insurrection, nor would he pledge himself to the Fourth Republic, as Auriol had asked. He had no desire or reason to save a regime that he had always fought and denounced as unworkable. As for the insurgents, he felt it was more important and realistic to discipline them and separate the genuine patriots from the fascist-minded seditionists after he had been invested with the power and authority of office, than to try to control them while he was still a powerless, retired army officer.

On the morning of May 28, after a soul-searching day of indecision, Pierre Pflimlin decided to offer his resignation to President Coty, to become effective if and when General de Gaulle agreed to be invested as premier under constitutional procedures. His resignation coincided with the delivery of de Gaulle's letter to Vincent Auriol. Meanwhile a mass demonstration for the defense of the republic was proceeding from the Place de la Nation to the Place de la République, the traditional public parade ground of the political parties ever since the Popular Front. A quarter of a million people marched behind such republican leaders as Mendès-France, François Mitterrand and André Philip; there were also, and significantly, great numbers of Communists, calling for a new Popular Front. The appearance of the Communists increased fears that the insurgents of Algiers might take it as a pretext to launch the landings in France that most authorities believed had been narrowly forestalled by de Gaulle's announcement the day before that he was forming a government.

The presiding officers of the parliament, National Assembly President André Le Trocquer and Senate Chairman Gaston Monnerville, sent a message to General de Gaulle asking urgently to meet with him that night to try to work out the terms of his legal election as premier. They met with de Gaulle at the same place where he had secretly conferred with Pflimlin two days before, in the residence of the Curator of the Park of Saint Cloud, a wartime resistant and "Companion" of General de Gaulle.

Their meeting lasted until one o'clock in the morning of May 29. The two parliamentarians alternately pleaded and fought with de Gaulle, trying to commit him to accept the legal procedures for appointment as premier and for the continuance of the republic. De Gaulle angrily denied that he had any intention of setting up a dictatorship. He reminded them that he had restored the republic after the war and was not now going "to come to power by the bayonet." However, he refused to "go through the ritual absurdities of parliamentary procedures." He would "respect the constitution, but not the practices of the politicians," he said. De Gaulle insisted that he had to have absolute powers for two years and must be free to send parliament into recess while he drafted a new constitution and put the affairs of France back in order again.

Gaston Monnerville, a moderate politician, conscious of his special role as a Negro and a symbol of the hopes of his people in the evolving societies of overseas France, was caught in the middle between the other two men. The Socialist firebrand Le Trocquer hated de Gaulle and kept needling him all through the meeting; de Gaulle despised Le Trocquer and became stiffer and more intractable every time Le Trocquer pressed him for a commitment or made an accusatory reference to de Gaulle's antiparliamentarianism. Monnerville played the role of the mediator and impressed upon de Gaulle the importance of keeping in mind the aspirations and the sentiments of the peoples of the French Union.

> For the peoples of overseas France you are the "man of
> Brazzaville" who proclaimed republican liberties as your
> war aim. You cannot now unilaterally draft a constitution
> by-passing the parliament and all the representatives of
> the people inside France and overseas. You cannot send
> parliament away for two years or even one year. There
> must be a fall term and there must be at least a constitu-
> tional committee on which parliamentarians share with
> government officials in drafting the text. You cannot do
> as Charles X did, and have the constitution written by the
> government alone.*

Monnerville and Le Trocquer went from Saint Cloud to the Elysée Palace and awakened President Coty to give him their report. He decided that his personal intervention was needed to bring the crisis to a head. At 10 A.M. on May 29 he announced that he would send an important message to parliament at 3 P.M. that day. The announcement set off a spate of rumors that Coty was going to resign and leave the republic without a president. There

* No precise notes were taken by any of the participants in this conference, but both Monnerville and Le Trocquer reported their statements to the parliamentary group leaders and to several reporters, including this writer, in personal interviews.

was a moment of panic throughout Paris, but it quickly passed when parliamentary group leaders spread the word that Coty would announce an agreement with de Gaulle for the General to form a new government.

At 3 P.M. Assembly President Le Trocquer read President Coty's message to a packed house. In the message, the President stated that "in this moment of peril for the nation and the republic" he was turning to "the most illustrious of Frenchmen, to the one who, in the darkest hours of our history, was our chief for the reconquest of liberty and who, achieving around him a national unanimity, rejected dictatorship and restored the republic." President Coty appealed to all patriots to put aside partisan politics and to support General de Gaulle.

The President said that the Le Trocquer and Monnerville meeting with de Gaulle "revealed that in the present state of things, very considerable difficulties remain to be overcome," but that he could not renounce his hopes for the return of "the incomparable moral authority that would assure the salvation of the country and the Republic." He expressed the hope that de Gaulle would confer with him "in the framework of republican legality." The President then shocked the assembly by confirming the rumor that had panicked Paris earlier in the day; he went on to state that "in the event of a setback to this attempt" he would feel obliged "to transfer immediately all my functions to the President of the National Assembly."

For the first time in the history of the republic, the chief of state, who was constitutionally the national arbiter, had intervened personally and directly in parliament. His threat of resignation was a powerful, publicly applied pressure, incompatible in spirit with republican principles. Nothing could have underlined the gravity of the crisis more than this departure from tradition by a man of honesty, integrity and love for the republic such as President René Coty.

General de Gaulle, at his retreat in Colombey, received a copy of the Coty message and a request to call upon the President of the Republic at the Elysée Palace. Until then he had refused to go to any government office and had met with the leaders of the state at Saint Cloud or, at times, in the Hôtel La Pérouse, where he had established a Parisian "crisis office." René Coty, however, was the chief of state and symbolized the republic as a national institution rather than the particular government of the time. De Gaulle

could not refuse a summons from France's chief magistrate. At
7.30 P.M. on that crucial night of May 29, while the parliamentarians were still hesitating about endorsing de Gaulle and the
insurgents were still on the verge of launching an invasion of
France, General de Gaulle came to the Elysée Palace.

In a tense negotiation with President Coty, General de Gaulle
cleared away the last obstacles to a procedure that would permit
him to form a government. He agreed to receive parliamentary
group leaders collectively but not individually as party leaders. He
refused to participate in a parliamentary debate on his bid to form
a government but agreed to go to the assembly and read his
investiture speech in person. Coty and de Gaulle further agreed
that a consultative constitutional committee would be created
which would give parliament a voice in the elaboration of a new
constitution and that all speed would be made to finish the draft in
time for a national referendum in the early fall. These compromise
solutions were worked out between Coty and de Gaulle in a
meeting that lasted a bit under two hours. Between 7.30 and 9.30
P.M. on May 29, 1958, France was saved, in extremis, from civil
war.

From the moment that General de Gaulle left the Elysée Palace
that night, events moved rapidly to a climax. It was reached on
June 1, when General de Gaulle presented to the national assembly
the program and the list of cabinet members of the government he
proposed to form with the approval of a majority vote that he
respectfully requested of the representatives of the people. The
politicians were relieved of their fears by his respect for the legal
form of procedure and by his inclusion in his proposed cabinet of
their traditional leaders: Socialist, Guy Mollet; Catholic, Pierre
Pflimlin; a moderate from Africa, Negro leader Félix Houphouet-
Boigny; and conservative, Louis Jacquinot—all as ministers of
state—and one of the most influential of the orthodox republicans, former Premier Antoine Pinay, as minister of finance. Only
one of the Gaullist revolutionaries, Senator Michel Debré, was
given a major post, as minister of justice—a curious choice of
mission for that most passionate of partisans. The other key
cabinet posts went to apolitical technicians: Maurice Couve de
Murville, foreign minister; prefect Emile Pelletier, interior minister; functionary Pierre Guillaumat, minister of the armies; while
Premier de Gaulle kept for himself the most important cabinet
post, minister of national defense, to deal personally with the

rebels of Algeria and Corsica.

Aside from Debré, whose personal devotion to de Gaulle was unquestionable and who had not taken an active public part in the seizure of power in Algiers, none of the conspirators and none of the antiparliamentary opposition leaders was given a role of importance in the de Gaulle government. The assembly was thus not being asked to approve a new governmental majority group, or to endorse the rebels; it was being asked to approve a new leader of the government, General de Gaulle, who had generously and wisely brought along with him the most eminent leaders of the former governments. No one had any illusions about the real importance of the roles that Mollet, Pflimlin, Pinay and the others would be permitted to play in a de Gaulle government. But they all appreciated the face-saving gesture and the meaning of de Gaulle's bid for cementing national unity and providing an honorable transition from the past to the future while rigorously excluding the principal engineers of the coup d'état.

General de Gaulle requested the grant of "full powers" to give him a free hand for six months; he asked for the right to revive Article 90 of the constitution in order to be able to organize a new constitutional referendum; he proposed to draft a new charter based upon "universal suffrage and separation of powers" but agreed that the government would still be "responsible before parliament"; he urged the speedy passage of three special laws to authorize him to proceed to carry out this program, after which parliament would immediately go into recess until the constitutionally prescribed formal opening of the fall term on the second Tuesday of October. These procedures would leave de Gaulle complete master of France for more than four months, which would push constitutional legality to the very limits consistent with law and honor but in conformity with the critical situation which existed.

The result was a foregone conclusion. The assembly had to yield to a situation of "force majeure," with its "honor" covered by the illustrious personality of General de Gaulle. The death epitaph of the Fourth Republic and the tone of resignation to the inevitable was delivered by a man who had often been described as "the de Gaulle of the Fourth Republic," former Premier Pierre Mendès-France, one of the few non-Communists who could not bring himself to vote for General de Gaulle. Mendès-France said, "The Fourth Republic has perished of its own faults. It dilapidated its

moral capital, the system failed to work, and many of the French
turned away from it. . . . Whatever my personal feeling about
General de Gaulle, I will not vote for his investiture. I cannot vote
under the menace of insurrection and a military show of strength.
The decision that is about to be taken will not be a free one: it is
a dictate."

Many of the deputies present shared the sentiments of Mendès-
France, but they knew, as he himself conceded, that they had to
put their hopes in de Gaulle or face a civil war that would destroy
France. They understood that Mendès, because of his great record
of service to the republic, could not bring himself to vote under
those circumstances, but the majority of members could not
permit themselves the personal satisfaction of adopting his position. They voted for de Gaulle by a majority of 329 to 224. Of the
224 negative votes, 141 were cast by the Communist Party group
and 49 by the dissident Socialists. The others belonged to scattered
dissidents from the other, smaller groups, including 18 radicals
who followed the lead of their party's former premiers who voted
against de Gaulle: Mendès-France, Edouard Daladier and Maurice
Bourgès-Maunoury. It was not a "triumphant" investiture, but,
in the circumstances, it was the biggest majority possible. What
mattered to de Gaulle, in any case, was not the size of the majority
in a parliament he held in contempt but the legal authorization to
dismiss it and erect a new regime on the wreckage of the old.

Charles de Gaulle did not seize power; he picked it up out of the
pieces of the shattered regime. It was also thrust into his hands by
those who had let their cabinets fall too often and too far into
public disrepute. The plotters would not have dared to stage their
clumsy and more or less feeble insurrection, which wavered and
faltered each day, had the regime not been exhausted and gutted
by its long struggles and internal divisions. Had they tried a coup
against a government with any authority or vigor, it would have
been swiftly crushed—as, in fact, similar coups were crushed later
when they were attempted against de Gaulle himself. The Fourth
Republic was stabbed in the back by the insurrectionists of Algiers,
but it was dying before the treacherous blow was struck. The coup
was more a coup de grâce than a coup d'état.

Charles de Gaulle did not come to power as a dictator, or as a
democrat, despite the face-saving rigmarole of a parliamentary
investiture. He came in as a receiver in bankruptcy, closed up the
shop, sent everybody away for six months while he cleaned up the

mess and set about restoring the country's morale and the nation's credit. At the age of sixty-seven Charles de Gaulle was indeed too old to start a career as a dictator, but not too old to begin a new life and a third career as a statesman, President of the Republic of France.

CHAPTER NINE

TOO LATE TO BE AN EMPEROR

> *We place no constraints on anyone. We ask you simply to say "yes" to us or to say "no" to us. If you say "no" we will draw the necessary conclusions. If you want your independence, you can have it. But if you say "yes" to us, then we will be brothers, marching side by side down the road to a great destiny.*
>
> CHARLES DE GAULLE, *speech in Dakar, August 27, 1958*

FROM THE INSURRECTION of May 13 through the investiture of de Gaulle as premier on June 1, the threat of civil war hung over France every hour of the long, tense days. Had anyone either precipitated events or suddenly put on the brakes, the complex, fast-moving crisis would have spun out of control. It almost did on a number of pressure fronts in Africa while the Fourth Republic was thrashing through its death throes in Paris.

On May 17 several thousand Tunisian troops tried to force the French garrison to evacuate the village of Remada. Shots were exchanged, and the local French commander radioed to the air force for help. Only the rapid intervention of French Commander-in-Chief General Gambiez and President Bourguiba, acting in concert to restrain their own forces, averted a pitched battle that could have provoked a French Army invasion of Tunisia. Similar trouble was brewing in Morocco, where news of the Remada incident incited the Moroccans to send reinforcements to their eastern provinces on the Algerian frontier.

On May 19—the day that de Gaulle held his press conference in

Paris to announce that he was too old to be a dictator but was holding himself ready to serve his country—the Moroccan prime minister demanded that French troops withdraw from the eastern provinces "in the briefest possible time." Moroccan and French troops clashed at Borj-Saf-Saf in an incident similar to the Remada conflict in Tunisia.

On May 24 another incident broke out in a shooting skirmish between French and Tunisian elements at Gafsa. President Bourguiba, nervously watching the maneuvers under way in Paris, not knowing whether de Gaulle would come back to power in time to restrain the French Army, appealed to America and Britain to send him arms and planes. He also sent a message to the U.N. Security Council, asking for a hearing on the threat to peace. The U.N. agreed to schedule a meeting, but the United States and Britain advised Bourguiba not to play with fire. They refused to send arms, and they told him to keep as calm as he could and trust them not to let his country be attacked and overrun. Above all, they warned him against giving the jumpy and angry French forces pretext for an assault. In the meantime tensions remained high in Algeria during the complicated negotiations between the political leaders and de Gaulle in Paris. The revolutionary Comité de Salut Public consolidated its grip in Algiers and also sent its agents into France to be ready to seize power by force if the politicians did not abdicate to de Gaulle.

During the critical days in May the fever spread like a plague throughout all the territories of French Africa. In Dakar, Senegal's strategic Atlantic port, a Committee of Defense was formed and the local authorities announced that "Senegal would welcome a government of General de Gaulle if his program includes liberal reforms for the overseas territories." The Africans sensed that the crisis of France gave them their opportunity to demand self-government. After Senegal, Madagascar announced that it would rally to de Gaulle, "the man of Brazzaville," making it clear, however, that support was dependent upon the extension of the wartime Brazzaville promise of evolution to self-government.

French colonial administrators were alarmed to see how the winds of freedom were blowing throughout Africa. In Brazzaville itself, a "Committee of Vigilance" was formed by the European settlers. The high commissioner there, Pierre Messmer, sent a telegram to Paris stating that "French Equatorial Africa expresses the hope that General de Gaulle will rapidly form a government."

Thus both the French colonials and the colonized Africans looked toward de Gaulle as the man to save the "French Union" and convert it into a new, progressive and evolving association of peoples.

As soon as de Gaulle was invested as premier on June 1, he promptly set himself to reassuring the Africans. His first official act on June 2 was to dispatch telegrams to President Bourguiba of Tunisia and to the King of Morocco. To Bourguiba he pledged his intention "to settle, with your agreement, the present difficulties between our governments and the conditions for good relations for the future." To the King of Morocco he sent personal assurances of the friendship and respect that he had for him and had had "ever since the time that Moroccans and Frenchmen fought together side by side for their liberty and for the liberty of the world."

The messages should have left no doubt in anyone's mind as to Premier de Gaulle's intentions in Africa. His reference to the solidarity of the French and the Moroccans in the fight for liberty could not possibly be construed other than as a commitment to the evolution of the African countries to independence. The King of Morocco had no such doubts and did not hesitate to express his sentiments in his answer to de Gaulle's message. "We remain convinced," he wrote, "that relations between France and the countries of North Africa will be made healthy and strong and that the conditions for a free and fruitful cooperation will be created by the realization of the national aspirations of the Algerian people and the establishment of peace in Algeria. May your name be linked to the success of this noble enterprise!"

This exchange of messages was greeted with satisfaction in Paris, above all by Senator Monnerville and Minister of State Houphouet-Boigny, the principal representatives of the African peoples in the French republic. General de Gaulle, knowing that the most difficult, dangerous and decisive problem was in Algeria, sought to free himself of all other entanglements so that he could concentrate all his energies on the main front. Thus, after reassuring Tunisia and Morocco, and through them the other African territories, he moved to win over and calm down the still suspicious, jittery parliamentarians in Paris. On the same June 2, the day of his messages to Bourguiba and the Moroccan king, Premier de Gaulle suddenly made a surprise visit to the assembly, which was discussing his request to pass three urgent bills before going into recess. The bills concerned the extension of special powers in

Algeria, the grant of full powers to the government in France for six months and the revision of Article 90 of the constitution to clear the way for the elaboration of a new constitution.

Charles de Gaulle showed a new personality to the deputies in his first appearance in the semicircular chamber as chief of government. Unlike the General de Gaulle who had presided over them haughtily and disdainfully after the liberation, the new Premier de Gaulle seemed to enjoy being in the assembly and made every effort to be pleasant and friendly. He shook hands with deputies who came to the government bench during a brief recess in the debate. He smiled and chatted with them, appeared to be completely at ease and at home in the house that he had so often covered with ridicule and scorn. The statesman was emerging in this latest reincarnation of the former soldier and savior.

De Gaulle went to the speaker's platform to assure the deputies of his dedication to republican principles. He said, "What I have done, I did so that the republic could continue. What I will do at all times will be done to make the republic stronger, healthier, more effective, indestructible." The surprised and gratified deputies burst into applause when Premier de Gaulle concluded his address with the words, "And I want you all to know how much I feel the honor and the pleasure of this occasion to be here among you tonight." Only the Communists sat frigid and motionless among the cheering deputies. Communist group leader Kriegel-Valrimont expressed their sentiments when he commented, "After Operation Sedition, we are being treated to Operation Seduction."

The seduction scene was successfully played. The final vote on the new constitutional authority was 350 to 161. Of the 161 negative votes, 142 were cast by the Communist group. Thus the great majority of the non-Communist deputies endorsed Premier de Gaulle much more enthusiastically than they had in the "under-the-gun" vote of investiture on June 1. With that endorsement strengthening his hand, and with the good wishes and trust of the African countries speeding him on his way, General de Gaulle flew off directly to Algiers for the first round of what would be the supreme test of the old man's new career.

* * *

The sky was as blue as the waters of the Mediterranean that sparkled beneath it. Tiny white clouds drifted back and forth like the sailboats scudding in and out of the harbor of Algiers. The hot African sun was cooled by the sea breeze, and the air was perfumed with the scent of orange blossoms. It was a perfect June day, in one of the most beautiful ports of the world, "Alger la blanche," the whitest, purest diamond in the crown of the old French Empire.

The "pieds noirs" were out in full force, in a festive mood to greet the king whom they had enthroned. They had every reason to feel as they did, for it was their uprising on May 13 that had brought down the Fourth Republic, and in that sense Charles de Gaulle was their creation. They were not particularly impressed by his repeated pledges of allegiance to the republic, for he had too often heaped scorn on the regime and too loudly called for a strong state to be taken seriously as a dedicated republican, at least by men who themselves despised the republican regime. They wanted and needed to believe in a strong leader who was also indebted to them. Giddy with power, overheated by the red-hot sun, the "tarheels" surged into the Forum on June 4, bearing banners, singing, shouting, laughing in an outburst of mass hysteria, as they gathered together to cheer the new sovereign and through him, in effect, to enthrone themselves as the new barons, dukes and princes of the realm.

At the gates of the Government-General Building, perched on a pyramid of camera cases, I could see de Gaulle on the balcony just above and behind me, and in front a vast sea of roaring people, contrasting with the calm waters of the Mediterranean in the distance. My colleague and good friend, CBS News cameraman George Markman, had set up his sound camera just in front of the gate, but he would go plunging deep into the crowd, carrying a hand-held camera, like a scuba diver spearing close-up pictures of the almost insane mob. Moslem women moaned, tore off their veils and clawed at their faces until they drew blood. Men jumped up and down, beating each other on the back, and every few minutes, first-aid stretcher bearers would push their way into the mob to rescue someone who had fainted or was throwing a fit. I kept staring up at de Gaulle, wondering what he was thinking and what words he would find to speak to the hysterical little kingmakers of Algiers.

General de Gaulle looked ten feet tall as he drew himself up to parade position and lifted his long arms high above his head in the famous gesture that converted his huge body into a giant V-for-victory sign. The mob moaned and shrieked, writhing like a monstrous animal with one mammoth body and a hundred thousand heads. It began to chant its battle cry: al-gé-rie-FRAN-ÇAISE-al-gé-rie-FRAN-ÇAISE. It was a cry and an incantation both, a plea to de Gaulle to join them in the chant, but also, one could feel, an underlying menace, a latent murderous rage if he did not. It was the most dangerous public challenge that de Gaulle had ever faced. If he joined in the chant, if he repeated the magic words, he would become the servant of that mob, irrevocably committed to carrying out its demands; if he did not join in or demonstrate his sympathies and allegiance, the mob might storm the building and tear down the balcony on which he stood. There could be no doubt about its intentions and the fearful power of its passions.

General de Gaulle met the challenge. He gradually lowered his arms, like a conductor signaling an orchestra to reduce its volume. Slowly he silenced the mob. Then he opened his arms wide, as though to embrace them all, and in his deep, powerful voice, calling out each word like an ancient oracle, he chanted the phrase, syllable by syllable: "JE-VOUS-AI-COM-PRIS!"

There was a split-second silence, an instant of total paralysis, almost as if the world had stopped turning. Everyone was caught in frozen motion, mouths open but breathless, arms stuck in the air, rigid, as in a trick movie sequence when a frame is suddenly stopped and the image fixed. Then a roar shattered the silence. Men began pounding each other again, European women, like the Moslems, tore their own dresses, while the stretcher bearers stood helplessly watching people fall by the hundreds. Cameraman George Markman fought his way back to our position, began to load a new film pack, then turned to me and said, "The hell with it! Nobody would believe it if I filmed any more of this. I don't believe it myself."

The uproar continued, but somehow de Gaulle managed to make himself heard again and continued his address for a few more minutes. It was the briefest speech in his career, lasting less than ten minutes. It did not matter. Nothing mattered, nothing was heard after the opening words, "Je vous ai compris," for what the mob wanted to hear and wanted to believe was that he was with them all the way, and this is what they understood him to mean when he said, "I have understood you."

How desperately these frightened, frustrated people wanted, needed, to be understood. They were not bad people, not the

majority of them, any more than the people of the American
South are bad people. In both Algeria and the South, however, a
minority of evil men have long exploited the fears of their fellows
and turned fear into hate, hate into repression, repression into
secession and secession into civil war. It was, in fact, this vicious
cycle of colonialism, racism and secessionism that de Gaulle
understood and that he had determined to bring to an end. This,
fortunately for de Gaulle, the mob did not understand to be the
true meaning of his oracular pronouncement.

Future historians may one day rank that opening phrase of de
Gaulle's address in the Forum among the greatest lines of all the
political speeches of history. It was a masterpiece of psychological
manipulation of the masses. It said nothing more than the simple
fact that he was aware of what they had done and what they
wanted. It was the mob that deluded itself into believing that
comprehension meant concurrence. De Gaulle might have meant
the exact opposite, and they could have sensed it if they had
considered his words carefully. "I have understood you" is an
elliptical phrase, ending in an implied parenthesis: "I have understood you, my friends," or "my enemies." It might have meant "I
agree" or "I disagree." The people in the Forum wanted to take
the phrase to mean, "I have understood you, my friends, and I
agree."

De Gaulle deliberately let the people deceive themselves, since
he could not at that point tell them the whole truth. At the same
time de Gaulle would not lie to them. He never deliberately lies in
his public statements on great issues. De Gaulle speaks publicly for
history, and he wants the record to do him honor. Unlike some
politicians, who are willing to lie in public and whisper the truth
only in private, de Gaulle tells the truth in public and practices
deception only in private. He will not always tell the whole truth
in public, but what he does say is nothing but the truth, perhaps as
little of the truth as possible, but never a lie. De Gaulle once told
this writer, "A statesman should never lie to the people; on the
other hand, he should be very careful about when and how to tell
the truth."

A lesser man than de Gaulle would not have been able to resist
the temptation to tell that delirious mob what it wanted to hear.
But Charles de Gaulle, despite his many faults, is not a lesser man,
he is a big and strong and very stubborn man. As President
Eisenhower said in a toast to de Gaulle at a state dinner in Paris,

"You are the most stubborn man I have ever known." De Gaulle will not let himself be pushed beyond the line he sets for himself. He will not commit himself publicly to policies he does not believe in—above all, not with the world listening and the world's scribes recording his words.

If the people of Algiers had listened carefully that day and had read the text of his speech the next day, they would have understood better what he meant when he said, "Je vous ai compris." All that de Gaulle really had promised in that speech was that he would end all of their colonial privileges. He had gone on to say he would terminate the segregationist electoral college in which Arab votes were counted separately from the European. He promised an equal voting opportunity to all inhabitants and pledged that the Arabs would elect their own representatives. Then he said—and this was the key phrase—"with those elected representatives we will see how to do the rest." The cheering crowd did not realize that "the rest" was a pledge to liquidate all that it was fighting to preserve.

Although the mob was induced to self-deception, some of the leaders of the May 13 insurrection, including the Gaullists, understood and resented what de Gaulle had said. This writer watched Léon Delbecque discussing the speech heatedly with members of the Comité de Salut Public. They were challenging him to explain the statement: "They will elect—and I repeat, in a single electoral college—their representatives for the public powers, exactly as all other French citizens." They were further outraged by de Gaulle's outstretched hand to the Algerian guerrilla forces in this invitation: "May even those participate who, in despair, are fighting on this soil, fighting courageously." De Gaulle took particular pains to address himself to the Moslem rebels: "I want to recognize this publicly, for there is no lack of courage in this land of Algeria. Their combat is courageous, although no less cruel and fratricidal for that fact. I, de Gaulle, open to all of them the gates of reconciliation."

Thus on June 4, only three days after he succeeded to the office of a premier whom the Algiers mob had overthrown for offering much less to the rebels, Charles de Gaulle faced the insurgents on their own grounds, inside their stronghold, and opened up the door to fraternization and integration for all the Arabs of Algeria, including even those who had killed and were on that very day killing Frenchmen in the guerrilla fighting. This was not what the insurgents had overthrown the Fourth Republic to bring about. This was treason.

Delbecque at first tried to persuade the ultras to trust de Gaulle. He assured them that de Gaulle was committed to keeping Algeria French. Nothing could persuade them other than an open declaration of devotion to Algérie Française, and this de Gaulle refused to make. In successive speeches in Algiers, Constantine, Oran, the only slogans that he shouted were "Vive la République, Vive la France!" Only once in the entire trip, in a speech at Mostaganem, did the words "Algérie Française" come from his lips, and when they did, de Gaulle looked as surprised as everyone listening to him. It may have been accidental, as some reporters thought. After all, it is almost impossible to make dozens of speeches among people shouting a slogan so that it is drummed into one's ears and not have it slip out of one's own mouth by accident. Or perhaps, as this writer suspects, it was deliberate, part of de Gaulle's Machiavellism, to confuse everyone and stir up a controversy. Deliberate or accidental, it could not be denied that the words were only pronounced once, in the smallest of the places visited, and to the smallest of crowds.

The main, consistent stress of de Gaulle's message to Algeria was less to keep it French than to offer full French citizenship rights to the inhabitants of Arab-Moslem origin. To the colonials of French origin his message was "total discipline, without qualification and without conditions." For the future de Gaulle promised only free elections, after which we "would do the rest" and "find the place for Algeria" in the French "ensemble"—a fine vague word which he refused to define or spell out in any detail. As for the Comités de Salut Public which had staged the uprisings and seized power, General de Gaulle dealt with them exactly as he had handled the resistance committees inside France after the landing in Normandy. He took steps to discipline them and warned them against "substituting yourselves for the public authorities."

De Gaulle would not tolerate the existence of revolutionary paragovernmental forces. They may have thought they had brought him to power, but this was not his interpretation of the situation. In his view, his power was derived from all the people of France, through his investiture by their delegates in parliament assembled. He owed no political debt to any special-interest group, nor would he, as chief of the government of the republic, permit

the existence of any armed force or public authority other than
that of the republic itself. There could be no misunderstanding on
this count. General de Gaulle stated this view publicly and privately, over and over again, and gave orders to this effect to the
army, the police and the civil authorities in Algiers. He had
crossed the Rubicon and was master of Rome, and the provinces
had only to obey.

The "provincials" were furious. They felt cheated and double-
crossed by de Gaulle, and were in no mind to obey. Even the most
fervent of Gaullists, Léon Delbecque, who had done more than
any other man to channel the coup toward de Gaulle, reacted
angrily to de Gaulle's orders to fall in line. He issued a communiqué addressed to "my compatriots of the metropolis" stating that
the Committees of Public Safety "emerging from the underground will organize themselves publicly and group themselves
around the national committee. It will be their task to denounce
and foil all the maneuvers of the dying system." And then, in a
scarcely veiled threat, Delbecque warned, "Princes of the system,
you thought you could choke off the revolution. Don't count on
it!"

By using the formula "princes of the system," invented by Debré
during the many months of opposition and plotting before the
coup, Delbecque was ostensibly addressing himself to the political
party leaders of the Fourth Republic. In fact, however, he could
only have been addressing himself to General de Gaulle, who was
the new ruling "prince" of a new system. If de Gaulle had chosen
to name the former princes to his cabinet, then it was he who was
trying "to choke off the revolution," and not the politicians who
were now powerless and derived their functions only from de
Gaulle. Thus within only a few days of the successful coup those
who had plotted and maneuvered together had rapidly split apart
in the inevitable fight among the victors for the spoils of power.
The conflicts between the committees of Algiers and the government of de Gaulle were ominous signs of the future test of strength
that would produce two more violent uprisings in Algiers in the
years ahead.

General de Gaulle saw this coming from the first day, and he set
about provoking the conflict himself, as he had at the liberation of
Paris, for, if there could be only one governmental power, the legal
power of the republic, then the sooner all paralegal and clandestine movements were stamped out, the sooner the republic could

be made secure. De Gaulle appointed General Salan as Delegate-General of the Government and ordered him to take action to bring the Algiers committee under control. He ordered his delegate to take disciplinary action when the committee of Algiers voted a motion opposing local elections and demanding the dissolution of political parties. De Gaulle told Salan, "In reference to the deplorable, untimely incident caused by the peremptory motion of the Algiers committee, I remind you that this committee has no other right and no other role than to express the opinions of its members to you and under your control. The regular authority, and in the first instance you yourself, cannot take any part in any issue that this committee or any other political organization may bring up, or put forward demands."

To prepare for the final test of strength with Algiers, General de Gaulle had first to win the support of the majority of the peoples both inside France and in the overseas territories. His appeal to the citizens of metropolitan France would be aimed at their principal aspirations: social progress and prosperity in a stable society. To overseas France only one appeal would be meaningful: a promise of self-government leading to independence in a freely consented assembly of sovereign nations. It was to those twin aspirations that de Gaulle set about addressing himself as soon as he had concluded the necessary first contact with the colonials of Algeria. Parliament had granted him full powers for six months, and he could not afford to lose one precious day preparing for the crucial test of strength in Algeria, a land torn by two rebellious forces: the French segregationists and the Arab fighters for freedom.

* * *

Premier de Gaulle moved first to make the home front secure. On his return from Algiers on June 10 he conferred at once with Finance Minister Antoine Pinay, who had been urgently drafting a plan to launch a new "national patriotic loan." The purpose was to demonstrate the popularity of the government and to raise funds to finance a new economic-recovery program. On June 13 Premier de Gaulle delivered a radio-television address to the nation to launch the loan. It was the first of such addresses that were to become the trademark of de Gaulle's "government by electronics." His technique is less a "fireside chat" than a cathedral chant, but it is a remarkably effective means of impressing the ungovernable but very guidable Gauls.

"Inside our country, a major effort is required," Premier de Gaulle told the people. "It is a very hard task, but absolutely necessary to restore the balance of our finances and our economy, failing which our country would head toward a stupid catastrophe, but thanks to which it will see the road to prosperity open wide for all." He asked the citizens to subscribe to the loan not only as "a first proof of national confidence and of confidence in themselves," but also "permit me to say, confidence in me, for I have a very great need of your help." Premier de Gaulle promised that he would "by early fall" propose new institutions to give the republic "powers strong enough, stable enough, sufficient enough to meet its destiny." He ended his address with a cry of hope and faith in France that is the essence of Gaullism: "The road ahead is a rough one, but it is beautiful! The goal is difficult to attain, but how great it is! Let us go ahead. The signal for departure is now given!"

The citizens saw, heard and were conquered by the appeal of their leader. They responded magnificently. The loan was the greatest success of its kind in French history. Not only did money pour in, but most of it was "fresh money," as the economists call savings funds rather than conversions of other assets. The supposedly mistrustful and miserly French people dug into the proverbial socks filled with gold that they keep hidden under city mattresses and buried in country gardens. They made de Gaulle the modern Midas of the republic. In the first four days of the loan citizens turned into the Bank of France a total of 34 *tons* of gold, more than all the gold the bank had been able to buy in the full seven weeks of a similar Pinay appeal in 1952. By the end of the "de Gaulle loan" citizens had turned in the astonishing total of 140 tons of gold and had subscribed a total of 320 billion francs—almost one billion dollars at the exchange rate of that time—of which 290 billions were in "fresh money." It was an economic and financial miracle, one of the most impressive votes of confidence that a people can give a president.

The success of the loan greatly enhanced de Gaulle's moral, as well as legal, authority for his test of strength with Algiers. It also increased his prestige throughout the overseas territories and in the watching world, where there were many doubts, hesitations and anxieties about the crisis of France and the nature of de Gaulle's regime. The world outside France did not merely watch events in France. World leaders conferred on French affairs and went to

Paris to meet with de Gaulle and personally to test the climate of France and the possible role of France in current important world problems. There was no lack of world problems in that first month of de Gaulle's return to office. He had to cope with them, and it is important here to note at least briefly what was going on in order to judge the magnitude of his task as the chief of government of the new republic. Despite his need to concentrate his energies in Algeria, the world was too much with him to permit a total concentration.

In the month of July he conferred in Paris with British Prime Minister Harold Macmillan, U.S. Secretary of State John Foster Dulles, NATO Secretary-General Paul-Henri Spaak and German Defense Minister Franz-Josef Strauss, while answering letters from Khrushchev calling for a summit conference and Eisenhower inviting him to Washington. At the same time a revolution erupted in Iraq, and the President of Lebanon appealed to the Americans and the British to land troops to prevent a Nasser-fomented revolution in his country. With all this buzzing around his head, de Gaulle had to keep his own hornets' nest under control in North Africa.

De Gaulle moved quickly to secure the eastern and western flanks of Algeria. In an exchange of letters with Bourguiba he agreed to pull back all French land troops in Tunisia and to regroup them in the coastal naval base at Bizerte within four months. He also proposed that negotiations begin on a new statute for Bizerte no later than October 1 and further agreed immediately to recognize Tunisian sovereignty over Bizerte. Similar assurances and steps toward a new cooperative relationship were taken by de Gaulle on Morocco while he prepared to make a second trip to Algeria and a full continental swing around Africa to the key territories of the French Union.

In the meantime, inside France, de Gaulle had launched the national loan campaign successfully despite these crises, which were not the best climate to encourage investment. He also instructed his minister of justice, Michel Debré, to move rapidly along with the consultative constitutional committee, to be ready to submit a new charter to the people in a September referendum. De Gaulle carried out all these activities in an Algerian and metropolitan French climate that was still at fever pitch. He and his government were far from secure. The situation was tersely summed up by his chief acolyte, writer André Malraux, who expressed a devout wish, rather than an accomplished fact, with these words: "There are today those who want a republic without de Gaulle; others who want de Gaulle, but not a republic. But the vast majority of Frenchmen want both a republic and General de Gaulle."

* * *

De Gaulle and the republic faced their first great test in the September referendum on the draft constitution. There were two testing grounds—one inside France, where he was assured a majority; the other, far less certain and far more important for the immediate future, in Africa, where the former colonial territories, nervously watching events in Algeria, wondered what de Gaulle had in mind for them. It was essential that he reassure the African peoples as a vital element in his over-all strategy of battening down the hatches for the storm through which he would have to steer the ship of state in Algeria. Therefore he scheduled an immediate speaking tour of the African territories, to be completed before the September referendum. Since he was tied down in Paris in July by the loan campaign, the organization of his internal defenses and the crises of world affairs, he was not free to go to Africa before August, in the worst heat of summer. Only a monumental iceberg like de Gaulle could have survived the kind of safari he decided to undertake.

The tour was a ten-thousand-mile sprint in African temperatures that boiled the blood by day and chilled the marrow of the bones at night, through deserts, over mountains, across the endless veld and jungles of Africa. It left everyone on the tour totally exhausted, except the extraordinary old man who seemed to get stronger and grow bigger with each lap of the race. In one week de Gaulle talked his way across the vast continent: On August 22 he toured the humid island of Madagascar, over roads steaming with heat and covered with viscous mud, thick as fudge; on August 24 he was in Brazzaville, deep in the jungle of Equatorial Africa, where the air was as hot and thick as the mud of Madagascar; on August 25 he visited Abidjan, bustling new river port of the Ivory Coast; on August 26 he spoke in Conakry, Guinea; and on August 27, far from the off-shore island of Madagascar southeast of Africa, the tireless Charles de Gaulle was haranguing the crowds at Dakar, on the far west coast, Africa's gateway to the Americas.

De Gaulle toured Africa as a liberator. He spoke as the emancipator, pledging liberty, equality and fraternity in the name of the French republic. He told cheering Africans that France would help them achieve self-government and guide them toward independence, with the hope that they would freely choose to remain closely tied to the motherland. He sought to distinguish between two kinds of independence while trying as much as possible to avoid using the word independence itself. He spoke instead of "sovereignty," making a distinction between national and international sovereignty. What he was doing was trying to sketch a picture of a new kind of commonwealth, based on the internal independence of member states but including an external interdependence with a greater guiding nation, like France. He called it the "Communauté Française."

The essential feature of this "French community" was the union of the member states overseas with metropolitan France in certain common institutions. The president of France would also be the president of the community, and the overseas peoples would participate in the election of the president through a special electoral college. There would be a council of the community with certain attributes for over-all community affairs. France, as the modern great power, would be responsible for the foreign affairs and the defense of the community. It was, therefore, far more centralized and formal an institution than the British Commonwealth. It sought, however, to be flexible enough to permit evolution and even outright independence if any nation wished to sever the ties of interdependence to assume full national and international sovereignty.

At every stop on the tour de Gaulle said, "I ask you to accept this new community by voting 'oui' in the constitutional referendum. But France will not raise any obstacles against those who wish to vote 'non.' I only tell you that to vote no is to vote to sever all ties with France. There is no responsibility without obligations and trust. Those who wish to be independent can do so by their free vote." Charles de Gaulle demonstrated that he was not only too old to be a dictator at sixty-seven, but that it was also too late, in the fifty-eighth year of the twentieth century, for any man to be an emperor.

To those who agreed to remain with France he offered economic, financial, spiritual and cultural aid, "all the treasures and advantages of being part of a huge, worldwide assemblage of self-governing free men, who would join together in the common defense of true liberties and the common construction of progress and prosperity." Premier de Gaulle was learning and liking his role of statesman. He still possessed all the qualities of Charles de Gaulle, the soldier, and General de Gaulle, the savior of France, but as a statesman he developed these qualities far beyond the more limited powers of his previous incarnations. The old man was a new man, reinvigorated and blazing with a charismatic magic that projected his own visions into the minds of other peoples.

The charisma of Charles de Gaulle was a powerful magic. It won for him the greatest popular mandate in modern history, as his draft constitution was approved by a 6 to 1 majority. These were the results of the September 28 referendum in those territories that returned a majority for the constitution:

TERRITORY	OUI	NON
Metropolitan France	17,668,700	4,624,511
Overseas France	9,221,585	632,606
Departments of Algeria	3,357,763	118,631
Overseas Departments	218,187	24,933
French citizens living abroad	355,163	15,246
Others	245,014	3,822
TOTAL	31,066,412	5,419,749

The vote was a triumph, particularly in Africa, where only one French territory returned a majority against the constitution, and thus, as de Gaulle had pledged, had voted for independence. Guinea's leader, Sekou Touré, had told his people they had to break all ties with France and they voted overwhelmingly "non" by 1,136,324 to 56,981, a vote of 20 to 1 to leave the French Union. But the percentages among the other African peoples were equally overwhelmingly in favor of the French community: 99.6 per cent in the Ivory Coast; 99 per cent in Upper Volta, Middle Congo and Oubangui-Chari; 98 per cent in Dahomey and the Chad; 97 per cent in Senegal and Sudan; 92 per cent in Mauritania. Only in Gabon, Niger and Madagascar did the percentage fall from the nineties to 78 per cent, but even that figure was a massive approval from territories that had suffered terribly from French repression of independence movements ten years earlier.

Sekou Touré sent a message to de Gaulle saying that the

negative vote should not be considered a hostile demonstration against France, but rather a political option to remain free and flexible in world affairs rather than a member of a bloc. He requested that Guinea be accorded the status of an "associate state" of the French commonwealth, if such a formula could be devised. De Gaulle courteously but coolly replied that the request would have to be considered by the member states; that France "did not command the new community of free nations."

France, of course, played the preeminent role, and anything that France opposed had little chance of being approved. De Gaulle had no intention of granting Guinea an associate status, for de Gaulle was an absolutist in such matters. One was with France or not with France, and there was no in-between. His rigidity always was his greatest weakness, along with his abrasive personality and the fallacious notion that "rightly to be great is not to stir without great argument." De Gaulle's principles were frequently sound, his policies drawn from those principles were just as frequently controversial, his practical application of the policies was almost always disastrous. He went out of his way to be disagreeable and exasperating in public relations, although he was, paradoxically, one of the most courteous of gentlemen in private, human relations.

De Gaulle could have kept Guinea as a friend of France, as the British kept Nehru in the Commonwealth although he refused to recognize any form, even a symbolic one, of British sovereignty. (This writer will never forget the extraordinary scene in Westminster Abbey when Nehru stood to honor the coronation of a Queen he did not recognize as the head of the Commonwealth which he had agreed to join.) De Gaulle, however, was a Gaul, not an Anglo-Saxon. De Gaulle was one of Caesar's children, his blood and brain imbued with Roman culture and Rome's dedication to statute law. Common law and custom are for Anglo-Saxons, not for Gauls.

The French community was open only to those who wanted to come all the way, not halfway, in. The door was slammed against Sekou Touré and the harsh slam shook the entire house. The house itself was thus doomed to collapse, for its frame proved to be so rigid that it could not bend with a storm. The first big blow-up would blow it down, soon after the institutions of the Fifth Republic were put in place. First, however, let us turn briefly to the home front, where de Gaulle achieved the victory that would give him the free hand he needed for the decisive battleground in Algeria.

* * *

The referendum triumph was followed by two more popular victories for de Gaulle in the legislative elections of November 30 and the presidential elections of December 21, 1958. The party that bore his banner although not his personal imprimatur, the U.N.R., captured a majority of the seats in the assembly. The Communists were virtually wiped out as a parliamentary force, less because of a loss of votes than because of an electoral system rigged against them. The Communists did lose some voters, about a 5 per cent drop from the elections of 1956, but they kept their roots deeply planted in the French working class. In terms of political power, however, de Gaulle had swept the Communists off the surface completely, forcing them underground. Some day those underground roots may push up new shoots, but for the first seven-year term of President de Gaulle, they stayed underground.

De Gaulle was then elected president by an almost unanimous vote of the non-Communist electors. Only two candidates ran against him: Communist Georges Marrane and Conservative Albert Châtelet. It was an indirect election by a limited electoral college of national and municipal delegates. The final vote was 62,394 votes for Charles de Gaulle against 10,355 for Marrane and 6,721 for Châtelet. President de Gaulle thus emerged from this triple test of the referendum, legislative and presidential ballotings with the greatest prestige and powers of any French leader since the election of Louis Napoleon in the last days of the Second Republic.

The Constitution of the Fifth Republic had swung the balance of power to the executive against the legislative. Its most controversial clause was Article 16, granting the president full powers in the event of an "emergency" or "serious crisis." It is so vaguely worded that it is tantamount to legalizing dictatorship. However, the history of France and Europe has demonstrated often enough that constitutions neither make nor prevent dictatorships. Experience will probably demonstrate that whether the clause itself is dangerous depends on the manner in which French affairs are conducted and the extent to which Frenchmen learn to coexist with one another. Aside from the exceptional powers of Article 16, the president has a number of other real powers not vested in that office of the previous Republic. In summary form, these are the principal attributes of the powers in the Fifth Republic, or, as some call it, the Republic of Charles de Gaulle:

THE EXECUTIVE POWER

THE PRESIDENT OF THE REPUBLIC:

Appoints the premier and presides over the council of ministers (government);

Negotiates and ratifies treaties;

May request a referendum on any bill dealing with the reorganization of the government authorities;

Possesses exceptional powers in the event of a serious crisis;

May dissolve the national assembly after consultation with the premier and the presidents of the two assemblies (except when exceptional powers are in effect or within one year of a previous dissolution).

(An amendment now provides that the president is elected by universal suffrage, rather than by the limited college that first elected de Gaulle.)

THE PREMIER:

Is responsible to parliament, but able to pledge its responsibility by requesting a vote of approval of his government's program;

May, like parliament, initiate legislation and introduce amendments;

May declare martial law.

THE LEGISLATIVE POWER

PARLIAMENT IS COMPOSED OF TWO ASSEMBLIES:

The national assembly—elected by universal suffrage

The senate—elected by indirect suffrage

THE NATIONAL ASSEMBLY *has the following principal attributes:*

Convenes in two ordinary sessions a year (five months in all) and may convene in extraordinary session at the request of the government or of the majority of the assembly's members;

Debates and votes legislation, the government being responsible for its agenda and possessing the regulatory means to restrict the right of amendment within reasonable limits;

Debates and votes the budget within very strict limits (70 days);

Shares with the government the right to initiate legislation and a revision of the constitution;

Controls the action of the government and alone may force its resignation if a motion of censure, signed by at least one-tenth of the deputies, is voted by an absolute majority, the government being able at any time to request approval of its program.

THE SENATE *plays a more limited role:*

Participates in voting on laws, expresses its opinion at the first and second readings, but in the case of conflict with the national assembly, a joint committee composed of an equal number of members from each assembly must meet to draft a compromise text;

May not challenge the responsibility of the government.

Constitutional experts and political scientists have been debating the strengths and weaknesses, democratic and antidemocratic, and all the other aspects of this document ever since its ratification in the September 1958 referendum. It is well to keep in mind that France has had about a hundred different constitutions in its turbulent history and that a constitution is not the vital, organic heart of French democracy, as it is of the American polity. Equally different from the other two is the British pragmatic concept of a body of principles and precedents, rather than a formal constitution. If it is difficult for Anglo-Saxons to understand each other's constitutional values, it is almost impossible for them to comprehend the French, except completely in the French context. In that context, the present constitution can be seen to be an attempt to solve the main problem of previous French republics: the weakness and instability of the executive.

There is no doubt that de Gaulle provided a stronger mechanical and procedural structure of governmental stability, both in his constitution and by his own personality. Whether or not the structure of law will prove as strong without de Gaulle as with him is highly conjectural. This writer's own guess is that the French people will not tolerate a return to the parliamentary games of the past. De Gaulle's successors may not have as much personal authority, but they will undoubtedly be stronger executive officers than any others of the past, partly because the constitution grants the President more power, partly because times and tempers have changed and past habits cannot be fully revived. The presidential elections of December 1965 and the new legislative elections that will follow thereon will provide only a first transitional indication of national trends. It will be many years before it will be possible to get the post–de Gaulle picture of French political forces.

It would be a safe guess to assume that the Fifth Republic is a midway house between parliamentary and presidential regimes, and the post–de Gaulle reajustments will be made as French society evolves along with European society. It is, moreover, futile to attempt to foresee the future of a still unsettled France that has been so dominated by the personality of one man but at the same time so subject to the contradictory forces at work in Europe today. No one can be sure whether the centripetal forces of the Common Market will prevail over the centrifugal forces of a continent whose body is split in half in Germany. Without knowing the outcome of those counterforces, it is impossible to foretell the evolution of a France that influences, and is in turn influenced by, those vital forces. This observer believes that the centripetal forces of unity will prevail and that the "French problem" will tend to fade away as France emerges into a greater European community, but in the reign of Charles de Gaulle this was more an article of faith than a demonstrable conviction.

* * *

The new Republic and Community of France began to function as soon as President Charles de Gaulle moved into the Elysée Palace in January 1959. No sooner had the institutions of the republic and the community been put into place, however, than they began to shake and to crumble. De Gaulle had crumbling materials to work with and had built on quicksand. His words could sway men but could not prevent his unreal world from swaying and buckling. Talk is cheap, the Anglo-Saxons say, but the great Gaul paid a high price for his own words. What saved de Gaulle from complete disaster was the fact that he was prepared to pay the price; he also kept on talking until he finally talked himself out of the trouble that he had talked himself into

at the outset of his return to power—1959 was the Year of the Word
in France and Africa.

The most costly word de Gaulle ever spoke was the word
"freedom"—a word beyond price. He had pronounced the word
and all its synonyms and corollaries in his first swing through
Africa in June 1958. He never stopped talking of liberties throughout 1959. Those who hate, fear, deplore or otherwise oppose de
Gaulle for many reasons must grant him the honor due to a man
who recognized and acted in cognizance of the reality of human
aspirations to freedom and independence. He had promised self-
government and even independence to Africans, if they wanted it,
and a free choice to Algeria, and he never once wavered in his
determination to make good on that pledge. He was often solemn
and stern, haughty and distant, but at times he indulged his
penchant for wit as a weapon in the service of the cause of
freedom. One of his most cutting stabs at the colonials came in the
course of a conversation with a deputy from Oran, Pierre Laffont,
director of the newspaper *Echo d'Oran*. De Gaulle ridiculed the
retrograde colonials of Algeria who, he told Laffont, were trying
to cling to "L 'Algérie de Papa." De Gaulle said, "What they want
is to have Papa's Algeria restored to them. But I tell you that the
Algeria of Papa is dead, and those who do not understand that will
die with it."

Laffont published these remarks in April 1959. They were
greeted with laughter and a round of cheers throughout the
world—except, of course, in Algeria, where they hit home. De
Gaulle knew they would. He was getting ready for the fight he
knew had to come. All through the year he poked and prodded at
the colonials until he finally stopped jabbing and hit them right
between the eyes, with a declaration of self-determination for
Algeria. He made the declaration at a press conference in Paris on
September 16.

At that conference President de Gaulle outlined a triple choice
offered to the inhabitants of Algeria. He said they would be called
upon in a special referendum to choose among these three solutions to the problem: outright "secession" from France (by which
he meant independence); or, "Frenchification" (by which barba-
rous word, invented by de Gaulle for the occasion, and which
reflected his own distaste for such a solution, he meant total
integration); or, a "federal solution" (which he explained as the
"government of Algeria by the Algerians, supported by aid from

France, and in a close union with France in the domains of education, economy, defense and foreign relations"). It was apparent from the tone of the declaration, and the comments of de Gaulle on each of the three "solutions," that the one he favored was the third, the same solution that he had already offered in much broader and more flexible terms to the eleven countries of the French African community and the island of Madagascar.

Two contradictory but logical reactions came from Africa. The French colonials of Algeria were enraged, the African peoples of the community were jubilant. The "man of Brazzaville" had remained true to himself. De Gaulle was hailed as the Abraham Lincoln of France. The joy and gratitude of the African leaders did not, however, mean that they would remain members of the French community. On the contrary, they saw the two-front war that de Gaulle was facing in Algeria and foresaw the inevitable results of the proclamation of self-determination: the Algerian guerrilla forces would fight all the harder for national independence now that de Gaulle had sanctioned it as a choice; the French colonials, their backs to the wall, would rise up once again and attempt to overthrow de Gaulle. The African peoples did not want to get caught in that two-front rebellion. They also knew that an embattled France would not be in a position to construct a meaningful community. They therefore decided to take de Gaulle at his word and opt for independence.

The Mali Federation was the first to express its desire to leave the French community; it so declared in a message from President Léopold Senghor to President de Gaulle on September 28, 1959, only twelve days after the proclamation of self-determination for Algeria. Madagascar followed soon after. Then, one by one, the member states resigned—1960 was the Year of Independence for French Africa. On April 2 Madagascar was granted independence; on April 4, Mali. The climax was reached in August with a continentwide freedom march: the Ivory Coast, Niger, Upper Volta, Dahomey, the Chad, the Central African Republic, the French Congo and Gabon all celebrated their independence between August 1 and August 17. It had taken less than two years for the French community, inaugurated by so massive a "oui" vote in the fall of 1958, to disintegrate completely.

The disintegration was, however, less a failure of de Gaulle's policy than a great achievement—perhaps the greatest of his new career as a statesman. He had been able to bring about the decolonization of France's old empire without bloodshed and had managed to make it look not like a defeat, but like a victory for a humanitarian France, which indeed the world acclaimed it to be.

By the end of 1960 President de Gaulle had finally secured his home front in France, had cleared himself out of the jungles of Africa and was at last ready to face his sternest challenge in Algeria. Having proved he was too old to be a dictator, and that it was too late to be an emperor, he was prepared to prove to Algeria that the moment of truth was striking.

* * *

There were some who thought that the moment of truth had already struck at the beginning of 1960. An insurrection had broken out in Algeria in January as a direct result of the September 16, 1959, proposal of self-determination. There had been immediate protests, at that time, from the colonials in Algiers and their representatives in Paris. Prominent parliamentarians had formed a new "patriotic" organization: Catholic leader Georges Bidault, right-winger Roger Duchet and some of the ultras of the Gaullist U.N.R. Party, Arrighi, Biaggi and Thomazo. They issued a communiqué declaring that "the hour has struck to reassemble all those who want to fight to the finish to keep Algeria French."

More serious than the grumbling of politicians was a spectacular denunciation of de Gaulle by one of his most faithful soldiers, General Jacques Massu, paratroop hero and commander of the Algiers region, who had decisively swung the balance to de Gaulle on May 13, 1958. Massu granted an interview to a German correspondent, Hans Kempski of the *Süddeutsche Zeitung* of Munich, a highly respected professional reporter. He told Kempski, "The army is disappointed to discover that de Gaulle has become a man of the left." Massu went on to say that on May 13 "General de Gaulle seemed the only man available to us. Maybe the army was wrong about that." In answer to Kempski's question as to whether the army would obey the President without question, General Massu was quoted as replying, "Naturally there are some people in the army who would obey without asking questions." Massu concluded the interview, according to Kempski's report, by saying, "Do not forget that we—the army—are in Algeria, and that we will never abandon it." *

President de Gaulle promptly ordered Massu back to Paris to explain himself. In Paris, Massu only made things worse by issuing a statement proclaiming his unquestioned loyalty to "the Commander-in-Chief of Algeria, without any intellectual reservations of any kind." This statement would have been very funny if it had not been so gravely impudent. The thought of Massu having any "intellectual" reservations is startling to those who know this brave but less than brilliant soldier. But it was incredible to hear him affirm his loyalty to his commander in Algeria, when it was to de Gaulle he had been disloyal in the interview.

De Gaulle immediately ordered the Minister of the Army to remove Massu from his Algiers command and replace him with General Crépin. This, in turn, brought a howl from Algiers, for Massu was the city's most idolized hero, the "conqueror of the Casbah," leader of the tough and feared paratroops, the glamorized modern "centurions" of France.

The most extreme elements, men who had long ago crossed the line of no return, banded together for action: Pierre Lagaillarde and Jean-Jacques Susini, leaders of the Students' Leagues, who had led the uprisings of May 13; a local fascist named Joseph Ortiz, one of Pierre Poujade's bully boys, who wore the Celtic cross as Hitler's Brown Shirts had sported the swastika; more ominously, Colonel Gardes, former chief of the army's psychological warfare service; and a number of embittered veterans of the Indochinese war. These men formed an insurrectional commando and called on their followers for a mass demonstration in the Forum as a replay of May 13.

The affair turned out very differently from May 13, for the situation was itself very different—a fact that escaped the self-intoxicated revolutionists. On May 13, 1958, a national hero, General de Gaulle, was in reserve, ready to rescue the nation. When the mob marched again to the Forum on January 24, 1960, no national hero was in the wings. The hero was on active duty as President of France. And the French people who would not fight to save the Fourth Republic, trusting that de Gaulle would clean up the mess, knew that they would have to stand or fall with de Gaulle and the Fifth Republic, or surrender to a Francolike fascist dictatorship. An insurrection against de Gaulle would only elec-

* Published by the *Süddeutsche Zeitung* on January 18, 1960.

trify, not terrify, Paris.

Paris was certainly electrified by what happened on January 24, when the mobs of Algiers fought a pitched battle with gendarmes. Frenchman shot down Frenchman on the monumental stairway of the Forum. No one knew who fired the first shot when the gendarmes began clearing demonstrators off the stairway, but everyone saw the bodies, dead and dying, that lay bleeding on the stairs and around the square at the end of that bloody Sunday. Among the rioters were a dozen dead, two dozen severely wounded and more than fifty badly hurt; among the gendarmes, fourteen dead, another dozen gravely hurt and dying, more than one hundred wounded and hospitalized.

President de Gaulle heard the full story of the fighting at his home in Colombey, where he had gone for the week end. At 2:30 A.M. he broadcast to the nation, calling the riots "a bad blow to the heart of France" and ending with the appeal: "I entreat those who have risen up in Algiers against the motherland, led astray by lies and calumnies, to restore national order. Nothing is lost for a Frenchman who comes back into the arms of Mother France." Then he telephoned to the Delegate-General in Algiers, Paul Delouvrier, and commanded him to restore and maintain order, saying, "You must settle this affair by tomorrow morning."

De Gaulle had seriously underestimated "this affair," just as the colonials had underestimated de Gaulle. It was not to be settled that next morning, or for a week of mornings to follow. Although not a generalized insurrection as on May 13, the revolt was a genuine uprising. The difference from May 13 was that, intense and deep as it was, it lacked a broad base and had no real hero. Massu was gone. Lagaillarde was only a comic-opera understudy as he pranced around in his leopard-spotted paratroop uniform. Susini was too old to be a student but too young, too shrill to be a man. Ortiz was a slack-jawed ape, and the French never follow the hairy unwashed know-nothings. If fascism ever comes to France, it will be high-domed and antiseptically sterile, as in Spain and Portugal.

De Gaulle may not like the French, but he knows them well, and he knew that the "buffoons of the barricades" who dug themselves into entrenched camps around the Forum could not win a mass following. He noted, too, that the Moslems, who had come out in great number on May 13 to shout "Vive de Gaulle," were brooding silently in the Casbah, refusing to join Lagaillarde and Ortiz. The Moslems were the only true Gaullists in French Algeria.

De Gaulle understood that time was on his side in this insurrection. The rebels were entrenched behind barricades at only two posts. Each day their morale sagged. The crowds did not come out to join them. The army high command remained loyal to de Gaulle. The paratroopers fraternized with the insurgents but contained them behind the barricades. They had no place to go, and an insurrection cannot succeed in a static defense position with no external support. So de Gaulle just let them blow off steam and cool off a little more each day.

De Gaulle had announced earlier that month that he would deliver a New Year's message to the people on January 29, and he decided to maintain his previously announced schedule. It took a man of steady nerves to keep silent during those tense days, but de Gaulle found no difficulty in following the rule of silence for a chief that he himself had laid down a quarter of a century earlier in *The Edge of the Sword*. De Gaulle is a man of words, many or few depending on the circumstances; from January 25 to January 29, 1960, he was a sphinx.

The scheduled moment to speak came on January 29 at 8 P.M. At exactly that hour President de Gaulle appeared on the television screens. Before he even began to speak, there was a gasp of astonishment, for he had put on his old wartime uniform and was appearing before them, not as President de Gaulle, but as General de Gaulle, savior of France, the wartime hero of the resistance. There was a double symbolism in that uniform: it was the uniform of a national hero and served also as a reminder to the army that the President of the Republic, Commander-in-Chief of all the armed forces, was a military man, a general talking to generals, not just a civilian politician of Paris.

De Gaulle wanted to make sure that the symbolism was understood by all. His very first words were: "If I have again put on my uniform to speak to you today on television, it is to stress the fact that I do so as General de Gaulle, as well as in my capacity of chief of state." As General de Gaulle he addressed himself particularly to "the community of French ethnic origin in Algeria": "You have known me well for many long years. You have seen me in your midst during the war, when your sons in great numbers served in the ranks of the army of liberation." De Gaulle's voice rose in pitch and volume, as he continued his appeal: "Frenchmen of Algeria, how can you listen to the liars and conspirators who tell you that, by offering a free choice to Algerians, France and de Gaulle want to abandon you, to withdraw from Algeria, to leave you in the hands of the rebels? Was it to abandon you, to lose Algeria, that we sent and maintain an army of half a million men?" De Gaulle asked the people to believe that "nothing would bring more joy to the country and to de Gaulle than the most French choice" in the process of self-determination.

De Gaulle then addressed himself to the army: "I say to all our soldiers: your mission is unequivocal and not subject to interpretation. You must liquidate the rebel forces that seek to drive France out of Algeria and impose their sterile, miserable dictatorship on the country. You must contribute to the moral and material transformation of the Moslem peoples, to win them over to France." De Gaulle warned the army that any other course would lead it into anarchy and break it up into "contemptible military feudal castes." He said, "I alone—and you know this—I am the supreme responsible authority. It is I who bear the destiny of the country. I must be obeyed by all French soldiers."

General de Gaulle concluded by conducting a dialogue with France: "Finally, I address myself to France. Well! my dear, old country, here we are, once again facing a harsh trial. By virtue of the mandate given me by the people and by the legitimacy that I have incarnated for twenty years, I ask each and every one of you to support me whatever happens." Then, deliberately echoing the famous words of his June 18, 1940, call to resistance, General de Gaulle said, "Once again I call all Frenchmen, wherever they are, whatever they are, to reunite with France. Vive la République! Vive la France!"

The performance was all de Gaulle, at his very best and at his very worst, depending on whether the viewer admired or deplored his style and character. The theatricality of the uniform, the high-pitched tremolos suddenly rising out of his deep chesty bass, the arrogance of his claim to represent twenty years of French "legitimacy," the pathos bordering on bathos of his dialogue with "my dear, old country," the deviousness of his expressed joy at "the most French solution" contrasted with the insistence on a "free choice" and "self-determination," the reiteration of faith in an army command for which he had little respect and less trust. All this elaborate staging and maneuvering made the address seem a caricature of reality.

In retrospect, it seems even more caricatured, but at the same time very real. It was a caricature because overgrown boys like Lagaillarde and Susini and apes like Ortiz were not really representative of the hundreds of thousands of genuinely distressed people who sincerely believed, no matter how wrong-minded, in a French Algeria. The patriotism of many of the French; their love for their native land, Algeria; the work they had done to build that country; their hopes and dreams—all these were real and worthy of respect. Many decent but misguided people merited a sympathetic understanding of their despair, but the majority could not sympathize with them, for their leaders were fools or desperados, and their mad defense of a dead past threatened the life of the French Republic.

The affair was rapidly brought to an end by de Gaulle's radio-television appeal. He had been heard throughout France and Algeria and had left no doubt in any mind that he would not yield to force, would maintain his policy of self-determination and was ready to order the army to use force to tear down the barricades if the insurgents did not surrender. The army had heard its commander-in-chief and knew he would insist on complete obedience or would himself give the signal for civil war. No one in the high command in Algiers that day would dare to try to lead the army in a rebellion against de Gaulle, and the Republic united behind him, not while there was still some hope of another way out, some hope that self-determination did not mean independence.

The army ordered its troops to close in around the barricades, either to cut off the insurgents from all help and make them surrender or to go in and take them by force. Early on the morning of February 1 it was all over. The "fight-to-the-death" slogans were forgotten. The insurgents surrendered. Lagaillarde's parliamentary immunity was lifted, because he had been caught in flagrante delicto, in the act of endangering the security of the state. He and the other leaders—except Ortiz, who had stolen away in the night—were arrested and sent off to Paris for trial and imprisonment.

The army and police mopped up remnants of the insurrectionists and kept embarrassed security patrols in the streets, not knowing exactly who were their enemies and who their friends, among the people of Algiers—Moslem and French.

General de Gaulle knew better than anyone that he had not won a decisive victory. The real danger for him was not the lunatic fringe of the colonial clique, it was the deeply troubled French Army. Twice the army had intervened directly in the political affairs of the Republic: in May 1958 and again in January 1960. De Gaulle had read intelligence reports on the fraternization between the paras and the insurgents. He knew that there was a junta of conspiratorial colonels working secretly with the colonials and planning plots of their own. The decisive test of strengh was still ahead.

* * *

There was a most deceptive calm before the coming storm at the end of 1960. The army behaved admirably during the referendum campaign on self-determination, and everyone breathed easier when it was over. The campaign had begun in December 1960, and as de Gaulle had ordered, the army maintained security in Algeria and permitted a relatively free vote. No completely free vote can be held in a colonial area under military occupation, in the midst of a rebellion. Some overzealous army officers herded a number of Moslems into trucks and "helped" them go to the polls to vote. But, given the circumstances, it was a remarkably fair performance over all, as the results in the vote of January 8, 1961, proved. A total of 23,986,913 citizens voted in metropolitan France and the Algerian departments. Self-determination was approved by the huge majority of 17,447,669 "oui" votes against 5,817,775 "non."

The French press was exultant. The independent, moderate *Figaro* of Paris headlined that de Gaulle "Facing Algeria is the Man of the Nation." The socialist *Populaire* headline read, "France voted for peace in Algeria." Only the extremes grumbled, the right against "abandonment of Algeria," the Communists saying, "Peace can only come by negotiations." President de Gaulle himself had no illusions about his "triumph." He wasted no time in self-congratulation. Instead, he sent a letter to General Crépin, commander of the Algiers sector, complimenting him on the conduct of the army but warning him to keep a close watch on discipline.

It had been essential, wrote de Gaulle, that there be no breach of discipline during the referendum, and he took note that such had been the case. He went on to say that he was the first to understand how "deeply the heart of soldiers is touched by the profound transformation taking place in Algeria." He told the General that "clear-sighted Frenchmen" must discern how vital it was for France to adopt freely and willingly the only possible solution consistent with the modern world. President de Gaulle knew how troubled the army was by the swiftly changing scene. It had remained steadfast for the vote on self-determination. Would it stay steady and loyal all through the process which de Gaulle had long ago determined would evolve toward independence? He had already taken the country step by step down the road, by progressively calling for unity, the peace of the brave, self-determination, an Algerian Algeria and an Algerian republic closely associated with France. He had seen army officers stumble, break step and then step out of line, from Massu to Salan. De Gaulle knew that many more were still wavering, shifting their weight, wondering where to step or jump next.

On the day that de Gaulle wrote to Crépin, January 12, 1961, General Salan was living in exile in Madrid with other insurgents who had fought de Gaulle. Some were fugitives from justice, others fugitives from reality. This writer saw Salan in Madrid that week. I had known the General in Indochina and in Algeria. Now he was a changed man. Known in the army by the nickname "The Mandarin," General Salan was noted for his caution and his ability to swim through troubled waters without making waves. He was one of the men most unlikely to become a rebel in exile. Yet Salan, like so many others, civilians and military alike, had been "intoxicated" by the drugs of colonialism and nationalism. He presided over a desperate group of bitter men in Madrid: Lagaillarde, Susini, Ronda and a number of lesser-known characters, some of whom were gangsters and hired guns, rather than patriots.

Salan, who had dyed his hair dark and grown a mustache to disguise himself, told me that the day of reckoning would come for "that traitor de Gaulle." He had with him a copy of a letter that had been published a week before, an "open letter to Frenchmen" that was signed by sixteen general officers who had commanded in Algeria. They had called upon the French people to vote "non" in the referendum. There were some illustrious military names on the list of signatories, including Generals Zeller, Boyer de la Tour, de Monsabert and Guillaume. Salan said to me, "You know these men. You served with them in the war. You know they are good men and good allies of America in the Atlantic Alliance. You Americans must help us, or de Gaulle will hand, first Algeria, then

France over to the Soviets, and the Atlantic Alliance will be doomed. All Christian civilization will be doomed."

This was a constant theme of anti-de Gaulle leaders in those days, and is indeed so again today. De Gaulle's anti-American policies and his opposition to NATO policies of integration keep alive the hope of his adversaries that there will be a break with America. They hope, too, that America's fear and hatred of Communism can be turned against de Gaulle, who has often "flirted" with Russia and China as a means of putting pressure on the Anglo-Saxons. As had been the case with several American writers, I had often been sought out by those who hoped to impress me with this line of argument and thus get it to the American government and public. They used the same techniques with embassy officials and CIA agents and were responsible for spreading stories that the Americans were backing them. These stories were untrue, but a French cabinet minister, who should have known better, actually went so far as to tell reporters that the CIA was involved in the revolt of the generals in Algiers.

De Gaulle was aware of the activities of the exiles and the brooding resentments of high-ranking officers, both active ones and those on the retired list. Yet he never took a step backward. He kept striding farther and farther down the road to granting independence to Algeria, thereby cutting out the cancer that was rotting the body and debasing the soul of France. Only one thing mattered to de Gaulle: to get it over with as quickly as he could.

On April 11 he spoke the truth to the French people, the whole truth, when he said at a press conference that the financial burden France was bearing in Algeria was so great that "France would consider with the greatest calm a solution that would end Algeria's attachment to her domain." Algeria, he said, will "be sovereign, in internal and external affairs both, I am persuaded. And France will raise no obstacles to this." De Gaulle knew, of course, that his confirmation of a willingness, almost an eagerness, to cut all ties with Algeria and grant it full independence, as he had just said unequivocally, was the ultimate challenge to the opposition. If the generals were opposed to independence, then they would have to act before de Gaulle completed the process or admit defeat. De Gaulle could not be sure that they would strike, but he had to provoke them to strike or surrender.

The generals struck early on the morning of April 22, eleven days after the deliberately provocative press conference. They made their move just after midnight. The conspirators used the First Regiment of Foreign Legion paratroopers as the spearhead of the coup. The Foreign Legion paras, toughest of all the troops in the army, occupied the buildings of the delegation-general, all official buildings in Algiers, the radio station and the central telephone and telegraph bureaus. They captured and held prisoner Delegate-General Morin and de Gaulle's Minister of Public Works Buron, who was visiting Algiers at the time, and to underline the nature of the rebellion, they seized Commander-in-Chief General Gambiez, who was loyal to de Gaulle.

At 9 A.M. that Saturday morning a junta of generals issued a communiqué announcing that it had taken power and decreeing a state of siege in Algeria. "No peace solution is possible except in a French Algeria," it stated.

The communiqué was signed by four of the highest-ranking, most illustrious generals of the French Army: Challe, Zeller, Jouhaud, Salan. Salan had slipped out of Spain, with or without the complicity of the Spanish authorities, who were supposed to have been keeping him under surveillance. But he did not take command of the junta, although he was the senior officer. He left the command to the younger, more popular Maurice Challe, who had been one of the finest officers in the army and who was very popular with allied officers with whom he had served.

The first news of the putsch had been flashed to Paris about 1 A.M. Saturday morning. President de Gaulle was informed as he was coming out of the Comédie-Française, where he had offered a gala performance in honor of President Léopold Senghor of Senegal, the first country to inform de Gaulle that it wished full independence. No novelist, not even the wildest movie scenarist, would have dared to write such a scene as that real-life drama of de Gaulle entertaining the first of the dissident leaders of Africa at the Comédie-Française, of all places, while a putsch was being carried out in Algiers.

It was absolutely ridiculous: the French Comedy indeed! With all the sympathy one might have for France, with all the aware-ness of the gravity of the putsch and the disaster for France and all her allies if it should succeed or erupt into the long-threatened civil war, one simply could not take it seriously. Even the ponderously serious and highly proper publication *L'Année politique,* which strives to be scrupulously objective and give no offense to the authorities, could not help but deride the coup. In its review of the generals' revolt story, it pours scorn on Prime Minister Michel Debré, whom it describes as appearing on television with "his face gray and badly shaved." It said that his speech was "very hashed up and tried to make itself dramatic." The review of the event continues with the comment: "Some people greeted the appeal to the nation with hilarity; it was indeed delivered in a somewhat ridiculous manner." Other people were infuriated that Debré should "call upon unarmed people to go out and throw themselves in front of invading paratroopers." *

All Paris roared with laughter or anger when Debré said, "As soon as you hear sirens, rush out to the airports and persuade the soldiers that they have been induced to error." Parisians called friends and suggested that they bring champagne to the airports and, when the paras were drinking, hit them over the heads with the bottles. Debré's pathetic performance somehow broke the tension in Paris and served a useful purpose, although this was by no means to his credit.

Even de Gaulle almost lost his unshakable calm in the course of the crisis. He was not shaken, however, when he first heard the news. As in the "affair of the barricades," he said nothing the first day but simply gave orders to his ministers to take certain basic security measures and went home to sleep. The next morning President de Gaulle sent a letter to the constitutional council, requesting its opinion on an eventual decision to put into application Article 16, which would give him full powers to take governmental decisions by decree at his own discretion. The council met urgently and approved such a move. He also worked on the drafting of a radio-television address to the nation, his principal instrument of government. His nerves held steady right up to the end of his radio-television address.

President de Gaulle appeared on the screen in full-dress uniform on Sunday night, January 23. He condemned the putsch and the "authors of the pronunciamento," deliberately using the Spanish word to characterize the generals as being similar to South American generals, so often held up to ridicule by French chansonniers. De Gaulle then coined a phrase that set all France to laughing, when he called the four rebels "that quartet of retired generals."

It is likely that the putsch collapsed at that moment. Everyone in France was listening to de Gaulle that night, and, more importantly, every soldier in Algeria was listening to a barracks radio

* *L'Année politique 1961,* Paris, Presses Universitaires de France, p. 53.

or to his own transistor. The putsch was to be dubbed by the press, later, as the "battle of the transistors," so completely did de Gaulle reach the entire corps and turn the soldiers against the generals. He said, "I forbid every Frenchman, and above all, every soldier to carry out any of their orders." This was an astute tactic based upon the memory of his difficulties in recruiting rebels for his own act of dissidence in 1940. He did not want to give any wavering soldier an excuse to follow the generals because they were superior officers.

De Gaulle was in complete possession of himself throughout the speech, playing the role of the unconquerable chief—calm, confident, stern, paternal, master of the situation. Then, suddenly, at the very end, his voice rose and broke on a high note, as it sometimes does naturally, but there was nothing natural about the words on which it broke: "Françaises, Français, aidez-moi!"

The whole nation caught its breath. No one ever expected to hear the giant of France appeal for the help of the little people of Paris. It was the sort of pathetic cry that could result in a massive arising of citizens to defend the republic or cause a nationwide panic. But de Gaulle knows the French, and all the French know de Gaulle; those who idolize him and those who cannot bear him, all know him well; and they could not believe that he himself had panicked. On the contrary, he roused them, as he had meant to do, and above all, he stirred the soldiers in Algeria. By far the majority were young citizen-soldiers, not professionals. They were metropolitan Frenchmen, not colonials of Algiers. If the paras jumped on France, they would be jumping on their homes, on their mothers, their families. Officers in Algeria later told this writer that they had watched the faces of the men as they listened to de Gaulle, and they knew they would have a bloody mutiny if they gave the slightest indication of sympathy for the putsch.

Soldiers demonstrated in favor of de Gaulle all over Algeria and swore to defend the republic against the putsch. It was all over very swiftly. By April 25, only three days after the first strike of the Foreign Legion paras, the generals ran up the white flag and surrendered. That is, General Challe surrendered. Zeller, Jouhaud and Salan fled and went underground to create a terrorist organization. They were eventually all captured and incarcerated. General de Gaulle had won his ultimate battle with the French Army in the fratricidal war that had begun back on June 18, 1940.

*   *   *

President de Gaulle was at last able "to do the rest," as he had pledged to do in his first speech at the Forum on June 4, 1958, after his return to power. The "rest" was not easy to do. War was still raging in Algeria on the first front, the war of independence. But it made little sense by then. De Gaulle had told the Arab rebels that they could have independence if they wanted it. He had put down all the opposition of French rebels. But it is easier to start wars than to stop them. It took a long time and many difficult negotiations to bring peace to Algeria, but there wasn't any doubt, after the farcical failure of the generals, that the Algerian period of French history had come to an end.

By July 1, 1962, more than a year after the putsch of the generals, a final vote was held on Algerian self-determination—not on the original three choices that de Gaulle had first proposed three years earlier, but on one choice, the ineluctable choice: independence. The result was, as expected, virtually unanimous for independence. On July 3 President Charles de Gaulle solemnly proclaimed the independence of Algeria, exactly 132 years after King Charles X had taken Algeria's independence away by his colonial conquest of that land.

* * *

President de Gaulle had decolonized Africa and brought peace to Algeria, but there was no peace or quiet for him. The insurgents turned from rebellion to terrorism and formed commando bands inside France, including assassination squads pledged to kill de Gaulle. They almost succeeded. On two occasions they missed him by a second and an inch.

The first escape from death came on September 8, 1961, when a fire bomb exploded as his car went over it at about sixty-five miles per hour, as he was driving home to Colombey. The second time President and Madame de Gaulle escaped death by a miracle on August 22, 1962, when his car was ambushed by assassins in a street in Petit Clamart, as he was driving to the airport. Almost one hundred bullets caught his car in a crossfire from each side of the street. One bullet pierced the chassis an inch from his head. He was covered with jagged shards of glass, but he remained unscratched. As he got out of the car after it reached the airport, he brushed off the glass, turned to his secret-service guard and said, "This is getting to be dangerous. Fortunately those gentlemen are poor shots."

There have been dozens of plots to assassinate de Gaulle. No respite, no tranquillity appears in sight. Assassins of the Secret Army of Algeria, the die-hard terrorists, just missed him in 1964, when a bomb exploded after he had left a ceremony during which he had been standing near the jar in which it had been placed. In May 1965 a similar plot was discovered when police caught some of the men who had planted the clay-jar bomb. They had been planning to plant another one at a statue to Clemenceau at which de Gaulle was scheduled to deposit a wreath.

De Gaulle is a fatalist about security, as all presidents must be. It is impossible to give a president full security, as we Americans have learned so tragically in our history. As he approached his seventy-fifth year, de Gaulle had naturally to be a fatalist about his destiny. His sense of humor was brought into play even on the subject of his own mortality. When asked about his health at his February 1965 press conference, he smiled and replied, "It's not bad. But be assured, one day I will not fail to die."

His exact physical condition was a closely guarded secret. His own closest advisors did not know it. In fact, one of his doctors, who supervised his postoperative care, told me that he had some difficulty persuading one of the men closest to de Gaulle that a prostate blockage that had been removed in an operation in 1964 was not cancerous. The doctor said, "This man was so devoted to de Gaulle and so worried about him that he had convinced himself that de Gaulle had cancer. He asked me whether it was not true that a prostate cancer in a man of seventy-four is less immediately dangerous because the cells multiply more slowly at that age. I assured him that the General had not suffered a cancer, but he smiled sadly and knowingly at me, assuming that, as the doctor, I would naturally conceal the truth. He begged me to answer his question."

This "cancer" story made the rounds of Paris and world capitals. Everyone professed to know a doctor who took care of de Gaulle or a doctor friend of a doctor friend of the doctor of de Gaulle. I myself knew some distinguished medical men who assured me "beyond a doubt" that de Gaulle had cancer of the prostate. Then I finally did make contact with primary sources who did know the truth. They may not have been telling the truth to me, but they would have little reason to lie. The circumstances of our talks were such that they could easily have refused to discuss the question with me. I am personally convinced that I heard the truth about de

Gaulle's physical condition, and some extraordinary insights into his character as well, in the stories I was told about his behavior before, during and after the operation.

General de Gaulle first suffered discomfort many months before the operation. When his doctor discovered the blockage, he wanted the General to be operated on immediately. But de Gaulle refused, saying that he had made a commitment to visit the President of Mexico and could not change the date. The doctor was appalled at the thought that de Gaulle, then seventy-three, meant to undertake a foreign tour in such a condition. He told de Gaulle that he would not permit him to go, and he even dared to bully de Gaulle by threatening to leak the information to the press if de Gaulle disobeyed his injunction. The President, impressed by the devoted doctor's concern, asked whether there was not some temporary medical relief possible that would permit delay of an operation for his malady. The doctor said that in some cases, where a patient could not be operated on for other reasons, the procedure would be to open up the blockage and insert a drain to keep it open until an operation could be undertaken.

The doctor was shocked when de Gaulle suggested this as a solution that would permit him to go to Mexico first and be operated on later. He assured de Gaulle that the pain and discomfort of a drain were considerable under any circumstances, but would be agonizing in a long air flight and the ceremonies of an official state visit. But de Gaulle cut him short: "I obey your injunction not to go without the necessary treatment, now you obey my command to put in that drain. We will not discuss this further."

The doctor did as ordered.

The surgeon said that de Gaulle, headstrong though he was in argument, was a most intelligent and obedient patient once agreement was reached. "The examinations and treatments for his malady are extremely unpleasant and, for a man of his dignity and prestige, somewhat humiliating—or, at least, most patients feel. But de Gaulle has a personal dignity that cannot be shaken. He also has an intellectual curiosity that carries him through difficult situations. He questioned me about everything that I was doing. By the time I had finished inserting the drain, he knew almost as much about it as I did. He said to me that he would like to meet and congratulate the surgeon who had devised this type of drain. I told him that it might be difficult to arrange, because he was an

American. De Gaulle flushed and snapped at me, 'American! Don't tell me that you have put an American drain into me! Great God, isn't there a French drain?' I hastily told him that the drain was manufactured under license in France so that, in effect, it actually was French. 'Good,' said de Gaulle, 'but not quite good enough. We ought to have our own design. Doctor, I do not wish it known that I have an American drain in me. You will regard this as a secret of state.'"

The doctor said that he had many misgivings about permitting President de Gaulle to go to Mexico in his condition. He said: "After de Gaulle arrived in Mexico City, I sat every night in front of my television set and watched pictures of the ceremonies taking place. I could not believe my eyes when I watched that fantastic old man, standing straight, walking through crowds, being jostled and pushed and pulled from all sides, and with a deep drain inside him. It must have been sheer hell. I don't know how he could have stood the pain and the discomfort. Yet only the physician in attendance in the presidential party, and those of us who inserted the drain here in Paris, ever knew the truth. Not by a word or a sign did de Gaulle show what he was going through and the most that the keenest-eyed reporters were able to see was that he appeared to be a bit tired and flushed. They thought it was due to Mexico's altitude. Ah, I tell you, he is a rare one, that old man."

When de Gaulle was finally ready for the operation, he instructed the doctors and his staff to maintain maximum secrecy. He wanted to tell the French people about it only after the operation. In order to fool the press and divert attention, he scheduled a television appearance for the very night that he was due to go to the hospital. He called in the national network and recorded his television speech on video tape in the afternoon and then left immediately for the hospital. At eight o'clock that night, when the people of France were watching and listening to their President, or thought they were, he himself was in a deep sleep, induced by sedatives administered by the doctor who was preparing to operate upon him. Yes, he is a rare one, that old man.

He gave the surgeon a bad time on the issue of anaesthesia. The source who described the scene to me was present at it, and he kept chuckling and also clucking in mixed admiration and professional disapproval as he relived the scene in the course of recounting it.

"I will *not* be put to sleep!" the General shouted.

"But, Mr. President, it is a rather disagreeable operation for any

layman, let alone the patient himself, and it would be dangerous—
inviting shock or nausea—to permit you to remain awake. Be
thankful, General, that your heart and respiratory conditions are
excellent and permit deep sleep."

"Nonsense! I have seen blood before. And if your confounded
meddling hasn't yet sickened me, nothing can. Do as I say. Keep
me awake."

"General, I cannot do that. It is quite impossible. You must calm
down. Why are you so determined about this? I assure you, you
would see nothing and would only suffer needlessly if you were
not in sleep."

De Gaulle fell silent and reflected for a long time. Then he said
to the doctor, "Sir, can you give me your word, on your oath as a
doctor and your loyalty as a citizen, that there is no possible danger
of death in this operation? Now, I want the truth, sir."

Astonished, the doctor replied, "Mr. President, I give you my
most solemn assurance by every oath of my career that, barring
unforeseen accident, of which the chance is so minimal as to be
negligible, there is no danger of death."

De Gaulle, pleased, smiled at the doctor and said, "So be it. Do
as you must. But I warn you—if I die, I'll come back to haunt
you."

The doctor, somewhat alarmed at the possibility that his patient's
anxiety about death might be a negative factor, said, "Forgive me,
Mr. President, but it is important for the operation that you be
calm and confident. You must believe me that there is no danger
of death. Tell me, if you will, why do you fear death?"

"Fear death! Good God, how can you be so dense?" de Gaulle
roared angrily. "I do not fear death, sir. I am ready whenever my
Maker wishes to call me. What I fear is what happened to my poor
friend, the Sultan of Morocco. Poor devil, he died on the operating
table, in blood and stench, in a mess of instruments, never knowing that he had died. What a tragic way to go. No, sir, I fear not
death. I fear only sleep. I want to know what is happening to
me."

The doctor paused in his narrative, looked at me and said, "You
know, I am convinced that he had prepared a few well-chosen
words for history—the last words of Charles de Gaulle—and
feared that I might be a bungler who would cheat him of his
curtain line. He is a devil, that old man." One could feel the
doctor's admiration in his voice, see it in his eyes. Yet, strangely

enough, this particular doctor was not a Gaullist politically and did not hesitate to criticize the man he so admired.

Many millions of French citizens share the doctor's mixed feelings of admiration and irritation. There are those in France called "les inconditionnels" who love de Gaulle unreservedly, without condition, and there are also almost as many "unconditionals" who hate him. The majority of the French, like the doctor, consider him to be a rare old man, half god, half devil.

At the moment of this writing early in 1966, Charles de Gaulle is still alive and kicking. The phrase is a kind of redundancy, for if he is alive, he is bound to be kicking. His favorite quote from *Hamlet* may well be rewritten as "Rightly to be alive is not to stir without great argument."

From the moment he returned to leadership in 1958, de Gaulle stirred great arguments. Occupied as he was with the reconstruction of the republic, the decolonization of Africa and the bringing of peace to Algeria, he was also deeply involved in world affairs throughout those troubled times of crisis inside France and the community. He conferred with Eisenhower in Paris and began a crucial negotiation on relations inside the Atlantic Alliance in the same month that he proposed self-determination for Algeria. He made state visits to England and the United States after the week of the barricades and presided over the aborted summit conference in Paris, all in that busy spring of 1960. In 1961, shortly after the revolt of the generals, de Gaulle received President Kennedy on a state visit to Paris. The world was ever with him in the peak periods of internal crisis. Uneasy rests the head of any sovereign, be he emperor or president.

For Charles de Gaulle it was too late to be an emperor, and he was too old to be a dictator, but he could never be too old, nor would it ever be too late, for him to devote himself to his main task: to make France great again, to restore her to her "rightful place" in the world. It was to this task that he gave himself above all others after he ended the Algerian war. It was the most exciting, most important and last chapter in the story of the three lives of Charles de Gaulle. It was, I suspect, the life that he enjoyed the most. What better opportunity for grandeur than to stir with great argument the entire world!

CHAPTER TEN

THE HOUR OF RECKONING WITH THE ANGLO-SAXONS

---

*No sooner had the sound of gunfire faded than the
world's appearance changed. . . . The ambition of
states reappeared in all its turbulence. The allies
revoked those considerations and concessions they
had necessarily granted each other in time of peril,
when they were confronting a common enemy.*

CHARLES DE GAULLE, *Memoirs III, Discord, 1959*

"YESTERDAY WAS THE TIME for battle; now the hour of reckoning
is striking." With those words Charles de Gaulle began the chapter of his memoirs entitled "Discord." He was referring to the
defeat of the Nazis and the conflicts that broke out between the
allies in their moment of victory. He called it "this moment of
truth" and charged that the wartime allies, freed of the necessity
of union against the common enemy, set themselves "to relegate
us to a secondary place among the nations responsible for conducting the peace." He added, "I have no intention of letting this
happen."

General de Gaulle was prepared for postwar conflict with the
Anglo-Saxon allies, for he had fought against them all through the
war itself. From June 1940 through May 1945 General de Gaulle
had fought a war within a war, an uncivil war with the Anglo-
Saxons behind their united front against the Axis powers. When
the Nazis surrendered in May, ending the war on the Western
front, the uncivil conflicts inside the Western camps grew more

heated. The boiling point was reached at the end of May in the Anglo-French conflict in the Levant, when British troops intervened against the French in Syria.

De Gaulle never forgot, not only the conflict in the Levant, but all the long years of rivalry between Fighting France and the Anglo-Saxon powers. There are those who think therefore that de Gaulle bore a grudge against Roosevelt and Churchill and revenged himself later on their successors. They underestimate de Gaulle. He was not motivated by anything so simple and human as a personal grudge. He was the guardian and champion of France, and it was as his mother's son that he defended her body and soul against all who would dominate her or deny her a place on the pedestal of the world.

Anyone who examines the record objectively will see that de Gaulle bore no personal grudge against the Anglo-Saxon leaders but rather, and more seriously, against the power politics of the Anglo-Saxon nations. Shortly after his return to power in 1958, de Gaulle invited Churchill to Paris, decorated him with the Grand Cross of Liberation, embraced him publicly as a friend and described him as "the greatest man of our times." De Gaulle also welcomed Eisenhower back to Paris in September 1959. He greeted his old wartime comrade and new presidential colleague, at the City Hall, in the most moving words: "I feel a profound joy as I find with me again President Eisenhower, the good, the dear, the loyal companion alongside whom I walked down the most difficult path on the route of history." There was thus no personal animus that poisoned relations between the chieftains of the Gauls and the Anglo-Saxons. Their animadversions grew out of conflicting ambitions and aspirations.

Men of goodwill in the rival camps wanted to believe that these conflicts were more superficial than deep, and they insisted that the common interests of the Western allies were greater than their conflict of interests. Alas, this was not true. The record shows that the only real tie between de Gaulle and the Anglo-Saxons was fear of the Slavs and the Mongols. When fear of Russia and China diminished to any extent in any of the Western camps, then their conflict of interests dominated relations.

The uncivil war between de Gaulle and the Anglo-Saxons that was the constant feature of their wartime relations broke out anew as soon as de Gaulle returned to power in 1958. It was always more constant and more bitter than the cold war with the Russians. If this truth is not faced and if measures are not taken to resolve or contain the conflicts, then a rupture of the most ancient friendship between the French and the Anglo-Americans cannot be ruled out as a real possibility.

Uncivil War I lasted for five years, from 1940 to 1945. Uncivil War II broke out in 1958 and is now—in 1966—in its eighth. It grew more uncivil each succeeding year, escalating from disagreements through disputes and divisions to a threatened rupture of an Atlantic Alliance which, if not yet broken, is badly bent and only barely functioning. A clear picture of this second uncivil war is difficult to see, partly because of the tight secrecy of presidential communications, but mainly because of the mass of public statements, texts, documents, communiqués, press conferences and speeches by which modern statesmen have learned to keep their secrets by overexposing them. The astute combination of the hidden, the partially revealed and the overexposed hides the truth in the dense, tangled jungle of public affairs.

This writer has been chopping his way through that jungle for a very long time, collecting bits and pieces of the puzzle along the way, some of them hidden nuggets of the truth, some of them found in sudden clearings in the heart of the jungle. The report that follows is not by any means the whole story, not a complete reconstruction of the jigsaw puzzle. It is, however, a basically accurate map of the jungle battlegrounds of the uncivil war, complete enough to permit us to see it as a whole, to follow the course of the battle and, hopefully, to consider ways and means of dealing with it.

This may be a pretentious aspiration for private citizens. But it is certainly a worthy one. Our leaders have fallen out and seem incapable of coming together again. By the end of 1965 there had not been a single substantive meeting between the presidents of the United States and France since John F. Kennedy went to Paris on May 31, 1961. More than four and a half years of total silence on the summits of France and America is much more than enough. If our presidents will not talk, then perhaps it is time for citizens to see what they can do. Clemenceau once said that war was too serious a business to be left to generals. Allied relations are, perhaps, too serious a business to be left to diplomats and statesmen. It would in any case be difficult for private citizens to make a greater muddle of allied affairs than is shown in this story of the uncivil war between de Gaulle and the Anglo-Saxons.

*   *   *

The second uncivil war began exactly where the first had left off thirteen years earlier, with almost exactly the same cast of characters. If there is an angel of destiny that charts the course of de Gaulle's career, it is certainly an angel with a Gallic sense of irony and logic. It selected as the site of the first international challenge of de Gaulle's second coming to power the very same arena where he had fought the last, most bitter battle against the Anglo-Saxons in 1945: the Levant. If General de Gaulle spoke the Anglo-Saxon vernacular, he might well have said, "Well, Ike, well, Mac, here we go again."

"Ike" and "Mac," the soldier and the diplomat of 1945, the "two old comrades," were the President of the United States and the Prime Minister of Great Britain in 1958. The fact that they were old wartime comrades of de Gaulle did not, however, necessarily mean the three would work in harmony as chiefs of government in times of peace, particularly in areas where they had clashed during the war. Memories of their first uncivil-war conflicts were very much alive in 1958. None of the leaders had forgotten that de Gaulle had warned the British that he himself would never forget that they had "betrayed the Occident" in their intervention in the Levant.

Macmillan, who had not forgotten the ominous words, sent de Gaulle a nervously friendly message of congratulation when he was invested as premier on June 1, 1958, and then, only five days later, flew off to Washington to confer with Eisenhower on how the alliance might be affected by de Gaulle's return.

Eisenhower and Macmillan spent a long session discussing analyses of de Gaulle prepared by their most experienced advisors and research analysts, who had pored over the records of de Gaulle's writings and actions in the years immediately preceding his return. The conclusions were gloomy: the analysts predicted serious trouble, for de Gaulle had consistently criticized the principal postwar structures of the Western alliance.

Eisenhower and Macmillan agreed that the prospects were not brilliant and that the world situation was too volatile and dangerous for a cautious wait-and-see attitude. They decided that the Prime Minister, as de Gaulle's cross-channel neighbor, should see him as soon as possible and that John Foster Dulles would be sent to Paris to follow up quickly on the Macmillan meeting.

Macmillan flew to Paris on June 29, accompanied by Foreign Secretary Selwyn Lloyd. Everybody tried hard to be pleasant. General de Gaulle went personally to the airport to greet the Prime Minister. He escorted him back to the presidential palace, where they had successive sessions on June 29 and 30. At the end of their meeting a joint communiqué stated blandly that the meetings had been most friendly and useful and that major questions of mutual interest had been fully discussed.

Upon returning to London the Prime Minister reported his "great satisfaction" at the frank and friendly atmosphere, adding that he could not recall "any other meeting of this kind in France which had been so successful," a statement that brought smiles to the faces of journalists who could not recall any British conference with de Gaulle that had had much success.

In a private "background session" with a few selected correspondents the Prime Minister insisted that the meeting had been cordial. He conceded that nothing had been agreed upon, but he argued that he had gone to find out what de Gaulle's thinking was and to reestablish personal contact, not to negotiate. Under grilling by persistent reporters he admitted that the exchange of opinions did not indicate any close identity of views, but he admonished us against being pessimists.

Secretary of State Dulles then flew into Paris on his follow-up mission and saw de Gaulle on July 5. As had been the case for Macmillan's meetings, the public atmosphere was warm and sunny. Indoors, however, the air-conditioners were turned on, for, although de Gaulle and Dulles respected each other, they shared no common experiences, and neither was a particularly warm, outgoing man.

Once again the final communiqué limited itself to anodyne generalities, but public discussion was excited and controversial, for everyone sensed that this was a more substantial and critical confrontation than Macmillan's. The public controversy centered around the triple-A issues of the day: the Algerian, Atlantic and Atomic policies that were known to be in dispute between de Gaulle and the Anglo-Saxons.

An unusual number of confidential "background briefings" were accorded correspondents by spokesmen and officials of both delegations. For once it looked as though the usual blackout curtains were being drawn. Officials were not exactly garrulous, but they did confirm the fact that there had been discussion of the Atlantic Alliance procedures. They denied that Algeria, as such, had been discussed, but they admitted the subject had come up in a general discussion of the urgent need to coordinate allied policies and to avoid cross-purposes in critical areas.

It was a brilliant performance by all the officials, a masterly demonstration of the subtle art of obfuscation. The essential truth was blinded out by the light of many nonessential truths: a classic case of secrecy by overexposure.

The topics of discussion between de Gaulle and Dulles that had been "revealed" to us seemed genuine, and of such primal concern that there was no reason to doubt that they were the heart of the matter. My own suspicions that something had been left out were not awakened until nine days later, when President Eisenhower announced that in the night of July 14–15 the United States fleet in the Mediterranean had carried five thousand combat marines to the beaches of Lebanon and that landings were in progress.

The Levant had been in turmoil all through the spring of 1958 as Nasser's agents spread dissension and fomented rebellions in the area. President Chamoun of Lebanon had to appeal to the West for help. Revolution broke out in Iraq on July 14, after the assassination of Prince Faisal and Nouri Said. The United Nations called a Security Council meeting on the night of July 14. The U.S Marines went to the rescue of Chamoun on the 15th. British paratroopers jumped into Amman, Jordan, on July 17 in response to a cry for help from King Hussein. Only one power was missing from the scene: France.

General de Gaulle presided over a cabinet meeting the day after the American Marines landed in Lebanon. The government spokesman announced that France was following the crisis closely and was "prepared for whatever action might be required." French reporters and editors were privately told that de Gaulle had not been consulted and had received only the minimum of advance information.

The French press had been incorrectly informed. The truth was exactly the opposite. It is now possible to reveal that Secretary of State Dulles fully informed President de Gaulle about the likelihood of American intervention and discussed this contingency at length in the meeting of July 6. This was a vital part of the essential truth that had been left out by officials. The full story of the Dulles–de Gaulle conversation has never before been told.* It is the key to what followed in the controversy that has been going on for the past seven years. The Dulles–de Gaulle meeting is not yesterday's dead headlines, it is today's explanation of current conflict.

Dulles was sent to Paris by Eisenhower at that particular moment, not only to establish an early contact with de Gaulle and to talk about the three "A's"—which was the official version—but also because Eisenhower knew that there would have to be a Western military intervention in the Levant. He had agreed on this secretly with Macmillan. It was essential to know where de Gaulle stood before launching a complex amphibian operation.

Dulles told de Gaulle at once that there would "very likely have to be military action in the Levant." He said that the United States held the view that it would be in the best interest of France and all concerned if the French would decide not to participate in that intervention. He offered to explain the reasons behind this thinking if the President of France requested it.

President de Gaulle thanked Secretary Dulles for his courtesy. He did not request any explanation. He simply stated, "If it becomes necessary to defend Western interests in the Levant, France will not be found absent."

De Gaulle and Dulles agreed that it was necessary for the two governments to keep in close touch with each other and with the British in this fluid situation.

Secretary Dulles said that there was nothing more important than being fully informed in all areas of concern to each of the allies and, since they were allies, the concern of each was always the concern of all. With this careful, respectful qualification, the Secretary asked President de Gaulle to evaluate the over-all French situation in the wake of "recent events" in North Africa. (The "recent events" were the uprisings in Algiers that had brought down the Fourth Republic and brought back de Gaulle.)

General de Gaulle said that the present was one of the most

* The details of this meeting were given to the writer by John Foster Dulles in the course of several conversations which were "off-the-record" at the time, and which have not been revealed until now. A transcript of my notebooks has been given to a historian preparing a biography of Dulles and collecting his papers for Princeton University. The minutes of the de Gaulle–Dulles talk, in the French and American government records, confirm the version given me in the talks with the Secretary.

critical moments in French history. The recent events in Algiers he considered to be symptoms of a deeply inflamed wound. The French people had suffered greatly in body and in spirit as a result of what had happened in Indochina. There was a real danger that the spirit might falter unless the morale of the people was preserved and strengthened in order to face the new trials ahead. De Gaulle said that there was a danger that the country might disintegrate under the strain of liquidating the French Empire in Africa if the people saw it as another defeat instead of the great new construction of a French-led "community of peoples." "That is why at this crucial moment there is nothing more important for the French people than to be made to believe again that France is a great power," de Gaulle told Dulles. He explained that "grandeur" is not a romantic notion; it is a reality, a tangible factor in a nation's efforts. The French "have the need to believe in themselves and the right to believe in themselves."

.Dulles said that he understood the need for the French to think of their country as the great nation it has been for so long and that this was in the highest interest of all France's allies. "The spirit of France is the spirit of Western civilization," said Dulles, adding, "It is certainly in our interest that this spirit be kept strong." He went on to warn, however, that there might well be a clash of wills if France, striving to maintain the status of a great power, were to appear to be setting herself up separately and above Germany and Italy. The Secretary pointed out that the Germans and Italians had their serious emotional and political problems; that they might misunderstand French motives and become mistrustful, and thereby severely strain the entire Atlantic Alliance.

General de Gaulle replied dryly that he was "not unfamiliar" with the problems of the Germans and Italians. He pointed out that Germany and Italy had been mainly Continental European powers throughout history, not world powers like France. Germany is certainly a great nation, but one must not confuse the power of Germany, and its spiritual and cultural contribution to Europe, with the power of France and its spiritual and cultural contribution to Europe and throughout the world.

De Gaulle pointed out that tiny Britain, smaller than Germany and very much smaller than the United States, had long been one of the greatest powers in the world. He took note of the fact, in ～～～g, that there was apparently no concern about a possible

and German mistrust of Great Britain's pretensions to

world power as there was of French ambitions. He further noted that there were no protests about Great Britain's status as an atomic power.

General de Gaulle concluded his comments by assuring Secretary Dulles of France's desire to improve relations with its Continental neighbors, and to move toward a durable, constructive reconciliation; but not at the sacrifice of France's interests and responsibilities in other regions. "France, Sir, has a world vocation."

President de Gaulle added that the Fifth Republic would, "of course," respect the treaties that had been entered into by France.

This conversation between de Gaulle and Dulles reveals fundamental difference of strategies, philosophies and attitudes that have divided the allies ever since. All the conflicts of the next seven years, up to and including today's crisis of relations, were there in embryo: America's view of France as a Continental power on a par with Germany and Italy, as opposed to de Gaulle's view of France as a world power; de Gaulle's concept of grandeur as a psychological imperative for the French people as well as a historical tradition and right; the American thesis of integrating allied forces and de Gaulle's unshakable conviction that full independence of action must be preserved at all cost by "cooperation," not integration with allies. "Cooperation between states is the only practicable basis for allied relations," de Gaulle told Dulles.

The basic characteristics of uncivil warfare can be seen in this opposition of views and aims and in the subsequent American anger at being accused of failing to inform and consult with the French, after Dulles had discussed the whole issue at length with de Gaulle.

U.S. Secretary of State Dean Rusk has told this writer, "When some nations complain about our failure to consult with them, they are, in reality, complaining about our failure to agree with them." There is a big measure of truth in this shrewd comment, but the greater truth is that de Gaulle wages political warfare in accordance with the rules of total war. He complains purposefully, not emotionally; when he seems most heatedly emotional, he is often most coldly purposeful. Above all, General de Gaulle is unconcerned with his allies' judgment of his conduct.

De Gaulle's statement to Dulles that France would not be absent in the Levant and his subsequent failure to follow through constituted, as the record will show, only one of many similar failures to do as he said he would. Puzzled American officials find it hard to believe that this is a deliberate Gaullist tactic. Yet it is. De Gaulle seeks to confuse, particularly in private talks. Public posture is more important to him because it is recorded by the journalists who provide the materials used by future historians. His private posture is less important, except for the written communications which are essential to the recording of history. In the uncivil war General de Gaulle sent off notes, messages and secret letters the way a military commander lays down a barrage of shells before an attack.

Within two months of his secret talk with Dulles, de Gaulle shot off a dispatch to Eisenhower that was the first of a series of secret letters by which de Gaulle wages a kind of epistolary war of words, a combat by correspondence. Since his sword was short, de Gaulle used his sharp pen as a secret weapon corresponding to the sharp tongue he used so effectively and exasperatingly in public. It was not surprising that de Gaulle began diplomatic negotiations with Eisenhower in a secret letter. After all, Charles de Gaulle was an accomplished man of letters.

The secret letter sent by General de Gaulle to General Eisenhower in September 1958 is the basic document of the continuing uncivil war with the Anglo-Saxons. It is also one of the prime examples of the twin technique of the hidden and the overexposed secret. Never has a letter been so widely discussed on the basis of such sparse information about it.

Presidential communications are not all secret. They range through several classifications, from the open letter, whose text is officially published, to the truly secret letter, whose existence is never even admitted. The letter of September 1958 falls in between these two extremes. Its existence is well-known, but its text has never been published. Its "broad outlines" and "general themes" have been reported by spokesmen, but always as "background information" and without many quotes or much supporting documentary evidence. Inevitably this leads to inaccuracies, misinterpretation, distortion, controversy and confusion, as each side gives out only a small part of its own version of the truth.

This writer has had access to the "secret letter" of September 1958 and also to several others that have followed in the course of the past seven years. They reveal the true reason for the bad split between France and the United States, a split that this writer now believes is unbreachable until after de Gaulle has gone from the scene. It is highly regrettable that these letters have not been published at least in an official, agreed summary. To the best of my knowledge the following description and analyses are accurate and reliable.

The first "secret letter" to Eisenhower was not, strictly speaking, a letter in the normal sense of the word. It was a document in two parts; the first was the "letter" part, a brief, personal greeting and reference to an attachment; the second was the attachment, a long, impersonal memorandum. There is an important motivation to the division of the letter in that fashion: it was designed to be used not only by the man to whom it was personally addressed in the first part, but also by his eventual successor, whom de Gaulle had in mind when he fashioned the memorandum.

General de Gaulle, then prime minister, was about to be elected president of the Republic for a *seven-year* term, whereas Eisenhower was concluding the final two years of his presidency. De Gaulle was thus opening negotiations not only with a particular president of the United States, but with the office of the presidency. This is one of the hidden facts that illuminate de Gaulle's tactics and long-range strategy.

One of the available facts of the greatest pertinence and significance has remained unknown for seven years, not because it was secret or hidden, for it is a part of the public record, but because its importance could not be seen or appreciated without the keys provided in the secret document. It is the fascinating relationship between two dates: September 14 and September 24, 1958. Each is a historic date in allied relations; but each is only a fragment of history until it is combined with two other valuable facts to reveal the hidden picture of the puzzle.

The first fact that led to the linked events of the month of September was hidden in the secret elements of the de Gaulle-Dulles talk of July 8, particularly the discussion of de Gaulle's demand for a three-power organization and Dulles' warning that it would be resented by the Italians and the Germans. De Gaulle listened intently to Dulles and came to the conclusion that the Secretary of State had already discussed the "de Gaulle problem" with the other nations.

Unwittingly or not, Dulles had done de Gaulle a good turn. Instead of being frightened off by the warning, General de Gaulle took it as a forewarning not to push his case with Eisenhower before overcoming or otherwise getting around the objections of his German and Italian neighbors.

This was the real motivation behind the missions to Rome and Bonn by French Minister Couve de Murville after Dulles had seen de Gaulle. These were not "goodwill visits" or "consultations," as the official explanation at the time would have it. General de Gaulle had sent his envoy on a reconnaissance mission to sound out the depth of the Italian and German fears and resentment of which Dulles had spoken. He also had his staff prepare exhaustive reports on official and public opinion in Italy and Germany. He did not press for a meeting with the German Chancellor until he had a full intelligence survey available. And he could not make a move toward the Anglo-Saxons until he had overcome or circumvented the Italo-German block. This is the second fragment that fits into the others to make the over-all picture.

De Gaulle was more than successful in his reconnaissance and his removal of the block. On September 14 he met with Chancellor Adenauer, in de Gaulle's private residence at Colombey, on the French-German frontier. General de Gaulle completely melted the Iron Chancellor of Germany. Adenauer was almost lyrical in his report on the meeting to a group of German journalists: "General de Gaulle was very frank, and I found him to be a completely different man from the one presented to us in recent weeks by the German press, and not only by the German press." The reporters were startled to hear the Chancellor add, "He is not a nationalist. He showed a perfect understanding of the international situation and the importance of French-German relations."

Adenauer's tribute was cheering, but the final communiqué on the talks was a triumph for de Gaulle. The communiqué stated that "Franco-German cooperation is the foundation of the European construction." It went on to say that this cooperation would "reinforce the Atlantic Alliance and serve the cause of all peoples in the domain of the great problems of the world."

In the diplomatic chess game the French knight had checked the Anglo-Saxon king and jumped right on the world square. The words, the tone and the themes of that communiqué were pure de Gaulle. He had won every point: the key word was "cooperation," not *integration* with other European countries; a "reinforcement" but not a *subordination* to the Atlantic Alliance; above all, German endorsement of a role for France in the "great problems of the world"—all of that without cost or counterpart, for Charles de Gaulle made no promises to Adenauer beyond the pledge he had already given Dulles that France would respect its treaties.

The conquest by charm of Adenauer is the final fragment that brings out the full picture when it is fitted into place, a picture of chain reaction. It was no coincidence that this bloodless conquest of Germany on September 14 was followed shortly by the secret letter to President Eisenhower; the chain of reactions had been forged link by link from Dulles to Adenauer to Eisenhower. This is confirmed in the secret letter itself, but only comprehended in its full significance when placed in the entire sequence of events.

In the opening remarks of the first part of his letter General de Gaulle told Eisenhower that events subsequent to his talk with Dulles in July had "served to affirm certain views" which could be found in full detail in the memorandum attached to the letter. He assured Eisenhower of his personal esteem but expressed his official concern about the mutual problems facing the French and Americans and the difficulties involved in the functioning of the Alliance.

The attached memorandum reviewed the crises of the past months, including the Lebanon landings, and stated that at one moment there was fear that the situation would get out of hand and explode into a general war. This demonstrated the "risks" that France had to take as a treaty ally of the United States, since the Alliance pledges all its members to join together if one is attacked. Therefore, any decisions taken by the United States that would lead to action resulting in hostilities were necessarily of concern to an ally that would share its fate.

President de Gaulle then complained that France did not get sufficient advance information and consultation on such decisions in many areas of the world. He pointed out that "France is a power with worldwide interests and responsibilities," in addition to being an ally whose own security could be affected vitally by American actions.

France, wrote de Gaulle, had gone through difficult years of occupation, liberation and reconstruction, when, "it must be admitted," the country had to devote its major energies to the task of recovery. But, recovery had been brilliantly accomplished and now, in the year 1958, France was ready and able "to assume its historic role in world affairs," General de Gaulle claimed. France could therefore no longer see justification for a delegation to the United States of the exclusive authority to make the vital decisions for the defense of the free world everywhere in the world. "It would be more realistic at this time to create a tripartite organization to take joint decisions on global problems."

The memorandum went on to state what de Gaulle meant by "joint decisions": the organization should be authorized to "draw up strategic plans" and also be empowered to "put them into effect" with specific application of this authority to "the use of nuclear weapons anywhere in the world."

There were detailed and closely reasoned arguments to support these theses and proposals, but the heart of the matter is contained in the key sentences cited above. The operative words, as valid a statement of de Gaulle's demands today as seven years ago, and just as totally unacceptable to the Anglo-Saxons, are: "tripartite organization," "joint decisions," "put into effect" and "use of nuclear weapons anywhere." When one thinks carefully of the full meaning of those words, it is difficult to see how de Gaulle could realistically expect the Anglo-Saxons to agree with his proposals, no matter how much they might agree with his general justification of France's right to an increased role in world affairs.

Since an "organization" is a formal institution, General de Gaulle was not only insisting upon the right to *participate* in *decisions,* he wanted this right to be *recognized officially and publicly* by creation of a formal institution.

De Gaulle would not have been satisfied even if Eisenhower had granted him all his extraordinary demands, including a full French voice in American strategy and the French veto over the Anglo-Saxons' decisive power implied in "joint decisions" on the use of nuclear weapons. Nothing less than the public formalization of these agreements would satisfy General de Gaulle. The secret history of the uncivil war demonstrates this time and time again.

Stunning as were these demands—and the full realization of what de Gaulle was asking did not immediately sink in—the greatest shock came at the conclusion of the memorandum. De Gaulle stated that henceforth France would "subordinate" her participation in NATO to the "recognition of French worldwide interests" and "equal participation" by France in global strategy.

The phrasing employed stopped just short of being an outright ultimatum, but its meaning could not have been more clear: the

Anglo-Saxons were warned to acknowledge publicly that France was one of the three great powers of the West, with full equality in the life-and-death decisions in the world, or de Gaulle would feel free to act independently of his allies. In the spirit of the French Revolution, applied to world affairs today, General de Gaulle had told the Anglo-Saxons in effect: Give me equality to reinforce our fraternity, or I will take my liberty of you!

Secretary Dulles, upon his return to Paris for the December meeting of NATO, went to see de Gaulle for a second time. He was particularly anxious to find out whether de Gaulle's use of expressions like "joint decisions" did specifically mean a veto power, in the sense that a "joint decision" can only come about if all parties concur. Under such definition, France, by withholding agreement, could prevent *joint allied* decision, thereby paralyzing the Anglo-Saxons. This was the kind of subtle legalism that appealed to Dulles and that he was well trained to spot in any contract or agreement.

After his talk with de Gaulle, the Secretary looked grim and glum. I had a chance to ask him about this "veto" issue shortly after he saw de Gaulle. Dulles was deeply distressed. He felt that de Gaulle had made an impossible demand and that there was no hope of an allied agreement. Soon after seeing Dulles, I interviewed French Foreign Minister Maurice Couve de Murville. He further confirmed de Gaulle's demand: "Yes, in effect, it does amount to a veto on the use of nuclear weapons anywhere in the world." The Foreign Minister explained: "If China attacks Taiwan, America may have to strike back with atomic weapons. This could lead to world war if Russia reacts. As your allies we would be plunged into war with you, without ever having been consulted or having participated in the chain of events. Do you think this is reasonable?"

Eisenhower had already replied to de Gaulle's letter before Dulles returned for the December talks. His reply, which was sent on October 20, was kept so secret that for more than five years thereafter there was a persistent legend that Eisenhower had not answered de Gaulle's letter. Washington silently suffered criticism of its failure to respond until it finally became necessary to put the record straight. This was done in May 1964 with an official "leak" to a Washington columnist. The "leak" put the record straight on the fact of a reply, but it was only a single droplet of the whole truth about the contents of that interesting secret letter of October

20, 1958. The following summary may not yet be the whole truth, but it is the most complete report that has been published thus far.*

President Eisenhower responded fully to de Gaulle's arguments. He began by agreeing that the threat to free-world defenses was a global one, long recognized as such by the United States. General Eisenhower had acted to meet it when he came out of retirement to head up the Atlantic forces in 1950. Three years earlier President Truman had moved to meet the threat in Greece and Turkey and had then created the Atlantic Alliance. President Eisenhower's administration had extended the network of allied defenses all around the world through regional defense pacts, such as CENTO in the Middle East and SEATO in Asia. He pointed out that France had joined two of these pacts, NATO and SEATO, and was therefore already enjoying the cooperation of the United States and other allies on a global basis. (This was addressed to but did not answer de Gaulle's demand for *three-power* global strategy, not membership in alliances.)

Eisenhower devoted a long passage to the importance of these pacts, not only for the obvious value of defense, but for the "frequently overlooked and invaluable habit of consultation among allies." Eisenhower argued that this "habit of consultation" must be continually strengthened, and become "broader and more frequent." He admitted that "you can lead a man to the table but you can't make him consult," but he insisted that it is almost impossible for even the most stubborn man to sit at a table frequently and for long hours with other men and not eventually join in and "acquire the habit of consultation."

The passage continued with Eisenhower's strong admonition that everything must be done to "avoid anything that would prevent or destroy the growing trust in consultation among all the members of NATO." He warned sternly of the peril of giving the impression "to our other allies that basic decisions affecting their own vital interests are being made without their participation."

President Eisenhower concluded by stating that "a Community association," in order to live and grow, must constantly look for means to make itself more useful to its citizens. He then kept the door open with these final words: "I am quite prepared to explore this aspect of the matter in appropriate ways."

This Eisenhower reply of October 20 is as vital a piece of the

* See Eisenhower interview, Chapter 11, pages 333–340.

puzzle as the de Gaulle letter it was answering. It is an enlightening document, with no information affecting state security other than the tradition of secrecy of presidential communications. The tight secrecy imposed for years on even the existence of the October 20 letter seems self-damaging in the light of the widespread discussion of the de Gaulle letter. The secrecy that was responsible for the inaccuracies in the discussions of de Gaulle's epistle was compounded by the misleading impression that Eisenhower had not even replied to it, or had just brushed it off. Both Paris and Washington have made their problems more difficult by their failure to make this exchange public.

The operative words in the Eisenhower reply that remain valid today are: *"regional* defense pacts," *"all* the members of NATO," *"our other allies."* They are shorthand symbols for America's faith in separate but interlocking regional pacts, as opposed to de Gaulle's proposal for a single worldwide organization for global strategy; they reflect America's determination to resist any narrowly based but widely responsible organization such as de Gaulle has never stopped demanding as his price for cooperation.

There is one curious inconsistency in the Eisenhower statement, on his point that other allies would resent basic decisions being taken without their participation. This was precisely General de Gaulle's own complaint about France not participating in American decisions that would affect French security. Eisenhower had replied in effect: since our allies resent being left out of basic decisions, we must leave you out too, although we do admit that allies do resent being left out. De Gaulle's logic was expressed quite differently. In effect, he had said to Eisenhower: since you will not make others happy anyway, you might as well meet my objections if you can, and you can if you wish. The fact is, you do not like my proposals in themselves and your references to other allies are hypocritical. If you really cared about the allies, you would let them share in basic decisions. General de Gaulle felt that General Eisenhower had told him to stay in the ranks without promotion to the high command. To say that de Gaulle was displeased would be an Anglo-Saxon understatement. In that first exchange the uncivil war that is raging today was made inevitable.

In an attempt to make at least a gesture toward de Gaulle's demand for joint planning, President Eisenhower instructed

Dulles to set up a "tripartite committee," but to keep it below cabinet level. Dulles did so in November, but made two moves that further enraged de Gaulle. He named de Gaulle's wartime nemesis, Robert Murphy, as the American member of the committee; then he told the Germans and Italians—who promptly passed the information back to de Gaulle—that the committee would *"discuss"* de Gaulle's proposals but not *"carry them out."*

When Dulles saw de Gaulle again on December 15, he received a sharp dressing down from the coldly angry President of France, who told him that the world situation was far too critical for "playing political games with committees." Officials close to General de Gaulle said he pointed out that, if war were to come, the Alliance was not in a position to react according to any common plan for action. "Correct, effective decisions cannot be made without the most careful advance planning," de Gaulle told Dulles. France, he pointed out, was not privy to any of America's war plans, nor, he commented sarcastically, were any of the other allies to whose resentments the Americans were so sensitive.

Under heavy pressure Dulles proposed that a start at three-power planning might be made in an area of common concern and interest, such as Africa, and said he would get busy on practical steps if de Gaulle agreed.

Unappeased, de Gaulle icily replied that he regretted the absence of such tripartite cooperation in Africa in recent years, particularly in North Africa. "Perhaps we French might have been spared some unnecessary difficulties had it existed before this." De Gaulle stated that he would nevertheless welcome genuine three-power planning in Africa, even if tardy. He then concluded with a comment that should live on as a collector's item in the memorabilia of Gaullism: "Of course, a common policy in North Africa would necessarily be a French policy."

There was no mistaking General de Gaulle's militant mood. The words and tone of his statements to Dulles dangerously skirted the line beyond which the Secretary of State might have been obliged to get up and walk out. Dulles left de Gaulle's office very despondent. On his return to Washington he warned Eisenhower to be prepared for a serious crisis.

The battle lines had been drawn, the first combat engaged. Uncivil War II was about to break out in the open.

* * *

General de Gaulle launched the first public battle of the uncivil war early in March 1959, when he instructed his representatives to inform the NATO command that France intended to withdraw its naval units assigned to the Allied Mediterranean Command. NATO was told that these units "would no longer be available in time of war"—a rather curious comment, since they were not supposed to be available to NATO *except* in time of war.

This is one of those complex, confused issues that de Gaulle knows how to exploit in provoking a controversy beyond the comprehension of the public. Since the public does not understand the complex technicalities, the tendency is to brush them aside and strike emotional attitudes. Nobody can strike an attitude quite like General de Gaulle, now that Roosevelt and Churchill, who were brilliant actors themselves, are no longer on the stage.

De Gaulle's curtain-raising posture in the second uncivil war was a stroke of genius; he had found an issue "full of fury and signifying nothing," for the number and importance of the naval units involved in the withdrawal were insignificant in themselves. It was the act of withdrawal rather than what he withdrew that caused the tempest.

De Gaulle could salve his conscience, assuming that he felt such a compulsion or had one in political affairs, by the thought that he had taken away almost nothing of strength from the allied Mediterranean fleet and that he could, in the event of war, return his units if need be. In short, there was no military or material significance of any kind to his action, yet the anguished uproar that it caused was quite satisfactorily thunderous. This is an essential characteristic of the manner in which de Gaulle wages this kind of warfare—by committing highly provocative acts of uncivility that wound without drawing blood or breaking bone.

The way de Gaulle used the navy to launch the uncivil war revealed techniques and characteristics pertinent to today's continuing struggle. Like the outbreak of the Civil War at Fort Sumter, which could hardly be classified as one of the great battles of history, the French naval affair, unimportant as a naval engagement, signaled the start of the second uncivil war between de Gaulle and the Anglo-Saxons. The analogy can be extended to the fact that the real issue of the Civil War was not slavery but states' rights; whereas the real issue between de Gaulle and the Anglo-Saxons is not the subordination of a few military units in NATO but the rights of the French state to be great and sovereign. General de Gaulle is a French "states' rightist." De Gaulle is the

Jefferson Davis of Europe and the Atlantic Alliance.

Unruffled by the tempest that he had blown up over the Atlantic, de Gaulle, hardly winded at all, picked up his pen and sent another secret letter to the Anglo-Saxons. Once again he addressed the letter to the American President and sent a copy to the British Prime Minister, thereby stabbing two birds with one nib.

The second secret letter, whose existence has still not been officially disclosed, was dispatched on the Ides of March, at the very moment that the Anglo-Saxons were being hit publicly by the naval affair. In that letter General de Gaulle admonished General Eisenhower to stand firm in Berlin and to resist every maneuver by Khrushchev, be it bluster or blandishment. This stern warning to get tough with the enemy came exactly at the moment that de Gaulle was getting tough with his allies, thus giving the enemy a chance to exploit their divisions. Only the "great Gaul" could have had the supreme self-confidence to advertise allied dissensions publicly while warning privately of a common danger.

The warning on Berlin was not, of course, the true purpose of the second secret letter. Its objectives could be read in the paragraphs which repeated the themes of the September 1958 letter, notably the "vital need to cooperate everywhere in the world on political, diplomatic and strategic joint planning." Those who read the second letter on the day that the navy was being publicly hauled away saw the link at once. NATO was the target, not Berlin. De Gaulle had simply fired a warning shot across the bows of the Anglo-Saxons' ships of state with his naval-unit withdrawal and the hint they might need his in case of crisis in Berlin—a harmless shot but well aimed to demonstrate that he could hit the target if he had to.

President Eisenhower replied at the end of March with his first sharply pointed rejection of de Gaulle's demand for tripartite cooperation. He wrote, "I attach the greatest importance to maintaining our military posture through the fullest, closest cooperation . . . in NATO." The pointed reference to NATO as the proper vehicle for "cooperation" came almost as a slap in the face of General de Gaulle, who had been insisting on his desire to break *out* of the NATO mold to become a world power. As a result of Eisenhower's reply, de Gaulle decided to take his case to the public before pressing it further in private.

On March 25 General de Gaulle staged one of his public performances, euphemistically called "press conferences," in the impressive red-velvet-and-gilt salon of the Elysée Palace, a fitting set for his act. In response to a series of questions, most of which had been suggested in advance to select "journalists," General de Gaulle made clear his view that there is a fundamental difference between the highly desirable "unity" of the Western alliance and the totally intolerable "integration" of forces that is the operating principle of NATO. In a union of sovereign nations it can be acceptable, under the exigencies of war, to put one's forces temporarily under a combined allied command; but integration—which means fusion, in which the individual elements lose identity and sovereignty—is nothing less than a "denationalization" and is intolerable, particularly in the absence of war.

Reporters were not aware on March 25 that de Gaulle had already secretly informed Eisenhower and Macmillan, not only of the navy withdrawal, but also of the philosophy behind it, which laid down conditions that could only lead to more and greater crises. While journalists were speculating how this act would hit London and Washington, Eisenhower had already drafted his sharp, secret riposte. One wonders what Woodrow Wilson, exponent of "open covenants of peace, openly arrived at," would have thought about de Gaulle's unique formula, "open discord, secretly arrived at." This formula has created one of the peculiar characteristics of the uncivil war: the worst incivilities are committed in the open forum, while secret discussions, even when contradictory, are generally courteous and closely reasoned, almost as though the principal protagonists were afraid to let their people know they are capable of reasoning with one another in a civil manner.

There is a reason behind this seeming madness, one that is most particularly pertinent to the modern electronic age. In this era of the talking stars and universal cameras, the "public view" has become a giant close-up, and the softest whisper is heard around the world. It is impossible to negotiate frankly in the public view. Statesmen now need secrecy to test out concessions that might be made but cannot be explored while their people watch and listen. Only if they fail to agree in private can they dare take their case to the public. The press conference is thus used as a means of public pressure to influence private negotiations, and no one knows better how to do this than General de Gaulle.

The Americans are not exactly amateurs at political warfare. They had a surprise in store for General de Gaulle—a secret exchange of their own with Russia. It came as a shock to all of Europe when Khrushchev and Eisenhower announced in August that they had accepted mutual invitations to visit each other's countries. European protests were so strong that Eisenhower had to fly off on a tour of Western capitals to calm allied fears about a direct Soviet-American "deal." It was on that tour that he stopped off in Paris on September 2, 1959, to see his "old comrade," de Gaulle. Eisenhower had to reassure Europeans about his meeting with Khrushchev, but he also had to reassure the Germans and the Italians that he would not yield to de Gaulle's demands to reorganize the alliance. He needed a united Europe behind him before engaging Khrushchev, whereas Europe was badly split by its fears, mistrust and conflicts on almost all issues. Eisenhower succeeded in reassuring the others, but he did not succeed in reassuring de Gaulle or resolving the disputes that had arisen in their exchanges of letters.

Only two months after de Gaulle had welcomed his "good, dear, loyal" comrade to Paris, he set off another political explosion in the most dangerous domain: nuclear policy. In an address at the Ecole Militaire on November 2, President de Gaulle announced that France would proceed to build an independent national atomic force. Excerpts of his address were given to the press that day. The full text was published in the *Information Bulletin* of the war ministry on November 13. These were the highlights:

> France must be in a position to defend herself by herself.

> The system that is called integration has outlived its utility. It is at an end.

> France will have an atomic striking force.

> There can be no separation between the political and the military. Military genius is at the service of a vast concept of over-all strategy.

> Defense of the nation is national defense; allies are essential but an alliance is not a substitute for the capability of self-defense; otherwise we could not maintain the state.

A week after the Ecole Militaire address, on November 10, 1959, in another spectacular press conference, General de Gaulle stated that France favored Soviet proposals for a summit conference and revealed that Khrushchev had accepted an invitation to come to France on March 15, 1960. In the span of one week he had openly revealed his break with the Anglo-Saxons on atomic and Atlantic policies and had rivaled the invitation they had themselves sent to Khrushchev instead of coordinating his invitation with theirs. The Atlantic Alliance looked like a Potemkin village in the late fall of 1959.

General de Gaulle was carrying out the policy he had explained to Dulles back in July 1958, when he had said that the morale of the French people could crack under the pressure of liquidating the old empire in Africa unless there was some corresponding sense of world mission. De Gaulle had proclaimed the policy of self-determination for Algeria in September. He knew that he had to sustain the spirit of the French by keeping their sense of greatness alive. In our times grandeur is atomic; there is no great power without atomic power. De Gaulle, to offset the liquidation of the African empire, was intent upon offering the French people and army the status of an atomic power at a summit meeting with the other great powers of the world. He felt he would not have a chance to regain control of the mutinous French Army unless he offered the army an independent nuclear striking force and showed the army and the French people how importantly represented they were on the world stage.

The "atomic" speech, the invitation to Khrushchev and his success in persuading the powers to choose Paris as the site of a summit conference all made it necessary for de Gaulle to pay his own personal respects to the Anglo-Saxons in their capitals. He went to London in early April 1960, then to Washington on April 22. In these capitals he conferred, without notable progress, with Macmillan and Eisenhower; then he returned to Paris to prepare to play host to the Big Four Summit Conference, that aborted affair which blew up when the Russians shot down the U-2.

In June, shortly after that luckless meeting, General de Gaulle reloaded his pen and shot off a new secret letter to President Eisenhower. It is interesting to note that de Gaulle found it necessary, even after a personal meeting, to carry on a secret correspondence on the very same points they had discussed in person in almost identical terms, just as though they had not just met. The written record is essential to writer Charles de Gaulle.

In the new letter, referring to the tripartite committee meetings that had been in process for about a year, de Gaulle told Eisenhower that the "habit of consultation" did not go far enough "to meet the essential aspect of our problem, which is global strategic cooperation." In this letter de Gaulle made it clear in unmistakable terms that France would settle for nothing less than "an equal voice in joint decisions on the use of nuclear weapons"—in other words, a veto right on America's essential weapon. He had talked about this before and referred to it in other letters, but in the June 1960 secret letter he made it specific and proposed that a "high-level planning group" be created to bring it about.

Eisenhower fired back a rocket complaining that de Gaulle kept making proposals but then took no action to follow through, even when the Americans had agreed to try to satisfy him. Back in December 1958 Secretary Dulles had proposed a tripartite committee for common action in Africa, to which de Gaulle had agreed and had promised to execute by appointing a French delegate. Eisenhower pointed out that he had been waiting a year and a half for de Gaulle to do so. He said that despite his discouragement he was willing to make another attempt, and he proposed that a "high-level" three-power military meeting be held to consider de Gaulle's demands for "global strategy."

This was not yet anything like the three-power "organization" or the "joint decision" demand of de Gaulle, but it was a step toward it, for it was the first time that Eisenhower had agreed to discuss "global strategy" and on a "high level."

With time running out on the Eisenhower term of office in that month of June 1960, de Gaulle moved fast and sent off another letter. In this secret letter de Gaulle answered Eisenhower's high-level committee proposal by counterproposing a three-power summit of the West. He stated that its purpose should be "joint planning of global strategy"; then he struck a new note by adding "and to reorganize the Alliance."

Eisenhower was appalled. Time and again the Anglo-Saxons had told de Gaulle that they could not risk the resentment of other allies by a public formalization of special status for France. Time and again they had pleaded with de Gaulle to work out the problems of the Alliance quietly and in detail. At the end of two years of constant repetition of these explanations, de Gaulle had not only reiterated his demands, but now also wanted to take them to the highest and most open forum and use it to reorganize the Alliance.

Eisenhower dispatched his last reply to de Gaulle's secret letters. He agreed "in principle" that a meeting with de Gaulle might be useful, but he avoided any reference to a summit meeting. He bluntly pointed out, moreover, that no useful discussion could be held on the "reorganization of the Alliance" until de Gaulle had sent him a detailed memorandum of his suggestions for Eisenhower to study. He curtly recalled that General de Gaulle had promised *twice before,* in the course of conversations about the Alliance, to send through such a memorandum but had never done so.

That was the end of the secret combat by correspondence between de Gaulle and Eisenhower. De Gaulle answered Eisenhower publicly on September 5, 1960, in a bitter attack on NATO at a press conference in Paris, with the statement that henceforth France would count only on herself, "for our only defense is our national defense."

This severe public summing up for the prosecution was not only a reply to Eisenhower's secret letter, it was a calculated advance warning to the man the Americans would select two months later to pick up the baton from Eisenhower in the presidential elections of 1960. De Gaulle was warning his next adversary. The next adversary was to be a very different man from any that de Gaulle had ever faced. The veteran French statesman, the oldest chief of state of the West, was about to test his steel on the youngest chief of state in modern American history.

John F. Kennedy was the first postwar American president who had never had any personal experiences with de Gaulle, good or bad. Whether this would prove to be good or bad was not a meaningful thought for General de Gaulle. An Anglo-Saxon chieftain, he assumed, would defend Anglo-Saxon interests. He had not noticed any significant difference between the Roosevelt-Churchill policies and the Eisenhower-Macmillan policies, despite the somewhat friendlier personalities of the latter.

General de Gaulle doubted that the advent of Kennedy would significantly change fundamentals. He believed that statesmen come and go but that the reasons of state remain. That was the attitude of the world-weary chieftain of the Gauls as he prepared to encounter the new, young leader of the Anglo-Saxons.

The uncivil war was moving to a new frontier.

* * *

General de Gaulle's oracular pronouncements had given him a reputation for Delphic prescience. By the accident of world time zones he was more than prescient in November 1960. He knew the name of the man who would be his new ally or adversary before John F. Kennedy himself knew that destiny had called. The Senator, exhausted by a long vigil, had gone to bed at 4 A.M. on November 9, before the tireless tabulators tapped out the decisive tally and flashed the news to a wakeful world. It was high noon in Paris when the Senator became the president-elect. John F. Kennedy was deep in sleep, blanketed by the darkness before dawn, when President de Gaulle began drafting a soothsaying message of congratulation.

Late that afternoon, after a victory speech and a final rousing game of touch football with the family, President-elect John F. Kennedy flipped quickly through his congratulatory messages, setting aside a few for more careful reading and reflection. Among them were the messages of Charles de Gaulle and Nikita Khrushchev.

Kennedy knew that he would face no more powerful and dangerous adversary than the Soviet leader. He also knew that he would have no more competitive and mistrustful ally than the man who was France. De Gaulle interested him particularly as the case study of a man who refused to admit defeat. General de Gaulle had long been one of the heroes in Kennedy's private gallery of profiles in courage.

He found de Gaulle's message encouraging, particularly the expression of hope that the new generation, "assuming the great tasks of leadership, would strengthen the traditional ties of friendship between our two countries." Khrushchev's telegram intrigued Kennedy most. The Soviet leader hoped that relations between America and Russia "might become again what they were in the time of Roosevelt." Kennedy wondered whether this was merely a genial desire for friendly relations or whether Khrushchev had any specific policy relationship in mind. He noted that Khrushchev and de Gaulle had put their emphasis upon improving relations, and he knew this to be no coincidence; relations of both men with President Eisenhower had been strained to a breaking point the previous year. Soviet-American relations had been virtually broken when the U-2 affair had blown up the Paris Summit Conference in May. At the same time General de Gaulle had been carrying on a running battle with his "old comrade" General Eisenhower, picking up where he had left off in the conflicts with Roosevelt. Suddenly it struck Kennedy that de Gaulle was counting on the new generation in America, whereas Khrushchev wanted to go back to the old Roosevelt days. Kennedy burst out laughing and said, "Well, one thing's sure; I can't make both of them happy."

Kennedy recalled that moment in the course of a "background interview" I had with him in New York a few weeks later. The President-elect speculated about the prejudices of the past. "Just how important is this so-called trauma of de Gaulle's?" he asked. He also wondered whether there were any lingering resentments about his 1957 senate speech criticizing the French in Algeria. I expressed doubts that de Gaulle would be concerned about a pre-presidential speech, or allow a personal grudge of the past to carry over against a different man in the present. However, the nature of de Gaulle's present conflicts with the Anglo-Saxons was undoubtedly influenced to some extent by traumatic experiences of the past. Kennedy nodded agreement and then said that he was determined to overcome de Gaulle's mistrust and make a fresh start.

This conversation took place on January 8, 1960, just two weeks before Kennedy's inauguration as president. France was very much in the news that day, for the voting had begun in the referendum on self-determination for Algeria. Kennedy viewed this as the crucial factor for the future of French-American relations. "De Gaulle just can't do anything constructive until he puts out that fire." Then, with a quick smile, he said, "I'm certainly glad my Algeria speech was made *before* de Gaulle came back to power. And I'm relieved that he now has a policy we can support. We ought to be able to get that thorn out of our sides."

Kennedy was to discover that Algeria was only one thorn; there were many others that would keep both sides constantly irritated. Relations between Kennedy and de Gaulle were to be further complicated by the changing nature of economic forces and the shifting balances of world power, not only between East and West, but inside each camp.

By 1961 Europe had recovered economically, while America was suffering from a dollar drain and drop in gold reserves. From this dollar drain to the disaster of the Bay of Pigs in mid-April, President Kennedy was bedeviled by one misfortune after the other.

General de Gaulle was beset by conflicts of his own, which climaxed in the revolt of the generals on the morning of April 22. De Gaulle's crisis came two days after the Bay of Pigs invasion had failed. However, he came out of the revolt in Algiers looking much better than Kennedy, who had taken an unsavory ducking in the Bay of Pigs.

General de Gaulle received many messages of solidarity and offers of total aid from President Kennedy during the Algiers insurrection. The American's public tribute to General de Gaulle at the moment of his victory was all the more generous, coming as it did so soon after Kennedy's own humiliating setback. Hope for an end to the uncivil war rose rapidly a month later when President and Mrs. Kennedy went to Paris and won the hearts of the French. The normally ceremonial state visit was converted by this handsome young couple into a gay public party.

The private working sessions were serious, but just as friendly as the public celebrations. General de Gaulle was impressed by the vigorous, intelligent young President, who looked very different from the distant image of the fumbling man who had suffered a severe humiliation. The loser of the Bay of Pigs showed no awe of the victor of Algiers. Kennedy was neither humble nor aggressively defensive. The young chief of state was respectful of the elder statesman, but he was quietly self-confident, looking and acting like a man who knew the value of the power that he represented. As a leader of the West, General de Gaulle was comforted; as the champion of French interests, he knew that he was facing a worthy opponent.

General de Gaulle had no illusions about his own "triumph" in Algiers. The French Army was still in a state of shock and not yet reliable; the French people remained dangerously divided and shaken. More than ever de Gaulle believed what he had told John Foster Dulles in 1958: he had to restore the morale of the people by reaffirming their sense of greatness; and he had to give the army both a mission and a weapon that would help end its manic-depressive torment.

De Gaulle's attitude to Kennedy was necessarily influenced more by these imperatives than by his appreciation of Kennedy's solidarity in his hour of trial, for he was a chief of state, and the state has reasons that the heart cannot know. General de Gaulle, like President Truman, believes that the presidential desk is ·the place where the buck stops; he would add, "This is where the heart stops feeling."

De Gaulle and Kennedy spent their first session reviewing in detail the complete history of all the exchanges with Eisenhower on the key issue of a three-power organization for joint global strategy. Kennedy had decided long before coming that here was the core of the matter.* He believed that each specific conflict over European unity, Atlantic integration and the nuclear striking force derived from or was essentially related to de Gaulle's determination to have an equal voice with the Anglo-Saxons on major decisions in any region of the world.

Kennedy suggested to de Gaulle that they break the deadlock on this issue by addressing themselves to specific urgent threats to peace in the world, such as Berlin and Laos. He proposed the creation of a three-power military group of senior officers to draft joint plans for these areas. De Gaulle promptly agreed. This was a giant step toward his objective. He said that he would instruct his foreign and defense ministers to work out top-level staff arrangements for such a meeting, to be held as soon as possible.

As in all the previous cases of similar agreements with Eisenhower, General de Gaulle failed to follow through on the plan for senior-level joint planning on Berlin and Laos. He never named a French representative to discuss these questions with the Anglo-Saxons. Kennedy, like his predecessor, was puzzled by the gap between de Gaulle's words and deeds. He kept asking officials and reporters with long experience of de Gaulle to try to explain it to him. I ventured a guess that de Gaulle was not interested in military meetings, not even at senior levels, since nothing is decisive below cabinet level and since, above all, they are always conducted in secret. De Gaulle wants *public* recognition, in an *organization* that would hold cabinet-level meetings at regular intervals, thus *formally* acknowledging France's great-power status. This derives directly from his conviction that France has a psychological need for grandeur.

The President did not like the "feel" of this explanation. He

---

* I had a long talk with Kennedy about this and then continued the discussion with his closest adviser, Presidential Counsel Theodore Sorensen, in the plane from New York to Paris en route to the presidential meeting.

thought it sounded logical enough but "it's a bit too pat," he told me. He suspected that perhaps de Gaulle might have developed this theory in order to rationalize his own deep-rooted desire for greatness; and that, with or without the morale-boosting value to the people, he believed in grandeur for grandeur's sake. Kennedy was disturbed and disappointed by his own analysis, for he knew there was no hope of resolving basic disputes if de Gaulle would accept nothing less than an equal vote on global strategy and action, particularly on atomic strategy.

The President was worried about de Gaulle's policies, not only in the allied uncivil war, which he had anticipated after studying the record, but also in the cold war with the East. For several years de Gaulle had played a lone hand in the cold war. When the question of a great-power summit in the Middle East had arisen, de Gaulle, insisting that it be limited to the Big Four, had opposed the "Anglo-Saxon" preference to meet in the framework of the United Nations. On Berlin and German reunification de Gaulle had opposed holding any kind of summit conference, arguing that the slightest concessions to the Russians would encourage Khrushchev to demand more.

De Gaulle had consistently opposed and had even shown mistrust of Kennedy's exploration of coexistence and a détente with Russia. They exchanged notes and views, before, during and after their June meeting. Kennedy sent Secretary Dean Rusk to Paris at the end of July to try to obtain de Gaulle's cooperation, or at least his passive endorsement of Kennedy's policies. Not only did Rusk get nowhere, he caught a diplomatic chill from de Gaulle's glacial disapproval. The patient, mild-mannered Rusk was shaken up by de Gaulle's treatment. He came very close to getting up and walking out on de Gaulle in the middle of the talk. Rusk gave Kennedy a report as gloomy as any that Dulles had ever given Eisenhower.

After the Russians put up the Berlin Wall on August 13, 1961, General de Gaulle sent a long secret letter to President Kennedy. The Berlin Wall and the allied disagreements on policy toward Russia were the occasions for the letter, but the arguments developed in it were variations on the same themes already played in the secret letters to Eisenhower and in the first personal meeting with Kennedy.

President Kennedy, unlike Eisenhower, just filed the letter away and did not reply. It was a break in the chain: Eisenhower had always replied. However, the letter writing had not ended; it was only being conducted differently. Kennedy bided his time and then sent a letter of his own to de Gaulle, not an answer but a new departure.

Kennedy dealt at length with the crisis of Berlin and with the dispute over nuclear policy. He made it clear that he appreciated de Gaulle's "tough line" on Berlin, but he also made it clear that firmness is most efficacious when backed up by substantial strength and by willingness to accommodate the adversary without abandoning vital positions. The reference to the "substantial strength" was a discreet but unmistakable reference to the relatively minor French contribution to allied covering forces in Germany. For many months American officials had been nettled by French admonitions to be firm without a corresponding firmness of French forces to back up the advice.

President Kennedy was particularly disturbed about the nuclear dispute. He sympathized with de Gaulle's desire for the weapon that had become the symbol of power, but Kennedy was genuinely concerned about proliferation of atomic capacities. He explained this fully to de Gaulle and said that the U.S. was always ready to hear suggestions on how to satisfy France's nuclear needs while avoiding the creation of precedents that led to proliferation. At one point during the secret negotiations of this period, a special American "formula" had been devised to provide de Gaulle with an atomic capacity if he would agree to cease all further French tests. It was turned down by de Gaulle out of hand. For the first time Kennedy began to believe the "grandeur theory," for it looked as though de Gaulle was more interested in the blast than the bomb.

General de Gaulle sent another letter to Kennedy in January 1962. He put forward another new proposal, this time for a permanent three-power political planning group and a combined military staff to prepare "common decisions and common actions"; he suggested this group might make a start in the area of the "nonaligned nations." He promised to send through a memorandum detailing the possibilities for working out common policies on this area of neutral and underdeveloped countries.

This was one of the most remarkable letters in the series of communications between Paris and Washington. It was the first time that de Gaulle had shifted toward the "third world" area and the first proposal for purely political and economic planning.

However, the particular stress on the permanent nature of the committee demonstrated that this objective was a long-range formalization of great-power status.

Although President Kennedy had been critical of de Gaulle's failure to follow through on his proposals for joint planning on Berlin and Laos, he nonetheless had a grudging admiration for de Gaulle's stubborn, single-minded pursuit of his own ideas. Above all, Kennedy marveled at de Gaulle's unabashed presentation of new proposals after failing to act upon any of the old ones. The promise to send through a "following memorandum" on how to deal with the nonaligned nations, after he had been prodded continually to send through the memorandum on Atlantic reorganization, is difficult to understand; moreover, the newly proposed memorandum was never sent either.

De Gaulle and Kennedy continued to communicate, once by telephone, but mainly by correspondence. Their exchanges soon became a "dialogue of the deaf," with each man talking but neither listening to the other. After January 1962, General de Gaulle gave up all hopes of reaching agreement on his basic proposal for a three-power organization of the West. He opened up a new front as a riposte to the New Frontier, resurrecting a "vast plan" that he had had in mind for many years: to group the western European nations into "an organization that would be one of the three powers of the planet."

The execution of de Gaulle's vast plan coincided with the launching of a vast American concept: Kennedy's proposal for an Atlantic partnership with Europe. In the middle was Great Britain, torn apart by conflicting commitments to America, Europe and its own Commonwealth. The uncivil war between de Gaulle and the Anglo-Saxons was about to enter its most bitter phase, "the Battle of the Grand Designs." The battlefield was principally Europe, but the conflict of interests spread around the world and involved the world.

CHAPTER ELEVEN

THE MOMENT OF TRUTH FOR THE FRENCH

Yesterday was the time for battle; now the hour of reckoning is striking. This moment of truth revealed France's continuing weakness in relation to her own goals and to the partisan calculations of other states.

CHARLES DE GAULLE, *Memoirs III, Discord, 1959*

IN THE HISTORY of every war—hot, cold, civil and uncivil—there comes a point of no return, where the antagonists commit themselves, sometimes by deliberate decision, sometimes by drift, to fight on without compromise, to victory, defeat or mutual exhaustion.

The point of no return in the uncivil war among the Atlantic allies was reached in the "dialogue of the deaf" between General de Gaulle and President Kennedy at the end of 1961; it was crossed in the extraordinary journey of Prime Minister Macmillan from Paris to Nassau at the end of 1962. From start to finish, 1962 was a year of open, fully committed, political warfare between de Gaulle and the Anglo-Saxons in the "Battle of the Grand Designs."

"Grand Design" was a phrase borrowed from French history, but it was the American President who used it to describe his vision of an "Atlantic Partnership" between the United States of America and a future United States of Europe. This Grand Design of President Kennedy collided in mid-air with the "Vast Plan" of General de Gaulle. De Gaulle's vast plan had first begun to evolve ın his mind in the final months of World War II. He explained in his memoirs that, as he watched the collapse of the old order, "It seemed to me that the new era would perhaps permit me to make a start upon the execution of the vast plan that I had formed for my country."

General de Gaulle described his "vast plan" in these words: "To collaborate with West and East and, if need be, to contract, with one side or else the other, the necessary alliances without ever accepting any kind of dependency." To accomplish this purpose, de Gaulle had a vision of bringing about "a political, economic and strategic grouping of all the states that bordered on the Rhine, the Alps and the Pyrenees." De Gaulle stated the objective of this "grouping" frankly and clearly: "To make that organization one of the three powers on earth and one day, if necessary, the arbiter between the Soviet and Anglo-Saxon camps."

A passage extracted from memoirs would not by itself be convincing documentary evidence; but there is impressive supporting evidence to prove it represented the current thoughts of President de Gaulle. The views of the President conform with the words of the author if those words are read in the light of the flames of the uncivil war. To anyone familiar with de Gaulle's speeches and secret letters one sentence fairly leaps out of the memoirs to hit the informed reader in the eye: "To make that organization one of the three powers on earth." This phrase of the memoirs runs like a leitmotif through all the presidential exchanges. There are other indications, moreover, which give it great significance. The most interesting phenomena are the dates of publication of the memoirs.

Volume III appeared in October 1959. The two previous volumes had been published successively in 1954 and 1956. The arithmetical progression of the first two volumes suggests that the manuscript of Volume III must have been finished, or very near completion, by the spring of 1958. De Gaulle's recall to power in June 1958 explains why Volume III was not ready to be published as scheduled but does not explain why another year and five months went by before its publication. If this unusual delay is measured against the secret and open negotiations between de Gaulle and the Anglo-Saxons, the answer suggests itself: de Gaulle delayed publication until he was convinced that he had run into a dead end in his explorations with Washington.

General de Gaulle had kept up the pressure from his first

meeting with Dulles in July 1958 to his first secret letter to
Eisenhower in September, through the naval crisis in NATO in
March 1959 and all through the spring and early summer of that
year. By then he knew that he had failed to persuade or force the
Anglo-Saxons to grant him the joint planning and action and the
public recognition of great-power status that was his no-compro-
mise objective. Only one month after the climactic Eisenhower
meeting of September 1959 Volume III of the memoirs appeared.

At that point the memoirs were no longer the twilight thoughts
of a fading old soldier. In October 1959 they were the official views
of the President of the French Republic. They were never disavowed as such, nor was any attempt made to qualify them as
history rather than as policy. It is fair to assume, therefore, that
the vast plan was in the mind of President de Gaulle in October
1959. He did not act upon it then; the publication of the plan in
the memoirs was more a warning and a last pressure. His actions
since January 1962 suggest that he began putting the substance of
this plan into execution immediately after the decisive disagreements with Kennedy on East-West relations and on atomic and
Atlantic policies.

Early in 1962 General de Gaulle instructed his envoys at Common Market headquarters in Brussels and in Germany and Italy to
push hard on the plan presented by French Ambassador Christian
Fouchet, featuring a high council and periodic meetings of the
chiefs of state as the basis for progress toward the political "unity"
of Europe. This was the plan that de Gaulle's critics decried as
seeking to create a "Europe of the Fatherlands." * General de
Gaulle has denied he had ever used such an expression. In a
"background conversation" the General explained to this writer
that the phrase he had used was "Europe of the States," † to
differentiate it from the "supranational Europe" of the Common
Market.

De Gaulle's campaign for his kind of Europe had begun in
January 1962, when the chiefs of state of the six Common Market
countries appointed a special committee of experts to study the
means of achieving political unity. The decisive meeting took
place in Paris on April 17, 1962, when, at the end of more than

* In French, "L'Europe des Patries."
† In French, "L'Europe des Etats."

three months of study, de Gaulle's project was vetoed by Belgium and Holland.

General de Gaulle, fighting harder with every setback, turned to his trump card—the German Chancellor, Konrad Adenauer. Once before at a vital moment de Gaulle had won him over, in their first meeting at Colombey in September 1958. He proposed that they go back to the letter and spirit of that first meeting, in which Adenauer had agreed that Franco-German cooperation was the keystone of any European construction and that it would advance the cause of all peoples in the world. Adenauer, under heavy fire at home, sensing that his days were numbered, agreed to negotiate a special Franco-German Treaty in that spirit. He was critical of Kennedy's "flirtation" with Moscow, but more than anything, "Der Alte" at that moment had to fight for his most passionate dream: the reconciliation of Germany and France. He was an eager partisan of de Gaulle's proposals for a replay of September in Colombey.

De Gaulle drove on relentlessly in a major diplomatic offensive as intense as a national election campaign. He went to Turin to see Italian Premier Fanfani and to Lake Como to confer with the vacationing Chancellor Adenauer, who then returned de Gaulle's visit by going to Paris in July. De Gaulle went to see Adenauer a third time, in Germany, in September. Finally there came the climactic secret meeting with Prime Minister Macmillan on December 15 and 16 in the forest of Rambouillet.

At that meeting in Rambouillet, General de Gaulle made his ultimate bid for cooperation with the British, proposing the fullest possible exchanges on all technical, scientific and atomic enterprises. De Gaulle recalled an earlier offer of January 1961 to rescue the "Blue Streak" missile project in a joint Anglo-French production of the missile after the British had had to abandon "Blue Streak" as too costly for them to produce alone. He also took a very hostile position toward British entry into the Common Market, and this shocked Macmillan.

Macmillan was in a most difficult position. He was facing a crucial meeting with President Kennedy at Nassau only two days after the meeting with de Gaulle. He admitted to de Gaulle that the Americans had decided to cancel production of the "Skybolt" rocket, which they had previously agreed to furnish to the British as a substitute for the "Blue Streak." The entire British atomic deterrent had been built on "Skybolt." The bitter quarrel that had broken out between Britain's Defense Minister Thorneycroft and Secretary McNamara over the cancellation made a Kennedy-Macmillan meeting essential. Macmillan flew from Paris to Nassau in a depressed mood. De Gaulle had given him no hope.

At the Nassau conference Kennedy offered to make American "Polaris" missiles available to the British, but they were to be assigned to a "multilateral Atlantic force." Macmillan accepted the offer with one condition, announced in the final communiqué: the British could withdraw the missiles from the international force "in the event that Her Majesty's Government should decide that supreme national interests were at stake." Kennedy and Macmillan sent off a message informing de Gaulle of the agreement and making him the same offer.

General de Gaulle turned down the offer, although there are indications that he hesitated for a moment.* The "multilateral" principle was exactly the kind of American-dominated device he had been fighting against for almost a quarter of a century. He was disdainful of what seemed to him a British surrender of their independent deterrent. The cancellation of "Skybolt" was enough evidence, if de Gaulle needed any, that it was not wise to build hopes on a missile supplied by the United States. De Gaulle did not reply to the Nassau offer in an official communication to Washington. He chose to denounce it publicly at his press conference of January 14. Once again he followed the formula of open discord secretly arrived at.

Several months later President Kennedy told me that some of his own advisors had thought he had made an error by offering de Gaulle the "Polaris," for it would have given de Gaulle a missile he could not produce for himself for a decade. Kennedy said, "If it was an error, de Gaulle saved me by not accepting it."

Nassau was the end of the road in the long journey since de Gaulle's first meeting with Macmillan in Paris in June 1958. De Gaulle had decided that the Anglo-Saxons would not let him join them on what he felt to be equal terms. Reversing a classic maxim,

---

* On January 2 a French spokesman told the press that de Gaulle had sent a note to Kennedy saying he was studying the offer. This was confirmed by Foreign Minister Couve de Murville in the national assembly on January 24. On January 4 President de Gaulle had received U.S. Ambassador Charles E. Bohlen, who said after his talk that there would be a long discussion of the Polaris offer.

de Gaulle decided, "If you can't join 'em, beat 'em." He promptly set out to beat them. The point of no return had been passed. In January 1963 the uncivil war between General de Gaulle and the Anglo-Saxons became a total war on all fronts.

Blow by blow General de Gaulle struck with full force. In his press conference of January 14, 1963, he slammed the door to the Common Market in Britain's face and then instructed French Foreign Minister Couve de Murville to break off negotiations in Brussels. He rejected the proposal for a multilateral force and then refused to sign the atomic test-ban treaty. De Gaulle told this writer, "The so-called test-ban treaty between America and Russia is another Yalta." In 1963 France virtually stopped participating as an active cooperative member of NATO.

One of the saddest incivilities in the light of subsequent events occurred in the summer of 1963, during the European tour of President Kennedy to Berlin, Rome, London and Ireland. Everyone thought that Kennedy was snubbing de Gaulle by flying over Paris and leaving him out of the tour. Official spokesmen deny this, pointing out correctly that Kennedy had paid a state visit to Paris in June 1961, so that it was up to de Gaulle to return the visit in Washington.

Some sources insist that Kennedy did want to visit Paris and that he sent several confidential messages to General de Gaulle saying that he would be pleased to stop off in Paris if de Gaulle invited him to do so. While in Germany he asked American Ambassador George McGhee several times a day to check the incoming messages to see if there was a reply from General de Gaulle.* He is reported to have done the same in Rome. General de Gaulle never replied. Whatever the truth of this affair, the two never met again.

The uncivil war turned bitter at the close of 1963 after the Kennedy assassination. President de Gaulle flew to Washington in November 1963 to pay his last respects to John F. Kennedy at Arlington. He met with President Johnson briefly after a state-department banquet for visiting dignitaries on the night of the funeral. President Johnson thanked de Gaulle for his earlier messages of condolence and his attendance at the ceremonies. He then said that he would be pleased if de Gaulle would reconfirm

---

* A ranking American diplomat assured me that this story is correct. Presidential counselor McGeorge Bundy, who was with Kennedy constantly on the trip, says that he was not aware that Kennedy wanted to see de Gaulle.

the appointment made earlier with Kennedy for a full-scale conference between the two presidents in Washington early in 1964. President Johnson pressed the invitation three times, in the friendliest manner. He genuinely wanted good personal relations with de Gaulle, and he felt the time was ripe and right for a "parley." General de Gaulle's replies were brief but seemed favorable to the suggestion.

As soon as he left de Gaulle, President Johnson went to another room to meet with the governors; he announced happily that President de Gaulle had agreed to keep with him the appointment made earlier with President Kennedy for a meeting in Washington. When French officials later denied that de Gaulle had agreed, the uncivil war had begun with Johnson, for the public disavowal of a president is a very grave affair.* There are two differing versions of what was actually said between the two men, one contained in a state-department summary of notes written shortly after the talks, the other in a French foreign-ministry document of the same kind.

The American version of the dialogue reports de Gaulle saying *positively,* "Yes, of course," and then adding that "the precise details can be *arranged* through diplomatic channels." The French version reports de Gaulle saying politely, "In principle, yes," and adding that "the details can be *discussed* via diplomatic channels." The subtle shadings between "arranged" and "discussed" add up to a not-so-subtle difference between yes and no. And the French phrase "in principle" does not guarantee agreement in practice.

A first attempt was made that night by French diplomats to suggest that de Gaulle had only agreed to confer but had not said where. The French then floated a trial balloon proposing that Johnson, as a new president, might want to make a swing around Europe, beginning in Paris. This was shot down by a sharp reminder that Johnson had already been in Europe, had represented Kennedy at a mammoth rally in Berlin, had met de Gaulle in Paris and could not leave the United States when there was no vice-president in office.

---

* The account of this conversation and the subsequent events described here have been transcribed from the notes I took that night. I was present at the state-department dinner and spoke with all the principals concerned during and after the events herein described. At one point a close aide of President Johnson asked me to see de Gaulle and Ambassador Alphand to clarify the confusion. It was undoubtedly based on a misunderstanding.

Undaunted, French diplomats suggested that President Johnson might perhaps meet de Gaulle "halfway," on the island of Martinique on de Gaulle's return from a state visit to Mexico. The American reply to this was a thundering negative. It would have been logical and convenient for de Gaulle, who was in any case flying home, to stop in Washington, rather than for Johnson, who was carrying a heavy burden alone, to make the totally unnecessary flight to a Caribbean island. The suggestion truly made the temperature rise in Washington.

It is difficult to see how a misunderstanding of this kind could arise between two chiefs of state on a question as simple as whether an invitation had been accepted. Yet there really was a misunderstanding of a special kind which frequently plagues Franco-American relations. It is not caused by a language barrier alone, nor is it just a misinterpretation of words, but rather it is a barrier of temperaments and personalities and a misinterpretation of customs and procedures.

President Johnson is very American in his impulsiveness and high spirits. He is also used to operating on the procedures of the flexible give-and-take of the congressional system of politics. Taking de Gaulle's words at their face value, wanting very much to have some good news on that sad night, the President could not resist making a public announcement of their agreement to meet early in 1964. He may have been pushing a bit hard, but it was an honest action.

General de Gaulle was never impulsive. He was a chess player, a master of evasive action and an artist in ambiguity. De Gaulle did not want to rule out the possibility of his coming to Washington, which is why he phrased his ambiguous reply in a positive manner, but he did not want to be committed to it. There is good reason to believe that de Gaulle became suspicious and then angered by Johnson's impulsive announcement, thinking that Johnson *was* trying to commit him publicly. This was a familiar, favorite device of Roosevelt and of Churchill and one of the chronic irritants of the uncivil war. It always made a bad situation worse, for de Gaulle resented and resisted this kind of pressure. Every time the "Anglo-Saxons" would try to force his hand, they only succeeded in stiffening his neck. His disavowal of Johnson was less a calculated act than an automatic action, a kind of Pavlovian conditioned reflex caused by the sight of an Anglo-Saxon hook.

This is the price of uncivil war. Mistrust becomes habit; the habit becomes so fixed that it is then impossible even to comprehend one another's positions, let alone to resolve differences between them. This explains how a misunderstanding that seems incredible is, in fact, inevitable. Discord finally becomes irreconcilable when the angry antagonists stop talking to each other. The total lack of intimate personal conversation between the American and the French presidents ever since that unfortunate meeting is a classic case in kind.

The year 1964 began with a bang when General de Gaulle recognized Communist China exactly one year after breaking off negotiations with the British. French delegates then voted to admit Communist China to specialized U.N. agencies. General de Gaulle broke ranks with America on policy in Southeast Asia by proposing neutralization of Vietnam. The uncivil war spread to South America when de Gaulle, who was too busy to visit President Johnson, found he was not too busy to visit the President of Mexico or to accept a half a dozen invitations from South American countries. A point of some kind, high or low, was reached on June 6, 1964, when instead of going to Normandy to participate in the twentieth-anniversary celebration of the liberation landings, General de Gaulle stayed in Paris to greet the new ambassador of Communist China.

The Anglo-Saxons were badly shaken up, but they were neither passive nor guiltless in this explosive phase of the uncivil war. Many impartial and anti-Gaullist observers agree with de Gaulle that the United States has not made full allowance for the increased strength of Europe and that it does run NATO largely as an American show. De Gaulle could also point out that America does not always practice what she preaches. She told her allies not to trade with Cuba but sold wheat to Russia, which was the principal supplier of Cuba. Then, after putting pressure on the British to cancel a sale to Rumania, the Americans negotiated with the Rumanians on the possible sale of nuclear reactors. As for Britain, she has broken ranks with her Anglo-Saxon partner almost as many times as de Gaulle and, upon occasion, before de Gaulle.

Britain recognized Red China as far back as 1950. Britain began to trade with Castro weeks before de Gaulle authorized such trade. The British are ill-placed to criticize de Gaulle's national nuclear program while maintaining one of their own, whereas America, which opposes de Gaulle's program, gives aid to Britain. Long before de Gaulle's "veto" the British refused to join European institutions and actively tried to hinder and halt the progress of a united Europe. There is still no evidence today that the British are much more enthusiastic about an integrated supranational Europe than General de Gaulle is.

This summary of the two cases is not meant to suggest that they balance out, but simply to point out that there is no one side to the case. It is not just de Gaulle against the Anglo-Saxons, but rather a mutual conflict between de Gaulle and the Anglo-Saxons. In this writer's opinion, there is certainly no doubt about who won or lost: in the "Battle of the Grand Designs" there have only been losers so far. Among the losers I believe that de Gaulle is the biggest loser and that in the long run the Kennedy design will prevail over de Gaulle's. Kennedy's vision of Atlantic partnership—undefined, it must be noted—has been dimmed by de Gaulle's refusal to proceed with the kind of united Europe upon which this partnership depends. But, although dim, it is not dead by any means. General de Gaulle's "vast plan" is, however, moribund, if it ever had been really alive.*

De Gaulle's much publicized "Franco-German treaty" had little reality, and the little that it had lost its original significance after the retirement of Chancellor Adenauer. De Gaulle himself demonstrated what he thought of his chances in Europe by concentrating all through 1964 on Africa, South America and Asia. The only new development in Europe that year was the French foreign minister's revival of friendly relations with Madrid, in a move that certain Paris wits acidly described as a "Franco-FRANCO" reconciliation.

In 1965 President de Gaulle used the press-conference platform for another of his "television spectaculars"—although it was considerably less spectacular than the big shows of 1963 and 1964, when he respectively vetoed Britain's entry into the Common Market and recognized Communist China. His 1965 show had a

---

* In October 1965 an official publication of the French foreign ministry proposed a new plan to reform NATO: to create a purely European combined defense force, with the United States excluded, but to coordinate Europe and America in NATO as the central organism of the alliance. This was taken to be a de Gaulle trial balloon for his tired old "vast plan" in a dressed-up version. It was unacceptable to de Gaulle's neighbors in Europe as well as to the United States. It only demonstrated de Gaulle's stubborn whipping of a dead horse.

much lower irritability rating. He merely cal
the Europeans," suggesting that the German
settled by Germany's neighbors.

This was even more unrealistic than most of
plans for Europe. The foreign minister had to pu
tion" later that day, saying that President de Gaulle
to exclude America from an eventual settlement o   ..ian
problem. An American Embassy official in Paris commented
dryly: "Indeed! How comforting to learn that President de Gaulle
has not abrogated unilaterally the four-power agreements on
Germany, and that our French friends concede that America,
which had a little something to do with defeating the Nazis,
would have a role in an eventual peace settlement in Europe."

The anger of the Americans did not impress de Gaulle. On the
contrary, he was rather pleased at their bitter reaction. They had
excluded France from Yalta and Potsdam, and, to use a French
expression, he was "paying them back in their own coin," or, in
Anglo-Saxon argot, "aping" those who had excluded him. However wrong Roosevelt may have been in his Yalta policy, de Gaulle
is surely not right in indulging himself in such diplomatic monkey
business. Two wrongs do not make a right, but, above all, de
Gaulle does not have the power to carry out his wrong policies.
Roosevelt could exclude de Gaulle from the postwar European
settlements, but de Gaulle cannot exclude the Americans from
Europe today. The United States has such tremendous power that
it can even make ill-conceived policies stand up for a long time,
whereas de Gaulle has so little real power that he would have a
difficult time making a correct policy succeed. Of all the naked
emperors who ever tried to hypnotize their subjects into thinking
them gorgeously arrayed, Charles de Gaulle is one of the most
ambitiously naked.

Like the naked emperor of the story, Charles de Gaulle has been
parading around the world pointing with pride to an atomic force
that is little better than a firecracker compared with the American
and Russian arsenals and delivery systems. He claims that it will be
an effective striking force by 1969, but this claim is disputed by
many authorities, including French scientists. Even if his own
estimate were correct, he acted in 1965 as though it were already
1969.

In the course of 1965 de Gaulle pulled France completely out of
SEATO, the Southeast Asia Treaty Organization, reducing his

...ation to the London Conference in May to a simple
...ver. The French Atlantic Fleet had already been taken out of
...ATO control, as had the Mediterranean units, as far back as
1959. The French Air Force just barely coordinates with the
NATO Command. Only two army divisions are effectively assigned in Germany. In June 1965 de Gaulle's military delegates
announced they would not participate in the annual FALLEX
strategic exercises.

The most painful moment of truth for the allies and those French
who believe in a united Europe and Atlantic partnership came on
September 9, 1965, in the last press conference of de Gaulle's
presidential term of office.

Reporters have learned that General de Gaulle used his conferences to announce major policy decisions. They were carefully
stage-managed to get maximum world attention. History had been
made at these press performances. Everyone in the Hall of Festivals
on September 9, 1965, knew that General de Gaulle would have
something very special to say in the last performance of his
term in office.

The audience was not disappointed. General de Gaulle put on
one of his best, or worst, performances, depending on the point of
view of the observer. He exploded, not one, but two, bombs on the
Anglo-Saxon capitals, rocking both London and Washington with
the shock waves and also shaking his allied neighbors in Belgium,
Germany and Italy. The only western European statesman who
was pleased by what he had to say was his trans-Pyrenean fellow
general, Francisco Franco, dictator of Spain, who had been excluded from the Common Market and from NATO, two organizations that General de Gaulle all but wrecked by the bombs he
dropped on them that day.

On the Common Market, whose meetings in Brussels had been
boycotted by General de Gaulle since June 30, he said, "Sooner or
later this crisis was inevitable," because of "certain errors and
ambiguities in the treaties of the European Economic Community." General de Gaulle stated that the treaties "were concluded
before the French recovery in 1958." He used the word "recovery"
as a euphemism for the coup d'état that brought him to power in
1958, and he made it sound as though there were something
sinister about a treaty that had been concluded before he came to
power. He said, "That is why these treaties cover, above all,
everything the other members sought," meaning, of course, that

since he, de Gaulle, had not been there to defend the interests of France, the midgets who preceded him had surrendered France to the wicked allies.

General de Gaulle made no mention of the fact that when he came to power it was his own government that signed the official instrument making the Common Market treaty the law of the land, and that he had undertaken solemnly to respect the letter of that law. Only those who followed these events closely could recognize his subtle justification in the statement that the "technocratic embryo made up largely of foreigners was not to our liking once we had decided to take our destiny into our own hands." In other words, de Gaulle's solemn undertaking to respect a treaty when France was weak meant nothing once France was strong enough to decide its own destiny.

De Gaulle argued that he had always favored European unity in the economic and political fields and that "for seven years we have worked to build up the European Economic Community properly. But what we wanted and still want is a fair and reasonable community." By fair and reasonable, General de Gaulle said, he meant a community in which agricultural products would be included along with industrial products. He made it sound as though this were being denied to France, whereas in fact all parties had agreed upon this principle. There had been disagreements, inevitably, on how to accomplish this end, with what speed and with what safeguards for the weaker agricultural systems. De Gaulle had seized upon those technical difficulties to break off talks on June 30, the deadline date on which a common agricultural policy should have been drafted.

The truth was that de Gaulle was all too pleased to have a pretext to break off the talks, for his real objective, as he finally admitted on September 9, was to cancel out the clauses in the Common Market treaty providing for the complete integration of the economies of the six member nations and the creation of a supranational high commission and European parliament that would assume sovereignty over the Market. This was the "technocratic embryo" that he wanted to destroy. The kind of Europe that de Gaulle sought was not the federated Europe of the Common Market, not the United States of Europe envisaged by Jean Monnet and the signatories of the Common Market treaty, but a revival of the Congress of Vienna, a congress of powers cooperating within the limits of their national interests and ambitions. He made this clear in these words:

> We know there is a different concept of a European
> federation, in which the member countries, according to
> the dreams of those who originated it, would lose their
> national identities. To this plan, which really seems un-
> realistic, France offers the alternative of organized coop-
> eration between the states, which would probably grow
> toward a confederation.

With those words General de Gaulle confirmed what his critics
had long been saying and gave the lie to his apologists. He was
unalterably opposed to any kind of European organization. He
sought only a Europe of completely sovereign and independent
states. And even his supposed passion for his kind of "unity" was
seen to be less than a glint, dismissed by the qualifying adverb
"probably" in his reference to a confederation; he would not even
commit himself to so mild a form of unity. He made this so clear
in that last press conference of his seven-year term that the
question could no longer be argued. And by so doing he aborted
the Common Market's embryo of union or, at the least, he froze its
further growth so long as he continued to exercise power in
France. It was a death blow to one of the most important projects
that had been long, painfully and expensively developed by his
neighbors—Germany, Italy and the three Benelux countries—and,
as importantly, by the United States of America. From General
Marshall's speech at Harvard, in June 1947, the basis of American
foreign policy in Europe, the very pillar of America's global
policies, was the unity of western Europe. Eighteen years of
constant, dedicated, brilliant efforts, and tens of billions of dollars
of investments, of which France was the largest single recipient (a
total of some nine billion dollars), had been effectively arrested by
General de Gaulle in that September 9 announcement.

The United States was even more directly shaken by a parallel
announcement in that same conference, when General de Gaulle
confirmed officially what had long been known: his intention
to take France out of NATO or, as some critics had put it, to take
the O out of NATO—that is, to pull France out of the *Organization* of the North Atlantic Treaty, retaining only the treaty
commitments on cooperation and mutual defense against aggression. He said that France had her own role to play in the world
and would not "abdicate" national responsibility to such interna-

tional organizations as "the United Nations, or NATO." He argued that "For us, it is a matter of keeping ourselves free of all subservience." De Gaulle admitted that France might have need of allies, but only under certain conditions: "So long as we consider the solidarity of the Western peoples necessary for the possible defense of Europe, we will remain the allies of our allies. But at the expiration of our present commitments—that is, at the latest in 1969—we shall end the subordination which is described as integration, which is provided for by NATO and which puts our destiny in the hands of foreigners."

Thus General de Gaulle delivered the coup de grâce to the basic principle of integration, the operative force of NATO and the Common Market both. His victims had no doubts that he meant what he said. Sharp criticism and protests were heard in all Western capitals. President Johnson did not reply directly to de Gaulle, nor did he name him, but, within hours of de Gaulle's news conference, a statement was issued by the White House reaffirming the faith of the United States in NATO and restating the belief that it was a fundamental indispensable pillar of Western security. Former President Eisenhower was even more pointed in his protest, which was a cry of alarm. He told *The New York Times* that "he did not see how the North Atlantic Treaty Organization could survive if France carried out her plan for ending the Alliance's joint military command." Eisenhower warned that de Gaulle's coalition view, as opposed to integration, would add to the burdens of the smaller countries, which would have to provide their own armies, navies and air forces, "perhaps even a nuclear unit—and that doesn't make sense." Eisenhower insisted that purely national coalitions of the Gaullist concept "never have succeeded and never will."

Although de Gaulle had no intention of recognizing the Caamano rebel forces in Santo Domingo, since such formal diplomatic recognition is contrary to France's tradition of de facto diplomatic relations, he nonetheless had his spokesman announce that he "is taking the matter under consideration." United States spokesmen and the press made the mistake of reacting angrily, which is just what de Gaulle wanted them to do. He was only trying to stir with great argument in an attempt "rightly to be great." De Gaulle ought to be ignored when he announces consideration of a move he has no intention of making. It should be American policy not to "holler until hurt," if at all. The more we reacted, the bigger we made de Gaulle seem.

In truth America was somewhat hurt by de Gaulle. His orders to his finance minister to convert dollars into gold increased the drain on the U.S. treasury and unquestionably weakened the prestige of the U.S. dollar, endangering its privileged position as a universal currency. The United States may be wrong in its insistence of maintaining the dollar as the prime instrument of international exchanges and currency reserves. Many economists in Europe—and indeed most European experts, including those who are pro-American and anti-de Gaulle—believe the United States has been stubbornly proud and wrongly inflexible on its monetary policy. Just as many friends of the United States disapprove of American policies and practices in Vietnam and Santo Domingo. But most of the allies, as good friends, tell America what they think in private and strive not to embarrass the United States and make its troubles worse by public criticism. De Gaulle alone constantly pulled Uncle Sam's beard in public. De Gaulle was not always wrong in his criticism, but the deliberately disagreeable and even damaging way he broke with his ally on major issues seems not only inexcusable but of little profit to France.

The alliance with America is still important to France, and de Gaulle brought it to the brink of a rupture that will hurt France more than America if they both go over the brink. De Gaulle's neighbors in Europe do not want to have to choose between an alliance with France and an alliance with the United States, but if such a choice were forced, they would unquestionably choose the United States. His own compatriots, including many pro-Gaullist Frenchmen, have no desire to reverse alliances. Few Frenchmen want to trade an alliance with the Red, White and Blue for Russia's monochromatic red banner. France's flag, like America's, is the tricolor, and the colors are the same even if they do run in opposite directions.

* * *

The real explanation of de Gaulle's foreign-policy posture is to be found in the American rejection of his original letter to Eisenhower proposing the creation of a three-power organization of the West to elaborate global strategy. In plain terms this meant that de Gaulle wanted to be one of the great powers of the world, the smallest of the big five perhaps, but one of the great powers nonetheless. Since he was refused this role, he chose to become the biggest of the small powers—that is, to become the champion of all the nations other than the colossi who tower over the world. This was essentially the motive behind his trip to South America, his frequent trips to Africa, his establishment of relations with China, his denunciations of American policies in Vietnam, Santo Domingo and the Congo and his attacks on the American dollar. A giant himself, he wanted France to be one of the giants. Failing that, he tried to play the role of David the Goliath-killer.

There was one basic contradiction in this game of de Gaulle's. He might have been able to achieve grandeur for France and a world-leadership role for himself had he embraced Jean Monnet's concept of a United States of Europe instead of his own idea of a Europe of the states. A Europe of the states is nothing more than the old coalition of nation-states dressed up in modern clothes but not much different from the Congress of Vienna. Whatever other virtues it might have, it is not a coherent force that can play the power role in the world envisioned in de Gaulle's "vast plan." A United States of Europe, however, could provide such a force and play such a role.

If Europe had started to integrate as one nation, it would have loomed up as big and as influential as Russia and America. Had de Gaulle endorsed such a Europe, France would have acceded to leadership in the new federal system just as surely as New England played a leadership role in the United States of America for so long. Only one man could conceivably have been elected the first president of the United States of Europe: Charles de Gaulle. But de Gaulle was a Frenchman, wholly a Frenchman and nothing but a Frenchman; because of that he was, in the final analysis, nothing more than a Frenchman. He was not the leader of Europe. De Gaulle was not the leader of a third force in the world either, nor could any Frenchman ever be, for if there ever is a third force, it will be African and Asian and its champion will not be a white European Catholic nationalist. It is not in the cards.

There is no doubt that Charles de Gaulle was seen as a great man by masses of peoples in South America, Africa and Asia. There is no doubt that he also had many admirers in Europe, east and west of the Iron Curtain. There is no doubt that he had the negative power of provoking the United States, flirting with Russia and China or suddenly reversing himself and provoking them as he has done often in the past. He could do many, many spectacular things and keep his name on the front pages and his

voice and face on the airwaves of the world. But when one adds it
all up, it was not much more than air. It was not truly a foreign
policy, it was a foreign posture. De Gaulle was able to maintain his
posture mainly because of the failure of the foreign policies of his
rivals and adversaries. If the Anglo-Saxons and the Russians had
had clear, coherent, consistent policies of their own, de Gaulle
would not have had a chance to play his game.

President Eisenhower's term of office was running out when de
Gaulle came in. President Kennedy was not in office long enough
to carry out a strong, consistent policy. He never worked out a plan
for an Atlantic partnership. The multilateral atomic force was
hastily improvised, and Kennedy did not give solid backing to the
men who were trying to execute it.

The British first tried to stop, then to sabotage, a united Europe.
Then they dragged their feet through endless slow negotiations.
Had they realized sooner how important the Common Market
was to them, they could have been in it before de Gaulle came back
to power. Socialist Harold Wilson opposed the Common Market
when he was out of office and showed no appetite for joining it
when he became prime minister in 1964. If de Gaulle had not
vetoed Britain in 1963 and had Wilson been prime minister then,
Britain would not have even tried to join. With a nation so divided
as Britain on this issue, it is not quite correct to blame de Gaulle
alone for keeping the British out. As for atomic policy, Macmillan
and Wilson were both nationalistic, just as Gaullist as de Gaulle.
Britain has not had a consistent, coherent foreign policy in the
postwar era.

The Russians are equally inconsistent and incoherent in their
policies. In the past ten years there have been a number of Kremlin
revolutions that have reversed both internal and external policies
in every power shift of Soviet leadership. Khrushchev blew hot
and cold on relations with the West. Kosygin and Brezhnev did
not set a clear line of direction. The conflict with China became the
overwhelming external problem of the Soviets and absorbed most
of their energies.

Who was there then to challenge de Gaulle? Or to hold him in
line? Or to offer effective alternatives to his moves on the world
chessboard? There was no one—not in England, not in Europe,
not in Russia and not in America.

Lyndon Johnson, like the Soviet leaders, had to devote most of
his attention in foreign affairs to Asia. Bogged down in the paddies

and jungles of Vietnam, to say nothing of the Caribbean hurricane that engulfed him, he had little time or energy to spare for the elaboration and execution of a global policy.

Lyndon Johnson once thought he might be able to get along with President de Gaulle. They met for the first time in Paris when Senator Johnson, then vice-president-elect, attended a NATO parliamentarians' meeting just after the November 1960 elections. Johnson was impressed by de Gaulle and pleased by the way the meeting had gone. With a broad grin he told this writer, "I discovered that de Gaulle and I are both six feet four inches tall, which permits us to see eye to eye." It was a happy thought, but it proved to be a false omen. It takes more than physical height to be able to see eye to eye with Charles de Gaulle.

* * *

The man who tried harder than all others to get along with de Gaulle was General Eisenhower. No other foreign statesman had known him as long or worked so closely with him. Of all Americans, Eisenhower was the one for whom de Gaulle felt the most affection. "He is a good man, a real man," de Gaulle said of Eisenhower. Eisenhower was also the only American leader who always felt friendship and respect for de Gaulle, no matter how they disagreed on major issues. Even after de Gaulle infuriated most Americans by his systematic opposition and unfriendly acts, President Eisenhower still had kind words to say about him.

On August 25, 1964, the twentieth anniversary of the liberation of Paris, I spent the day with General Eisenhower in Gettysburg and talked to him about General de Gaulle. Earlier I had sent Mr. Eisenhower a copy of the first draft of the chapter in this book in which I had written about their exchange of letters and their negotiations from 1958 through 1960. He told me on arrival, "I hope you make it clear that de Gaulle and I had remained mutually respectful of each other all through the worst moments of friction during the war years. And this carried over into the presidency period many years later, when we were both presidents of our countries."

President Eisenhower went on to talk at length about de Gaulle and the great issues of their presidencies. He spoke for almost two hours, with complete frankness and an almost total recall of events and arguments. The discourse was recorded, transcribed and submitted back for verification of facts and precise dates. It is a revealing, illuminating document. The following excerpts are most pertinent contributions to an understanding of the relations between de Gaulle and the Anglo-Saxons.

> You know, de Gaulle and I got along fine personally. . . . Of course, he and I were never Charles and Ike—never—not like with Winston, for example. Winston and I—why, we were just as warm, personal friends as we could be under the circumstances. De Gaulle never was that. He never had time, for one thing, and, for another, he's rather remote and I think he believes that his position requires it. He tries to create this feeling of a remoteness, of mystery—or you might say mystique. . . .
>
> Now, I'll tell you how I felt about de Gaulle. About two years before de Gaulle came back into office, I began to tell Dulles, I said, now look, Foster, our only hope in Europe is to get de Gaulle back in. He is the only man that will save that country. Now, let's make no mistake—this man is not easy to deal with, and I said, as a matter of fact, that I was probably the only American that was welcome in his house. But the thing is, only he can save France, and France is going down the drain. Every economic index we have is pointing this out and on top of that these troubles with Tunisia, Morocco and later Algeria, and, of course, they'd gone through this terrible Gethsemane of Vietnam—it's going down the drain and, by golly, you've got to do something. Well, Dulles said, look, I agree with you, Mr. President, but, now don't forget, when we get him back, you're going to have to be the one to deal with him. . . .

General Eisenhower paused, picked up my manuscript, flipped the pages to recheck a passage he wanted to comment upon, and then said:

> De Gaulle was difficult, yes, but everybody has some rough edges, I don't care who it is. His were just a little bit more pronounced, that's all. So, while I don't object to your calling it an 'uncivil war,' because a great deal of it was that—an uncivil war—there were, I think, some peaceful interludes in it. Let me put it this way—in my

own memory, as I look back over my relations with General de Gaulle, during the whole time I could class them as much more pleasant than they were with some people, and they were more fruitful.

Roosevelt's relations with him were, of course, very different. Well, Roosevelt—you see, he would make a pronouncement and that would be like the laws of the Medes and the Persians. Now, I had disagreements with de Gaulle, but I never insulted him or fought him personally. And Winston, you know, he had to stay close to the President, he had to go with Roosevelt when de Gaulle kicked the traces. Now, I don't believe that he, himself, would have been so tough on de Gaulle if he had been free to act his own way and handle things his way. But, in any event, that's between those two, Winston and de Gaulle. Finally they became good friends. And that's important in an alliance.

I've constantly argued you cannot have really good allies unless there is at least a mutually felt good faith. I have to have faith in you and you in me. Now, you can't do that unless you're pretty good friends. And if you're good friends you will show your good faith even on the most sensitive issues. That's the reason I was always for giving my allies some nuclear capability. I always said, why should I treat them like second-class people? I just don't believe that they're going to start wars just because they got a weapon that we have, and after all, the principal adversary has the weapon and all the so-called secrets, so why are we withholding from a friend secrets that an enemy already has?

Look, I could have reached a satisfactory agreement with de Gaulle on the atom thing except for the law. I told de Gaulle time and again. I said, look, Mr. President, I'll go as far as I can today and I'm going to try to get Congress to change some of the provisions in the atomic-energy law. He believed me and I did do it. I changed the law twice, but we never did get all we needed. The atomic-energy act ought to be repealed, because it's a futile thing—those restrictions on the president. But there's a joint committee down there in Washington, a very powerful one, and it became an emotional issue.

Now, of course, the atomic weapon is not only bigger, it is different in kind from any weapon in history. And, of course, there is the terror aspect of it. So the greatest care should be taken in how it is handled, not just the bomb, but the whole atomic business, politically, in the world, the whole thing, atoms for peace—I started that program, the search for disarmament. But, that doesn't mean turning against an ally who is going to be with you if there is a fight. . . . Now, when I go into battle I want the guys with me to feel they've got the same chance I've got. After all, your ally has as much to lose as you have and not only as much to win. That's why I think we ought to help de Gaulle on his nuclear programs.

De Gaulle knew where I stood on this question of being a loyal ally and good friend, so he did not doubt my motives when I disagreed with him on the big pitch he made for a three-power directorate, or triumvirate of the West. He knew I was sincere and not just being, well, selfish or trying to monopolize power, because he knew I was trying to help him on atomic power. But the three-power thing—I just couldn't see it. . . . Our biggest argument as presidents came out of this idea he was sold on, to have a publicly proclaimed triumvirate. You've got that right in your book, that tripartite business and public recognition of France as a great power. That is exactly what he wanted.

I would say to him, look, I'll do everything else. I'll consult you as you request. I'll promise to make no move and neither will the British unless we've all agreed that we'll do this thing by study, but let's don't proclaim it publicly as a three-power directorate. But de Gaulle would have none of it, nothing less than his demands. I'd say to de Gaulle, now, Mr. President, this is trouble. I can't do it. I'd say that I believe that in the long run we've got to have the support of West Germany, of Italy and of the rest of western Europe, as well as France. Now, Mr. President, if we are going to just tell them that they are going to have to do such and such—while we are going to do so and so—why, pretty soon they are going to say, now hold on there, you are making us second-class citizens and then they will desert us.

And de Gaulle said to me, well, Mr. President, France, Britain and the United States have worldwide responsibilities and these other nations do not. That was always de Gaulle's argument. . . . De Gaulle's one obsession since 1940 has been to restore what he referred to as the rank, the honor and the prestige of France, and I don't think it's fair to put this always down just to his personal ambitions, as a lot of people do. He is a patriot. His proposal to set up a three-power kind of triumvirate was designed to demonstrate that France stands as an equal, along with Britain and the United States, and that France must be recognized as such.

He finally made his biggest pitch for it when we were alone together—at Rambouillet, it was, in September 1959. Just the two of us and one interpreter—nobody else. That's when he took up all the world issues, you know, Vietnam, Laos and so forth, and French interests and influence there, and how we really needed to work out tactics and strategy together and how he could help us there, too, because we were going to have a big problem there. . . . De Gaulle, of course, was not president of France during the Indochina war. He was not personally marked by that French failure and he felt he could talk objectively about the problem and had influence there. Well, I told him how I felt about that Vietnam problem. We Americans had to move into a vacuum there after the French pulled out in 1954.

What bothers me most about de Gaulle's policy is that he does not give enough weight to the vital importance of this whole Southeast Asia struggle and what would happen if we let the thing go. What is India going to do then? India would become totally isolated. I think that really the defense of Southeast Asia today, in my opinion, is the defense of India, and if that whole subcontinent of some 400 million people and more falls to the Communists or breaks with the West, well, I'll tell you, then we become more and more isolated in this world. Now de Gaulle is pretty good and clear in saying what we do that's wrong and how Vietnam is in a mess, but we don't get much from him on how to clean it up, or any offer to help on it.

But, to get back to the tripartite directorate. It's part of his obsession about the Anglo-Saxons—you know, the special relationship he thinks we have with the British. Now, that's just not true and the record proves it. Why, the British wanted us to agree in advance with them on certain plans in Suez, for example, and we wouldn't do it. Now, that Suez thing—it was the British and the French together. So where was this Anglo-Saxon thing de Gaulle always talks about? And de Gaulle knows I always tried to give him everything he needed and wanted to conduct the war and to help him unify the French. And I spoke out for his Algerian policy and tried to help him on the nuclear program when I was president.

Why, back in the war we talked about this allied relationship problem all the time. He brought this up with me many times—this thing about the British special relations. What happened was because of the war itself. We and the British had the only supplies and resources. When France did come back in the war, after its surrender, why, it came in by the back door, you might say, and with the things we gave de Gaulle and his Free French. They were dependent completely on us. They had no manufacturers or factories or anything else because they were occupied and then their factories were destroyed. And, of course, I can't blame Roosevelt and Churchill for just keeping the combined chiefs of staff as a British-American combine, because that was the reality—the fact of life. But de Gaulle always resented that he wasn't brought into it.

But after all, it was my influence, more than anybody else's, that got the French sector in Germany, because I believed already that they had to have something to help them up after the war. And I believed in de Gaulle and in his own belief that the French needed grandeur, that they needed to restore self-respect by a sense of greatness and mission. Yes, de Gaulle was right on that and he knows I backed him up all the way and did everything I could to build up their morale. I worried more about the French and helped them more than I did for the British. There was never any special English-speaking favoritism, and de Gaulle should know that. And, then, much later in

NATO, we set up the Standing Group of the French, British and American military advisors meeting in Washington. We brought them in. But I do admit that, no matter what we did, de Gaulle had this fixed misconception and he would never forget it. But he's wrong and I told him so, over and over again.

You can't have just two or three pals acting as a self-contained unit in the diplomatic and strategic world without just losing all your other friends, and that's all there is to it. And I just couldn't go along with this plan of his for joint global strategy—what you call in your articles here his veto on our strategic air power. You're right, that's what joint planning as de Gaulle requested would amount to—a veto. Why, he said we shouldn't use our nuclear weapon anywhere in the world without consulting him, and his sharing in the policy decisions. Now, he must know we couldn't do that. Why, the British haven't got any such kind of deal. That's where I stood on this business and I told him so as often as he brought it up.

I was willing to recognize de Gaulle as an important world figure, but he didn't have any means of exercising real world power. He had no real air force, he had no fleet, he had nothing else, so when we were trying to defend ourselves in Formosa, in Korea, Vietnam, or carrying out things all around the world, I wasn't going to be saying to my commanders: Are you going to consult now with these people and wait for them to do something. Good gracious, if you try to conduct our United States foreign policy and defense policies on the basis of not being able to do anything until you went and consulted everybody and said, here now, they've got to agree before we do it, well, you'd be in an awful lot of trouble, I'll tell you that. But short of just delivering our initiatives over to him and submitting ourselves to his judgments, well, short of that, I really did try to meet his desire and need for some kind of world position and prestige.

I'll tell you how far I went. I said to de Gaulle: Now, this is the way we can do it, Mr. President. We'll set it up in London—you've got a big embassy there, and so have I. I'll make special appointments—I'll strengthen the embassy with special people, high-ranking people, both in the political and military world, and you can do the same. Britain can do it, of course, because they're right there in London. We will have all these top people there and we will put them, if you want, under a director, or some such title, and they will be authorized to take current plans, current problems, emerging problems— and we will give them authority and plenty of time to coordinate our view so we can plan to be in a position to operate in unison, anywhere in the world, on any prob- lem, or at least not to act in disunion. We can map out broad areas of agreement, for there are many, and can identify and contain the disagreements.

I tell you I was offering him everything it was possible to offer and very far toward his requests. But he wouldn't have it. It was all or nothing with him. He wanted it at the top, all the way like Cicero and Pompey and Caesar. I recognized what he wanted to do and why. I knew that there were some things you couldn't get through to him —and you had to ignore—but I still think it's a good thing we had him, because there wouldn't be any France today without him.

I asked General Eisenhower if he felt the same way about de Gaulle's value today. General Eisenhower thought a long time before finally answering:

Well, I don't know what's going on now. You'd better put that question to the fellows dealing with him now. But you make it clear that he and I were always friends, even when we disagreed. The disagreements get a lot of publicity, of course, but we got along personally very well and there were a lot of areas of agreement, too. Be sure you put that on the record, because that's part of the whole truth about what you call the uncivil war. Now, as I told you, I don't object to that title—it's right enough— but it should be all right, not just the truth, but the whole truth.

* * *

The most objective and tireless of historians would find it difficult to tell the whole truth. Part of the truth is still guarded as secret by governments. Even governments do not know the whole truth, for presidents keep many of their papers for themselves. De Gaulle compiled personal files of state documents that were withheld from the national archives; Truman and Eisenhower took many of their papers with them when they left the White House. There is, moreover, no single truth, but rather many truths as seen by different men, the whole truth being, therefore, vast, complex and difficult to ascertain.

Within these limitations many revealing truths have become available thanks to the cooperation and candor of General Eisenhower and a number of necessarily unnamed officials in Washington, London, Paris, Rome and Brussels. One of these essential truths is that Charles de Gaulle's foreign policies are as inconsistent and contradictory as his objective is consistent and coherent. His fixed immutable purpose is to achieve for France a leadership role in the world without sacrificing any parcel of French sovereignty to achieve it. This explains the otherwise confusing pattern of his many shifts of policy in the Fourth and Fifth Republics.

De Gaulle's policies on Germany, European unity and relations with America and Russia have shifted and crisscrossed throughout the years. In 1944 General de Gaulle proposed that France occupy the right bank of the Rhine and dismember Germany into small, decentralized provinces. But in 1945 he conceived a "vast plan" for a European coalition, including Germany, a coalition that he saw as a third force in the world independent of East and West both, playing one against the other. In 1950 he denounced the Coal and Steel Community, which was a first step toward a European coalition, and in 1957 he denounced its extension in the Common Market treaty. But in 1958 he endorsed the Common Market and pledged himself to respect the text of the treaty. In that same year he proposed that France join America and Britain in a three-power directorate of the West. But from 1963 to 1965 he refused to respect the Common Market provisions for integrating the six member nations, and he denounced Anglo-Saxon leadership of a Western bloc, presenting himself as the champion of the nations caught in a squeeze between the two colossi, thus reverting to his third-force concept of 1945.

In a radio-television address to the nation on April 27, 1965, President de Gaulle referred to France as "a nation whose hands are free" and said that this fact "modifies the world interplay which, since Yalta, seems to be limited to two partners." But, said de Gaulle, "since this division of the world between two great powers, and therefore into two camps, clearly does not benefit the liberty, equality and fraternity of peoples, a different order, a different equilibrium are necessary for peace." President de Gaulle concluded his analysis of the world of tomorrow with the question: "Who can maintain this better than we—provided that we remain ourselves?" He then answered his own question, as he so often does: "Men and women of France, as you can see, for us, for everyone, as ever, France must be France!"

The contradiction is apparent between this denunciation of the Yalta "division of the world" and his own proposal to Eisenhower that a Western directorate be created. The Western directorate that he wanted would serve to deepen the division of the world that he denounced. If he did not approve the splitting of the world into blocs of East and West, then why did he seek to join America at the head of the Western bloc? It seems clear that what de Gaulle really disapproved was not the division of the world but America's refusal to share its half of world leadership with France. De Gaulle was much less opposed to Yalta than to France's exclusion from Yalta.

All through June 1965, in the last barnstorming tour of his presidential term, General de Gaulle hammered away at this theme of an independent, renascent France providing a third force between the two hegemonistic colossi. His campaign reached a climax in his speaking tour of the Paris region on the last lap of the seven-year marathon of series of personal visits to every one of the ninety "departments" of Overseas and Continental France. He completed the tour in Chartres with a peroration that carried him to the very extreme limits of rationality in a passage in which he gave new ammunition to those who charge that he suffers from a Joan of Arc complex. He admitted that he heard voices.

Standing in the shadow of the Cathedral of Chartres, which towers over the golden wheat fields of Beauce, General de Gaulle looked out upon the people and said, "Very often I seem to hear a murmur—even if the voices are not raised loudly—but I sense that it is a murmur which corresponds to a world sentiment, a general call: 'Go France! Go France! Go!'"

Veteran reporters watching this grotesque performance by a great man whom many of them had served as soldiers in the ranks of the army of liberation were visibly embarrassed. They did not seem to know whether to laugh, cry or steal silently away. One could perhaps view it objectively and unemotionally if it were just an act, a bit of political cynicism or demagoguery. What was chilling was the realization that it was not just cynical or demagogic but that he really believed what he had said. He genuinely believed that France had a world mission, "her eternal mission of peace, equilibrium, liberty and equality," although one thousand years of French history offer overwhelming testimony to deny that this has been France's "mission de toujours."

It is true that as much as any people, and more than many, the French have made invaluable contributions to the ideals of peace, liberty and equality. But it is not true that these contributions have been constant and consistent, as he claims in the phrase "mission de toujours." France has frequently upset the peace, restricted liberty and shared its resources and treasures inequitably. More often than not the French have mocked fraternity inside and outside of France. The French are more xenophobic than most peoples, and brotherly love is almost unknown among the French themselves. As for "equilibrium," one wonders how a student of history like Charles de Gaulle could possibly make the obviously false assertion that France has always been a factor of equilibrium in the world. If there is anything that France is not, it is a balanced force at home or in the world. There never was a France like the Madonna that Charles de Gaulle worships in the fresco of his imagination.

To say that France is not the France of Charles de Gaulle's personal fairy tale is not to say that France is not a great nation or that the French no longer have an important role to play in the world. One can refuse to believe in the mystique of France and still have great faith in and affection for her people. The French have given much to the world and, as the last exponents of individualism, may have an even greater role to play in the crowded, collectivized communities of the future. If they are to play that role, however, it will be not as servants or crusaders of the French state nor as members of the French nation, but as members of the human race.

MORTALITY AND IMMORTALITY

I fear not death. I fear only sleep.
I want to know what is happening to me.

CHARLES DE GAULLE *to his surgeon,*
before an operation, 1964

THE MORNING of December 5 was dark and stormy throughout most of France. The North Wind howled its hate of Brittany, lifting huge waves and dropping them against its cliffs. Only the gulls were fishing. The men, walking from the chapel to the schoolhouse to vote, bowed low to the wind as though they were still stooped in prayer. Their small stocky wives, wearing white, starched coifs pinned firmly to tightly coiled buns of hair, turned their backs on the wind and the village and headed homeward to prepare the Sunday dinner. They would vote after their men had eaten.

No one doubted how the dour, devout Bretons would vote. They would give a big majority to dour, devout Charles de Gaulle, partly a Gael like themselves. And so would the equally Catholic, if less austere, people of Alsace and Lorraine, for Charles de Gaulle was part of them, too. His cross was the cross of Lorraine, and he had made his home in Colombey-les-deux-Églises, on the foggy

354

eastern marshes facing the frontier of Germany. Frost covered the golden vineyards and daffodil beds of the East, but the churches were filled and so were the streets leading to the polls.

The French are a voting people. From 70% to 75% of the registered voters turn out consistently for all forms of national expression, whether elections or referenda. It would take more than wind, frost, or the "crachin" (the light spittle-rain that swirled around that day as though sprayed from an atomizer), to prevent citizens from voting in the first direct presidential election in French history to be decided by universal suffrage. A century earlier, Napoleon III had decreed a direct election for the presidency, but it was more a plebiscite than a popular election, and it was for men only.

The women of France had first been granted the vote, after the liberation in 1945, by the man whom they would reward on that rainy Sunday in December. The women, by two to one, are Gaullist. And they are, if not the stronger sex, the bigger sex, by numbers one and a half million more than the men. France is a martial land with a heavy blood tax, ironically the only tax most Frenchmen willingly pay for their country. The election of December 5 was a milestone election in this sense; it was the first time in twenty-five years that Frenchmen went to the polls without any Frenchmen fighting some kind of war somewhere in the world.

Like the women, the young citizens were out in greater numbers than ever before, with more than two million voters under the age of 24 to cast their débutant ballot—almost 10% of the electorate, a not inconsiderable segment. If this election might decide the future of France, as some observers thought, then it was *their* future which would be decided. In an important sense, this election was the election of French youth, and that, too, was an historic "first." Before 1965 youth played only an insignificant role in French affairs.

Young voters were out not only in greater numbers than ever but with a new éclat, for, even in old France, this is the age of youth, and the young are making themselves heard as never before. Singing stars Johnny Hallyday (22) and Sylvie Vartan (21), the husband-wife "pop-duo" of the year, drove hard all night after a singing engagement to get to their home election district in time to vote. So did tall, lissome, blonde, Françoise Hardy, the idol of the teenagers. And photographers were waiting to record this exercise of the franchise.

High up on the summit of the age pyramid, performing his civic duty at the age of 105, was Martial Jeuvaine of Benac in the Haute-Vienne. Eldest voter Jeuvaine was closer in age to the majority of the electorate, for, although more than half of the French population is now under 32 (because of the big post-war baby-boom), 70% of the registered voters is still in the upper and advanced age-group, over 45 years old. Of the twenty-four million citizens who voted on December 5, 1965, a historic day, some seventeen millions were 45 and over. This was one of the last elections dominated by that middle-and-older citizen group. That was one of the reasons why it was a historic day, the end of an epoch in many ways, as the results would show.

One could sense the approach of an hour of destiny in the unending queues of citizens who kept coming to the polls in numbers never seen before, not even in voting France. The government radio and television stations had told the people to vote very early, during lunch hour and early evening, instead of bunching up after mass, after dinner or at the last minute. They followed the suggestion, but found themselves facing long lines all through the day without a break. By the time the polls began to close—7 p.m. in most districts, 8 p.m. in the great agglomerations—the greatest number of citizens ever to turn out for a national expression of opinion had set a record at 24,002,093, an amazing 85% of the total qualified electorate, higher than in any other free nation. If one considers that on any given day as many as fifteen out of a hundred people could be prevented from voting because of illness, absence or a host of natural reasons, it amounts to a turnout of almost 100% of those able to vote.

French elections, even the percentage of the turnout, are usually not difficult to predict. They have been extraordinarily consistent in the post-war decades. The French are a literate and mature people. Their favorite aphorism, "the more things change the more they stay the same," is an accurate expression of a French reality. Ever since Julius Caesar first observed that all Gaul was divided into three parts, there has been some kind of trinity division of France and French society: the church, the army, the nobility; the robe, the cloak, the sword; the King, his Ministers, the people; the blue, white and red; the royalists, the republicans, the revolutionists; the capitalists, the bourgeoisie, the proletariat; the right, the left, the center. There were constant changes inside the ruling trinity, but basically things stayed the same in French society not matter what the seismic disturbances on the political level.

The sense of a more profound change was felt on December 5, 1965, and had been felt in a series of political, economic and social upheavals that had been rocking the country through the fifties and sixties, and most particularly since the return to power of Charles de Gaulle in 1958. It had been his destiny to preside over the most violent and important of the changes in modern French life: the historic process of decolonization that would finally clear the way for the other pent-up forces of change that had been set in motion by the great wars and technological advances of this century. De Gaulle had succeeded. He had completed the process of decolonization. But he had done little to release the other forces of change.

To the two million young French men and women marching to the polls on December 5, 1965, Charles de Gaulle was an old man whom they did not understand and who had never paid much attention to them. His fame as the Liberator, his heroic war record, all the exploits and legends of his great career, all this was history to them but not part of their own experience. In all the thousands of speeches, radio-television addresses, news conferences and other forms of public incantation in the seven years of his presidency, General de Gaulle had not once delivered a major address to the youth of France.

De Gaulle had cultivated the grass roots of the country but not its most important roots, its young men and women. He did, of course, congratulate himself and France on the "belle jeunesse" of the nation, but he spoke only *about* youth, not *to* youth. Yet of all the great tasks of construction for any leader of a great nation, and most particularly of France, none is so important as the future of its youth. After a century and a half of declining or slow-growing population rates, France was revitalized after World War II and began literally to be reborn. If de Gaulle were truly concerned about restoring French grandeur, in the most fundamental and enduring terms, he should have concentrated on the youth that is the grandeur and the future of France. But de Gaulle was handicapped by his own advanced age and his own paternalistic personality. Youth was distant from him. It never occurred to him that it is not enough to congratulate oneself on having fine, strong children. Parents, and most particularly the father of a nation, must give their children hope, must prepare them to take their places rapidly and effectively in society, must give them their chance.

French youth, in the reign of Charles de Gaulle, was not encouraged. It was discouraged, disillusioned, disciplined. It was told to work and study harder, but young people watched sulkily as their increasing numbers overflowed the small, inadequate classrooms of the past. The cruel, feudal system leading to the baccalaureat degree, the dread "bachot," which takes its toll in suicides, nervous breakdowns and broken lives each year, has been "reformed" no less than four times in five years, so that no class knew exactly what its course of study or requirements would be. Half the candidates fail the "bachot" the first time they take the examination, and more than a third never pass it, thus losing their chance for the higher education that is so vital a social symbol of success and advancement in life.

No one could be sure just how the two million first voters would divide politically, for, if they had little or no contact with or feeling for de Gaulle, the youth had shown no clear trend in its choice, or lack of choice, of political parties. This was one of the unknown variables of that first direct presidential election, which, for once, made it difficult to predict exactly what the results would be.

Public opinion polls in the months preceding Sunday, December 5, had shown a split between de Gaulle and the five other candidates running against him in the general proportions of 50-50, but with as many as 25% of those questioned saying they had not yet made up their minds. And there was another new variable, as unpredictable but as powerful as any political force that had ever arisen in France: television. Television was to prove the one undisputed winner of the presidential elections.

Television is not new in France. More than half of French families have a television set, or access to one. But until the presidential elections of 1965, television had been dominated by the State, which runs it as a government monopoly. French TV was the voice and face of de Gaulle and the Gaullist regime. The opposition was given an insignificant share of air-time. But it had to be granted a fair share of time for the election campaign. General de Gaulle made the double mistake of granting unaccustomed, and therefore highly novel, exposure to the opposition, while taking the incredible decision of passing up his own allotted share of time, as though he would not even deign to run against the "rabble" opposing him.

The result was the biggest audiences nightly in French history. The people were spellbound to see men attacking the government on the government's own television programs. After years of controlled news, poorly presented and loaded with propaganda, they suddenly saw and heard men denounce their regular fare as ersatz and fraudulent. They heard information that the government had strained to keep from them, and it sounded more important and true than it really was. It was almost as though censored and banned sex films, only whispered about in private, were shown free in all neighborhood theatres. Almost everything they had been told, night after long night, by government spokesmen, was suddenly contested and contradicted.

Where Gaullist economists had been telling the people about the great efforts made to build more lodgings, citing figures of increasing percentages of construction, opposition candidates told the people that Britain, Germany, and even Italy had built more houses and lodgings than France. Finance Minister Valerie Giscard d'Estaign said that France's rate of industrial production had been rising more rapidly than that of Britain, Germany, or the United States. Opposition critics quickly pointed out that Giscard was using figures for the period 1960–1964, a favorable period in France, whereas if one took the entire period of de Gaulle's presidency, from 1958 through 1965, then France was far down on the list.* On food prices, for example, the Minister's figures showed France at an index of 117 in the year 1964 on the base of 100 in the year 1960, as against corresponding figures of 119 for Britain, 121 for Belgium and 126.5 for Italy, demonstrating how much more prices had risen in other countries. But the opposition demonstrated that when one took 1958, the year de Gaulle came to power, as the base year of 100, then the price indices for 1964 were: Germany 106, Italy 117 and France 125. On industrial production France, during the de Gaulle years, ends up next to last in growth among the European nations.

This was heady stuff for French viewers, and public opinion polls showed just how heady it was. The French Institute of Public

---

* The economic situation and Giscard's handling of it cost him his post. He was dropped from the Cabinet after President de Gaulle renamed Pompidou Prime Minister of the first government of the second term, in January, 1966.

Opinion (IFOP) did a special study of the influence of television during the election campaign. It showed that more than half of the people admitted that their vote had been significantly influenced by watching the new television programs. As many as 26% said that it had actually changed their vote. The factor they pointed to as most influential was the revelation of economic, industrial and social failures.

Of all the many paradoxes in the career of Charles de Gaulle, the strangest was his failure to use the television medium to his advantage in the presidential election campaign. De Gaulle, the man born on radio who won the battle of Algeria on the air, failed at the high point of his political life with his strongest weapon. He may have been the victim of overconfidence, as some suggest; he may have been the victim of his old age, which showed up painfully in contrast with his youthful rivals, as others suggest. These were undoubtedly important factors. But perhaps most important of all, de Gaulle underestimated and never fully understood the democratic process and how it functions.

He so despised political parties and held politicians in such contempt, with rare exceptions, that it never occurred to him that politicians could match him in a direct appeal to the people. He did not understand how starved the public was for truth and respect in his authoritarian, paternalistic regime. Above all, he, who had so thoroughly understood the value of rarity in public appearances and appeals, had underestimated the rarity factor of the fresh opposition faces. And they were very attractive new faces for the French public.

Only two of the five opposition candidates were important enough to affect the outcome seriously: François Mitterand and Jean Lecanuet. The other three were not serious threats: extreme right-wing lawyer Tixier-Vignancourt; respectable but dull Senator Rene Marcilhacy, a moderate conservative; finally, a kind of intellectual eccentric, Marcel Barbu, the self-styled champion of the victimized tax-payers.

Both Mitterand and Lecanuet made handsome, dynamic television candidates. Lean and athletic at 49, Mitterand is a skilled tennis player and looks like a Morre Star. There is a fire in his black eyes, a passion in his face and manner. He has been described by the French press as a "Florentine," a Medici-like political intriguer. Although he was a prominent political figure all through the Fourth Republic, serving in its cabinets a dozen and more times, the general public, outside of political initiates, knew little about him. As the candidate of a Popular Front coalition of the Socialist Party, the Communist Party, and left Radicals, he rode into the arena like the mysterious black knight, on a powerful charger blowing steam from flaring nostrils. In a few television appearances he became one of the most exciting and controversial personalities of France, as he called for all citizens to put aside "outdated prejudices"—meaning anti-communism—and join together to save the Republic from "one-man rule."

Equally lean and athletic, tall, dark and handsome, his principal rival, Jean Lecanuet, was the very opposite of a mystery-man or intriguer. He was the clean-cut type, a white knight, a Christian crusader carrying a golden cross, unmasked and open-faced, striding into the arena on foot, smiling and unafraid. These descriptions are deliberately put in the simplest terms, almost a cartoon depicting the promise of good and the lure of possible evil. If this is caricatural, this is true to what the men did to portray themselves in a campaign that was a kind of caricature of the democratic process, as the French, sophisticated and mature though they be in politics, naively discovered the democratic process.

Lecanuet, an excellent man, with a brilliant record of service to his country as a wartime resistant and a postwar participant in political and governmental affairs, was so consciously playing a planned role that he was saved from being a grotesque—he practically ran as a foreigner—only by his evident sincerity in the role he was playing. Youngest of the major candidates at 45, leader of the Catholic party MRP, he presented himself as the candidate of all who believed in continuing effort toward further integration of Europe, in the concept of Jean Monnet's vision of a United States of Europe. He proclaimed himself to be a faithful advocate of the Atlantic alliance and ever closer friendship with the United States of America. Thus he took deliberate issue with General de Gaulle in the two most important areas of foreign policy, despite the warnings of many friends who told him that these were not profitable issues.

The most astonishing role that Lecanuet played was his presentation of himself as the "French Kennedy." He did not do this subtly. He did not try only to project a Kennedy-like image. He frankly said that he was in fact the French John F. Kennedy, and called upon all citizens who had admired Kennedy to vote for him. Surely there is no parallel, in the political history of any major country, to this example of a candidate for the highest office in his nation standing on the platform of a foreigner. There never was an election like that almost incredible French presidential election of December 5, 1965.

An indication that something almost unbelievable was going to happen came in the ten days preceding the balloting. The IFOP polls had begun to show a sudden, startling drop in de Gaulle's percentage, as the "don't-knows" started to make up their minds. In the space of four weeks, from October 25 to November 25, de Gaulle had fallen from about 55% to 45% in the samplings taken. The Minister of the Interior, Roger Frey, thoroughly alarmed and surprised, sent urgent messages to the government's prefects, the administrative governors of each of France's ninety "departments," calling for new surveys and new efforts for the President. On the Wednesday night before the fatal Sunday, the reports were all in and they showed that de Gaulle would get less than the needed 50% plus one for election.

All the pollsters and experts, private and governmental, knew before a vote was cast that de Gaulle would be defeated for the first time in his career. They knew it but they still found it hard to believe, so deeply ingrained was the belief in his infallibility.

Charles de Gaulle, outwardly calm and confident, left the presidential palace and drove to his home, La Boisserie, in Colombey to cast his vote on Sunday, just as all the candidates and principal personalities of Paris do on each day of election or national referendum, for few of them are electoral residents of the capital. And like the pollsters, everyone in Colombey knew that something was wrong.

Colombey is one of the smallest municipalities of France, with a total electoral list of only 200 and a voting record of more than 90% turn-out, for, as the home district of the Great Man, it is a highly political hamlet. As in every small village, gossip and local scandal are the principal entertainment of the people, and Colombey had its own scandal to whisper about on that election Sunday: a reputed feud between "le Général" and "M. l'Abbé." The village curate, Abbé Druot, had been heard to speak critically of the General. And the General had not appeared for mass on that Sunday morning, preferring to call in another curate to hold mass in his private chapel at La Boisserie. Local gossips said that the Abbé had voted against the Gaullists in the last legislative elections and would vote against de Gaulle himself, a virtual sacrilege in Colombey.

At 11:30 in the morning, voter number 49, Charles de Gaulle, appeared, asked for his ballot, shook hands all around and disappeared into the isolated booth. Heads nodded, voices murmured, "Another vote for the General." When Madame de Gaulle cast her ballot in the secrecy of the curtained booth, there were smiles all around: "That's a vote against the General." Local wits insist that the single negative vote cast against the General in the first vote after his return to office, was cast by "Tante Yvonne" who wants him to retire, according to Colombey "insiders."

On December 5, 1965, there was more than one vote cast against the general in his home fiefdom. Of the 200 registered voters, 193 cast valid ballots: 175 for de Gaulle; 9 for the communist-socialist-radical candidate, Mitterand; 7 for the "Kennedy" candidate, Lecanuet; and, to everyone's astonishment, 2 votes for the extreme right-wing Algérie Française rabble rouser, Tixier-Vignancourt. Eighteen opposition votes out of 193, represented almost ten percent against General de Gaulle inside his own fortress-hamlet. It was a sign of the times and the tides that were running against the old general.

The rumbles of thunder that reverberated across France on that stormy Sunday began to echo in the election headquarters tally room at the Ministry of the Interior within an hour after the last polls had closed down at 8 p.m. Interior Minister Roger Frey, his thin lips twitching with tension, picked up his baroque-style XIXth century telephone—a gift from his daughter Marianne—and called Prime Minister Georges Pompidou, waiting anxiously in his office at the Hotel Matignon across the Seine, and pronounced one word, the dread word: "Ballotage!"—run-off.

Ballotage means literally split ballot, and this was what polls had been predicting in the last two weeks of the campaign. The people of France had so split their ballots among the candidates that de Gaulle had failed to get the absolute majority needed for re-election. His failure was personally humiliating, more than for any other candidate because he had asked for a massive vote of confidence in his person and his regime.

A mere politician can be satisfied with 51% and could call 55% a landslide, but Charles de Gaulle was not running as a politician. He was running as a national hero, not even for the presidency alone, but for the role of savior of the nation. In one of his most arrogant and ill-conceived statements, Charles de Gaulle on November 4, announcing his intention to run for a second term, had told the French people that the choice was between him and chaos. He claimed to be the indispensable man, the sole bulwark of France against collapse and ruin. In effect, he told the French people that they were not yet ready or able to govern themselves. A man with that concept and that platform is not asking for a majority, he is asking for a popular mandate, for the laurel crown to be put upon his noble brow by a grateful populace. For a man shouting "Salvation!", the answer "Run-off!" is a personal rejection, a profound humiliation, no matter how far ahead of all other rivals he might run.

"Ballotage" was the shout heard throughout the country and most particularly in the homes and headquarters of de Gaulle's opposition candidates. "They're splitting, it's a run-off," said Senator Marcilhacy, as he listened to the running reports of early returns on a transistor radio he had set on a marble bench in the garden of his home at Jarnac, where he lives in an old mill. At Sannois, Marcel Barbu finished dinner, predicted a run-off, refused to listen to the returns, played a Bach fugue and went off to bed unconcerned. He of all candidates was able to be detached, for he had no chance of making even a respectable showing. His candidacy had been absurd, a personal entertainment. He received 277,644 votes or 1.16% of the total. Senator Marcilhacy, too, retired early, physically and politically. On awakening the next morning, he learned he had come in next to last, with 413,125 or 1.46%.

The three significant candidates, whose votes could influence the outcome—de Gaulle, alone, of course, was the only one with a chance of being elected without a second Sunday run-off—all stayed up late to listen to the results. By an unusual coincidence two of them dined in the same Paris restaurant, La Mediterranée, the chic seafood restaurant with wall murals by Cocteau on the Place de l'Odéon. Tixier-Vignancourt and his wife were in the rez de chaussée dining room when Jean Lecanuet, who had reserved a first-floor private salon, walked through with his friends and political allies, Maurice Faure, Bertrand Motte and Joseph Fontanet. The rivals merely glanced silently at each other.

The Mitterand family dined at home, but it was not a quiet dinner.

"Dad! Dad! You've got the run-off!" his young son shouted from his post at the radio set in the corner of the room.

Mitterand grinned, looked over his shoulder at his son and said, "Go do your homework, *you* have to get the 'bac.' " Mitterand could not resist getting up and going over to join his son at the radio set, tuned in to the program broadcast by France's most listened-to station, the semi-autonomous Europe 1, the only independent French station free of government information controls. Europe 1's able, uncompromisingly professional news chief, Jean Gorini, was giving the returns and the predictions of the IFOP vote-analysis, as spewed out by an IBM machine that they had programmed. Gorini had long finished with predicting the final result. He was saying flatly that de Gaulle had failed in his bid for re-election that day and would have to face "ballotage." The only predictions still being made were the final percentages of the rival candidates.

At the seat of government no one was shouting, smiling or supping, although a sumptuous cold table for 200 guests had been laid out in the grand salon of the Hotel Matignon office of Prime Minister Georges Pompidou. The Prime Minister and his guests were moodily and uncomfortably watching the returns on TV. At 11:30 p.m. an usher in wing collar and swallow-tail coat, looking in at circumstances like an undertaker's assistant, walked slowly across the room toward the Prime Minister, who watched him come like a man who knew for whom the bell was tolling. The usher leaned over and whispered the expected words, "Colombey is calling." The Prime Minister lifted himself wearily out of his Louis XV fauteuil and made his way to his private office to speak with General de Gaulle.

Slowly, with somber mien, he walked back to join his guests and fellow Cabinet ministers who grouped themselves around his chair to hear the message from the Mount. "We have made a serious miscalculation. We underestimated the discipline of the communist voters. Some of them—many, indeed—did break ranks to vote for the general. But not enough, not enough." He looked up at his ministers, saw in their eyes the question they did not dare ask, and after a moment's hesitation answered it with utmost discretion: "He did not say. I do not know."

The unasked question, to which he could not give a clear reply, was finally answered an hour later, after a second call from Colombey. This time M. Pompidou stepped briskly back into the salon, shedding his fatigue and grinning widely as he walked over to a waiting television crew with a live camera ready to transmit

his words. As the Prime Minister began reading a statement
jotted down during his talk with de Gaulle, "Diversionary movements have postponed the creation of the broad, national unity
that is needed for the continued . . . ," the ministers and other
guests relaxed, winked at each other, began shaking hands and
making the victory sign, whispering, "He's going to fight. It's a
run-off. He won't quit."

President de Gaulle had not told his Prime Minister that he
would agree to carry on in a run-off, man-to-man contest with
the candidate who came in second. He would keep people guess-
ing for a little while as he kept his silence and seemed to be considering retirement. But the keys to the mystery of his decision
were to be found in two words of the Prime Minister's "authorized" statement: "postponed" and "continued." Only de Gaulle
could *continue* to fight for a victory that had been *postponed,*
for only de Gaulle had been running as the Gaullist candidate.
Those who knew de Gaulle were not surprised. He could not
possibly end his career on a defeat. He could not run away from
a fight, no matter how humiliating the need for Goliath to
descend into the arena with a "little David" like François Mitterand.

For it was Mitterand, the communist-socialist-radical "man of
the Left," as he described himself, who had come in second and
would, under the electoral law, be the opponent of the leader of
the lists, Charles de Gaulle. The final results were these:

Number registered voters 28,235,002
Number valid ballots cast 24,002,093 (85%)
Abstentions or invalid votes 4,477,000 (15%)

Candidates	Votes	Percent of votes cast	Percent of registered voters
Charles de Gaulle	10,386,734	43.71	36.78
François Mitterand	7,658,752	32.23	27.12
Jean Lecanuet	3,767,408	15.85	13.34
Tixier-Vignancourt	1,253,959	5.27	4.44
Marcilhacy	413,125	1.73	1.46
Barbu	277,644	1.16	0.98

Charles de Gaulle had been defeated and badly wounded, although it was not his first defeat nor were these his first battle
scars. As a soldier of the Third Republic, Captain de Gaulle had
been defeated in a bloody battle for a hill outside Verdun, and he

had been taken prisoner, his body badly torn and wounded. As the savior of France, in World War II, General de Gaulle had lost a number of battles, the expedition to Dakar, for one, and his political clashes in the uncivil war with Churchill, Roosevelt and Truman. His pride, if not his body, had been wounded when he was forced to back down and withdraw from the occupation zones of Stuttgart and the Val d'Aosta. His worst defeat was his failure to win a parliamentary majority for his "Rally of the French People" movement in his post-liberation bid to rule the Fourth Republic. This defeat sent him into retirement and a premature political death. He had known defeat and wounds during his incarnations as the soldier and savior of two French Republics. But, on December 5, 1965, President de Gaulle, in his third role as the statesman and ruler of the Fifth Republic, his very own creation, suffered his first and most wounding defeat in the final incarnation of his lives and times.

The Gaullists tried to rally their supporters and to put the best face upon the defeat, which was even more theirs than his; without de Gaulle the "professionals" in the government would retire to private business, while the politicos would largely disappear into the recesses from which they had come. Prime Minister Pompidou, questioned by reporters on the lesson to be drawn from the results, said, "Until now we have been preoccupied with administering the country. From now on we will concentrate on the political fight to win the country. And we will win the first great victory in this fight on December 19. Forward! For the second turn!"

The man who would stand up against de Gaulle for the second turn of the electoral wheel of fortune, François Mitterand, exulted as he had every reason and right to do: "Now we can see how false it is to say that nothing can be done against de Gaulle. France has lived before General de Gaulle and France will live after de Gaulle." As for the "Battle of the second turn," Mitterand realistically predicted that de Gaulle would win a man-to-man contest, particularly because a frightened bourgeoisie, although disenchanted with de Gaulle, was more terrified by the spectre of a communist-backed Popular Front coming to power. "My aim," said Mitterand, "is to hold de Gaulle to less than 14 million votes," that is, less than half of the total of 28 million registered voters.

This was a shrewd statement, for the target could almost certainly be attained, thus giving Mitterand a chance to claim a moral

victory even though de Gaulle would win the election. The reason
this was a safe prediction was that it was based on the total of
registered voters, that is 100% of all qualified voters, an impossible
figure. There had been a 15% abstention on the first turn, the
lowest such percentage in modern history. Mitterand could count
on at least the same percentage, and most likely a much higher
one. It was then thought that many citizens, reluctant to vote
either for a communist-backed candidate or for the Old Man, would
sit home and watch television. Thus de Gaulle's chances of getting more than half of an impossible 100% would be almost nil.
Clearly, Mitterand, looking beyond December 19, 1965, was aim-
ing at discrediting de Gaulle and the Gaullists and building himself for the long-term fight ahead, the fight for the legislative elections of 1967.

Mitterand's major support in the press, and his principal advisers on public relations, the brilliant journalists of the left intellectual weekly, *Le Nouvel Observateur*—Jean Daniel, Hector de
Galard, Claude Krief and others—were convinced that he could
hold de Gaulle down to something close to thirteen and a half
million votes, well within the range of his official target figure.
They counted heavily on television to swell their political support.
They based this reasoning on the results of the Kennedy-Nixon
debates and cited passages from Theodore H. White's *Making of
the President—1960* to prove their case. For "New Left" analysts, Mitterand, relatively unknown compared to de Gaulle, was
in a similar position to Kennedy, relatively unknown compared
with incumbent Vice-President Nixon. He could only profit from
a man-to-man contest with de Gaulle, for the debate would elevate
him to the position of being de Gaulle's peer, if not his equal, to
say nothing of the national exposure that the campaign would
give him as the unique rival, instead of only one of five opposition candidates as on December 5.

The "third man" of that December 5 tournament, Jean Lecanuet, agreed with Mitterand that something fundamental had
changed, that France could get along without de Gaulle. "The
post-war period of politics has ended," he said, "the time of tempests has passed." This was a clear reference to de Gaulle's former
appeal as the wartime liberator and the man of the tempest of
Algeria. "The hour of the present and the future is striking," said
Lecanuet, thus stressing the importance not only of the December
19 run-off but also of the legislative elections of 1967 and, appro-

priately for a man of 45, the fact that his generation was thinking further ahead to the day when de Gaulle would have disappeared from the scene.

On the morning after the vote, political observers, the press, the people of France, and their neighbors in Europe and the United States analyzed and argued about the meaning of the split ballot and re-examined their own feelings in the light of the changed circumstances that would prevail in the run-off of December 19. Both de Gaulle and Mitterand would have to be sure they knew why some five million citizens had not voted for either one of them, and try to find ways to rally that five million, each to his own standard, for the final test. This was more important than trying to analyze their own votes, for they assumed that they would hold almost all of their first-round voters on the second round. Their main concern about their own supporters was to keep them keyed up and to bring them to the polls. This was not unusually difficult, for neither side suffered from the kind of over-confidence or hopelessness that causes important abstentions. The Gaullists knew their man would win, but they also knew he needed a much bigger margin to preserve his prestige and authority; the Left coalition knew it could not defeat de Gaulle, but it also knew that a big vote would be in itself a victory and a guarantee that the "New Left" coalition would endure.

Minister of Information, Alain Peyrefitte, who would later lose that portfolio* because of errors made in his handling of public relations and information, made at least one correct judgment when he said, "On the first turn one chooses; on the second, one decides." The comment was apt. Citizens angry with de Gaulle with no real opportunity to express their disapproval for years, realized that they could afford to choose to vote against him without losing him and without putting a communist-backed candidate in office, for there was no chance that enough people felt this way to give Mitterand a majority. They could punish de Gaulle and teach him a lesson without risk. Others, who had a positive choice rather than the negative one, could, in the same way, afford to vote for the man of their choice without affecting a final, dangerous deci-

---

* On January 8, 1966, on the occasion of his second inauguration as President, General de Gaulle renamed Georges Pompidou as Prime Minister but reshuffled the Cabinet. In the reshuffle Peyrefitte lost his status as Cabinet Minister and was appointed the Prime Minister's "Delegate" for scientific and space research.

sion. It was truly a free vote of December 5, a vote free from all
kinds of political pressure and blackmail. The detailed results are,
therefore, the most reliable guidelines and, until the spring legislative elections of 1967, the only reliable and up-to-date map of
French political geography.

"France ought to have two Presidents," a Paris wit observed, as
the results showed a de Gaulle predominance in the North and an
opposition majority in the South, along a dividing line running
from the coastal city of La Rochelle on the west to the Alpine slopes
of eastern France facing on Geneva. North of that line de Gaulle
scored heavily in the old irredentist, Catholic provinces of the
Vendée, Brittany, Normandy, Alsace and Lorraine. In each of
these Gaullist fiefdoms, however, there were strong red cordons
around the ports, the coal mines, the industrial suburbs of Paris,
Nancy and Strasburg. Similarly, Mitterand and Lecanuet won
heavily in the South, along the Mediterranean coast from Mar-
seilles to Monaco, but with strong de Gaulle bastions in the southwest from Bordeaux to Toulouse down the foothills of the Pyrenees. In broad, general terms, Gaullist strength was drawn mainly
from Catholic women, the urban middle classes, the gentry, the
old families, the cadres and the upper age groups; whereas the
opposition was drawn from the urban proletariat, the small peas-
ants, the civil service, the schoolteachers, the intellectuals, big
industry, particularly those in the export trade, bankers and finan-
ciers alarmed by de Gaulle's foreign and economic policies, and
finally the middle and lower age-group of voters. In each case,
however, there were minority groups of each sector that crossed
lines, with many communists and socialists voting for de Gaulle
and many Catholics, conservatives, cadres and urban middle class
voters casting their ballots for the opposition.

The figures are, therefore, open to conflicting interpretations.
Some are unclear, confusing and contradictory; but some have
generally been accepted by most objective observers. One general
comment reflects fundamental consensus: the French by their
majority vote against de Gaulle told him in effect that they wanted
more freedom and better, friendlier relations with their European
neighbors and with the United States; at the same time, by their
strong plurality for de Gaulle they also demonstrated to the Left
their desire for a stronger executive power and a more stable political regime than in the past. This conclusion is based upon the fact
that Mitterand and Lecanuet, who totaled a bigger vote together

than de Gaulle, campaigned vigorously for more freedoms and better foreign relations, whereas de Gaulle's principal argument has consistently been that his regime produced a strong, stable government.

France's allies were justifiably pleased by this demonstration, and most particularly by the astonishing total of 15.85% won by Jean Lecanuet, who was virtually unknown to the general public before the campaign. The fact that he had received the rare endorsement of "Mr. Europe," Jean Monnet, who almost never took a position on France's internal politics, was a source of satisfaction and encouragement to the frustrated officials in Brussels, headquarters of the Common Market, besieged by de Gaulle. The fact that he was also the "Kennedy" candidate added to the satisfaction and encouragement of Washington, although Washington was not happy about the nature of the "red-front" coalition of Mitterand. For Washington the decision on December 19 between de Gaulle and Mitterand would be a choice between the devil and the big red wave. In such a choice, Washington had to hope for that "old devil" de Gaulle, an adversary less dangerous, because certainly more temporary, than communism.

Most authorities also agree on the following conclusions: 1) there has been a "rupture of generations," with pro-de Gaulle votes mainly in the over-50 year range (except on the left) and anti-de Gaulle votes generally in the under-35 group across the spectrum; 2) TV played an important role but only because of the shock caused by the new faces; it would play a smaller role if there were more equitable exposure for all parties; 3) the myth of "legitimacy" and national unity had been exploded, for de Gaulle was surely no longer the father of the country, the national hero, but only a chief of a party, the most powerful vote-getting politician, but no more than a politician, the biggest man but not superman; 4) that the anti-de Gaulle opposition would have to search for sharper self-identification over and beyond anti-Gaullism; 5) the opposition forces must then go beyond self-identification and search for compromises that would permit the eventual consolidation of a coalition that could achieve a majority permitting the kind of stability achieved under de Gaulle, but with the democratic freedoms the people insisted upon preserving; 6) the vague outlines of three groupings emerged in the opposition: a) a democratic-socialist tendency, composed of anti-communist Socialists, Radicals and other left-of-center splinter groups, roughly similar to such American groupings as the ADA, the New York Liberal Party, the mid-western Progressive movements; b) a similar grouping of the center and right-of-center by Christian Democrats of the Lecanuet persuasion and an assortment of moderates, conservatives and independents who believe in a united Europe and a strong NATO; c) the "New Left" led by Mitterand and the *Nouvel Observateur* magazine intellectual clan, based on co-existence and cooperation among the Communist Party, the Socialist Party and left Radicals; 7) the sharp decline of the extreme Right to the level of a minor splinter group; 8) the need for a purge and reorganization of de Gaulle's party, the UNR, to try to build it into a more effective political machine and classic political party.*

Although Mitterand and the "New Left" received the largest opposition total, most observers agreed that de Gaulle failed to get the absolute majority because of the almost 16% vote attained by Jean Lecanuet, for it was Lecanuet's liberal Catholic internationalist and anti-communist appeal that cut most into the ranks of the Gaullists. Many Catholics who disapproved de Gaulle's foreign policies would, observers believed, have voted for de Gaulle anyway, rather than for Mitterand and the communist coalition, if they had not had the more satisfactory alternative of Lecanuet. This theory would be proved out in the run-off elections of December 19.

The *Nouvel Observateur* analysts did not deny this theory of the Lecanuet sabotage of the Gaullists but argued that the very large vote for Mitterand, much bigger than anyone had expected, had made the "New Left" rather than Lecanuet the true opposition leader, and had prevented Lecanuet from becoming the "arbiter" of the opposition. This was the argument advanced by editor Jean Daniel in the special "Election Edition" of the *Nouvel Observateur*. He said that the best the Left had hoped for was to come out ahead of Lecanuet and to hold de Gaulle to "a painful victory." However, it had actually prevented de Gaulle's victory and had doubled Lecanuet's vote. It was a real victory but "only a first victory, the first grouping of the Left, not yet on a program but in the context of a perspective." Daniel said that "the second round must prepare the campaign for the legislative elections of

* Some fifty UNR deputies who failed to control their districts or were negligent in their attempt to do so were to be dropped from the party's electoral lists.

1967." He called for redoubled efforts to increase the vote on December 19 and added: "Who, tomorrow, would dare try to break the unifying spirit that would be engendered if François Mitterand were to advance from 32% to 40% of the electoral corps? How could one doubt that this would generate and, in any case, facilitate a rebirth of the Left?"

Daniel tried to present the run-off as a direct confrontation of the "Republican Left" and the "classic, conservative, reactionary Right." In a clear reference to liberals and leftists who voted and might again vote for de Gaulle, he said, "It is a matter of deciding whether, on December 19, a man of the left can vote with the banks, the bosses, the clerical hierarchy and financial lobbies of all kinds." This language revealed a key characteristic of the so-called "New Left," which is not really new at all, but rather the generation of 45–55-year-olds who were young students or young men in the depression-ridden, fascist-menaced thirties, and who still cling to the nostalgia of all the old slogans against "the bankers, the bosses, the bishops, the brokers, the businessmen and the brigadiers."

Some of these classic enemies of the Left certainly can be found in the Gaullist camp, but perhaps as many are anti-Gaullists. The splits and ideologies of the sixties are not the same as the thirties, and General de Gaulle, who gave France universal suffrage, nationalization of key industries and banks, decolonization of Africa, is certainly not the representative of the "classic, conservative, reactionary Right." There are many effective and accurate arguments to be used against de Gaulle, but the "New Left" will not be effective or look like anything but a tired, old Left, if it pursues the arguments advanced in the editorial of Jean Daniel, or similar arguments put forward in the same edition by leftist philosopher Jean-Paul Sartre. Sartre repeated all the hoarse slogans of anti-Americanism, anti-fascism, anti-trustism, all the shibboleths of the class struggle, without addressing himself primarily to the real challenge to a new Left: the need to find a genuine basis for a common program among the communists, socialists, radicals and liberals who make up the disparate, disorganized "Left," and a common approach to the real problems that face France in the sixties and the decades ahead—unification of Europe, technological progress and its social pressures at home—problems that are almost totally different from the problems of the thirties.

The final shape of the opposition to de Gaulle and the Gaullists will not be determined until after the legislative elections of 1967, for the fight for power inside the opposition can only be resolved in the greater fight for power in the nation. Electoral pressures will force compromises not easily reached between elections, but it will not be until well after the elections that one can tell whether the coalitions were mere electoral expedients or political realities. This was dramatically illustrated by the shifts that took place between December 5 and 19 and the real doubts that persisted after the 19th on the durability of the anti-de Gaulle pacts among groups whose only real cement was anti-Gaullism, such as anticlerical socialists and Catholics, urban liberals and rural conservatives, social democrats and right-wing reactionaries of the Tixier-Vignancourt camp, "Europeans," "Atlanticists" and rabid nationalists of the embittered "Algerie Française" colonialists.

Jean Lecanuet, whose candidacy blocked de Gaulle on the first turn, refused to take a clear-cut position on the run-off and left his partisans free to decide for themselves whether to vote for Mitterand or de Gaulle. Tixier-Vignancourt had no such scruples. He hated de Gaulle more than he feared the communists. He called upon all his supporters to vote against de Gaulle. In this sense the run-off was less a contest between de Gaulle and Mitterand than between de Gaulle and de Gaulle. Most citizens voted mainly for or against de Gaulle, rather than positively for de Gaulle or Mitterand.

De Gaulle himself in one sense also ran against de Gaulle. It is true that he made no substantive concessions on any of his major policies, despite the evidence that charges of economic stagnation and isolationism hurt him badly and made concessions necessary. He did, however, alter his style of campaigning, recognizing belatedly that his arrogant announcement of his candidacy on November 4, his habit of talking down to the people, and his failure to use his full, allotted time on television had all combined to cost him votes and could seriously cut his final margin on the 19th.

This observer first learned of de Gaulle's decision to change his style when he received a call on Saturday morning, December 11, from an old friend and colleague, Michel Droit, editor-in-chief of *Le Figaro Littéraire* and a leading television personality. I am a contributor to his paper and have appeared often on his television-interview program. The excitement in Droit's voice was apparent even before he broke the big news to me: "David, I have been asked by General de Gaulle to do a series of three half-hour interviews with him on the principal issues that the oppoistion has raised against him." The news was, indeed, something to be excited about, for de Gaulle had never allowed anyone to interview him in public. Even the question-answer period at his news conferences is carefully rigged and controlled to protect him against embarrassing or hostile questions and to permit him to say precisely what he intends to say.

When the decision was announced, there were the usual cynics to say that the interviews would also be rigged because Michel Droit was an avowed Gaullist and because it was unthinkable that de Gaulle would permit a spontaneous, unrehearsed interview. But the cynics were essentially wrong. The interviews by Michel Droit were certainly not fully spontaneous, any more than the interviews prepared by Mitterand were—in fact the de Gaulle-Droit interviews were livelier and more in the nature of a free exchange than the Mitterand "interviews." They were, however, not rehearsed and they were astonishingly hard-hitting, with Droit asking de Gaulle every tough, critical, even disagreeable question that the opposition itself could have put to him, with only one notable exception, a question de Gaulle refused to have put: the issue of amnesty for the hundreds of rebellious citizens arrested during the resistance to de Gaulle's policy of self-determination for Algeria.

There was high drama that week before the elections as the proud Old Man stepped down into the arena, his face powdered, his lips rouged for the bright lights of the camera, and sat down opposite the handsome, young television interviewer whose own rugged, ruddy health added an unavoidable editorial note to his sharp questions. The very first question set the tone of the three interviews. Michel Droit began by telling General de Gaulle that many fellow citizens believed that his love and devotion for France were not matched by equal sentiments for the French people. From that first question on Monday night, December 13, through the successive interviews on Tuesday and Wednesday, General de Gaulle submitted himself to a cross-examination by Michel Droit, who played the role of the People's Interrogator. Even the cynics and the critics of de Gaulle admitted that it was extremely effective.

The funniest and perhaps most apt comment on the interviews, which set the entire nation laughing, came from cartoonist Jacques Faizant, in the paper *Paris–Presse*. His cartoon showed a hotel room, an open suitcase containing slippers, and panties on the floor next to an armchair in which a tall old man with a familiar big-nosed face is seated with a cute little "baby-doll" wearing the cap of Marianne, symbol of the Republic, cuddling in his lap. He had a rather confused frown and smile on his face, as she looked up at him adoringly and said, "You see, Big Silly, if only you had talked like this to me sooner."

Whether or not de Gaulle could have seduced Marianne by talking sweetly sooner cannot be proved, but many political experts believe that he could have won the election on the first time around if he himself and his television network had worried more about pleasing and informing the people of France, instead of controlling and distorting the facts and sermonizing them on special occasions. "Sweet talk" alone would surely not have accomplished this purpose. To achieve victory would have required greater sensitivity to the people's desire to live in closer amity with neighbors and allies, particularly the United States. And this Charles de Gaulle was not prepared to do. In his talk with Droit, the President did deny that he was "anti-American" but he continued to criticize American policies and to oppose the principal programs that his European and American allies favored.

On the Friday before the final run-off election, the campaign came to an end. De Gaulle decided against another interview, preferring to close with a direct speech to the people. He startled Michel Droit by lapsing into "franglais," the broken French-American slang he and his government had always denounced. He told Droit, "Vendredi je ferai un talk." The effect of de Gaulle's using the word "talk" instead of the French equivalent was heightened and made grotesque by his French accent, which made the word sound as though it were "toke," so that for a few seconds Michel Droit had no idea what the President was talking about.

The people of France, however, knew what de Gaulle was talking about, and on December 19 they proved at the polls that, although they still preferred de Gaulle to the alternative offered them, they were not cuddling up in his lap adoringly. They gave him a majority, re-electing him to a second seven-year term, but they did not give him the national mandate he had sought, and, in fact, did not even give him a majority of the registered voters. The final totals were:

Candidate	Total votes	Percent votes cast	Percent registered voters
C. de Gaulle	12,645,315	54.49	44.77
			(Abstentions 17.85)
F. Mitterand	10,557,480	45.51	37.38

A study of the detailed figures showed that Mitterand, who had increased his totals by almost three million votes and more than 13%, had won these votes from two sources: a very large proportion of the votes that had been cast for Tixier-Vignancourt on the first ballot; about half the votes that had gone first to Lecanuet. This was not a brilliant result for the "Man of the Left," whose gains came mainly from the extreme Right, but it was, nonetheless, a strong showing to have held his first-round support and increased it to a total of more than 45% in a direct man-to-man contest with Charles de Gaulle. It was, indeed, if not brilliant in some respects, extraordinary as an overall achievement. And however much the Mitterand vote may have been essentially an anti-de Gaulle vote, his partisans could legitimately argue that the man himself must have impressed the voters favorably for them to have accepted him as the recipient of their anti-Gaullist sentiments.

Mitterand and his friends rejoiced, claimed an "historic victory" and called upon "all good Republicans" to join him for the ultimate fight for control of the Parliament in 1967. Mitterand rejected the traditional salute of congratulations to the victor. He would send no message to de Gaulle. He told reporters: "I am convinced that this election is contrary to the true interests of our country."

Tixier-Vignancourt congratulated Mitterand rather than de Gaulle but was bitter about Lecanuet, saying that if Lecanuet had asked his supporters to vote for Mitterand as *he* had, then de Gaulle would have been defeated. This was, of course, theoretically possible. Lecanuet's 16% had split in two, with some 8% going to de Gaulle, without which de Gaulle's total would have been only 47% and Mitterand would have been elected. The theory was, however, highly unrealistic, for hardly anyone but Tixier-Vignancourt believed that Lecanuet's supporters would have voted for Mitterand even if Lecanuet had begged them to do so.

The Gaullists were just as furious with Lecanuet, for, with much the same mentality as Tixier-Vignancourt, they believed that de Gaulle would have had a triumph well above 60% if Lecanuet had supported de Gaulle in the run-off. The Gaullist argument had a bit more validity to it than the Tixier-Vignancourt thesis, for Lecanuet's supporters were mainly drawn from the Gaullist camp and might possibly have been persuaded back had Lecanuet recanted. But it was unrealistic to ask Lecanuet, who had made a brilliant debut in national politics, to throw it all away. He had to do what he did, which was to keep himself clear of the current contest and hold himself uncommitted in reserve, for the fights ahead.

The French relaxed, pleased at the results, for it meant they had avoided a grave crisis which would surely have ensued had Mitterand been elected without any real majority program; but, at the same time, they had cut de Gaulle down to the size of a man, an extraordinary man to be sure, but a man not a demigod. It was just the proper appetizer for a festive holiday season, and, within days of the run-off, the French were off on the run to their favorite holiday resorts in the Alps, the Riviera, Spain and the Balearic islands.

In foreign lands the results were generally accepted as the best that could have been expected. De Gaulle's old friend, ex-chancellor Adenauer in Germany, rejoiced, but most official Germans considered the result the "lesser of two evils." In Rome, with its own problems of coming to terms with communism, the reaction underlined the importance of the communist emergence from almost twenty years of quarantine from the French body politic. North African countries were generally satisfied, but Black Africa, unhappy about de Gaulle's policies in the Congo and Rhodesia, grumbled. The Soviet Union was evidently satisfied, for the Russians had won a political "daily double": their allies, the communists, had made important gains; and the biggest trouble-maker in the western world, Charles de Gaulle, would be back in power making trouble for the Common Market and NATO, more trouble than Russia could make on its own. In Washington, Lyndon Johnson gritted his teeth, maintained his wise policy of silent suffering and concerned himself with his greatest, most urgent problem: the search for an honorable peace in Vietnam —hoping that de Gaulle would, at least, keep out of his way.

The election of December 19 had settled nothing. It had only postponed the ultimate moment of truth for the French, the moment some half of the people could not wait to see come, and that the other half has kept putting off, the moment after de Gaulle. As the year 1966 wrote itself into history, no one could be sure just how near or far was the post-de Gaulle period of French history. Legally, it would not have to come until January 1973, when a new President would be inaugurated to succeed de Gaulle, who, by then age 82, would be most unlikely to run or get re-elected to a third term. There are many observers, perhaps the majority, who feel that the moment will come sooner, that de Gaulle does not wish and would not be able to carry on through the full seven years of his mandate.

This writer believes that it is idle speculation to try to guess how long de Gaulle will want to or be able to rule. As he entered his second term, he was certainly strong enough, vigorous enough to carry on. No doctor would predict the future of a man of 75, so that it is futile for laymen to speculate. De Gaulle has told no one, insofar as we know, whether he desires to serve out his term, although his second inaugural address, promising to defend the constitution for the next seven years, seemed to hint at continuity. Those close to him know that he yearns to complete his memoirs, to write his own version of the record of his presidency. But he also thoroughly enjoys the making, even more than the writing, of history. Personally, I doubt that Charles de Gaulle will retire until his health or an irreversible political defeat makes it impossible for him to govern. That is not scheduled to happen politically until the legislative elections of 1967 at the earliest.

Since events evolve rapidly in our times, no one can be sure what circumstances will prevail at that time. If I had to judge in the context of 1966 I would predict a defeat for de Gaulle and the Gaullist party in 1967, a defeat more serious than the humiliation of December 5. De Gaulle cannot govern France without a parliamentary majority. Some astute observers disagree with such a prediction. On the night of December 19, in the course of a long talk at the offices of the *Nouvel Observateur* while watching the returns, Mendès-France told me that he believed de Gaulle would revise the electoral law in such a way as to force run-off elections in most districts between the pro-Gaullist and communist-backed candidates, and that, as in the contest with Mitterand, a majority of the French would vote against the communist-front candidate. He may well be right, and one hesitates to take issue with so brilliant an analyst of French politics as former Premier Pierre Mendès-France. But Mendès, brilliant though he is, is an embittered, disappointed man, inclined always to look at the gloomiest side of any picture. I think he is overpessimistic, and I find it impossible to believe that Gaullism can win an election in which de Gaulle is not personally a candidate. Perhaps no one could beat de Gaulle for the presidency in 1965 but that is very different from saying that the Gaullists could win a parliamentary majority either alone or in coalition. I am convinced that they passed their peak in their victory of 1962, a victory brought about by the desire of the people to help de Gaulle end the Algerian war and withdraw rapidly from North Africa. Without that stimulus I do not believe the Gaullists can even come close to a majority.

Whatever happens, however, it is not likely to change in any important respect the judgment of history on Charles de Gaulle. He has lived three-quarters of a century, thus the greatest part of his several lives is far behind him. It is so unlikely as to be almost impossible for de Gaulle to suffer the cruel fate of his former mentor, Marshal Pétain, who was given a burden too great for a senile, small man to bear. De Gaulle is no Pétain, and the very example of Pétain would move Frenchmen to retire de Gaulle should such improbable circumstances come to pass. A contemporary historian can, therefore, permit himself to review the lives and times of Charles de Gaulle now, as he enters into his second term of his third incarnation, with little risk that significant changes might occur.

* * *

For all his reputation as a visionary, despite his early perception of the changes in warfare tactics brought about by mechanization, Charles de Gaulle was a misfit out of tune with his times during most of his career. At the time of his birth, France had already begun to decline as a world power after its defeat by the Prussians of Bismarck. But France still lived on its past reputation and managed one last burst of glory during the young manhood of Charles de Gaulle when Clemenceau, "the Tiger," led the allied coalition to victory over the Kaiser in World War I. It was the last "victory" of an exhausted, declining French nation.

The decline of France is not absolute. As a nation it grows steadily, if slowly, in population and economic strength. But the relative decline is great. By the end of this twentieth century France will be a very small country of only seventy million people, compared with one hundred million Germans, three hundred and fifty million Americans, four hundred million Russians and nine hundred million, perhaps even one billion, Chinese. Will any future de Gaulle, in the year 2000, be able to repeat his empty boast that "France must be France for everyone"? And in so unlikely an eventuality, what echo would his words evoke in the world of tomorrow? Where would he find anyone, let alone everyone in the world, to agree that what matters is for France to be France?

France is not the only great nation to have experienced a relative decline in power. England and Germany have walked down the same road. They are all living in the twilight zone of their world power. When they finally acknowledge to themselves the passing of their preeminence as world powers, the people of England, Germany and France will sooner be able to walk through the twilight and into a new dawn of achievement, for there has been no decline of individual human potential. It is the nation-state that has passed its peak, not the peoples of those nations. Some day this new fact of life will be recognized even by the Americans, Russians and Chinese. In the mid-twentieth century those nations entered in a rising cycle of power, but even as they approached their peak they began to discover how small even the biggest nations were in a rapidly expanding world. They too began to experience the limitations of power.

The world rejected de Gaulle's pretentious claim to France's leadership role. Rarely was France so alone as in the reign of Charles de Gaulle. And rarely was the world so unbalanced as in the years during which he vainly offered France as the equilibrium of a new order. A new order and equilibrium were certainly needed in the world, but de Gaulle presented no new blueprint of the new order of which he spoke. Never did he explain where he put China in his vision of a world dominated by the twin hegemony of Russia and America. What balance, what orderly relationship did he ever propose for India and Pakistan, between the Arabs and the Israelis, the North Africans and the South Africans, among the South Americans and the Southeast Asians? De Gaulle only indulged himself in sweeping statements asserting the world's longing for a France that is France.

In the course of making France France again, President de Gaulle came close to wrecking all the alliances and friendships that have provided so much security and progress for the French people. The recognition of Communist China weakened the ties between Paris and Washington without truly establishing ties between Paris and Peking, for the Communist Chinese leaders did not recognize any special role for de Gaulle. There was no appreciable increase of trade between France and China, no significant Peking counterpart to compensate the loss of trust in Washington. There has been a net loss of confidence in France and a dangerous strain on relations between France and the United

States resulting from de Gaulle's diplomatic recognition of Communist China.

It was not the fact, but rather the act, of recognition that caused the trouble. De Gaulle always had a perverse genius for doing the right thing in the wrong way. In the abstract there was nothing wrong or harmful in his decision to establish diplomatic relations with China. One could conceive of circumstances in which it would have been a useful move. The West needed listening posts and interlocutors in China. But de Gaulle's recognition was not made in the abstract or for any purpose of common interest to the Western allies. He announced his decision publicly at a press conference, with almost no prior consultation with his allies, and in a manner that left no doubt that he was less interested in recognizing China than in deliberately defying the United States. In this sense it was part of his cold, uncivil war with the Anglo-Saxons, a deliberate provocation, and not the evocation of a diplomatic reality, as his apologists attempted to argue.

General de Gaulle and his sycophantic propagandists seriously underestimated the damage that they inflicted on France by the unfriendly manner in which they conducted themselves in the alliance. They committed a grave error in failing to distinguish between disagreement and disagreeableness. It was certainly true, as they often charged, that the United States and Great Britain were not always reliable allies of France—witness Suez, the French trauma of our times. But the Anglo-Saxon disagreements with the French were not systematically envenomed by a deliberately disagreeable treatment of the discord. They did not, as de Gaulle so frequently did, add insult to injury. De Gaulle's tongue was sharper than the edge of his sword, and he made more enemies by his words than by his deeds.

America rarely went out of its way to ridicule, scorn and insult the French. American official spokesmen were remarkably patient with de Gaulle and spent years turning cheeks for him to slap—and de Gaulle rarely missed an opportunity to slap the Anglo-Saxons. He went out of his way to do so, as in the case of Santo Domingo, where French interests were not deeply involved. He not only instructed his ambassador at the U.N. to introduce a motion critical of the United States, he also had his spokesman in Paris tell the world press how thoroughly he disapproved of American actions. On Vietnam he went beyond all tolerable limits by personally characterizing American intervention as "a dirty war." * He did not use the epithet as Americans did, in the physical sense, but in the moral sense, as the Communists once used it against the French in Indochina.

American and British leaders did not personally attack France in this extremely disagreeable manner; they never publicly imputed bad faith and wicked designs to their allies. At least, until recently they did not. In the course of the year 1965 American patience was exhausted and nerves strained to the point where even the normally mild-mannered, soft-spoken Secretary of State Dean Rusk began snapping sharply. He came closer to telling de Gaulle publicly to mind his own business on Santo Domingo than a diplomat ordinarily would. And President Johnson denounced "narrow nationalism" in a speech clearly aimed at de Gaulle.

The years of governmental discord began to poison relations among the citizens of France and America. Thousands of American tourists bypassed France or went through quickly in the summer of 1965. Businessmen began to reexamine their plans and programs for commerce with the French. One of the most francophile of Americans, Stanley Marcus of Nieman-Marcus, the great specialty store of Dallas, was one of the few leading merchants who decided to maintain his public relations with, and his purchases from, France, but only after much soul-searching and public opinion soundings. After a number of other men had canceled plans to hold traditional "French Fortnight" festivals, Stanley Marcus decided to maintain his program. In correspondence with this writer he agreed that this was a time for private citizens to keep the channels open, particularly since the leaders of their countries were burning their bridges. He conceded it would be an error to boycott French producers and punish them for de Gaulle's policies when they themselves might well be pro-American and opposed to de Gaulle's actions.

The positive decision of the Dallas merchant brings to mind one of the comments of General Eisenhower that friendship is a necessary ingredient of an alliance; that an alliance cannot endure or succeed "unless there is a mutually felt good faith . . . unless you're pretty good friends." That statement was pure "Ike,"

* De Gaulle pronounced these words at his annual garden party for French parliamentarians in June 1965. He also said that the United States republic was built upon the bones of the native Indians whom the colonists had slaughtered.

General Eisenhower at his best, the simple humanist who believes that over and above reasons of state, the heart has reasons that the state does not know. Unlike General Eisenhower, General de Gaulle put reason above heart in his conduct of the affairs of State. Or perhaps more accurately, all of his heart belonged to France, and there was no room for any other affection. De Gaulle did insist that there was a sentimental side to his character. At the outset of his memoirs he wrote that his thoughts about France were "inspired by sentiment as much as by reason." He then referred to the "affectionate side of me" as he explained his image of France as the princess of the fairy tales. This "affectionate side" of de Gaulle is, however, strictly limited to France. He felt no affection for any other country.

De Gaulle's rejection of friendship hurt France and the Western alliance. The fact that it began to affect relations between the peoples of the alliance as well as between their governments was equally grave. Governments come and go, but not peoples. Genuine friendship between peoples is slowly built over years, even centuries. Once lost, it can take a very long time to regain. There is no human quality more fragile than friendship. The bad feelings generated by de Gaulle have caused damage that may last longer than the time it took for him to do the damage. Destruction is almost always swifter and more easily wrought than construction. And in his career de Gaulle has proved more apt at destroying evil than in constructing permanent good. It is, however, still too early for de Gaulle's contemporaries to make final judgments or to view the whole of his career with the necessary detachment and objectivity. I would guess that, as in the case of Napoleon, the legend of Charles de Gaulle will grow throughout the years. Much of the angry criticism provoked by the bruised feelings and frustrated plans of his contemporaries may not seem so important to our unborn grandchildren, who will never have suffered from his arrogant superiority.

His great achievements are many. He was one of the most courageous soldiers and farsighted military theorists of French history. Charles de Gaulle, five times decorated for valor by the Third Republic, prophet of mechanized warfare, won a permanent niche in history as a soldier of France. Similarly, nothing that he did later could mar the memory of his finest hour as General de Gaulle, the Liberator and Savior of the Fourth Republic. The man of June 18th earned his place in the Pantheon of French history. It was in his third incarnation of France, as the father of the Fifth Republic, that Charles de Gaulle became the stormy petrel of a troubled world. It was in this period that he most angered the intellectual elite of his country and almost all the other powers of the world. It is extremely difficult for his contemporaries, so often insulted and injured by him, to view the last great period of his life with fairness and objectivity. Moreover, the great achievements of the last years of his life were essentially negative achievements. He came to power as the result of a coup d'état engineered and executed mainly by extremists and retrograde forces. He overcame them, but, as he himself once admitted to this writer, "If one walks through mud, one cannot but be stained." President de Gaulle's achievement in bringing the Algerian war to an end and the skill and courage with which he liquidated the old colonial structure in Africa may be judged one day to have been the greatest achievement in French history, but, unfortunately for de Gaulle, heroic and brilliant as it was, it was fundamentally negative in the same sense that a life-saving operation for cancer is negative. He cut out a fatal tumor, keeping France alive, but, as in all major cancer operations, the cut was deep and the treatment was long and painful. One has great admiration and gratitude for a doctor, but cancer surgeons are not popular hero types by the very nature of their mission. In this sense, de Gaulle's great achievements may seem even greater in the glamorizing process of history, and future historians, whose vanity and ambitions are not challenged as ours are, may judge him to be an even greater giant when measured against some of his predecessors and contemporaries.

Mark Antony in his funeral address assured his friends and fellow Romans that he had come to bury Ceasar and not to praise him. He argued that the evil that men do lives after them but that the good is oft interred with their bones. This writer, in the course of a quarter-century of world experience, has seen the opposite come true as often as not. Looking back upon that quarter-century as a whole, I would conclude that if evil was done, it will be interred with his bones, but the good of Charles de Gaulle will live on long after him.

Index

David Schoenbrun

DAVID SCHOENBRUN, reporter, broadcaster, author, is one of America's outstanding authorities on world affairs. He has won top awards in the fields of radio, television, magazines and books, including the Alfred E. du Pont Award as "Commentator of the Year" and the Overseas Press Club selection of *As France Goes* as "Best Book on Foreign Affairs in 1957."

His CBS news broadcasts over a period of nearly two decades won him a reputation as one of America's foremost foreign correspondents. His daily reports, now syndicated by Metropolitan Broadcasting, are heard nationwide.

Born in New York, Mr. Schoenbrun began his career there as a teacher of Romance Languages. During the war he served as an army combat correspondent and was decorated with the Croix de Guerre and the Légion d'Honneur. His wife, also a native New Yorker, studied painting in Paris, and their daughter, born in Paris, took her baccalaureate degree there. Internationally renowned, David Schoenbrun writes and broadcasts in several languages and his reports are carried throughout the world.